Software Engineering for Agile Application Development

Chung-Yeung Pang
Seveco AG, Switzerland

A volume in the Advances in Computer and Electrical Engineering (ACEE) Book Series

Published in the United States of America by
IGI Global
Engineering Science Reference (an imprint of IGI Global)
701 E. Chocolate Avenue
Hershey PA, USA 17033
Tel: 717-533-8845
Fax: 717-533-8661
E-mail: cust@igi-global.com
Web site: http://www.igi-global.com

Library of Congress Cataloging-in-Publication Data

Names: Pang, Chung-Yeung, 1954- editor.
Title: Software engineering for agile application development / Chung-Yeung
   Pang, editor.
Description: Hershey, PA : Engineering Science Reference, an imprint of IGI
   Global, 2020. | Includes bibliographical references and index. |
   Summary: "This book explores concepts, principles, and techniques for
   agile application development in software engineering"-- Provided by
   publisher.
Identifiers: LCCN 2019040433 (print) | LCCN 2019040434 (ebook) | ISBN
   9781799825319 (hardcover) | ISBN 9781799825326 (paperback) | ISBN
   9781799825333 (ebook)
Subjects: LCSH: Agile software development.
Classification: LCC QA76.76.D47 S654 2020 (print) | LCC QA76.76.D47
   (ebook) | DDC 005.1/112--dc23
LC record available at https://lccn.loc.gov/2019040433
LC ebook record available at https://lccn.loc.gov/2019040434

This book is published in the IGI Global book series Advances in Computer and Electrical Engineering (ACEE) (ISSN: 2327-039X; eISSN: 2327-0403)

British Cataloguing in Publication Data
A Cataloguing in Publication record for this book is available from the British Library.

For electronic access to this publication, please contact: eresources@igi-global.com.

Advances in Computer and Electrical Engineering (ACEE) Book Series

Srikanta Patnaik
SOA University, India

ISSN:2327-039X
EISSN:2327-0403

MISSION

The fields of computer engineering and electrical engineering encompass a broad range of interdisciplinary topics allowing for expansive research developments across multiple fields. Research in these areas continues to develop and become increasingly important as computer and electrical systems have become an integral part of everyday life.

The **Advances in Computer and Electrical Engineering (ACEE) Book Series** aims to publish research on diverse topics pertaining to computer engineering and electrical engineering. **ACEE** encourages scholarly discourse on the latest applications, tools, and methodologies being implemented in the field for the design and development of computer and electrical systems.

COVERAGE

- Analog Electronics
- Algorithms
- Computer Science
- Computer Architecture
- Applied Electromagnetics
- Computer Hardware
- Qualitative Methods
- Electrical Power Conversion
- VLSI Design
- Programming

IGI Global is currently accepting manuscripts for publication within this series. To submit a proposal for a volume in this series, please contact our Acquisition Editors at Acquisitions@igi-global.com or visit: http://www.igi-global.com/publish/.

Titles in this Series

For a list of additional titles in this series, please visit: https://www.igi-global.com/book-series/advances-computer-electrical-engineering/73675

Novel Approaches to Information Systems Design
Naveen Prakash (Indraprastha Institute of Information Technology, Delhi, India) and Deepika Prakash (NIIT University, India)
Engineering Science Reference • © 2020 • 299pp • H/C (ISBN: 9781799829751) • US $215.00

IoT Architectures, Models, and Platforms for Smart City Applications
Bhawani Shankar Chowdhry (Mehran University of Engineering and Technology, Pakistan) Faisal Karim Shaikh (Mehran University of Engineering and Technology, Pakistan) and Naeem Ahmed Mahoto (Mehran University of Engineering and Technology, Pakistan)
Engineering Science Reference • © 2020 • 291pp • H/C (ISBN: 9781799812531) • US $245.00

Nature-Inspired Computing Applications in Advanced Communication Networks
Govind P. Gupta (National Institute of Technology, Raipur, India)
Engineering Science Reference • © 2020 • 319pp • H/C (ISBN: 9781799816263) • US $225.00

Pattern Recognition Applications in Engineering
Diego Alexander Tibaduiza Burgos (Universidad Nacional de Colombia, Colombia) Maribel Anaya Vejar (Universidad Sergio Arboleda, Colombia) and Francesc Pozo (Universitat Politècnica de Catalunya, Spain)
Engineering Science Reference • © 2020 • 357pp • H/C (ISBN: 9781799818397) • US $215.00

Tools and Technologies for the Development of Cyber-Physical Systems
Sergey Balandin (FRUCT Oy, Finland) and Ekaterina Balandina (Tampere University, Finland)
Engineering Science Reference • © 2020 • 300pp • H/C (ISBN: 9781799819745) • US $235.00

Handbook of Research on New Solutions and Technologies in Electrical Distribution Networks
Baseem Khan (Hawassa University, Hawassa, Ethiopia) Hassan Haes Alhelou (Tishreen University, Syria) and Ghassan Hayek (Tishreen University, Syria)
Engineering Science Reference • © 2020 • 439pp • H/C (ISBN: 9781799812302) • US $270.00

Major Applications of Carbon Nanotube Field-Effect Transistors (CNTFET)
Balwinder Raj (National Institute of Technical Teachers Training and Research, Chandigarh, India) Mamta Khosla (Dr. B. R. Ambedkar National Institute of Technology, Jalandhar, India) and Amandeep Singh (National Institute of Technology, Srinagar, India)
Engineering Science Reference • © 2020 • 255pp • H/C (ISBN: 9781799813934) • US $185.00

701 East Chocolate Avenue, Hershey, PA 17033, USA
Tel: 717-533-8845 x100 • Fax: 717-533-8661
E-Mail: cust@igi-global.com • www.igi-global.com

Table of Contents

Detailed Table of Contents

Section 1
Requirements

This section covers requirements analyses, which are the first activities of a software development project.

The combination of software engineering and agile development process can bring great benefits to the development and maintenance of enterprise applications. This chapter introduces the engineering of requirements in an agile Scrum development process. In Scrum, requirements are usually defined as user stories in a product backlog. Since many enterprise applications do not have intensive user actions, stories cannot be linked to users. Topics such as user and enabler stories, non-functional requirements, considerations of architecture and business components, business workflow, and breakdown of user stories are addressed. The requirements engineering of PBIs is illustrated by practical examples. Using UML use cases and collaboration models is recommended to transform the stories in the product backlog into formal requirements specifications. The proposed approach can be part of the agile development framework for flexible software products that are easy to customize and maintain.

Section 2
Software Design and Architecture

This section covers various techniques for software design and architecture.

The health framework introduces the concept of sustainability because of its dynamics as individuals' needs change with everyday life and environmental changes. It is well known that, despite grave concern, the implementation of health policy is particularly affected in developing countries. This chapter is about creating a healthcare framework that is sensitive, insecure, and flexible. The medication process is dependent on laboratory tests and the techniques vary from time to time, which affects the services that the experts provide to patients. This increases the overall cost of the medication process and can be sustained by the concept of health insurance. For this purpose, the well-planned and defined software is obligatory due to the non-functional requirements up to the concepts of the software architecture. The designed framework is an integrated approach that conveys factual awareness of personalized and competent health services and facilitates agile principles and practices.

The interaction of distributed applications raises an integration problem that consists in how to satisfy the minimum interoperability requirements while reducing coupling as much as possible. Current integration technologies, such as Web Services and RESTful APIs, solve the interoperability problem but usually entail more coupling than required by the interacting applications. This is caused by sharing data schemas between applications, even if not all features of those schemas are actually exercised. This has its toll in application development agility. This chapter proposes compliance and conformance as the concepts to minimize coupling without impairing interoperability by sharing only the subset of the features of the data schema that are actually used. In addition, data binding between messages and the receiver's schema is done structurally in a universal and application-independent way. This eliminates the need for application-specific stubs and allows clients to use any server with which they comply and servers to replace any server to which they conform.

Most enterprise IT systems are very complex with a combination of COBOL and Java programs running on multiple platforms. What is needed is a solid IT architecture that supports the operation and growth of a cross-platform IT system. It must enable the iterative and incremental development of applications that are foreseen in an agile development process. The design concept of such an architecture with its infrastructure and development tool is presented in this chapter. This design concept is based on the design principles and architectural patterns of software engineering. The architecture is a combination of layered, component-based, and service-oriented architectural patterns. The agile development process is based on a model-driven approach. The architecture and development approaches were first introduced in 2004. Since then, many applications have been developed on time and within budget.

Web applications today play a significant role, with a large number of devices connected to the internet, and data is transmitted across disparate platforms at an unprecedented rate. Many systems and platforms require applications to adapt quickly and efficiently to the needs of consumers. In 2000, the Representation State Transfer (REST) was introduced, and the developers quickly adopted it. However, due to the growth of consumers and the different needs, this architectural style, in the way it is used, revealed some weaknesses related to the performance and flexibility of the applications. These are or can be addressed with GraphQL. In this chapter several alternatives to use GraphQL are explained and their benefits in terms of performance and flexibility. Some prototypes were implemented in an organization, and the results of some experiments were analyzed in light of possible gains in performance.

Chapter 6

    Pedro Aguiar, Instituto Superior de Engenharia do Porto, Instituto Politécnico do Porto, Portugal
    Isabel Azevedo, Instituto Superior de Engenharia do Porto, Instituto Politécnico do Porto, Portugal

Gamification has been applied in diverse areas to encourage participation, improve engagement, and even modify behaviors. However, many gamified applications have failed to meet their objectives, and poor gamification design has been pointed out as a recurrent problem, despite a growing number of gamification frameworks and their valuable guidelines. Model-driven engineering approaches have been proposed as possible solutions to the deficient, and incoherent, inclusion of several dynamics and mechanics. They allow achieving a formalism that can avoid many errors and inconsistencies in the process. Moreover, these efforts are necessary to achieve a conceptualization of gamification that facilitates its inclusion in applications. Three proposals are analyzed, all based on domain-specific languages (DSL), which allows users to design complex gamification strategies without requiring programming skills. The MDE approach can be used to enrich gamification design by providing a platform that involves various concepts and the necessary connections between them to ensure harmonious designs.

Chapter 7

    Chung-Yeung Pang, Seveco AG, Switzerland

Reusability is a clear principle in software development. However, systematic reuse of software elements is not common in most organizations. Application programmers rarely design and create software elements for possible future reuse. In many agile software development processes, the project teams believe that the development of reusable software elements can slow down the project. This can be a misconception. This chapter examines various ways to reuse software. Three approaches to developing reusable software artifacts from 15 years of experience in the agile development process are presented. The first approach is to create generic programs or configurable frameworks that support similar solutions for a variety of use cases and environments. The reuse of patterns is the second approach presented. Another effective way is to use a model-driven approach with model patterns. These approaches help to speed deployment software. The final product is flexible and can easily be adapted to changes. This is one of the main goals of an agile approach.

Testing software is a process of program execution with the intent to find errors. For this purpose, various testing techniques have been used over time. Testing software is an intensive field of research in which much development work has been done. This field will become increasingly important in the future. There are many techniques for software testing. This chapter gives an overview of the entire range of software testing with suggestions for their implementation. One focus is on testing in an agile development process why the different types of software tests are important, and their cycle and methodology are described. In addition, different levels, types, and a comparative study on different types of tests are presented. The chapter also includes suggestions for performing the various tests and an effective approach to testing a software system.

Agile methodologies have become the preferred choice for modern software development. These methods focus on iterative and incremental development, where both requirements and solutions develop through collaboration among cross-functional software development teams. The success of a software system is based on the quality result of each stage of development with proper test practice. A software test ontology should represent the required software test knowledge in the context of the software tester. Reusing test cases is an effective way to improve the testing of software. The workload of a software tester for test-case generation can be improved, previous software testing experience can be shared, and test efficiency can be increased by automating software testing. In this chapter, the authors introduce a software testing framework (STF) that uses rule-based reasoning (RBR), case-based reasoning (CBR), and ontology-based semantic similarity assessment to retrieve the test cases from the case library. Finally, experimental results are used to illustrate some of the features of the framework.

Given the large dimensions of software algorithms, the creation of unit test sets is both very difficult to use as an assurance of software quality and also very resource consuming. Some of the industry has already focused on this issue, and several methods are being used to cope with traditional testing shortcomings. Property-based testing has been one of these techniques and has been gaining traction, mainly due to the shift to functional programming techniques which can be seen in most of the popular languages and platforms. To give students tools that can increase the quality of their production as software developers, property-based testing has been taught in the Advanced Programming Techniques course of the master's program in Informatics Engineering of the Instituto Superior de Engenharia do Porto.

Chapter 11

Shanmuganathan Vasanthapriyan, Sabaragamuwa University of Sri Lanka, Sri Lanka

Software testing, which is a knowledge-intensive and collaborative activity, is a sub-area of software engineering. Software testing knowledge can be applied to different testing tasks and purposes. Since software development is an error-prone task, in order to achieve quality software products, validation and verification should be carried throughout the development. This study, using qualitative methods, investigates the current practice of software testing practices in two software companies on the basis that they both claimed to apply software testing practices in their software development work. Interview results revealed some interesting latest trends in software testing from both companies.

Chapter 12

Shanmuganathan Vasanthapriyan, Sabaragamuwa University of Sri Lanka, Sri Lanka
Kuhaneswaran Banujan, Sabaragamuwa University of Sri Lanka, Sri Lanka

Software testing is a sub-activity of software engineering, and it is also a knowledge-intensive activity. Software testing experts need to gather domain knowledge to be able to successfully test and deliver a software system. In particular, novice software testers, who have joined the company, need to acquire enough knowledge to perform their tasks. Since software development is an error-prone task, in order to achieve quality software products, validation and verification should be carried throughout the development. This means that knowledge transfer to novice software testers must be quickly and effectively performed to facilitate the onboarding process. One way to understand the knowledge transfer process is by analyzing the software development context and the involved team members. This study, using qualitative methods, investigates the current practice of knowledge transfer in software testing practices in one software company.

Chapter 13

Shanmuganathan Vasanthapriyan, Sabaragamuwa University of Sri Lanka, Sri Lanka
Kalpani Madushika Udawela Arachchi, Sabaragamuwa University of Sri Lanka, Sri Lanka

Software maintenance is an important phase in the lifespan of a software system. This chapter examines the effectiveness of Scrum and Kanban methods in terms of their impacts on project management factors for a software maintenance project. The six-point star model defines project management factors like schedule, scope, budget, risk, resources, quality, and study, and uses two other non-quantitative techniques such as team commitment and work organization. A quantitative survey was carried out together with the questionnaire distributed to IT industry professionals in Sri Lanka. Each question in the questionnaire was related to one of the above factors. The Pearson correlation coefficient was used to find the correlation between the coefficients. A strong correlation was identified. Based on the results of multiple linear regression modeling, a model has been proposed. Scrum-based software maintenance projects can improve project quality by managing work organization and resources whereas Kanban-based can improve project quality by controlling the risk and scope of the project.

Preface

In the early days of software's history, programmers tended to develop their programs in an ad hoc style, with no documentation. A result of this was the software crisis of the 1960s, 1970s and 1980s (Software Crisis, 2010). Typical phenomena of the software crisis were:

- Many problems arising in software development.
- Software projects tending to run over budget, be late or completely fail to deliver.
- Mission critical programs becoming obsolete and unmaintainable.
- Enterprise IT systems becoming increasingly complex and difficult to manage.

Software engineering (2010) is a discipline that provides solutions in order to counter the software crisis. It defines standards, disciplines, methodologies and processes for software development. In the past few decades, many new methodologies, standards, programming languages and paradigms have been developed. Programming styles like structural programming (Yourdon & Constantine, 1979; Jackson, 1975), object-oriented programming (Booch, et al., 2007), etc., have been introduced. Programming languages such as ADA, C++, Smalltalk, Java, Prolog, etc., have evolved in order to enable developers to program while using better structures and to adapt to new programming styles like object-oriented programming, as well as concepts of artificial intelligence and expert systems (Winston, 1992). Various CASE tools have become available to assist software development through modelling. The Unified Modelling Language (UML) (Fowler, 2004) has also evolved. Developers can build different software artefacts in different phases of a software-development process in the form of UML models. For the software-development life cycle (SDLC), we have the waterfall model (Royce, 1970), the spiral development model (Boehm, 1986; 1988), the rational unified process (RUP), the agile development process (Kay, 2002), etc. Extreme programming, rapid application development (RAD) with prototyping, Scrum and Kanban, etc. (Stellman & Greene, 2015), provide different programming paradigms (SDLC, 2013). There has been a great evolution of software technologies since the period of the software crisis.

THE CHALLENGES

Despite the advances in software technologies, the problems related to the software crisis do not seem to have been solved. The Standish Group's 2009 CHAOS report (Standish Group, 2009) shows that only 32% of software projects are completed successfully, 44% are challenged (making them late, over budget and/or having fewer features and functions than is required) and 24% failed, meaning that they were cancelled prior to completion, or were delivered and never used. "These numbers represent a downtick in the success rates from the previous study, as well as a significant increase in the number of failures", says Jim Crear, Standish Group CIO, "They are a low point in the last five study periods. This year's results represent the highest failure rate in over a decade".

Enterprise IT systems involve a complex interplay of people and processes. Technologies alone do not provide solutions for managing the complex IT landscape. Development styles, budget pressures and project deliverables, followed by the need to deliver short-term results in an over-constrained environment, led to the rapid creation of huge amounts of proprietary code. Programs are developed as required. Cross-references are made between modules when extensions of existing modules for new functionalities are required. This results in a "mountain-of-spaghetti" of code. The maintenance and operation of such a system represents a logistical nightmare. The re-engineering of current IT systems turns into a process of continuous cycles.

Ambler challenged the CHAOS report in a LinkedIn debate and argued that the agile approach to software development has a far more successful rate (Saravanan, 2013). In a vote, many participants shared views that their projects had been successful (Ambler, 2013). However, most of them also faced great challenges in their projects. Recently, a software engineer celebrated the success of a software project in his company. The project was originally planned to take two years; however, it took four years to complete and cost three times the original budget. For the team, it was a success, as they argued that the final product has many functionalities that are different to the original concept of the product. It is difficult to define success; however, software development still remains a challenge.

A few of years ago, the Swiss government announced the complete failure of a software project for tax management after an investment that was the equivalent of over 100 million USD. In the press, we were informed that the central office divided the whole project into the development of many software packages and subcontracted these packages to different contractors. These software packages did not work together.

All the existing discussions of the problem show that software development is still a challenge, 40 years after the start of the software crisis period. The causes of failure in software projects vary. They could be flaws in the development process, such as consuming most of the budget in requirement specifications, flaws in architectural design and implementation, the inability to handle the complexity of the software system, particularly when a huge system should be developed in one go or, finally, poor project management and understanding of what is really required to manage a software project.

SEARCHING FOR A SOLUTION

In the traditional development approach, business analysts would try to begin with requirements analysis and specification (Bell & Thayer, 1976). Once this task is completed, the specification is signed off and development begins. This approach has not proven effective as requirements are often moving targets. In fact, many projects failed because the development teams did not develop suitable requirements specifications.

Not content with the traditional development approach, several prominent software developers gathered to create a new foundation for the software development approach. As a result, the *Agile Manifesto* was introduced in 2001, first outlining the basic concepts of agile development (Agile Manifesto Group, 2001). The Agile Manifesto is based on 12 principles:

1. Customer satisfaction through the rapid delivery of useful software.
2. Welcoming changing requirements, even late in development.
3. Working software is delivered frequently (every few weeks rather than months).
4. Close, daily cooperation between business people and developers.
5. Projects are built around motivated individuals, who should be trusted.
6. Face-to-face conversation is the best form of communication (co-location).
7. Working software is the principal measure of progress.
8. Sustainable development, which is able to maintain a constant pace.
9. Continuous attention to technical excellence and good design.
10. Simplicity — the art of maximizing the amount of work not done — is essential.
11. Self-organizing teams.
12. Regular adaptation to changing circumstances.

The agile software development process has become very popular in the software industry in recent years. There is extensive literature on agile development processes and practices (Ambler, 2010; Larman, 2003; McGovern et al., 2004). The Agile Alliance has provided a comprehensive online collection with an agile application practice map (Agile Alliance, 2019).

The most popular agile approaches include extreme programming (XP), Scrum, Kanban, etc. These processes follow the evolutionary and iterative approach of software development (Ambler, 2010; Larman, 2003) and focuses on adapting to change. The concept fits in well with enterprise application development to improve business and IT agility. The Standish Group has named the "agile process" as a factor of success (Hartmann Preuss, 2006; Krigsman, 2006). In an agile development process, concrete requirements are identified together with the development process through successive implementation of prototypes.

The 2015 Standish Group CHAOS report (Hastie & Wojewoda, 2015) shows that the success rate for an agile approach is more than three times higher than for a waterfall approach. An agile approach is certainly the better choice than a traditional waterfall approach. However, the report also shows a 39% overall success rate for the agile software development approach. There is further need for improvement. One should try to consider applying the principles of software engineering that have developed after so many years of experience.

There are many articles on why an agile approach can still fail and how it can be improved (Ballard, 2013; Fleming, 2018; Harlow, 2014; Ismail, 2017 & 2018; Kiggundu, 2014; Zaytceva, 2019). Most of the suggestions are about improving the agile process, managing it properly, building a dynamic team, and so on. Using software engineering methods in the agile development process is rarely an issue. One author even suggested that no more documentation be written, as the code should be self-documenting and comprehensible enough (Zaytceva, 2019). For enterprise applications with their inherent complexity, thousands of components have to interact with each other in many different ways. You cannot expect a new team member of a project to go through the code to understand how the applications work. Documentation that can help a new team member understand the overall structure and mechanism of how the applications work is essential.

Software development is not just coding. It needs good engineering. An agile process like Scrum is a good practice. However, the process alone does not guarantee the success of a software project. There are many other factors. Attempts to use only the agile approach to software development can still fail. Software engineering is a discipline that has evolved since the seventies. The combination of software engineering practices and the agile development process should provide techniques and mechanisms to ensure the success of IT projects and improve the quality of applications. The final applications should be easy to maintain and adapt to the changes.

THIS BOOK AND ITS ORGANIZATION

This book aims to give readers a better understanding of the agile application development approach and related issues. Readers should also better understand software engineering with its concepts, principles and techniques. They should get insights into the architecture of the software so that the product has an agile quality that adapts to changes and is easy to maintain. The presented materials combine theories from current empirical research results as well as practical experiences from real projects. The target audience of this book are IT experts such as software developers, software engineers, software project managers as well as scientists and researchers from the fields of computer science and information technology.

Most of the chapter reviewers for this book are authors who work at the academic institutes. There are also a few invited reviewers who are experienced software engineers. It is interesting to see the focus of reviewers. Academics usually focus on the research topic and see how the presentation builds on the topic. References are very important. On the other hand, the experienced software engineers would look for content with practical examples that they can apply to their daily work. In this book, one will find contributions to both academic research and software development. This covers the interest of IT professionals as well as academics and researchers.

The book is divided into three sections with a total of 13 chapters. Here is a brief description of each chapter:

Section 1: Requirements

Chapter 1 deals with requirement engineering in an agile development process using Scrum. In Scrum, requirements are usually defined as user stories in a product backlog. The chapter covers topics like user and enabler stories, non-functional requirements, considerations of architecture and business components, business workflow and breakdown of user stories. Using UML use cases and collaboration models is recommended to transform the stories in the product backlog into formal requirements specifications.

Section 2: Software Design and Architecture

Chapter 2 describes the effective development of a framework that meets the needs of the healthcare industry. The framework is constantly undergoing technological changes to ensure the updating dynamics for an efficient restructuring process. An agile framework is therefore the most important innovative prerequisite for the successful functioning of the system. The authors showed how such a framework can be built.

Chapter 3 describes a structural data binding mechanism for solving the integration problem of distributed applications to meet interoperability requirements while reducing coupling. The author suggests compliance and conformity as concepts to minimize coupling without compromising interoperability by sharing only the subset of the data schema features actually used. The mechanism increases the flexibility and ability to adapt to changes in applications in a distributed environment.

Chapter 4 presents the design concept of an agile architecture based on the design principles and architecture patterns of software engineering. The architecture is a combination of layered, component-based and service-oriented architectural patterns. It provides a plug-and-play mechanism for component integration that, according to the author, is essential for the iterative nature of an agile development process. The agile development process is based on a model-driven approach. Implementations in COBOL and Java are described.

Chapter 5 is a case study on the performance of GraphQL. The author shows how GraphQL can solve application performance and flexibility issues when using the REST API. It discusses several alternatives to using GraphQL and their benefits in terms of performance and flexibility. The author also presents the results of various prototypes and shows potential performance improvements.

Chapter 6 introduces Model-Driven Engineering approaches to gamification. Gamification is not just for creating games. It can be applied in different areas to promote participation, improve engagement and even change behavior. In this chapter, Model-Driven Engineering approaches are proposed as possible solutions to the poor and incoherent involvement of multiple dynamic and mechanical aspects of gamified applications. Three proposals are presented, all based on Domain-Specific Languages (DSL). They allow users to design complex gamification strategies without the need for programming skills.

Chapter 7 presents three approaches to the systematic reuse of software elements in agile development processes. The first approach is to create generic programs or configurable frameworks. The reuse of patterns is the second approach. The third is to use a model-driven approach with model patterns. These approaches accelerate the delivery of software. The final product is flexible and can easily be adapted to changes.

Section 3: Testing and Maintenance

Chapter 8 provides an overview of the software testing lifecycle and techniques. The authors give an overview of the entire spectrum of software testing with suggestions for their implementation. One focus is on testing in an agile development process. Various levels, types and a comparative study on different types of testing are presented. The chapter also includes suggestions for performing the various tests and an effective approach to testing a software system.

Chapter 9 presents a framework for reusable test case generation in software systems testing. The author shows the use of software test ontology to represent the software test knowledge of the software testers. He argues that reusing test cases is an effective way to improve software testing and introduces a software testing framework that uses rule-based-reasoning, case-based-reasoning, and ontology-based semantic similarity assessment to retrieve the test cases from the case library. Experimental results are used to illustrate some of the features of the framework.

Chapter 10 shows why and how to teach property-based testing. Property-based testing is a type of model-based testing in which properties play a dominant role and generated random data is used to evaluate previously defined properties that the system is expected to meet. The authors give a good description of property-based testing. They presented the approach and experience of teaching property-based testing to students of advance programming technique courses.

Chapter 11 contains a report on investigating software testing practices in two companies in Sri Lanka. The author conducted a qualitative methodology survey to examine the current practice of software testing practices in two software companies, based on the claim that both use software testing practices in their software development work. This chapter gives a report of the approaches and techniques for testing of these two companies.

Chapter 12 contains a qualitative analysis of knowledge transfer between senior and novice software testers in a software company in Sri Lanka. The authors emphasize the importance of acquiring knowledge for novice software testers from senior testers to get their work done. They conducted a qualitative methodology study to examine the current practice of knowledge transfer in software testing procedures of a company. The survey results showed some interesting recent trends in knowledge transfer in software. The results can help other software companies improve knowledge sharing and learning practices.

Chapter 13 reports on the effectiveness of Scrum and Kanban on agile base software maintenance projects. A quantitative survey was conducted with the questionnaire distributed to IT professionals in Sri Lanka. The questions relate to a six-point star model that defines project management factors such as schedule, scope, budget, risk, resources, quality and study and uses two other non-quantitative techniques such as team engagement and work organization. The results show that Scrum-based software maintenance projects can improve project quality by managing work organization and resources, while Kanban-based projects can improve project quality by controlling the risk and scope of the project.

Chung-Yeung Pang
Seveco AG, Switzerland

REFERENCES

Agile Manifesto Group. (2001). Manifesto for Agile Software Development. *Agile Manifesto*. Retrieved from http://agilemanifesto.org

Ambler, S. W. (2010). Agile Modeling. *Ambysoft*. Retrieved July 26, 2010, from http://www.agilemodeling.com/

Ambler, S. W. (2013). *What Was Final Status*. Retrieved March 20, 2013, from http://www.linkedin.com/groups/What-was-final-status-most-1523.S.222770182

Ballard, M. (2013). *Why Agile Development Failed for Universal Credit*. Retrieved December 11, 2014, from http://www.computerweekly.com/news/2240187478/Why-agile-development-failed-for-Universal-Credit

Bell, T. E., & Thayer, T. A. (1976). Software Requirements: Are They Really a Problem? In *Proceedings of the 2nd International Conference on Software Engineering*, (pp. 61-68). IEEE Computer Society Press.

Blocher, M., Blumberg, S., & Laartz, J. (2012). Delivering Large-Scale IT Projects on Time, on Budget, And on Value. *McKinsey & Company*. Retrieved December 11, 2014, from http://www.mckinsey.com/insights/business_technology/delivering_large-scale_it_projects_on_time_on_budget_and_on_value

Boehm, B. (1986). A Spiral Model of Software Development and Enhancement. *Software Engineering Notes*, *11*(4), 14–24. doi:10.1145/12944.12948

Boehm, B. (1988). A Spiral Model of Software Development and Enhancement. *IEEE Computer*, *21*(5), 61–72. doi:10.1109/2.59

Booch, G., Maksimchuk, R. A., Engle, M. W., Young, B. J., Conallen, J., & Houston, K. A. (2007). *Object-Oriented Analysis and Design with Applications* (3rd ed.). Upper Saddle River, NJ: Addison-Wesley.

Fleming, S. (2018). 5 ways to make agile work for your organization. *DigitalDirections*. Retrieved July 11, 2019, from https://digitaldirections.com/5-ways-to-make-agile-work-for-your-organization/

Fowler, M. (2004). *UML Distilled: A Brief Guide to the Standard Object Modeling Language* (3rd ed.). Boston, MA: Addison-Wesley.

Harlow, M. (2014). Coconut Headphones: Why Agile Has Failed. *Code Rant*. Retrieved December 11, 2014, from http://mikehadlow.blogspot.ch/2014/03/coconut-headphones-why-agile-has-failed.html

Hartmann Preuss, D. (2006). Interview: Jim Johnson of Standish Group. *InfoQ*. Retrieved July 26, 2010, from http://www.infoq.com/articles/Interview-Johnson-Standish-CHAOS

Hastie, S., & Wojewoda, S. (2015). Standish Group 2015 Chaos Report - Q&A with Jennifer Lynch. *InfoQ*. Retrieved May 26, 2019, from https://www.infoq.com/articles/standish-chaos-2015

Ismail, N. (2017). UK wasting 37 billion a year on failed agile IT projects. *Information Age*. Retrieved May 26, 2019, from https://www.information-age.com/uk-wasting-37-billion-year-failed-agile-it-projects-123466089/

Ismail, N. (2018). Why IT projects continue to fail at an alarming rate. *Information Age*. Retrieved May 26, 2019, from https://www.information-age.com/projects-continue-fail-alarming-rate-123470803/

Jackson, M. A. (1975). *Principles of Program Design*. Cambridge, MA: Academic Press.

Kay, R. (2002). System Development Life Cycle. *Computerworld*. Retrieved January 18, 2016, http://www.computerworld.com/article/2576450/app-development/app-development-system-development-life-cycle.html

Kiggundu, A. (2014). Agile – Theory vs. Practice. *ThoughtWorks*. Retrieved December 11, 2014, from http://www.thoughtworks.com/insights/blog/agile-theory-vs-practice

Krigsman, M. (2006). Success Factors. *ZDNet*. Retrieved July 26, 2010, from http://www.zdnet.com/blog/projectfailures/success-factors/183

Larman, C. (2003). *Agile and Iterative Development: A Manager's Guide*. Reading, MA: Addison-Wesley.

McGovern, J., Ambler, S. W., Stevens, M. E., Linn, J., Sharan, V., & Jo, E. K. (2003). *A Practical Guide To Enterprise Architecture*. Upper Saddle River, NJ: Prentice Hall PTR.

Royce, W. (1970). Managing the Development of Large Software Systems. *Proceedings of IEEE WESON*, (28), 1-9.

Saravanan, G. (2013). *Why Software Engineering Fails! (Most of the Time)*. Retrieved March 9, 2013 from https://www.linkedin.com/groups/Why-Software-Engineering-Fails-Most-1523.S.221165656

SDLC. (2013). Software Development Life Cycle. *SDLC*. Retrieved December 11, 2014, from http://www.sdlc.ws/

Software Crisis. (2010). Software Crisis. *Wikipedia*. Retrieved July 26, 2010, from http://en.wikipedia.org/wiki/Software_crisis

Software Engineering. (2010). Software Engineering. *Wikipedia*. Retrieved July 26, 2010, from http://en.wikipedia.org/wiki/Software_engineering

Standish Group. (2009). CHAOS Summary 2009. *The Standish Group*. Retrieved July 26, 2010, from http://www.standishgroup.com/newsroom/chaos_2009.php

Stellman, A., & Greene, J. (2015). *Learning Agile: Understand SCRUM, XP, Lean, and Kanban*. Sebastopol, CA: O'Reilly.

Winston, P. H. (1992). *Artificial Intelligence* (3rd ed.). Reading, MA: Addison-Wesley.

Yourdon, E., & Constantine, L. L. (1979). *Structure Design: Fundamentals of a Discipline of Computer Program and System Design*. Upper Saddle River, NJ: Yourdon Press.

Zaytceva, O. (2019). Why Agile Doesn't Work for Large Projects. *DZone*. Retrieved June 25, 2019, from https://dzone.com/articles/four-problems-of-software-development-complexity-a

Acknowledgment

The editor would like to acknowledge the help of all the people involved in this project and, more specifically, to the authors and reviewers that took part in the review process. Without their support, this book would not have become a reality.

First, the editor would like to thank each one of the authors for their contributions. My sincere gratitude goes to the chapter's authors who contributed their time and expertise to this book.

Second, the editor wishes to acknowledge the valuable contributions of the reviewers regarding the improvement of quality, coherence, and content presentation of chapters. Most of the authors also served as referees; I highly appreciate their double task.

The editor especially thanks Thomas Miller and Jannik Pfister for participating in the review process so that the review process can be completed on time.

Chung-Yeung Pang
Seveco AG, Switzerland

Section 1
Requirements

This section covers requirements analyses, which are the first activities of a software development project.

Chapter 1
Product Backlog and Requirements Engineering for Enterprise Application Development

Chung-Yeung Pang
https://orcid.org/0000-0002-7925-4454
Seveco AG, Switzerland

ABSTRACT

The combination of software engineering and agile development process can bring great benefits to the development and maintenance of enterprise applications. This chapter introduces the engineering of requirements in an agile Scrum development process. In Scrum, requirements are usually defined as user stories in a product backlog. Since many enterprise applications do not have intensive user actions, stories cannot be linked to users. Topics such as user and enabler stories, non-functional requirements, considerations of architecture and business components, business workflow, and breakdown of user stories are addressed. The requirements engineering of PBIs is illustrated by practical examples. Using UML use cases and collaboration models is recommended to transform the stories in the product backlog into formal requirements specifications. The proposed approach can be part of the agile development framework for flexible software products that are easy to customize and maintain.

INTRODUCTION

An important aspect of software development is the requirements analysis. "You need to know what you need to program before you can program it," is the reason for the requirements analysis. Once you have identified the need in the application, you must also document it. The document would become the requirement specification. It is a daunting task to create a proper requirement specification for a business application. There has been a lot of research in this area (Wiegers & Beatty, 2013). The way to do requirements specification, which we usually call requirements engineering, is a discipline in itself.

DOI: 10.4018/978-1-7998-2531-9.ch001

In the traditional development approach, business analysts would try to begin with requirements analysis and specification (Bell & Thayer, 1976). Once this task is completed, the specification is signed off and development begins. This approach has not proven effective as requirements are often moving targets. In fact, many projects failed because the development teams did not develop suitable requirements specifications.

As software technology advances, we recognize that software development is an iterative process. Requirements analysis and specification are also part of the iterative process. Business applications need to be flexible at all times to meet new requirements and changes. The agile approach to software development has been developed for this reason (Larman, 2003). It is widely used in the software community, especially in the IT development teams of large companies.

There are many methods for an agile development process. This chapter focuses on Scrum (Stellman & Greene, 2015) which is widely used in the software community. For Scrum, there is no activity for the requirement specification. Requirements in the Scrum product backlog are usually user stories. These user stories are taken out in the iterative development process with sprints from the product backlog. There are many literatures for writing user stories (Abdou et al., 2014; Rehkopf, 2019; User Story, 2019).

User stories are not detailed requirements specifications (what a system should do), but negotiable declarations of intent (it needs to do something about like this) (Scrum Expert, 2016). They are short, easy to read and understandable to developers, stakeholders and users. Therefore, user stories should be turned into more stringent requirements specifications before implementation. Another problem is that user stories are great for capturing functional requirements, but they do not work well with design constraints and non-functional requirements (Cohn, 2015; Galen, 2013; Badri, 2016). Solutions to these problems are presented in this chapter.

The materials in this chapter are based on the techniques given in the literature and 15 years of experience of the author in the agile development. The aim of this chapter is to provide concepts and mechanisms for agile requirements engineering based on practical examples. Emphasis is placed on applications with architectural and design constraints and non-functional requirements, as well as formal requirements documentation that is not normally covered by user stories. The chapter is structured as follows. The Background section discusses the historical background of software development and software / system life cycle (SDLC). The next section focuses on both traditional and agile requirements engineering. The following section is about product backlogs and user stories. This is followed by two sections with practical examples on agile requirements engineering based on user stories. The following section provides an explanation of the UML use cases introduced as an approach to formal specification. This section also describes the implementation approach using UML collaboration models. The chapter closes with a vision for the future section and a final conclusion.

BACKGROUND

As background, the following subsections discuss software engineering and the traditional and agile development process lifecycle.

Figure 1. Waterfall model for software development process

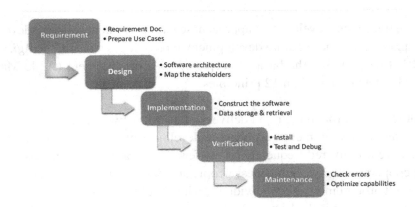

Software Engineering and Software Development Life Cycle (SDLC)

In the early days of software history, programmers tended to develop their programs without documentation in an ad-hoc style. The programs are usually not structured and organized. With the development of many new features, the underlying software became unwieldy. Software Engineering (2010) is a discipline that provides solutions to the increasingly complex nature of software systems. In recent decades, many new methods, standards, programming languages and paradigms have been developed.

In the 1970s, software engineers discovered that there are a number of software development activities. They present logical structures of the various activities that are involved in the life cycle of an IT system. Since then, much research has been done on the activities and processes in the software / system development lifecycle, also known as SDLC (SDLC, 2013). SDLC is used to describe the process of creating software systems in a very deliberate, structured, and methodical way, repeating every stage of the system's life. The waterfall model is one of the first models for SDLC (Royce, 1970; Bell & Thayer, 1976). As shown in Figure 1, the waterfall model provides a simple and logical structure of the various activities and defines clear results in a software development process. It is still popular today.

As we see in Figure 1, the first phase of a software project is the collection of requirements. This is an important step in the software development process, as everything that will be developed later depends on the requirements collected. One sub-discipline emerging from software engineering is requirements engineering. Requirements engineering defines the process and the techniques for In all text books on software engineering, requirements engineering is one of the main topics (Geetha et al., 2015; Sommerville, 2015; Tsui et al., 2016). There are also text books just on this subject (Wiegers & Beatty, 2013; Sommerville & Sawyer, 1997).

Despite its popularity, the linear sequential flow of activities in the waterfall model has many shortcomings. One major flaw concerns the concept that one-phase activities must be completed before activities of the next phase begin. A requirement is often a moving target, as we can see from the fact that most software packages have different versions. As development progresses, we can gain new understanding and insights into the problems of our project. Requirements specifications and designs can be changed constantly. In short, the software development lifecycle is usually an iterative and incremental process.

Agile Manifesto and Development Process

Not content with the traditional development approach, several prominent software developers gathered to create a new foundation for the software development approach. As a result, the *Agile Manifesto* was introduced in 2001, first outlining the basic concepts of agile development (Agile Manifesto Group, 2001). The Agile Manifesto is based on 12 principles:

1. Customer satisfaction through the rapid delivery of useful software.
2. Welcoming changing requirements, even late in development.
3. Working software is delivered frequently (every few weeks rather than months).
4. Close, daily cooperation between business people and developers.
5. Projects are built around motivated individuals, who should be trusted.
6. Face-to-face conversation is the best form of communication (co-location).
7. Working software is the principal measure of progress.
8. Sustainable development, which is able to maintain a constant pace.
9. Continuous attention to technical excellence and good design.
10. Simplicity — the art of maximizing the amount of work not done — is essential.
11. Self-organizing teams.
12. Regular adaptation to changing circumstances.

The agile software development process has become very popular in the software industry in recent years. This process follows the evolutionary and iterative approach of software development (Ambler, 2010; Larman, 2003) and focuses on adapting to change. The concept fits in well with enterprise application development to improve business and IT agility. The Standish Group has named the "agile process" as a factor of success (Hartmann Preuss, 2006, Krigsman, 2006). In an agile development process, concrete requirements are identified together with the development process through successive implementation of prototypes.

There is extensive literature on agile development processes and practices (Ambler, 2010; Larman, 2003; McGovern et al., 2004). The Agile Alliance has provided a comprehensive online collection with an agile application practice map (Agile Alliance, 2019). This chapter introduces only Scrum. Scrum is designed for teams of three to nine members who split their work into actions that can be completed within a timeframe (sprint) that lasts no more than a month, usually two weeks. The software development process with Scrum is shown in Figure 2 (Scrum, 2019). A product backlog is used that contains a complete list of all allowed requests. The elements in the product backlog are usually user stories. The idea of using user stories comes from Cockburn (1998). This chapter addresses the technical requirements using the product backlog.

REQUIREMENTS ENGINEERING

Regardless of the SDLC model used, software development begins by identifying the requirements of the project. The international ESI survey of 2000 business professionals from 2005 shows that 50% of the reasons for the failure of software projects are due to an insufficient definition of requirements (Abdou et al., 2014). This shows how important the correct engineering of the requirements is. This section

Figure 2. Scrum for software development process

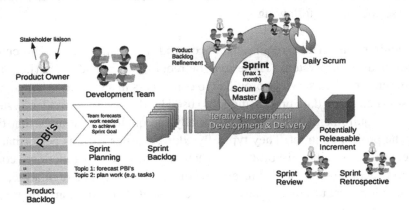

contains a brief description of requirements engineering. The first subsection deals with requirements engineering, which has emerged from traditional software engineering. The second subsection describes requirements engineering in an agile development approach. The last subsection discusses design constraints and architectural considerations that are imposed on the requirements.

TRADITIONAL REQUIREMENTS ENGINEERING

According to IEEE Standard 610.12-1990, requirement is defined as "a condition or capability needed by a user to solve a problem or achieve an objective" or "a condition or capability that must be met or processed by a system or system component to satisfy a contract, standard, specification, or other formally imposed documents" (IEEE SA, 1990). Requirements engineering is the process of defining, documenting and maintaining requirements. According to Sommerville (2015), these include the following activities:

1. Requirements inception or requirements elicitation – Developers and stakeholders meet, the latter are inquired concerning their needs and wants regarding the software product.
2. Requirements analysis and negotiation – Requirements are identified and conflicts with stakeholders are solved. Both written and graphical tools are successfully used as aids.
3. System modeling – Some engineering fields (or specific situations) require the product to be completely designed and modeled before its construction or fabrication starts and, therefore, the design phase must be performed in advance.
4. Requirements specification – Requirements are documented in a formal artifact called a Software Requirements Specification (SRS), which will become official only after validation. A SRS can contain both written and graphical (models) information if necessary.
5. Requirements validation – Checking that the documented requirements and models are consistent and meet the needs of the stakeholder.
6. Requirements management – Managing all the activities related to the requirements since inception, supervising as the system is developed and, even until after it is put into use (e. g., changes, extensions, etc.)

The software requirements are classified into functional requirements and non-functional requirements. They are described in the following:

- Functional requirements: These requirements cover all the main features and characteristics that are to be provided by the system. These may be requests from end users (i.e., user requests) or requests from services (i.e., services provided to consumers in a service-oriented architecture) and from processes (i.e., batch data processing jobs) used by the service provider System be provided.
- Non-functional requirements: These are essentially the quality constraints that the system must fulfill under the project contract. They typically address issues such as performance, availability, reliability, security, scalability, usability, etc. There may also be non-functional constraints related to organization, deployment, platform, architecture, infrastructure, regulation, legislation, and more. Non-functional requirements may be more critical than functional requirements. If these are not met, the system may be unusable. A non-functional requirement, such as a security requirement, may generate a number of related functional requirements that define system services that are required.

Geetha et al. (2015) also suggested that an interface specification is required. They argued that most software systems do not work alone and need to interact with other systems to work. They interact with many other systems to receive and send data, obtain help in processing logic, store information in other systems, and so on. The interaction requirements of one system with another system are defined in the interface specification.

Basically, requirements engineering should deliver a complete and consistent SRS. In practice this is rarely the case. The author has learned that in a number of projects, the effort and cost of pursuing a complete and consistent SRS accounted for most of the project budget. Many of these projects have never achieved their goals.

AGILE REQUIREMENTS ENGINEERING

In the waterfall model, requirements engineering process is the first phase of the SDLC. The main difference between traditional and agile development is not whether to do requirements engineering but when to do it. In the waterfall model, requirements engineering must be completed before going to the design phase. Agile development, on the other hand, assumes that requirements engineering will continue throughout the life cycle of the system. It welcomes new requirements at any time even late in the SDLC. Agile requirement engineering applies the focal values mentioned in the agile manifesto to the requirement engineering process. It encourages iterative analysis and design, user collaboration with face to face communication, short planning cycles and frequent iterations.

An agile method, such as Scrum, documents requirements in the product backlog, which contains a list of request items. The product backlog items are usually user stories. A high-level user story can form an epic. An epic is a high-level user story that is too big to fit in a sprint (Rubin, 2012). It can be broken down into a collection of related user stories. A theme can be used to indicate that a series of stories or epics have something in common, such as being in the same functional area. The product backlog usually includes themes, epics, and user stories.

Table 1. Summary of activities of traditional and agile requirements engineering processes

Traditional Requirement Engineering Process	Agile Requirement Engineering Process
Elicitation	Formulation of product backlog by product owner Stakeholders and business analysts collaborate with users to write user stories.
Analysis	Iterative analysis and design with user collaboration Backlog refinement meeting. Test cases analysis and design Prioritization of product backlog items
Specification	User stories, code, acceptance criteria and test cases, unit test cases
Validation	User collaboration, acceptance tests
Management	Iteration planning cycle (e.g. Sprint planning) Backlog item tracking Backlog grooming

The product backlog is formulated by the Product Owner. User stories can be written by any stakeholder and business analyst. Often, user stories are based on interviews with users. The product backlog should contain all the requirements that the development team must meet (Drumond, 2019).

There are a number of articles comparing the activities involved in agile requirement engineering and traditional requirement engineering (De Lucia & Qusef, 2010; Kuehl & Hawker, 2019; Sebega & Mnkandla, 2017). A summary of the differences in the activities of the two approaches is given in table 1.

DESIGN CONSTRAINTS AND ARCHITECTURAL CONSIDERATION

The design is subject to constraints that depend on factors such as the hardware platform, software platform, network properties, or database. Enterprise applications also have enterprise architecture limitations. For example, architectural patterns such as SOA (Service Oriented Architecture), component-based architecture, or layered architecture define a set of rules for designing and implementing all software components and elements. They may be parts of non-functional, interface, or implementation requirements in the software system that need to be documented in the requirements engineering process.

The operating domain of the system imposes requirements on the system. For example, in a batch job, synchronous communication between two systems is not allowed, so there should be no timeout that could cause the job to abort. Domain requirements can be constraints on existing requirements. If they are not satisfied, the system may not work (Sommerville, 2015).

Basically, the requirements should specify what the system should do, and the design should describe how it does so. In practice, requirements and design may not always be separable. As mentioned earlier, enterprise architecture can impact the requirements of an application. For example, integrating an application into an SOA may be a domain requirement that the functional requirements are services with interfaces for service consumers.

PRODUCT BACKLOG AND USER STORY

Regardless of which development approach we pursue, we must have requirements. Scrum uses product backlog to list all the features, functionalities, requirements, enhancements, and fixes that represent the changes to be made to the product in future releases (Rubin, 2012). Product backlog items (PBIs) have the attributes of a description, an order, an estimate, and a value. PBIs often contain test descriptions that prove their completeness "Done". They should include the key features that make planning and prioritization easier. Each iteration of the development process, the developers remove the work items from the product backlog and into the sprint backlog. The items should be prioritized in the list so that the developers know which ones to select for a new iteration.

The product backlog belongs to the Product Owner. The work items can be described by user stories. User stories can be written by any stakeholder, business analyst and even customer. In most cases, business analysts can interview the users and put all their stories in the product backlog. The prioritization can be based on business values. Once they are done, developers can easily build the software according to the user stories.

User Stories

A user story is the smallest unit of work in an agile framework. It is an end goal, not a feature, expressed from the perspective of the software user. User stories are often expressed in a simple sentence that is structured as follows (Agile Business Consortium, 2019; User Story, 2019):

As a <user role> I need <requirement>, so that <business reason/value>

The sentence contains three following major parts:

- who is the primary stakeholder (the role that derives business benefit from the story)
- what effect the stakeholder wants the story to have
- what business value the stakeholder will derive from this effect

User stories should not describe technical requirements. Often, however, requirements are required that result from technical perspectives. Badri (2016) recommended using technical stories instead of user stories in these cases. Recently, technical story was referred to as enabler story (Scaled Agile, 2019). Enabler stories support exploration, architecture or infrastructure. The author suggests expressing enabler stories in a technical language rather than a user-oriented language in the following format:

<Technical actor> needs to <feature / functional requirement> so that / to / for <reason / value>

User stories focus on solving problems for real users. They define requirements with the intention of working with the users to find out what they really need. Enabler stories define architecture or infrastructure requirements to implement some user stories or support components of the system. A user story or enabler story in the product backlog is short and requires a more detailed discussion of the development. User stories and enabler stories are not intended as a complete specification of requirements. They can have different granularity.

Some guidelines for creating effective user stories have been proposed in Wake's INVEST model (Wake 2003):

- **Independent (I)**: A story should be self-contained, in a way that there is no inherent dependency on another story.
- **Negotiable (N)**: Stories are not explicit contracts and should leave space for discussion.
- **Valuable (V)**: A story must deliver value to the stakeholders.
- **Estimable (E)**: One must always be able to estimate the size of a story.
- **Small (S)**: Stories should not be too big as to become impossible to plan/task/prioritize within a level of accuracy.
- **Testable (T)**: A story or its related description must provide the necessary information to make test development possible.

The last guideline of the INVEST model is Testable. When writing a user story, we would also specify the acceptance criteria. Acceptance criteria can be functional and / or non-functional. They are directly related to the functional and non-functional requirements. Below is an example of a user story:

User Story

As a client care representative at the help desk, I need to be able to search a client's trade orders so I can answer a customer's questions about their trade orders.

Acceptance Criteria

Functional:

1. To start a search, I must enter the client number.
2. I can optionally enter the date and time period to restrict the search range.
3. The search result should include all trade orders made by the client.
4. A pop-up dialog box with a warning should be displayed if no trade order is found for the client with the given search criteria.

Non-Functional:

1. I can only search for trade orders for clients of the area for which I am responsible.
2. The search system must be available every working day from 9:00 to 17:00.

Theme, Epic and Splitting Of User Story

A person cannot work on more than a few concepts and their relationships at the same time. In software development, an abstraction makes it possible to suppress unimportant details and to emphasize the important information. Abstraction is the process of identifying a set of essential features of an entity without paying attention to its details. Abstraction helps manage the intellectual complexity of software. It provides a higher-level concept that ignores certain detailed properties altogether. This actually applies to writing requirements respectively user stories particularly at the starting phase of a project. One can start writing high level user stories and these user stories would be broken down into small Stories that can eventually be implemented in individual sprints.

As previously described, high-level user stories are epics that can be broken down into a series of more detailed user stories. We can also use theme for a set of stories or epics have something in common, such as being in the same functional area. To give an example, when an application to be developed would run under SOA, the Stories related to the services the application provides are themes. The Stories related to components a service required are epics and the stories for individual modules that make up a component are small user stories that can be implemented in individual sprints.

High-level user stories for themes and epics must be split up smaller user stories. Lawrence (2009) has suggested the following 10 strategies to break down large user stories:

1. Breaking down by workflow steps
2. Breaking down by business rules
3. Breaking down by happy / unhappy flow
4. Breaking down by input options / platform
5. Breaking down by data types or parameters
6. Breaking down by operations
7. Breaking down by test scenarios / test case
8. Breaking down by roles
9. Breaking down by 'optimize now' vs 'optimize later'
10. Breaking down by browser compatibility

Another set of split patterns proposed by Wake (2018) are:

1. Workflow Steps Pattern
2. Business Rule Variations Pattern
3. Simple/Complex Pattern
4. Variations in Data Pattern
5. Data Entry Pattern
6. Operations Pattern
7. Defer Performance Pattern
8. Break Out a Spike Pattern

The breakdown strategies of Lawrence and the split patterns of Wake have a lot in common. Some of these patterns are used in the examples to break high-level stories in the next section.

PBI FOR APPLICATION IN SOA

This section describes an example of creating PBIs for a Client Trade Order application. The application would be part of a corporate IT system. The application must integrate with the existing enterprise system architecture, which is a component-based layered SOA. The system infrastructure is already in place. The infrastructure architecture defines a set of rules and program structures that the application must follow. They form the design constraints and architectural considerations that lead to domain and non-functional application requirements.

The following subsections illustrate the phases of the PBIs development process. It starts with project inception and requirements elicitation. The next step is requirement analysis with a breakdown of the business workflow. Further breakdowns are required to refine the stories to meet the INVEST principle and be ready for implementation in sprints.

Project Inception and Requirements Elicitation

A project is usually initiated when needed. Before the project is formed, there are some ideas about the need of the project from different stakeholders. Typically, these stakeholders come together to share their ideas and develop a common understanding of the need for an application. At some point, they did a brainstorming session to work out the features and scope of the project. Business users and technical experts may be invited to comment on the use and constraints of such an application. This can be a first feasibility study of the project. Different companies have different approval procedures for the project. After the project has been approved and budgeted, it starts and the Product Owner can formulate the product backlog for the project. Very often, PBIs are taken from old projects that did not fall within the scope of former applications. This example assumes everything starts fresh.

In this inception or elicitation phase, the following activities are performed:

- Perform some high-level requirements envisioning
- Gain a common understanding of the scope of the problem among the stakeholders
- Define business goals
- Start iteration 0 of the agile project
- Layout the architectural and design constraints as well as the domain and non-functional requirements that apply to the entire application

In this phase we can create the first user story in the form of a theme like the following:

User Story

As a client advisor, I must capture an order for foreign exchange so that a client can request such a service.

Acceptance Criteria

Functional:

1. To start the application, I must log into the system.
2. The system must provide me with the steps and screens for data entry to capture the order.
3. To capture an order, I must provide the client information, exchange currency pair, amount of traded currency, and other business data concerning the order.
4. The system must validate the data that I enter.
5. The system must ensure the business rules and constraints are kept for the order I enter.
6. I must be able to select the accounts for the bookings of the trade.
7. I need a quote for the currency exchange rate.
8. I can accept the quote within the period that it is valid.

9. I should be able to correct or update the order data I have entered before the order capture process is completed.
10. When the order capture process is completed, it must be sent to service for trade settlement and booking.
11. When the order capture process raises a warning or error, I must be informed through a message in pop-up dialog box and advise me what I can do.
12. I must be able to search the trade orders that I have captured.

Non-Functional:

1. I can capture orders on a GUI application running on my browser.
2. I need to be authenticated before I can capture any order.
3. I can only capture trade orders for clients of the area for which I am responsible.
4. The system must be available every working day from 9:00 to 17:00.
5. The data entered through GUI on the browser must be sent to the services running on the host provided by the application.
6. The communication between GUI and services must be in XML format.
7. The GUI would react with a proper screen or a pop-up dialogue box according to the reply of the host service.
8. The service must commit the transaction when a step of the order capture is processed successfully.
9. The service must roll back the transaction when an error occurs during the order processing.

The above user story is the result of a stakeholder brainstorming session to identify the features that the application must provide. These features are the functional requirements in the acceptance criteria. In other words, the application will not be accepted if one of these functions is missing. Architecture and design constraints as well as domain requirements form the non-functional requirements of the acceptance criteria. At this stage, the user story and its acceptance criteria requirements are high-level abstractions. The user story needs another breakdown. The requirements can be converted into fine-grained user stories. The idea is to divide the stories until they are small and clear enough to be implemented in an iteration and to follow the principle of INVEST.

Requirement Analysis With Business Workflow Breakdown

The first refinement strategy is to break the top-level user story into workflow steps. User stories describing the steps of the business workflow in our example are listed below:

1. As a client advisor, I need to enter an order for foreign exchange when requested by a client so that I can start an order capture process.
2. As a client advisor, I need to select the client account for the order so that the settlement and booking can be made on the selected client account.
3. As a client advisor, I need to review the quote and the total price of the order so that I can inform the client about the cost of the order.
4. As a client advisor, I have to accept the quote and fee of the order on behalf of the client when the client agrees so that the order can proceed.

5.   As a client advisor, I have to look up my orders based on a few criteria so that I can check the orders at any time with their details and status.

The first four of the five stories above contain the sequential steps of the trade order capture workflow. The last story offers the search function for orders placed by a client advisor.

Data Entry, Operation and Business Rule Breakdown

The complete user story with the acceptance criteria for the first workflow step is listed below:

User Story

As a client advisor, I need to enter an order for foreign exchange when requested by a client so that I can start an order capture process.

Acceptance Criteria

Functional:

1.   I must enter client information for the order.
2.   I must enter the currency pair and the amount for the order.
3.   I must enter the business data required for the order.
4.   When the data entry is completed, I need to submit the order to the backend service.
5.   The service needs to validate the order input data in order to ensure the accuracy of the order.
6.   The service needs to verify the customer's entitlement for a trade order.
7.   The service must check the currency pair is tradable.
8.   The service must check the amount is within the limit that is allowed for a foreign exchange trade.
9.   The service must fetch the client accounts for the traded and exchanged currencies.
10. The service must return the lists of accounts for the traded and exchanged currencies to the frontend GUI application.

   Non-Functional:

1.   A service must be provided for the trade order initialization process.
2.   The service must commit the transaction when all the validations, checks and account retrieval are successfully completed.
3.   Standard exception handling should take place when any validation, check or account retrieval fails and the transaction must be rolled back.

The above user story can be subdivided into the following user stories and enabler stories according to the data entry, the operations, and the business rule:

1. As a client advisor, I must enter the data required for the foreign exchange order so that the data required for the order can be sent to the backend service.
2. The order entry service needs to get the client data from the client information business component to ensure that the client is valid client and the client is entitled to place and order.
3. The order entry service needs to verify that the currency pair is given in the tradable currency pairs table to ensure that currency pair is tradable.
4. The order entry service needs to check amount is lower than the upper bound and higher than the lower bound of the allowed limit of the traded currency given in the configuration table to ensure that the amount is within limit.
5. The order entry service needs to retrieve the customer's accounts for the traded and exchanged currencies from the client information business component to allow the client advisor to select the accounts for booking.

All five stories fulfill the INVEST principle. They are small enough to be implemented in iterations. Two of the above stories must interact with the client information business component developed by a team in another business unit. The client information business component may already provide the required interfaces for these stories so that no other development is required by the other team. Otherwise, a negotiation of the interface requirements between the project team and the client information business team would have to take place. Such interface requirements must be implemented.

In an agile process, the emphasis is on rapidly deploying functional software to end users. Once these five stories are implemented, the client advisor can perform the initial acceptance test for the order initialization process.

HAPPY / UNHAPPY FLOW WITH EXCEPTION HANDLING BREAKDOWN

Stories 2 through 4 presented in the previous subsection include validation and checking. The related processes may fail, resulting in an exception. The default exception handling is mentioned in the non-functional requirement in the acceptance criteria of the parent user story. The non-functioning requirement may lead to another breakdown of the unhappy flow. An example is given below.

1. The order entry service needs to terminate the process and generate an error message if the eligibility check fails to ensure that an ineligible client cannot place an order.
2. As a client advisor, I need a message dialog to inform me that the client is not eligible to request the trade order I entered, so that I know that the order will be rejected and I can inform the client.

TECHNICAL CONSTRAINTS AND PROCESS BREAKDOWN

This section presents another example of PBI development in two subsections. In this example, there is a technical constraint that requires a special design solution. Solving the problem leads to further requirements in the product backlog. It shows the iterative nature of an agile process in which the design starts before the completion of the requirements capture.

Requirements Elicitation of a Batch Process

The first user story (theme) describing the application is shown below:

User Story:

As a product manager, I need a process to execute daily foreign currency exchange transactions after each business day so that the transaction amount of the foreign currency is converted to a local currency amount and this local currency amount is debited or credited to the customer's account for each day.

Acceptance Criteria

Functional:

1. Scan and retrieve the daily trades that involve foreign exchange from the trade order table.
2. Validate the trade data.
3. Skip the trade when the trade data is invalid and log the error into the error log.
4. Retrieve the account of the client for the trade.
5. Request the exchange rate from the quote engine.
6. Transform the traded amount into local currency.
7. Credit or debit the client account for sell and buy.
8. Update the trade data after booking for settlement process.

   Non-Functional:

1. The process must be in batch mode.
2. The process must run at midnight.
3. The process cannot be stopped when some errors occur and it must run through every time.
4. Errors must be recorded in a log file and handled manually by the support team.
5. There is no synchronous communication between the process and the system on which the Quote Engine resides, to avoid a time-out error.

   Similar to the first user story of the previous section, the above user story contains the first general information about the application to be developed. PBIs should not contain design solutions. However, the requirements and system constraints of the user story force us to create PBIs that can eventually be implemented as described in the next subsection.

Requirements Analysis and Technical Process Breakdown

As one can see, the features required for the top-level user story are all technically related. The breakdown of the user story would lead mainly to the following enabler stories:

1. The process must retrieve all trading data created relating to the exchange of foreign currency on that day, so that daily trading transactions with the exchange of foreign currencies can be settled and booked.
2. The process must validate the trade data to ensure a trade is valid and can be booked.
3. The process must retrieve the client account for the local currency of the transaction so that the transaction can be booked to the client account.
4. The process must receive the exchange rate from the quote engine so that the amount traded can be converted into an amount in local currency.
5. The process must calculate the amount in local currency based on the exchange rate received from the quote engine for crediting or debiting the account.
6. The process must credit or debit the account for sale and purchase for the booking to be made.
7. The process must update the status of the business data to "booked" for the settlement process to begin.

With detailed functional and non-functional requirements in the acceptance criteria, the implementation for the stories described above can be started. There is a big problem. The process cannot call the quote engine hosted in another system synchronously. Therefore, one cannot have a sequential step for the above stories for each trade. The system constraint forces the split of the process into two batch jobs. The first one would do the steps of the first three stories. Upon completion of the first batch process, a quote request must be sent to the quote engine in the other system to determine the exchange rate of all currencies involved in all transactions. After the response from the quote engine, the second batch process must be triggered to do the rest of the booking activity. Therefore, the identified constraint requires a solution, and once this solution is established, a new set of requirements may come out. They can be formulated as enabler stories. The enabler story of the first batch process is shown below:

Enabler Story

The first process must prepare a message with all currencies involved in daily trading along with the traded total for each currency and send the message to the quote engine when the process is complete for the quote request to be asynchronous.

Acceptance Criteria

Functional:

1. Record all different traded currencies involved in the daily trades.
2. Calculate the total traded amount for each currency by adding the traded amount to the total amount for the purchase and subtracting the traded amount from the total amount for sale.
3. Generate the message for quote request.
4. Send the quote request message to the quote engine.

Figure 3. Example of Use Case Diagram

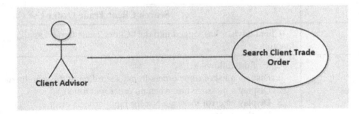

Non-Functional:

1. Quote request message must be in XML format.
2. The message is sent to the quote engine in a fire and forget mode.

This example shows that the design may need to be created during the requirements analysis. The design may create new requirements to solve a problem. This actually corresponds to the concept of the agile approach to software development.

FORMALIZE REQUIREMENTS WITH USE CASES AND IMPLEMENTATION

In the Scrum development process, a sprint is an iteration in which certain development work must be completed. Developers would create the programs or modules according to the user and enabler stories of the PBIs.

As mentioned earlier, a user or enabler story in a product backlog does not contain the full specification of the request. To get started with implementation, we need more formal specifications for the user and enabler stories. For example, the data structure associated with the interface of a service or component should also be included in the request specification. They are very important when different teams are responsible for components of different business areas. They are usually not part of the user stories.

One approach is to use the UML use case to capture the requirements of a user story (Scrum Expert, 2016; Madanayake et al., 2016). This approach is discussed in the first subsection. The second subsection introduces the collaboration implementation based on the collaboration model. The following subsection deals with the topics architecture and process flow. The section concludes with prioritizing the implementation of PBIs.

User Story Mapping and Use Case

Use cases was introduced by Jacobson more than 20 years ago (Jacobson et al., 1992). They describe the functional requirements of the system from the point of view of the actors. A use case describes how an actor wants to use a system. An actor can be a user or a system or an entity, such as a company or an institution. A functional requirement can be captured by three elements, the actor, the use case, and the relationship between them. Figure 3 shows the use case diagram for a feature request.

Table 2. Requirement documentation of a use case

Description	Search Client Trade Order Use Case
Pre-condition	Client advisor has logged into the "Client Trade Order" application and selects the search function.
Post-condition	One of the following: 1. Display a list of trade orders found according to the search criteria 2. Display a message box when no order was found 3. Display an error message box for input criteria error 4. Display an error message box for technical error on the backend server

Flow of event: basic path	1. The client advisor enters search criteria in one or a combination of the following options
	    a. Enter date-time period
	    b. Enter the number of orders to be returned (the most recently created orders, if no other option is selected)
	    c. Enter client number
	2. Client advisor clicks Submit button
	3. Message sent to backend server to invoke the "Client Trade Order" search service
	4. Format the service output from the response.
	5. Display the list of trade orders found.

Flow of event: alternative path	1. In step 1, the client advisor selects Cancel. The search is ended and return to the main screen. 2. In step 4, if no order has been found for a particular search criteria, a message box appears stating that no order was found.
Flow of event: exception path	1. In step 4, if the back-end server returns an error message stating that the input criteria are incorrect, an error message box appears showing the incorrect input. 2. In step 4, if the back-end server does not return a message within the time-out period, an error message box will be displayed with a back-end server technical error (Timeout). 3. In step 4, if the back-end server returns a technical error message, an error message box with technical errors is displayed.

Figure 4. Use case diagram for daily settlement of trades

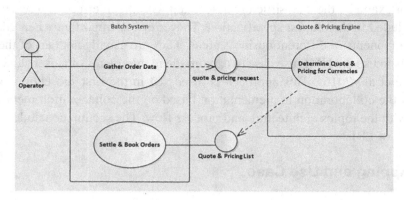

Full documentation of the requirement would provide more detailed information. An example of the use case shown in Figure 3 is given in table 2.

The mapping of user stories to use cases is not necessarily a one-to-one basis. We can have multiple user stories for one use case. It may happen that a user story is mapped to several use cases. This is not advisable because it has to be a very big story that would violate the INVEST principle. The story should

Figure 5. Refinement of capture trade order use case

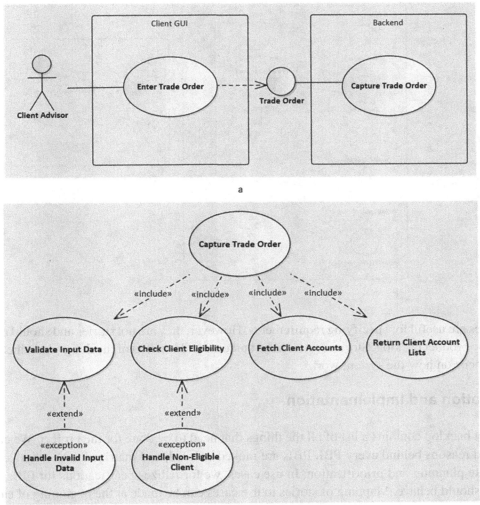

be refined and divided into a series of smaller stories in the product backlog before being selected for a sprint.

Another example given here are the use cases for the daily settlement of trades described in the previous section. Figure 4 shows the use case diagram. The diagram shows how use cases in different systems interact with each other.

We can have use cases with high-level abstraction. Figure 5 shows the use case of the example "Capture Trade Order". In this example, we map the big user story to a high-level use case, as shown in Figure 5.a. At some point in our iteration development process, we refine the use case to include low-level use cases for our sprint backlog, as shown in Figure 5.b.

Figure 6. Collaboration model for search client order use case

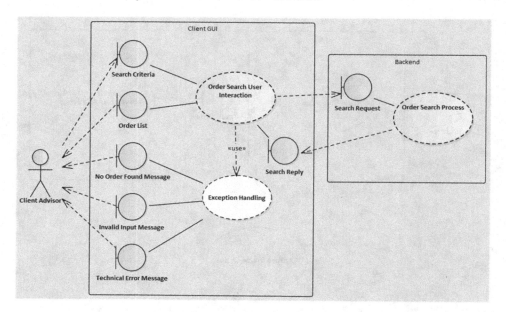

Use cases are useful for specifying requirements. However, they are not stories and should not replace stories in the product backlog. Stories focus on the outcome and benefits of the things described, whereas use cases focus on how the system works.

Collaboration and Implementation

The product backlog contains a list of all the things that need to be done for the project. We can see the benefits and reasons behind every PBI. PBIs are ranked ordered, and matrixed with other key features that facilitate planning and prioritization. In use cases, we formalize specifications for PBIs as to how the system should behave. Mapping of stories to use cases can be made at the beginning of each sprint. Once use cases have been created, we can perform further modeling and designing and then implement the programs according to the use cases.

UML uses collaboration to implement use case (Richardson, 2006). Figure 6 shows the collaboration model for the "Search Client Trade Order" use case. In this model we identify objects that are involved in the collaboration. The dynamic behavior of the collaboration can be represented by a UML activity diagram as shown in Figure 7. Note that the "Search Client Trade Order" use case in Figure 3 does not include the interaction between the front-end GUI program and the process in the backend system. This is captured in the collaboration model.

One of the main advantages of the collaboration model is the ability to capture the interactions between different collaborations. The physical implementation behind a collaboration can be a component, a service, or an infrastructure. As shown in Figure 6, the "Client Order Search" collaboration interacts with the "Exception Handling" collaboration. The implementation of "Exception Handling" collaboration contains a set of infrastructures that are used for all processes of the application.

Figure 7. Activity Diagram for dynamic behavior of Client Order Search Collaboration

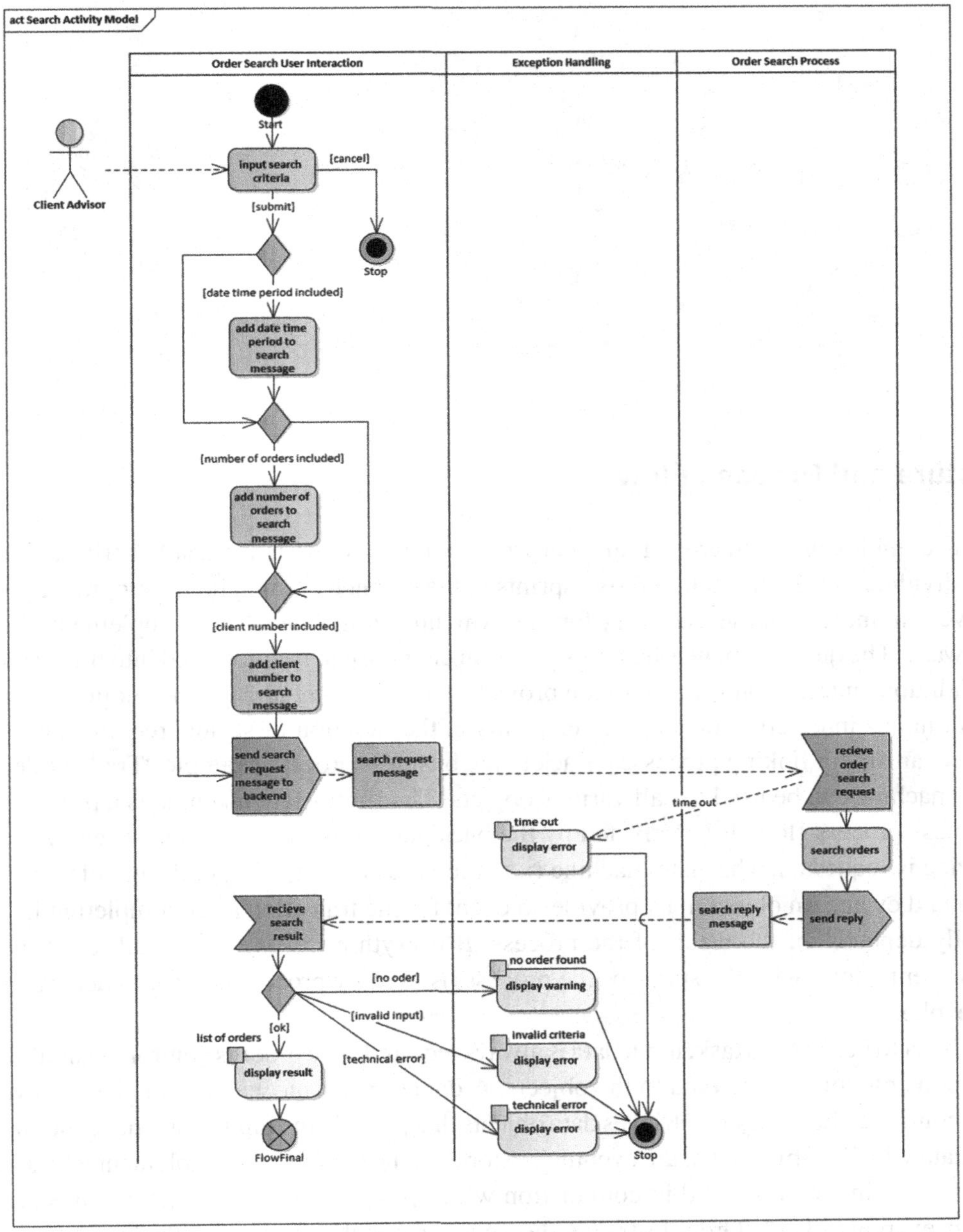

Figure 8. Collaboration model for trade order entry showing the architecture

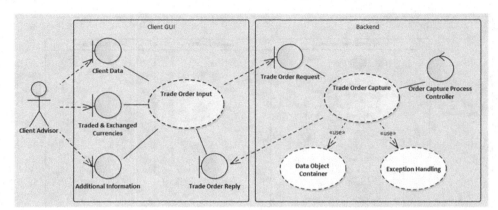

Architecture and Process Flow

Splitting the complex problem area of an enterprise application into manageable PBIs and then implementing individual pieces through iterative sprints is the essence of an agile development process. For example, we can implement the user story for the "Amount Limit Check". The implementation is rather straightforward. The question now is how this program element can be integrated into the overall system. In fact, continuous integration is a key to the project's success using an agile development approach.

The continuous integration of program elements in the iteration of sprints requires an architecture with the mechanism for linking processes. Back to the business process example "Trade Order Entry", a finite-state machine can be used to call various objects. The finite-state machine is a process controller of the business process flow. It is activated by the backend infrastructure when the entry of the Trade Order Service is requested. The state machine (i.e., the process controller) calls an object based on the actual state and event. An object must provide an event for the transition after completing its task. This event usually depends on the result of the process. If everything is ok, the default event is an "OK" event. This event, along with the status of the process, is used by process control to determine the next object to invoke.

For an object to perform its task, input data is always required. The process controller should be generic and not responsible for passing data to the objects. A data transfer mechanism can be achieved using a data object container. Each object retrieves data objects that provide the input from that container and fills the output data with the objects that are eventually stored in the container. If implemented in Java, Spring Application Container can be used in conjunction with Spring dependency injection mechanism. The design of the example "Trade Order Entry" is shown in the collaboration model in figure 8 and figure 9.

The activity diagram shown in Figure 9 can simply use the name of the action taken as the process state. By default, each action completes with an "OK" event that is not displayed in the chart. An action can generate another event, such as the "Invalid Input" event generated by the Validate Data Entry action. This would cause the process control to trigger the action to handle the invalid input case as shown in Figure 9.

Figure 9. Activity diagram for trade order entry collaboration showing the architecture

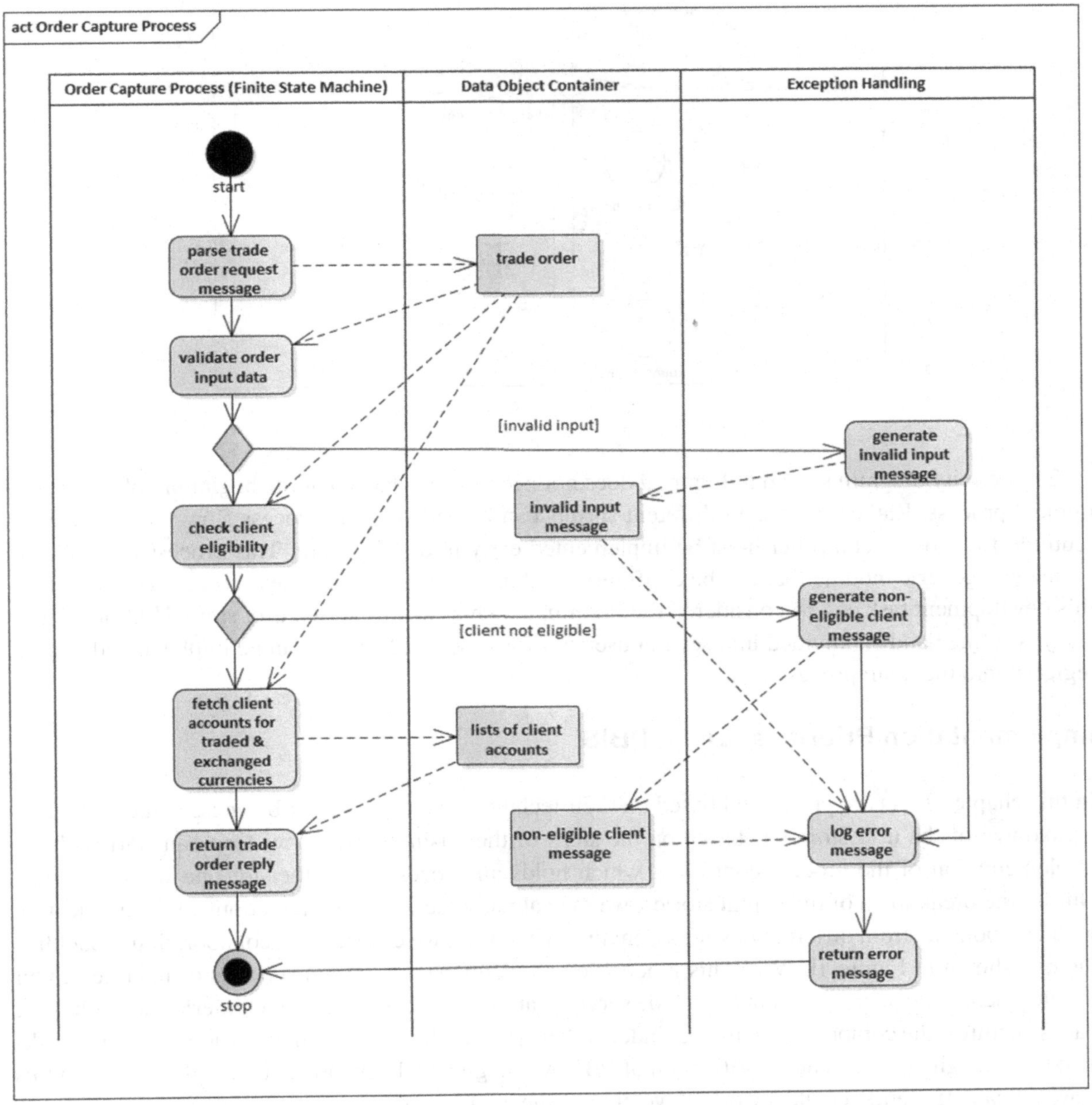

Figure 10. Collaboration model for components

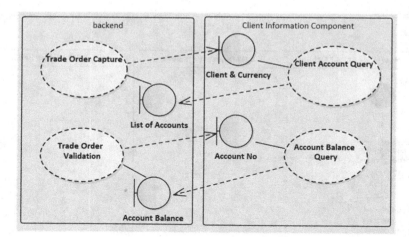

The activity diagram shown in Figure 9 does not need to be finalized at the beginning of our development process. Rather, actions in different sprints can be added to the process flow. The basic code required for process controller must be implemented early in development. This process controller is typically a generic module that can be configured and used for various business process flows. In fact, this development task can be considered the first implementation of the first user story. High-level user story is refined and subdivided into several user stories. Low-level stories can be implemented and integrated into the main process flow.

Implementation Prioritization Of PBIS

In this chapter, PBIs are prioritized based on their technical values, not their business values. The first breakdown of the user stories is based on the steps of the business workflow. One can start with the implementation of the process controller, which holds all processes together for one workflow step. During the breakdown of the parent stories, we may already identify the interactions of the application with components from different business domains. Therefore, we can sketch a collaboration model like the one shown in Figure 10. With this model we can identify the required services or interfaces. Our development in the next sprint could include service data structures or component interfaces. With these data structures, the component teams can independently begin their development. Therefore, these tasks also have a high priority. The prioritization of PBIs would give PBI dependencies a high priority. In this way, we can efficiently create a working version of the application.

User interaction is considered very important in an agile development process. In the example with the project "Client Trade Order" the main users are the client advisors. They should be heavily involved in the design of the GUI with which they would interact actively. For the backend process, business experts and stakeholders are more important in defining business rules and processes.

VISION FOR THE FUTURE

This chapter introduced requirements engineering for creating product and sprint backlog items. This can be part of an application development framework in Scrum. What we need is a framework for the entire SDLC for an agile development practice. Models offer a high-level of abstraction. They provide overview, mechanism and structure of the underlying programs. They are a great documentation for applications. Models can be changed relatively easily. If we have a concrete framework and tools to transform the parent models into working software, we have an agile IT system that allows us to quickly develop applications and easily adapt to changes.

In recent years, great advances have been made in the fields of artificial intelligence, pattern recognition, machine learning and natural language processing. With these modern techniques, user stories and their requirement models can be analyzed to identify the underlying business and technical patterns. For many companies, we have a variety of existing software components that cover most of the business and technical patterns. If we can extract the code of these components and override it with the variations required for certain requirements, we can automate application development. This should become a focus of research as it would have a significant impact on the development process.

CONCLUSION

Many enterprise applications are not user-oriented. Many business processes, such as trade settlement, ledger bookings, order completion processes, etc., have no user interaction. Development teams can be organized by business domains. That is why we may not focus solely on user-related stories. There are stories related to architectural constraints, such as batch processes, business components, services, and so forth. In addition, complex enterprise applications require appropriate requirements engineering.

In this chapter, the requirements engineering of PBIs is presented by means of practical examples. The Scrum development process is selected. Emphasis is placed on applications with architectural and design constraints and non-functional requirements that are usually not adequately captured by user stories. The chapter offers approaches with illustrations of techniques and mechanisms to address the following issues and issues:

- Requirements inception and elicitation with high-level first user story.
- Break down high-level user stories into user stories and enabler stories until they conform to the INVEST principle, especially when architectural and design constraints are imposed.
- Requirements that require an early design solution to continue agile development.
- Formalizing user and enabler stories with UML use cases.
- Providing detail specification through UML collaborations.
- Technical architecture issues in solution proposals for requirements analysis and implementation in agile development with continuous integration.
- Prioritization of PBIs according to business values as well as architecture and component interfaces.

Using the requirements engineering approaches suggested in this chapter, one can develop software products that are flexible, easy to customize, and easy to maintain.

REFERENCES

Abdou, T., Kamthan, P., & Shahmir, N. (2014). User Stories for Agile Business: INVEST, Carefully! *ResearchGate*. Retrieved May 25, 2019, from https://www.researchgate.net/publication/267515016_User_Stories_for_Agile_Business_INVEST_Carefully

Agile Alliance. (2019). *Agile Alliance*. Retrieved July 26, 2019 from https://www.agilealliance.org/

Agile Business Consortium. (2019). Chapter 15: Requirements and User Stories. *Agile Business Consortium*. Retrieved July 26, 2019 from https://www.agilebusiness.org/page/ProjectFramework_15_RequirementsandUserStories

Agile Manifesto Group. (2001). Manifesto for Agile Software Development. *Agile Manifesto*. Retrieved July 26, 2010, from http://agilemanifesto.org

Ambler, S. W. (2010). Agile Modeling. *Ambysoft*. Retrieved July 26, 2010, from http://www.agilemodeling.com/

Badri, A. (2016). User Stories and Technical Stories in Agile Development. *Seilevel*. Retrieved May 26, 2017, from https://seilevel.com/requirements/user-stories-technical-stories-agile-development

Bell, T. E., & Thayer, T. A. (1976). Software Requirements: Are They Really a Problem? In *Proceedings of the 2nd International Conference on Software Engineering*, (pp. 61-68). IEEE Computer Society Press.

Cockburn, A. (1998). Origin of story card is a promise for a conversation. *Alistair.Cockburn*. Retrieved May 26, 2017, from http://alistair.cockburn.us/Origin+of+user+story+is+a+promise+for+a+conversation

Cohn, M. (2015). Not Everything Needs to Be a User Story: Using FDD Features. *Mountain Goat Software*. Retrieved May 26, 2017, from https://www.mountaingoatsoftware.com/blog/not-everything-needs-to-be-a-user-story-using-fdd-features

De Lucia, A., & Qusef, A. (2017). Requirements Engineering in Agile Software Development. *Journal of Emerging Technologies in Web Intelligence*, 2(3), 212–220.

Drumond, C. (2019). What is Scrum? *Atlassian*. Retrieved July 11, 2019, from https://www.atlassian.com/agile/Scrum

Galen, R. (2013). Technical User Stories – What, When, and How? *RGALEN Consulting*. Retrieved July 11, 2019, from http://rgalen.com/agile-training-news/2013/11/10/technical-user-stories-what-when-and-how

Geetha, C., Subramanian, C., & Dutt, S. (2015). *Software Engineering*. Delhi, India: Pearson Education India.

Hartmann Preuss, D. (2006). Interview: Jim Johnson of Standish Group. *InfoQ*. Retrieved July 26, 2010, from http://www.infoq.com/articles/Interview-Johnson-Standish-CHAOS

Jacobson, I., Christerson, M., Jonsson, P., & Oevergaard. (1992). *Object-Oriented Software Engineering*. New York: ACM Press.

Krigsman, M. (2006). Success Factors. *ZDNet*. Retrieved July 26, 2010, from http://www.zdnet.com/blog/projectfailures/success-factors/183

Kuehl, R., & Hawker, J. S. (2019). Requirements – Architecture – Agility. *SWEN 440-01 Software Requirements and Architecture Engineering*. Retrieved October 28, 2019, from http://www.se.rit.edu/~swen-440/slides/instructor-specific/Kuehl/Lecture%2026%20Requirements%20Architecture%20Agility.pdf

Larman, C. (2003). *Agile and Iterative Development: A Manager's Guide*. Reading, MA: Addison-Wesley.

Lawrence, R. (2009). Making Agile a Reality. *Agile for All*. Retrieved July 20, 2019 from https://agile-forall.com/patterns-for-splitting-user-stories/

Madanayake, R., Dias, G. K. A., & Kodikara, N. D. (2016). Use Stories vs UML Use Cases in Modular Transformation. *International Journal of Scientific Engineering and Applied Science*, *3*(1), 1–5.

McGovern, J., Ambler, S. W., Stevens, M. E., Linn, J., Sharan, V., & Jo, E. K. (2003). *A Practical Guide To Enterprise Architecture*. Upper Saddle River, NJ: Prentice Hall PTR.

Rehkopf, M. (2019). User Stories. *Atlassian Agile Guide*. Retrieved May 22, 2019, from https://www.atlassian.com/agile/project-management/user-stories

Richardson, M. (2006). Guideline: Use-Case Realization. *IBM Corp*. Retrieved May 22, 2019, from http://www.michael-richardson.com/processes/rup_classic/core.base_rup/guidances/guidelines/use-case_realization_C690D81F.html

Royce, W. (1970). Managing the Development of Large Software Systems. *Proceedings of IEEE WESON*, (28), 1-9.

Rubin, K. S. (2012). *Essential Scrum: A Practical Guide to the Most Popular Agile Process*. Reading, MA: Addison-Wesley.

Scaled Agile. (2019). Story. *Scaled Agile Framework*. Retrieved July 20, 2019 from https://www.scaled-agileframework.com/story/

Scrum. (2019). Scrum (software development). *Wikipedia*. Retrieved July 20, 2019 from https://en.wikipedia.org/wiki/Scrum_(software_development)

Scrum Expert. (2016). User Stories Are Not Requirements. *Scrum Expert*. Retrieved July 20, 2019 from https://www.scrumexpert.com/knowledge/user-stories-are-not-requirements/

SDLC. (2013). Software Development Life Cycle. *SDLC*. Retrieved December 11, 2014, from http://www.sdlc.ws/

Sebega, Y., & Mnkandla, E. (2017). Exploring Issues in Agile Requirements Engineering in the South African Software Industry. *EJISDC*, *81*(5), 1–18.

Software Engineering. (2010). Software Engineering. *Wikipedia*. Retrieved July 26, 2019, from http://en.wikipedia.org/wiki/Software_engineering

Sommerville, I. (2015). *Software Engineering* (10th ed.). Essex, UK: Pearson Education Limited.

Sommerville, I., & Sawyer, P. (1997). *Requirements Engineering: A Good Practice Guide*. West Sussex, UK: John Wiley & Son.

Stellman, A., & Greene, J. (2015). *Learning Agile: Understand Scrum, XP, Lean, and Kanban*. Sebastopol, CA: O'Reilly.

Tsui, F., Karam, O., & Bernal, B. (2016). *Essentials of Software Engineering* (4th ed.). Burlington, MA: Jones & Bartlett Learning.

User Story. (2019). User Story. *Wikipedia*. Retrieved July 26, 2019, from https://en.wikipedia.org/wiki/User_story

Wake, B. (2003). INVEST in Good Stories, and SMART Tasks. *XP123*. Retrieved May 25, 2019, from https://xp123.com/articles/invest-in-good-stories-and-smart-tasks/

Wake, B. (2018). Back to basics: Writing and splitting user stories. *Medium.com*. Retrieved May 25, 2019, from https://medium.com/agile-outside-the-box/back-to-basics-writing-and-splitting-user-stories-8903a931499c

Wiegers, K., & Beatty, J. (2013). *Software Requirements* (3rd ed.). Redmond, WA: Microsoft Press.

KEY TERMS AND DEFINITIONS

Agile Software Development Process: An evolutionary and iterative approach to software development with focuses on adaptation to changes.

Document-Based Database: A database designed for storing, retrieving, and managing document-based information, also known as semi-structured data.

Generic Software: An implementation of an algorithm with elements that have more than one interpretation, depending on parameters representing types.

INVEST: A mnemonic for agile software projects as a reminder of the characteristics of a good quality Product Backlog Item commonly written in user story format.

Model-Driven Approach to Software Development: A model centric rather than a code centric approach to software development with code generated from models.

Pattern: A reusable solution to a common problem in a particular software context.

PBI (Product Backlog Item): An item in the Product Backlog such as a feature, defect, or technical work that is valuable from the product owner's perspective.

Product Backlog: An ordered list of everything that is known to be needed in the product.

SCRUM: An agile process framework for managing knowledge work, with an emphasis on software development.

Software Component: A software unit of functionality that manages a single abstraction.

Software Development Life Cycle (SDLC): The process, methods or a set of methodologies applied to create or alter software projects.

Software Engineering: The application of engineering to the development of software in a systematic method.

Spring Framework: An application framework and inversion of control container for the Java platform.

Sprint: A time-box of one month or less during which a "Done", useable, and potentially releasable product increment is created.

UML (Unified Modeling Language): A general-purpose, developmental, modeling language in the field of software engineering that is intended to provide a standard way to visualize the design of a system.

UML Activity Diagram: Graphical representations of workflows of stepwise activities and actions with support for choice, iteration, and concurrency.

UML Collaboration: An illustration of the relationships and interactions among software objects.

Use Case: A representation of a user's interaction with the system that shows the relationship between the user and the different use cases in which the user is involved.

User Story: A short, simple description of a feature told from the perspective of the person who desires the new capability, usually a user or customer of the system.

Waterfall Model: A sequential design, used in software development processes, in which progress is seen as flowing steadily downwards (like a waterfall) through the phases of Conception, Initiation, Analysis, Design, Construction, Testing, Deployment, and Maintenance.

Section 2
Software Design and Architecture

This section covers various techniques for software design and architecture.

Chapter 2
Software Architecture Framework of Healthcare Using Nonfunctional Artifacts

Umesh Banodha
Samrat Ashok Technological Institute, India

Kanak Saxena
Samrat Ashok Technological Institute, India

ABSTRACT

The health framework introduces the concept of sustainability because of its dynamics as individuals' needs change with everyday life and environmental changes. It is well known that, despite grave concern, the implementation of health policy is particularly affected in developing countries. This chapter is about creating a healthcare framework that is sensitive, insecure, and flexible. The medication process is dependent on laboratory tests and the techniques vary from time to time, which affects the services that the experts provide to patients. This increases the overall cost of the medication process and can be sustained by the concept of health insurance. For this purpose, the well-planned and defined software is obligatory due to the non-functional requirements up to the concepts of the software architecture. The designed framework is an integrated approach that conveys factual awareness of personalized and competent health services and facilitates agile principles and practices.

INTRODUCTION

The truth of one's life is that one undergoes the medication throughout the life span. Therefore, medicines must be available to all communities and natives of the societies in each country. It is one of the most important, demanding and flexible areas where family, society and health are at the centre. There are currently several treatment methods in the world, such as: **Homeopathy** is one of the oldest systems for curing diseases with the aim of eradicating diseases from the roots, without side effects of the drugs, but it is a lengthy process and takes a long time Cure illness. Allopathic System uses the concept of

DOI: 10.4018/978-1-7998-2531-9.ch002

multidisciplinary current to cure the patients and the majority of drugs that are made with the combination of chemicals. **Ayurveda** is one of the oldest, most popular and effective systems to cure patients with medications from different plants and herbs. **Siddha** is the oldest system to cure patients with the help of matter and energy found in vegetables, fruits and metals (solvable and insoluble), supported by the concepts of metal, yoga and philosophy. **Unani** uses the concepts of chemistry and pharmaceutical processes to make medicinal oils, powders and ointments and to use the alcohol (in admissible amount) for treatment. The feature of the allopathic system has become extraordinarily popular and effective for three centuries. The allopathic system is easily accessible to citizens and medications are very effective in providing immediate relief to the patient. The system is less time-consuming to provide relief and, most importantly, it helps to cure diseases such as ischemic heart disease and strokes, chronic obstructive pulmonary disease, lung cancer, diabetes and many more. According to the WHO report, the diseases mentioned above are the world's most common diseases, and in 2016 nearly 22 million people died. The Health Metrics Network (2008) also found that measuring one's own health was inadequate and therefore needed the appropriate tools to strengthen the medical information system, which plays the crucial role in this area.

As a result, there has been a need to bring the medication process to the changing needs of the health organization based on the needs, requirements and government policies of patients, and most importantly, to dynamically revolutionize the worldwide diagnosis and treatment of the diseases. This area is very sensitive, as the highest priority is to save the patient's life economically with the least ethical side effects. Therefore, the methods must respond to radical changes in the health field without affecting the defined structure of the area due to the availability of current techniques. The functionality and capabilities of agile methodology can lead to the solution of the above situation with uninterrupted perfection, in order to adapt to the health framework that best exploits the approach while maximizing the economic and principal return. McKinsey Global Institute (October 2006) provides the stable backbone for the uncertain area where dynamic agile changes are made. One such area is healthcare, where agility helps authorities make a quick decision in a flexible scenario to empower them. It will expand the domain by redesigning the innovative affiliation, reconfiguring and improving the diagnostic process by investing only once in state-of-the-art technologies that complements efficiency by reducing costs and promoting the growth of lifesaving. This will not only improve precision at the health care level - clinically and non-clinically - but will also enable the supportive staff of the domain to meet the on-demand needs of patients and experts as needed. Thus, mobility will facilitate the health sector by adjusting the change without restructuring the process. The whole process will be flawless, smooth and natural, starting from the bottom up instead of top down. The framework accepts the dynamic changes and formulates them with the flexible and dynamic characteristics to respond according to the scenarios.

Figure 1. Medical components

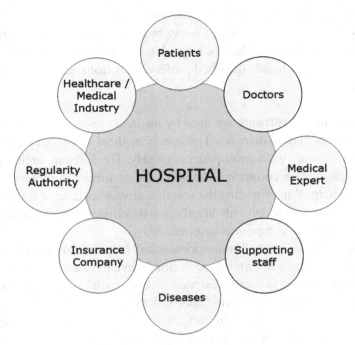

Medical Components of Healthcare System

The health care system is extremely extensive, and the detection of disease symptoms is complex. To reduce complexity, the most important active components of the healthcare system are as follows:

- **Patient**: A person who suffers from physical or psychological problems must use the services of the appropriate experts to cure the physical or mental problem.
- **Disease**: A disease is a condition of patients, animals or plants that are affected by bacteria, infections and dysfunctions, so that the patient cannot work efficiently.
- **Physician / Medical Expert**: A medical / medical expert is an authorized person or entity that provides remedies to patients, animals or plants.
- **Auxiliary Staff**: They provide service / support to patients from the first phase (arrival) to the discharge of patients. They also help doctors, lab technicians and medical experts.
- **Hospital**: A hospital is a unit / organization of medicines in which medical experts or a team of medical experts, together with assisting staff, can conveniently remedy the patient with the help of medical devices.
- **Insurance Company**: A health insurance is an activity offered by authorized health authorities / companies that reimburses the amount according to the plan chosen by the individual when someone falls under the standards of the authorities / companies responsible for the disease. All health insurances must obtain approval from the Insurance Supervision and Development Agency.
- **Regulatory Authority**: A legislative society that sets rules, regulations and controls for the medication facility to improve patients. Only a few law enforcement agencies are regulatory au-

thorities for pharmaceuticals, drug regulatory authorities, the Medical Council of India, and the International Association of Medical Regularity Authority.

- **Healthcare / Medical**: A combination of many industries provides the equipment (present and progress) and a variety of services that are helpful in the treatment and exclude patients from various diseases. It is a group of highly qualified professionals from various disciplines who meets the need for medicines.

The computer equipment and software are used by medical experts in the lab to predict the details of the signs and symptoms of certain diseases. The role of medical software is significant and there is a need for the appropriate software to monitor patients closely. The software architecture (Garlan, 2000; Clements et al., 2010) provides a common solution to the recurrence problems, so various types of software architecture are helpful in providing the solution at various levels / stages of problems. While various types of software architecture provide health-care functionality, the chapter focused on the nonfunctional parameters of medical-component architecture.

The aim of the chapter is to design the framework that will help improve health conditions and reduce mortality rates. The health system will provide the various services to accelerate health worldwide. This is only possible if the framework is properly designed with impartial and efficient features. This can be achieved by supporting the powerful monitoring approach that enables decision makers to closely monitor health progress and performance, assess impact and ensure accountability at the country and global level. It always raises the question of what significance the health system has. To understand it, one can express the state of the health system. A system to manage the improvement of health problems, either by focusing on the factors directly or indirectly related to health or by strengthening the awareness-raising activities of the citizens of a country. This is the responsibility of the citizen and the government authorities according to the structure of the country, e.g. For example, in INDIA, the structure of the governing body begins in the district and ends at the provincial level. The purpose of the system is to identify the causes of the disease as well as the impact of nature on health at an early stage and to provide those in need with rehabilitation, health, prevention and insurance / subsidiary / financial services. To provide the information, the system must be well known, as (Schoen et al., 2011) illustrated the survey of eleven countries and noted that lack of attention is due to poor care. The information may come from different sources, e.g. from historical data, environmental conditions, disease trends, government policies, and more. Smooth operation of the system requires well-trained staff, financial resources, pre-processed information, medical facilities, consultants and consultants, and more importantly, leadership that can guide and support the smooth operation of the system. In order to strengthen the system, it is therefore necessary to focus on the most important limitations of the above requirements in various areas.

The healthcare system needs input, processing and output. As shown in Figure 2, the input consists of the demographic information of the patient, the expert and other staff, the health status of the patient and the staff, the patient's insurance status, alternating with the quality of the available staff, planning and the coordinated inputs. Processing begins with the registration process of the staff and the patient, the emergency process, the technical support / care, the diagnostic and laboratory test process and the insurance process. The results may be hospital admission, discharge and death. Given the complexity of the health system, the proposed framework of the health system remains abstract. This will help generously strengthen the system, identify and tag the data sources, collect, analyze, evaluate, and ultimately monitor the system.

Figure 2. Healthcare system

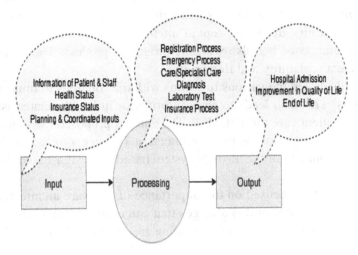

LITERATURE REVIEW

(Al-Baity, 2013; Macedo et al., 2016) focused on the reuse of code, framework and architecture at various levels such as abstraction, object, component and system. They also focus on software products where changes do not affect the source code, as COTS deals with the concept of design, implementation and testing of the HSSF, i.e. the Health Surveillance Software Framework, leading to a reduction in overall development will cost with the introduction of the reuse functionality.

(Ammenwerth et al., 2002) proposed the systematic health system application framework by defining the roles and responsibilities, information processing and tools, communications, business processes and team structure at five levels for analysis - organization, components of organization, employees, their roles in the organization and the task performed by them. (Clements et al., 2007) dealt with the effective use of teamwork in health care with the improvement of conditions based on research and expert opinion. In addition, (Conway & Clancy, 2009) have highlighted the need for quality improvements that relate to collaboration, comparability, quality measurement, and payment execution in order to change the healthcare frontline.

(Lina et al., 2015) conducted the comparative analysis of healthcare reference architectures, assessing their completeness on the basis of the reference architecture and research direction selection process in order to improve the reference architectures for healthcare. After the evaluation FeelGood and Continua are the mainly complete and consolidated reference architecture.

(Oh et al., 2015) presented health information services based on cloud-based computing. The platform is used as SaaS with the features Cost Effective, Clinical Values High and Usability High. Using the layered architecture, the following requirements were analyzed: enterprise services, cloud SaaS, multilingual quality capacity, privacy and security, and the conclusion that the system can easily accept mid-size hospitals with low system operation and maintenance costs.

(Kouroshfar et al., 2015) focused on architectural restoration procedures and identified the impact of procedural changes in the models. The focus is also on the impact of predicting the correlated error through improved software architecture accuracy.

(Al-Sakran, 2015) worked on the conception of e-Healthcare in terms of the health care components of the interoperability problem. The techniques that help patients with their routine work, information transfer, and increased reliability are the concept of intelligent agents and case-based technology. This not only helps with the diagnosis, but also with the prognosis process. The proposed architecture is characterized by intelligent scalability and flexibility.

(Steele et al., 2012) illustrated the various functions with the solutions to improve the quality of life of patients with certainty. This also leads to early informatics in health-related issues decisions with competent and effective patient care through HSP. The authors proposed the ubiquitous technological baseline and connectivity coverage for the PHR architecture. (Khajehpour & Raheleh, 2013) have continued to advance the development of the medical system based on design-based thinking and purpose-based thinking.

(Andrade & Crnkovic, 2019) focused on the importance of software architecture in heterogeneous computing to overcome the architectural challenges that can cope with the heterogeneous computing use, based on the spaces and the propensity of computing are determined from the 28 studies conducted by the authors.

(Oreizy et al., 1999) illustrated the need for software to adapt itself due to the nature of dynamic behaviour. The main focus was on system evolution and system customization, which analyzed the circumstances in which the changes had an effect on the software and the changes required to be made in both the planning state and the deployment state.

(Shaw, 2001) worked on software development issues with key settings such as feasibility, characterization, methods / means, generalization, and selection. The research projects are qualitative / descriptive, empirical predictive models, analytical models must learn to determine the validity of the research and long-term projects.

(Mehta, 2017) focused on the current conditions in India, as the health program is poorly understood for certain people's cadres and the implementation of programs. Demographic conditions are also to some extent responsible for poverty and the lack of availability of the right medicines at the right time. Therefore, it requires infrastructure, technology, investment and awareness of health. The author has tried to propose some solutions as health systems that are accessible, efficient and above all affordable, governance in the formation of the health system and the market drivers, all of which contribute at different levels.

(Piña et al., 2015) discussed the framework that describes the progress of the health system in comparative effective research. The focus is on the constitution and its functions to provide the health system. The entire process can be divided into three phases: (i) initial development, (ii) prioritization exercise for committees and full interest groups, and (iii) finalization of the elemental table. The framework presented with the 26 elements of 6 domains for clear understandability and well-planned to take on the changes occurred. The frame case study was described for the USA concept.

(Wendt et al., 2009) illustrate the need for a framework that examines the health care system with its various revolutions. The problem persists in health care in the robustness that such a flexible system can handle. The authors examine the system through the three structures of system transformation (i) financing, (ii) service delivery, and (iii) health care regulation.

The McKinsey Global Institute, (2006) worked on the seven basic elements of health care reform. They actively control supply and demand in the healthcare sector. (Ganton, 2018) shows the involvement of the patient and the family in the health and health framework. It works at the level of engagement, consultation, engagement and partnership, and shared leadership. It also looked at the earnings aspect and the risk factor for the engagement activities.

(Bielecki & Nieszporska, 2019) proposed the analysis of functional activities for the agent-treated healthcare. The concept was based on game theory, which dealt with the payment table and stability with the degree of cooperatives. This helps to identify the causes and suggests ways to eliminate them.

(Itumalla et al., 2016) describes the problems and challenges of health insurance, especially in relation to INDIA. Here, most employees work in disorganized sectors. Therefore, a group insurance is required, which is implemented and mandatory for all. It has also been suggested that awareness-raising programs should be implemented to highlight citizens' rights, tax benefits and related issues.

FRAMEWORK

The conception of the health framework starts with the organization, which takes care of the patient information, and ends when necessary, including the insurance. The incitement process of the healthcare framework differs significantly from the traditional domain framework because of its dynamic behaviour. The health framework requires deep knowledge and is useful if it is already taken into account in the early stages of the design. The key features required must be robustness, reliability, adaptability, availability and simplicity. Therefore, the software architecture plays an important role in creating the health framework. The software architecture emphasizes the patterns, styles and functional and non-functional attributes with the different methods. The healthcare framework will work well with architecture practices in the software development process to improve the efficiency and robustness of the system. According to the current concept of the medical industry, the framework design approach must be well planned and executed well to handle the situations in a consistent and secure manner that integrates with the system workflow. Second, it facilitates the users of different calibre. Therefore, the appropriate arrangements must be timely planned, which on the one hand reduces development costs and on the other hand helps end users to ensure the significant health quality. The continuous process increases the robustness of the system with the construction of the medical unit. In short, the health framework needs to adapt itself so that the following issues can be dealt with efficiently and successfully.

- Data adaptation based on the expert requirement

Identifying the relevant and exact requirements is a challenging task in healthcare due to the different operational practices of the experts. Therefore, the design team must constantly contact the professionals with sound expertise. The requirements may be summarized for ease of understanding. This speeds up the collection of requirements.

- Privacy on demand eases of use

In every health organization, protecting the privacy of patients is a top priority. Therefore, one has to be very careful in accessing the information while at the same time not preventing end users from doing their job efficiently.

- The architecture model proposed

The integrated process in every health organization is very important and cannot change. Therefore, the architectural model must propose its self-bearing capacity before it is implemented. This is the repetitive process that not only adds future aspects to the system, but also accustoms end users to its applicability.

- Time efficiency

The framework must be time-efficient, as the reality, especially in developing countries, increases the number of patient queues day by day. Experts should not be patient when the system takes too much time, and the system must accelerate the process. It also needs to be able to handle the situation when an error occurs.

- Validation versus verification

In the conventional software, the emphasis is on verification, but on the validation process in healthcare. Ensuring a correct and accurate process for this task is very important as the expertise is carefully considered. Therefore, validating and testing all possible exceptions can help to ensure proper functioning under unusual conditions.

- Flexibility in design

The organization of the healthcare system is very flexible due to changes in the organization's work policies, government policies and the adoption of new treatment standards. Each time you cannot buy or develop the new system, the existing system must be able to handle such changes. Therefore, the database design must play the crucial role to cope with changes, and the architecture must be designed to work with such limitations. During the design of an acceptable mode, the continuous improvement process of the request update will more easily take on the challenges. The attributes must be derived to speed up the input process in a time-efficient manner.

- Heterogeneous organizational structure

However, the workflow defined for the job seems irrelevant when the question arises for an unusual case. From organization to organization, the workflow structure varies, and the team tries asynchronously to solve the problem. On the other hand, the organization needs to interface with systems that are not part of the current organization. This gives the concept of the collaborative system within the organization as well as between the organizations. When designing the framework, it must therefore be taken into account that the organization is heterogeneous and users are not only experts but also want to do their work.

- Self-adaptability

The health framework must be self-adaptive (open and closed) due to the nature of the health area. In general, health is dynamic because the framework needs to be designed so that the changes made in the system can be easily applied. The self-adaptive concept was about changing its functionality in relation to changes in the health environment. The health environment in the health framework refers to the inputs, outputs, medical devices, insurance, rules and much more, which are referred to as remarkable changes in the existing system. The notable changes are an improvement in response time and recovery from a subsystem failure. While self-tuning is a challenging task and is also cost effective as it improves performance, it also increases the memory management and monitoring management overhead that predicts the appropriate time and circumstances to make changes to the system and the cost of the system update the system (hardware as well as architecture).

Framework Building Blocks

Researchers are aware of the following building blocks of the framework: (i) medical theories based on technology, (ii) necessary and required information, (iii) service delivery, (iv) financial aspects, (v) healthcare system and (vi) Leadership & Governance. Figure 1 shows the health care components that are part of an organization, resources, and institutions, and non-functional building blocks that contribute to the improvement of primary health and health improvement activities. In order to strengthen the system, the non-functional attributes play a crucial role in defining the most important constraints and may have the functions of the above-mentioned framework. Figure 3 shows an example of the software architecture of the health domain, which works with the non-functional building blocks of the health domain. The software architecture consists of two layers, the outer one consisting of the basic factors that form the basis of the framework and the inner one used to provide functionality according to the non-functional building blocks such as (i) patient and expert engagement, (ii) Governance and Governance, (iii) Trust, (iv) Analysis and Improvement, and (v) Dissemination.

Engagement of Patients and Experts

The involvement of patients and experts in the proposed framework facilitates the support of administrators, physicians, policy makers, technicians and the entire team in creating an environment that meets the required conditions, with comfort and meaningful support for patients and their families. The correct information must be communicated to you within the valid period. Undoubtedly, the commitment requires its contribution at various levels of planning and development of activities in relation to the area mentioned. Members of the inclusion process incorporate the knowledge and insights into design and decision-making, with the values and requirements of individuals / families being improved with limitations, i.e. improving the workflow of architectural drivers. The level of engagement contributes to the direct involvement of patients / experts and other co-staff, leadership, governance, policy makers and decision-makers at various levels.

Patient information can be demographic and general information, medical history, education, and health-related information (just to name a few). The information of the expert can be demographic and general information, advice, experience, specialization. Healthcare Service Providers (HSP) information may include policies, rules, and practices, cultural, regulatory, and social norms. Inclusion methods included focus group, face-to-face meeting, audio, video or written recording, patient shadowing, patient travel mapping, empathy mapping, medical trip, collaboration with community agencies, social media, educational presentation, ongoing membership and advice or guidance and preparation for the challenging situation, i.e. trust.

Figure 3. Software architecture of the healthcare domain

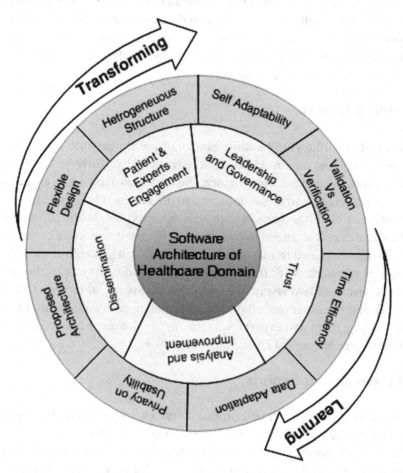

Trust

One very important aspect is the trust, as if the patients had confidence that they opened up with their problems with the health professionals. This leads to greater patient satisfaction and helps to share better decision-making. Trust is the key factor, especially in health care, due to the nature of the uncertainty and the involvement of the risk factor. In the current scenario, society has no confidence on either side of the healthcare sector, causing the experts to experience unforeseen events. The literal meaning of trust depends on reliability. Therefore, the reliability factor is of great importance. On the one hand, how much patients trust the hospital, the doctors and the support staff, and on the other, the patient and the family, i. e. confidence must be reversed. Trust must have the benefits of caring, accepting medicines and trust in the facilities provided by the HSP. Confidence arises when the following elements are present in a health sector / software development: knowledge literacy, competence in social / communication skills, honesty, confidentiality, care, and respect.

Competence in Knowledge

It is only possible if the professionals and staff of the HSP ensure lifelong learning according to the development and requirement of the system. This not only increases the quantity of knowledge, but also improves the quality of the treatment process with the appropriate role and responsibility. Confidence comes about automatically when knowledge speaks. The system must be able to acquire knowledge and transform it as needed. This can result from (i) training, (ii) work skills, (iii) transparency in conducting the analysis, (iv) error / grievance handling, and (v) assessment procedures. The following points should be considered, especially when the machine responds to (i) timeliness, (ii) statement, (iii) information, (iv) ongoing support, (v) confidentiality, and (vi) ongoing care.

Competence in Social/Communication Skills

On the one hand learning is important and on the other hand listening is too important. The system must be capable of paraphrasing, summarizing, clarifying and reflecting the information collected. Experts and the team have to keep the patient at the centre of the decision as they need to know all the consequences of the options. Therefore, the involvement of patients and the family must be included in the decision-making process. If necessary, the experts / team can go through the consultation process, but the system must accept and respect the patient's decision to update the personal information.

Honesty

HSP must act transparently and honestly in order to maintain public trust and maintain the reputation of the medical profession. The system must also have the ethical version to treat the patients without concealing the real situation and the prospects of survival.

Confidentiality

HSP must have the confidence of patients that no information may be disclosed to third parties without the consent of the patient. This creates confidence in maintaining the confidentiality of patient information. This is a statutory requirement with periodic reviews to maintain confidentiality.

Showing Respect and Care

Every patient and staff must be treated with dignity and respect, regardless of caste and belief, educated or uneducated. The system must maintain confidence even in the event of unforeseen events and stressful working conditions.

Analysis and Improvement

There are several approaches to analyzing HSP, to name but a few: systems theory approaches, socio-political approaches, and systematic approaches. Since it is very clear that the area is very uncertain and highly complex, this requires flexibility according to the conditions, by observing the standards up to the secured state. To create an environment in which patients, experts, employees and administrators keep the role of analysis intact, this is crucial. It must be done on the interference of leadership and governance (Kaufmann D., Kraay A., 2007) in the HSP. The role and responsibilities must be clearly defined and include the correct hierarchy of all HSP participants and patients. Singh S. et. al. (2018) improved the involvement of the family counsellor with the patients in the research group. Here, the technology selection for information processing plays a central role. The collected information must be pre-processed and analyzed using the analysis tools. One must also remember that no redundancy can be found because at the time of registration, billing, checking, etc., the same information was needed. The reality of the domain is that the health professional also communicates with different roles and needs responsibilities. The exchange of information may take place directly or indirectly in the form of decisions in the meeting, briefings, posting, etc. The business process influences the analysis in terms of schedule activities to simplify the routine work with the feedback process. Team structure and collaboration within the team must clearly define the goal for which the team should work with patients, taking into account the current situation.

Leadership and Governance

It is a new concept to health care. The concept of governance introduces the roles and responsibilities of the HSP team and shapes them in relation to the goal and limitations of the HSP. Many government guidelines are based on the papers that require transparency for actual implantation with effective and strong accountability. The process works at both levels - society and policy makers. The analysis is based on collective, operational and constitutional reasons.

Dissemination

Finally, the learning process for improving the framework is continued throughout the lifecycle and transformed into the information requested, according to the stakeholders' needs.

HEALTHCARE FRAMEWORK COMMENCE PROCESS

The goal of HSP is to efficiently treat the problems with a powerful decision support system to facilitate patient treatment and to ensure transparency in medication and financial matters. In general, the data collection problem arises because of the bad historical record, which somehow speeds up the processing time. Second, the framework must be made up of a number of special problems, as the health system cannot be limited to a single area. In healthcare, the importance of treatment at the required time is very important and the practice must be very careful. Therefore, the concept of the timeline plays a very important role in terms of care and the same point and the care of the entire team of experts, all concerned with the situation of the needy patients. Since the above issues clearly indicate that the system is not easy to build, the framework and therefore the detailed analysis of the developers must be necessary to simplify the development process. The analysis must include the simple communication between the various teams, the time at which the interaction should be performed, the framework with the clear goal to be created, and finally how it can be easily implemented in the application. The agile principles and methods will facilitate the whole process of creating the health framework.

Figure 4. Agile approach based working model

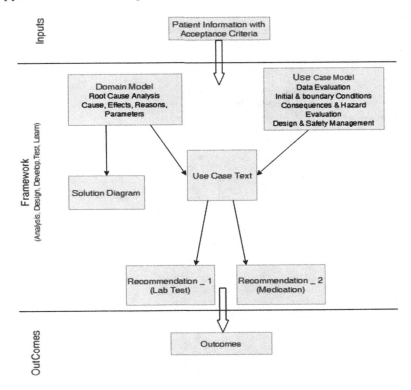

Agile Principles and Methods

The health framework is the iterative process performed by the right team of specific expertise and associated stimuli using agile principles and methods. The agile principles are more beneficial in the health field because they better manage the flexible situations with the feedback process without starting from scratch. The grip and the pace remain the same due to the sprints according to the agile principle in the development process. The sprints interpret the mistakes of each component in time and can later cause damage. It also reduces the impact of cumulative errors. The second advantage is that it can communicate healthier with customers to make sure the requirements are taken into account or not. This is more suitable in the health sector because the highly complex system with its risk characteristics can also be addressed in the work modules. It also addresses the confidentiality of patient information and helps maintain the standards of healthcare organizations.

The development processes include various teams such as teams of experts, quality assurance, analytics, finance (insurance) and information processing. As development progresses, the main problem lies in the diverse backgrounds of the knowledge team members. Therefore, the mutually understandable documents must be prepared in order to avoid the confusion of the problem space and the solution space with the correct state space. The process is to use the simplest tools, use the truthful artifacts, and create the understandable and robust content extracted from the group discussion. As a result, the Agility Principle framework provides for clarifying the needs of the individuals (patient / expert / authorities / staff) in the presence of the requirements of the HSP, rather than examining the solutions in general

Figure 5. Registration: domain diagram in healthcare framework

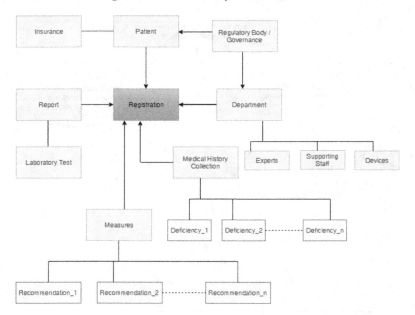

for all members of the HSP who were directly or indirectly indirectly involved. Thus, at the time of registration (the entry level), HSP will understand the pros and cons of the problems before symptoms of the remedial process occur. Similarly, the experts can recommend the laboratory test to identify the disease by severity. The framework focuses on outcomes based on non-functional parameters such as satisfaction (patient / expert / authorities / staff), time scalability, optimization, efficiency, performance, availability, and more. The framework will be constantly exposed to technological changes to ensure the update dynamics for an efficient restructuring process. This will strengthen the HSP through the experienced and trained staff. Therefore, one can recommend the agile framework as one of the most important innovative prerequisites for the successful functioning of the HSP.

For the framework, the models can be referred to as either UML standard models or non-UML models. Figure 4 shows the healthcare working model that requires detailed architectural processing of the system. This is the structure and behavioral process of the framework, i. e. a policy for building healthcare software using agile principles and methods.

Figure 6. Use case of the information gathering (Registration process)

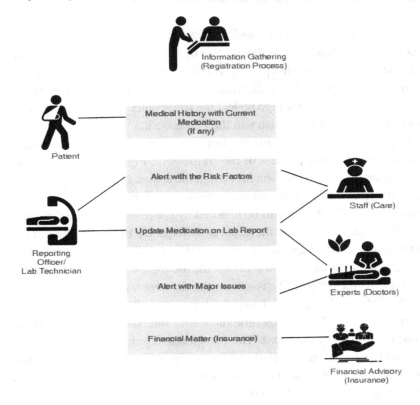

Figure 7. Alert solution diagram

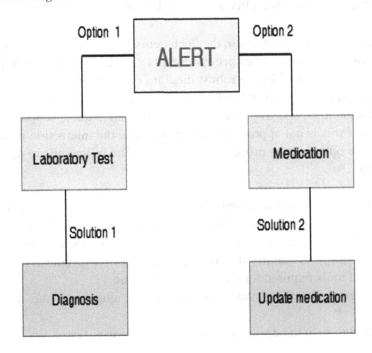

Patient Information With the Acceptance Criteria

The aim is to define patient admission standards for the benefit of health improvement under the signs and symptoms established by the regulatory authority and by the experts. Such patients log in and therefore need the registration system with detailed patient history. This helps in determining the actual condition of the patient and has the change in the medication process (if necessary). One has to identify the main classes and the relationship between them to reflect the irrelevance. Figure 5 shows the domain diagram with a few classes that are part of the registry in the framework.

The use case diagram helps to determine the important behaviour of the team members with their specific actions in the development process of the framework. Figure 6 shows the use case diagram of the information collection for the registration process in the frame. In general, the required information is patient information (medical history and current medication) of the patient. The reporting or laboratory technician can create the ALERTS that will be handled by the assistants and, if changes are needed, the experts will follow the requirements and the experts will specify the risk factors. Finally, the financial adviser will make the insurances and update the information according to the facts and the current situation.

Similarly, the decision tree is used to uniquely define the logic used in evaluating the input conditions (one or more) to determine the output. The issue may be the generation of the risk warning and to whom and when it should be addressed. Figure 7 shows the decision made at the time of the ALERT generation as an alarm resolution diagram. Finally, the graphical user interface will represent the visualization of the system with respect to the use case text. The use case text helps to understand the behavior of end users when dealing with the system. To eliminate the confusion of end users, the author needs to define a complete roadmap to make the system look the way it can and to solve the problems that end users could face. The roadmap can be in the form of a solution diagram that shows the relationships between the objects used in the framework.

Agile Knowledge Enhance the Development Process

The healthcare framework is flexible because the documents are up-to-date and events can vary before they are completed. This feature sometimes becomes impractical if it is not handled properly at the time of designing the condition. To do this, the robust diagram can support the development process. The table may contain information on required and essential specifications, machine / programmed validation, final stage regression tests, and live system documents. Validation is supported by feedback from the affected team, and if this is not appropriate for an instance, the interaction process is re-analyzed. The process leads to the optimization process in the design. The following are the benefits that Agile knowledge can provide.

- Patient information: The complete anamnesis with the current state of knowledge is taken into account. The acceptance criteria of the patient guide the measures to be taken for the patient into the desired criteria. This facilitates the boot process that starts with the registration.
- The domain model helps to identify the structure, conditions, procedures in the current scenario, and the operational tools required for the present and future.
- The use case diagram illustrates the warnings and warnings with the recommendations and solutions.
- The decision tree will help to be wary of ambiguity at an early stage.

General Benefits

- Support recognition of important design patterns with reusability options.
- Enhance the pace to learn the new skills and transform into the desired shape.
- The whole framework with the adaptability of the design process is visualized through feedback.
- Allow developers to analyze the results of the process to ensure patient care and improve quality of life.

CONCLUSION

The framework consists of the medical components that together make up the following key areas of the healthcare system: patients and experts, lifesaving services, leadership and governance, trust and insurance. The framework highlights the various non-functional conceptual artifacts used by the software architecture. The determination of the artifacts helps to find the area of reusability with the evaluation patterns over time and the development of the architectural framework. The assessment is based on the analysis and design of the framework architecture along with the internal deployment complexity and the final creation of the system deployment. Thus, the scaffolding artifacts not only affect the research base, but also illustrate their ease of use by users and professionals. The framework will reduce the unexpected situation that has occurred, especially in active medical-sector deployment, by properly developing artifacts for non-functional requirements. Agile framework development with timely iteration has a major impact on the effective development of the framework to meet the needs of the healthcare industry. The agile knowledge process promotes the insightful, non-functional requesting and design process by clearly mapping the mental process. The event diagrams speed up the design process of the framework that was linked to the medical components and the derived components.

REFERENCES

Aggarwal, A., Kapoor, N., & Gupta, A. (2013). Health Insurance: Innovation and challenges ahead. *Global Journal of Management and Business Studies*, *3*(5), 475-780.

Aitken, A. (2014). Dual Application Model for Agile Software Engineering. *47th Hawaii International Conference on System Sciences*, 4789-4798. 10.1109/HICSS.2014.588

Al-Baity, A. A., Faisal, K., & Ahmed, M. (2013). Software reuse: the state of art. *Proceedings of the International Conference on Software Engineering Research and Practice (SERP)*, 1–7.

Al-Sakran, H. O. (2015, February). Framework Architecture For Improving Healthcare Information Systems using Agent Technology. *International Journal of Managing Information Technology*, *7*(1), 17–31. doi:10.5121/ijmit.2015.7102

Ammenwerth, E., Ehlers, F., Eichstädter, R., Haux, R., Pohl, U., & Resch, F. (2002). Systems Analysis in Health Care: Framework and Example. *Methods of Information in Medicine*, *2/2002*, 134–140. PMID:12061120

Andrade, H., & Crnkovic, I. (2019, May). A Review on Software Architectures for Heterogeneous Platforms. *IEEE 25th Asia-Pacific Software Engineering Conference (APSEC)*.

Anita, J. (2008). Emerging Health Insurance in India–An overview. *10th Global Conference of Actuaries*, 81-97.

Bielecki, A., & Nieszporska, S. (2019, April). Analysis of Healthcare Systems by Using Systemic Approach. Hindwani Complexity, Volume 2019, Article ID 6807140, 12 pages.

Clements, D., Dault, M., & Priest, A. (2007). Effective Teamwork in Healthcare: Research and Reality. *Healthcare Papers*, *7*(sp), 26–34. doi:10.12927/hcpap.2013.18669 PMID:17478997

Clements, P., Bachmann, F., Bass, L., Garlan, D., Ivers, J., Little, R., Merson, P., Nord, R., & Stafford, J. (2010, October). *Documenting Software Architectures: Views and Beyond*. Pearson Education.

Conway, P. H., & Clancy, C. (2009). Transformation of health care at the front line. *Journal of the American Medical Association*, *301*(7), 763–765. doi:10.1001/jama.2009.103 PMID:19224753

Devi, S., & Nehra, V.S. (2015). The problems with health insurance sector in India. *Indian Journal of Research*, *4*(3), 6-8.

Ganton, J. (2018, June). *Engaging Individuals with Lived Experience A Framework*. Primary Health care Opioid Response Initiative.

Garlan, D. (2000, June). Software architecture: a roadmap. In *The Future of Software Engineering 2000, Proceedings 22nd International Conference on Software Engineering*. ACM Press.

Itumalla, R., Acharyulu, G. V. R. K., & Reddy, L. K. V. (2016). Health Insurance in India: Issues and challenges. *International Journal of Current Research*, *8*(2), 26815–26817.

Kaufmann, D., & Kraay, A. (2007). Governance Indicators: Where Are We, Where Should We Be Going? *The World Bank Research Observer*, *23*(1), 1–30. doi:10.1093/wbro/lkm012

Khajehpour, S., & Raheleh, E. (2013). Advancements and Trends in Medical Case-Based Reasoning: An Overview of Systems and System Development. *Iran J. Medical Informatics*, *2*(4), 12–16.

Kouroshfar, E., Mirakhorli, M., Bagheri, H., Xiao, L., Malek, S., & Cai, Y. (2015). A Study on the Role of Software Architecture in the Evolution and Quality of Software. *12th Working Conference on Mining Software Repositories*, 246-257. 10.1109/MSR.2015.30

Lina, M. G. R., Ampatzoglou, A., Avgeriou, P., & Nakagawa, E. Y. (2015, June). A Comparative Analysis of Reference Architectures for Healthcare in the Ambient Assisted Living Domain. *28th International Symposium on Computer-Based Medical Systems*, 270-275.

Ludík, T., Barta, J., & Navrátil, J. (2013). Design Patterns for Emergency Management Processes, World Academy of Science, Engineering and Technology. *International Journal of Economics and Management Engineering*, *7*(12), 3026–3033.

Macedo, A. A., Pollettini, J. T., Baranauskas, J. A., & Chaves, J. C. A. (2016, August). A health surveillance software framework to design the delivery of information on preventive healthcare strategies. *Journal of Biomedical Informatics*, *62*, 159–170. doi:10.1016/j.jbi.2016.06.002 PMID:27318270

McKinsey Global Institute. (2006, October). *A Framework to Guide Healthcare System Reform*. San Francisco, CA: Author.

Mehta, P. (2017, January). Framework of Indian Healthcare System and its Challenges: An Insight. In *Healthcare Community Synergism between Patients, Practitioners, and Researchers* (pp. 247-271). IGI Global.

Nicolini, D., Powell, J., Convile, P., & Martinez-Solano, L. (2008, August). Managing knowledge in the healthcare sector, A review. *International Journal of Management Reviews, 10*(3), 245–263. doi:10.1111/j.1468-2370.2007.00219.x

Oh, S., Cha, J., Ji, M., Kang, H., Kim, S., Heo, E., ... Yoo, S. (2015, April). Architecture Design of Healthcare Software-as-a-Service Platform for Cloud-Based Clinical Decision Support Service. *Healthcare Informatics Research, 21*(2), 102–110. doi:10.4258/hir.2015.21.2.102 PMID:25995962

Omar, W., & Bendiab, A. T. (2006). *E-Health Support Services Based on Service-Oriented Architecture*. IEEE Computer Society.

Oreizy, P., Gorlick, M., Taylor, R. N., Heimbigner, D., Johnson, G., Medvidovic, N., ... Wolf, A. L. (1999, May/June). An Architecture-Based Approach to Self-Adaptive Software. *IEEE Intelligent Systems, 14*(3), 54–62. doi:10.1109/5254.769885

Piña, I. L., Cohen, P. D., Larson, D. B., Marion, L. N., Sills, M. R., Solberg, L. I., & Zerzan, J. (2015, April). A Framework for Describing Health Care Delivery Organizations and Systems. *American Journal of Public Health, 105*(4), 650–659. doi:10.2105/AJPH.2014.301926 PMID:24922130

Powell, M. (2007). The mixed economy of welfare and the social division of welfare. In M. Powell (Ed.), *Understanding the Mixed Economy of Welfare* (pp. 1–21). Bristol, UK: Policy Press. doi:10.2307/j.ctt1t89b4m.6

Ramesh, M., Wu, X., & He, A. J. (2013). Health governance and healthcare reforms in China. *Health Policy and Planning, 29*(6), 663–672. doi:10.1093/heapol/czs109 PMID:23293100

Saha, S., Beach, M. C., & Cooper, L. A. (2008). Patient centeredness cultural competence and healthcare quality. *Journal of the National Medical Association, 100*(11), 1275–1285. doi:10.1016/S0027-9684(15)31505-4 PMID:19024223

Schoen, C., Osborn, R., Squires, D., Doty, M., Pierson, R., & Applebaum, S. (2011). Survey of patients with complex care needs in eleven countries finds that care is often poorly coordinated. *Health Affairs, 30*(12), 2437-2448.

Shaw, M. (2001, May). The Coming-of-Age of Software Architecture Research. *Proceedings of the 23rd International Conference on Software Engineering, ICSE 2001*, 656-664. 10.1109/ICSE.2001.919142

Shaw, M., & Garlan, D. (1996). *Software Architecture: Perspectives on an Emerging Discipline*. Prentice Hall.

Singh, S., Burns, K. K., Rees, J., Picklyk, D., Spence, J., & Marlett, N. (2018). Patient and family engagement in Alberta Health Services: Improving care delivery and research outcomes. *Healthcare Management Forum, SAGE Journal, 31*(2), 57-61.

Steele, R., Min, K., & Lo, A. (2012). Personal Health Record Architectures: Technology Infrastructure Implications and Dependencies. *Journal of the American Society for Information Science and Technology, 63*(6), 1079–1091. doi:10.1002/asi.22635

Wendt, C., Frisina, L., & Rothgang, H. (2009, February). Healthcare System Types: A Conceptual Framework for Comparison. *Social Policy & Administration, Wiley, 43*(1), 70–90. doi:10.1111/j.1467-9515.2008.00647.x

World Health Organization. (2008). *Framework and standards for country health information systems.* Geneva: Health Metrics Network.

Chapter 3
Structural Data Binding for Agile Changeability in Distributed Application Integration

José Carlos Martins Delgado
https://orcid.org/0000-0002-2536-4906
Instituto Superior Técnico, Universidade de Lisboa, Portugal

ABSTRACT

The interaction of distributed applications raises an integration problem that consists in how to satisfy the minimum interoperability requirements while reducing coupling as much as possible. Current integration technologies, such as Web Services and RESTful APIs, solve the interoperability problem but usually entail more coupling than required by the interacting applications. This is caused by sharing data schemas between applications, even if not all features of those schemas are actually exercised. This has its toll in application development agility. This chapter proposes compliance and conformance as the concepts to minimize coupling without impairing interoperability by sharing only the subset of the features of the data schema that are actually used. In addition, data binding between messages and the receiver's schema is done structurally in a universal and application-independent way. This eliminates the need for application-specific stubs and allows clients to use any server with which they comply and servers to replace any server to which they conform.

INTRODUCTION

Agile software development methods (Hoda et al., 2018) aim to improve productivity in developing complex applications by attempting to better match human programming capabilities and problem requirements. From an application integration point of view (Panetto & Whitman, 2016), *agility* is defined as the ability to prompt and cost-effectively adapt an application (reactive and / or proactive) to changes in its interoperability requirements with other applications.

DOI: 10.4018/978-1-7998-2531-9.ch003

A complex software system usually involves many interacting modules, with many compromises to consider and many decisions to make, not only in each module, but also in the way the various modules interact. Object-oriented modeling is a classic paradigm designed to minimize the semantic gap between a problem specification and the software application's architecture. It addresses this issue through close correspondence between entity establishment and the corresponding software models (classes). However, this is not enough.

Ideally, classes should be completely decoupled, without mutual restrictions and completely independent life cycles. This would allow separate development of each class and eliminate inefficiencies in software development and programming due to the interaction between the class specifications, which usually results in iterations of the requirements for other classes and resulting changes. However, the classes must interact and cooperate to work together to achieve the goals of the system. A fundamental principle in agile software design is to reduce class coupling as much as possible (Bidve & Sarasu, 2016) without compromising the interoperability required to support the required class interaction (Queiroz et al., 2018). A weaker coupling means a higher:

- **Changeability**: A change in one class is less likely to have a significant impact on other classes.
- **Adaptability**: Fewer constraints require less effort to adapt to changes in other.
- **Reusability**: A class with fewer requirements and constraints has an extended scope of applicability.
- **Reliability (In a Distributed Context)**: A smaller set of requirements simplifies the search for an alternative application in the event of a failure.

The correct tuning of the decoupling is not an easy task in practice. The basic problem of application design in terms of interaction is to provide (at most) the least possible coupling while ensuring (at least) the minimum requirements for interoperability. This means that the main goal is to ensure that each interacting class knows enough about the others to work with them and avoid unnecessary dependencies and restrictions. This is particularly relevant when agility is one of the main concerns.

Software development methods emphasize decoupling, changeability and agility. This means structuring classes of an application so that implementing a change takes only a short time and other classes are not badly affected. Interoperability between classes of a local application is not a big problem, as classes are implemented in the same programming language. Type names and inheritance are generally shared.

The interaction between distributed applications is completely different. Interoperability is difficult as these applications are developed, compiled and linked independently. This most likely results in different type names, inheritance hierarchies, programming languages, execution platforms, and data formats. The interoperability of current technologies is based on a strict data format alignment (Data Schema Sharing). Although decoupling is of paramount importance, it has been treated as a secondary issue in distributed contexts where best efforts are made after the primary objective of interoperability has been achieved.

The two most commonly used application integration approaches are Service-Oriented Architecture (SOA) (Erl et al., 2017) and Representational State Transfer (REST) (Fielding et al., 2017). They achieve interoperability, but do not solve the coupling problem because the schemas used by the interacting applications must be identical. SOA is good at modeling distributed systems based on the service paradigm (an extension of the class-based paradigm for distributed applications). However, it involves complex and static software specifications. It also requires the sharing of schemas between the interacting applications, which creates a strong coupling between the applications. Changing the interaction between Web services is not a trivial task. REST is much easier and is becoming increasingly popular. On the other hand, it is rather low-level and not the best solution for general behavior-oriented distributed applications. It also hides a high degree of coupling because both interacting applications must have the same media type specification.

This chapter reiterates the problem of application integration without being limited in advance by technologies such as Web Services for SOA and RESTful APIs for REST. The only assumption is that there are applications that need to interact with messages. The main goal is to propose and promote the concepts of *compliance* (Czepa, Tran, Zdun, Kim, Weiss & Ruhsam, 2017) and *conformance* (Carmona et al., 2018) as the underlying solution for reducing application coupling and increasing agility in software development.

Compliance and conformance allow for partial interoperability rather than relying on the sharing of data schemas to provide interoperability that entails strong coupling. If the interaction does not fully exercise the range values, the coupling is higher than required.

Compliance and conformance test compatibility between data and applications at a structural level. That makes the difference. Unlike Web Services, a client does not have to use declared. Unlike RESTful applications, the client and server do not have to agree on a particular data type. Every data resource has its own schema, which results from its own concrete structure. The interoperability check between two data resources (e.g., between a message and the parameter required for an operation) is recursive until primitive data resources are found. This means that data binding between a message and the recipient's message schema is structural and universal, without the need for prior agreement on a particular messaging schema.

The primary goal of *structural data binding*, based on compliance and conformance, is to reduce the coupling between distributed applications, increase the extensibility of the overall system, and make a significant contribution to the agility of software development.

The rest of the chapter is structured as follows. First, changeability and agility in application development are discussed. It then describes the basic problem of application integration with a model of application coupling. The concepts of compliance and conformance are presented and proposed as a solution to reduce application coupling and increase agility in software development. This includes structural data binding with an underlying data model and rules for compliance and conformance at the data and service levels. Examples are presented to illustrate how to implement these concepts.

BACKGROUND

One of the biggest challenges in agile application development is *integration* (Panetto & Whitman, 2016). Integration is the ability to work meaningfully and efficiently with other subsystems to pursue the goals of the overall system. Integration can be observed at all levels of abstraction and complexity. It can be low-level cyber-physical systems (Zanero, 2017). It can also be high-level corporate functions such as governance and management for features like dynamic outsourcing and re-configurability. These features are critical to enterprise agility (Samdantsoodol et al., 2017) and to the value chains of companies focused on the capabilities required for the fourth industrial revolution known as Industry 4.0 (Liao, Deschamps, Loures & Ramos, 2017).

For interaction, applications must be interoperable. *Interoperability* (Agostinho et al., 2016) is the ability of two or more systems or components to exchange information and use the exchanged information as defined by ISO / IEC / IEEE 24765 (ISO, 2010). So mere information exchange is not enough. Interacting systems must also be able to understand and respond to each other's expectations.

Another problem is *coupling* (Bidve, & Sarasu, 2016), which shows how strongly applications depend on each other. Interoperability and low coupling must be combined to achieve effective collaboration in the integration of distributed applications, especially in complex applications like enterprise domain applications (Popplewell, 2014; Rezaei et al., 2014).

Coupling is of paramount importance in distributed contexts, but has traditionally received less attention than interoperability. This is the case for the two most commonly used integration approaches, SOA and REST. Their corresponding technological solutions for distributed interoperability are Web Services (Zimmermann et al., 2012) and RESTful APIs (Pautasso, 2014). These are based on data description languages such as XML (Fawcett et al., 2012) and JSON (Bassett, 2015). Although they have achieved the basic goal of connecting independent and heterogeneous applications and supporting distributed interoperability, they are not effective solutions for coupling, since the message data schemas used by the interacting applications must be identical.

Various metrics (Pantiuchina et al., 2018) have been proposed to evaluate the maintainability of service-based distributed applications based essentially on structural features, namely, service coupling, cohesion, and complexity (Babu, & Darsi, 2013)., Other approaches focus on dynamic and not static coupling with metrics to assess coupling during program execution (Geetika, & Singh, 2014). There are also approaches that try to combine structural coupling and other coupling levels, such as semantics (Alenezi, & Magel, 2014).

Compliance is a concept that can serve as a basis to make sure partial interoperability and thus minimize coupling. Conformance is another concept that underlies partial interoperability and allows one application to replace another if it conforms the other application (supports all features of the application).

THE CONTEXT: CHANGEABILITY AS THE BASIS FOR AGILE DEVELOPMENT

Change-Oriented Application Lifecycle

Simply and quickly making changes to a software system, possibly with many interacting applications, is a prerequisite for software development agility. Many systems, especially at the organizational level, are so complex that changes are required while being developed. Therefore, a software system must be designed primarily for changeability throughout its life cycle.

Figure 1 shows a typical life cycle of a complex software system, an Enterprise Information System (EIS). Its focuses are on changeability that can be applied to the entire EIS from the beginning or to one of its subsystems. The environment represents other EIS or applications into which this EIS must be integrated.

This model is maximalist, in the sense that an EIS (or a subsystem thereof) should at least conceptually go through all phases, but the degree of emphasis and level of detail in each phase need not always be identical. The higher the level of the subsystem, the more important the vision and strategy becomes, but they must reach the point of operation if they are to function. Lower-level subsystems will focus on development and operations, but must also have a vision and mission.

Figure 1. The lifecycle of an EIS, emphasizing changeability

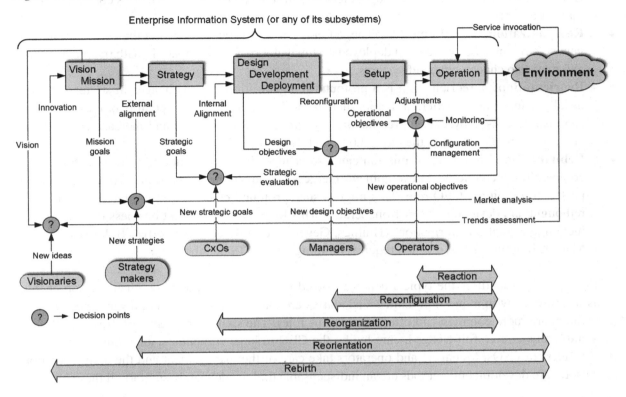

In figure 1, the lifecycle of an EIS is modeled using a pipeline of phases that are more concrete and detailed than the previous one and have multiple enhancement loops. Each of these loops assumes that metrics (indicators) are defined so that goals and objectives can be evaluated. If the difference between the desired and the measured indicator is greater than an acceptable level, the loop should be iterated to decide and implement what needs to be changed to minimize this difference.

The inner loops deal with lower levels and more details, while the outer loops deal with higher levels and less details. Figure 1 looks at the following loops, though others are possible by detailing the pipeline phases:

- **Reaction**: All changes only affect the state. Therefore, the cost and time for detecting (monitoring) and generating a change (a state) is usually very small. The changes can be very frequent and occur in response to events or predictable trends in adaptive systems. This is the loop that is more accessible to automation. However, without considering self-changing systems, which are particularly difficult to build in complex systems, every possible change must have been incorporated into the design.
- **Reconfiguration**: Some EIS, for example in manufacturing, especially in relation to Industry 4.0 (Liao et al., 2017), support re-configurability (Farid, 2017). Reconfiguration does not mean designing a new EIS, but more than just changing the status. Some of the subsystems are used in a different configuration or parameterization, for example to produce another product in a production line. However, this must be included in the design of EIS. Otherwise, a new version of the

EIS is needed, which is the next loop. A reconfiguration can be as frequent as its cost and benefits make it effective.

- **Reorganization**: The EIS must be changed in a way that is not included in the current design. A new version must be created and deployed that may not be fully compatible with the previous one and may also change other subsystems.

- **Reorientation**: A reorientation is a profound reorganization due to changes in strategy. This is usually determined by external factors such as the development of competitors or customers, but can also be caused by internal restructuring to improve functionality and increase competitiveness. An example of this is the latest 4.0 trend (Dornberger, 2018).

- **Rebirth**: The vision and / or mission can also change significantly due to factors such as fierce competition, technological development, mergers / acquisitions, or even the replacement of the person fulfilling the CEO role. This implies such profound changes that in practice it has to be rethought and designed almost from scratch. This loop may also reflect business diversification, including digital transformation ((Hinings, Gegenhuber & Greenwood, 2018; Bohnsack, Hanelt, Marz & Marante, 2018)), which requires building a new EIS or subsystem.

Figure 1 also identifies the typical actors involved in the decision points on change / non-change decisions (circles with a question mark). Visionaries are hard to find and do not always exist as such (innovators are more common and often take on this role). The strategy makers vary from small business entrepreneurs to a full-fledged team led by the CEO in large companies, including various chief level officers or CxOs. Managers and operators take care of the management and the daily operation. Agile software development methods are an indispensable tool to adequately support all these changes.

Agility in Application Development

Typically, a change is made to a complex software system, such as the EIS whose lifecycle is shown in figure 1, if an actor determines that the benefit of a change (BoC) is greater than the cost of implementing that change (CoC)., Agile software development requires little change cost (Tooranloo & Saghafi, 2018), so changes can often occur, either in response to changes in the environment or as proactive anticipation (Pulparambil, Baghdadi, Al-Hamdani & Al-Badawi, 2018).

Because an application is not necessarily synchronized with other applications in its environment, it increasingly deviates from it over time. The misalignment of the software system and the need for change are increasing (Delgado, 2019). To realign the system, more and more changes are required and the CoC will increase, as shown in figure 2.

If the BoC increases faster than the CoC, as in the case of figure 2a (a not very complex software system), the change will be cost effective and ideally should be done at time T_c when the BoC equals the CoC. If the change is made too early (at T_{c-}), the costs outweigh the benefits. If the change is made too late by waiting too long (at T_{c+}), some benefits will be lost.

However, if the software system is very complex and uses diversification (creating a new version or introducing an adapter) rather than promoting agility to cope with changing requirements, the CoC will become higher and never lower than that be appropriate BoC. as shown in figure 2b. In this case, the change time (T_c) is determined by the need to limit the CoC (*max*) rather than its cost-benefit effectiveness. Having a lightweight software system that only contains what is currently needed to make

Figure 2. Change benefits versus cost of changes in a light (a) and complex (b) software system

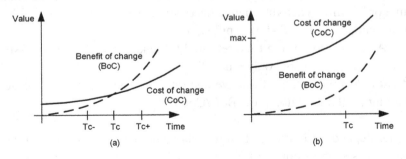

Table 1. Types of changes

Timings	Type of change	Description
$T_c \pounds T_s < T_d$	Reactive	Completely reactive change, since its implementation does not start until one realizes it should be in place
$T_s < T_c < T_d$	Mixed	Change with a proactive and a reactive part. It starts before T_c, but some time later, the change still needs to be completed
$T_s < T_d \pounds T_c$	Proactive	Fully proactive change as the implementation begins and ends before it is needed. There is no point in having T_d long before T_c
$T_s < T_d = T_c$	Just in time	Change is done precisely when it is needed. The ideal case

it reasonably easy to change is preferable to a complex and very comprehensive system, which takes a lot of time and effort to change.

It should be noted that T_c is only the time when the change is deemed necessary and ideally must be complete and operational. However, the implementation and deployment of the change will take some time. For example, the change is implemented at T_s and implemented at T_d, which would result in several cases described in table 1.

Although proactive action is desirable, guessing the future is still an art and many things can happen between T_s and T_c. In the worst case scenario, given the recent events and trends in the environment, the change can be completely wrong and result in losses compared to no change at all. In many cases, therefore, a fast response is the best approach.

In this case, the *change delay* $(T_d - T_c)$ determines how fast the software system is able to reorient and adapt to changing requirements. If the average value is small compared to the MTBC (*Mean Time Between Changes*), the system can be classified as very agile or even real-time.

Taking into account the various factors that characterize a change and taking Table 1 into account, the following definitions (considered as averages) can be made:

- **Agility**: An indication of the change delay in terms of the speed at which changes are required $((T_d - T_c)/MTBC)$.
- **Dynamicity**: An indication of the implementation time of a change in the speed at which changes are required $((T_d - T_s)/MTBC)$.

- **Proactiveness**: An indication of the proportion of the proactive part of the change in the implementation time or the time when the change needs to be decided compared to the time required to implement the change ($(T_c-T_s)/(T_d-T_s)$). Applicable only when $T_s \pounds T_c$
- **Reactiveness**: An indication of the time required to make the change with respect to the change delay ($(T_d-T_s)/(T_d-T_c)$). Applicable only when $T_s > T_c$
- **Benefit/cost ratio**: An indication of the average ratio between the benefit value of a change and the corresponding implementation cost (BoC/CoC).

Agility should not depend on implementation costs or proactivity, as this is a need that is mainly caused by external factors such as competition or technological advances. However, in complex software systems such as EIS, the environment only recognizes whether a particular organization responds quickly enough (or too slowly) to a developing context. The cost of this responsiveness, or how much in advance the organization must anticipate the need for change, is an internal matter of that organization. Sometimes it is preferable to pay more for a faster solution and implement a change less efficiently just to beat the competition and gain the competitive edge of being first in the market. If the time pressure is not high, optimization may focus on implementation costs rather than minimizing the change delay.

It is also important to acknowledge that these indicators can be measured in each of the loops of figure 1, but all must be considered according to the theory of constraints (Şimşit, Günay & Vayvay, 2014). For example, if an organization is very agile in terms of innovation and environmental perception (reorientation loop) but only slowly implements and deploys changes (reconfiguration loop), the overall agility will be affected by this slower loop (Queiroz et al., 2018).

THE PROBLEM: COUPLING IN APPLICATION INTEGRATION

The Fundamental Integration Problem

Among the many problems in software development, integrating applications or application modules is one of the most important issues with agility. Integration means dependency or coupling. When the coupling is high, changes are costly and agility is compromised.

Applications that interact in a distributed environment need a network to send each other messages. Each message transaction (sending a request and processing a response) requires both the sender and the recipient to understand and respond appropriately to receiving request and response messages. A particular application, in the role of the server, publishes the set of request messages to which it can respond, and defines the interface of the functionality offered by that application (its application programming interface API). In the role of the client, another application can send one of the allowed request messages to the server and invoke the corresponding functionality. Applications can also expose their APIs in terms of disclosed features such as operations. Each operation can accept its own set of request messages.

Figure 3 shows a typical client-initiated interaction that sends a request message to the server over the inter-connecting network. This usually causes the server to respond with a reply message when executing the request.

The server must be able to understand the client's request and respond to the client's expectations. Otherwise, the interaction does not lead to the intended effects.

Figure 3. Message-based interaction between two distributed applications

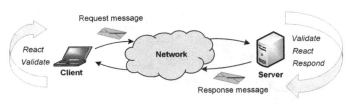

In a distributed environment, interacting applications evolve independently and cannot rely on names of local data types or inheritance hierarchies. However, the exchanged messages must be accurate and meaningful in both contexts of the interacting applications. The goal of a simple interaction, as shown in figure 3, can be divided into the following goals:

- There must be an addressable interconnecting network and a message-based protocol supporting a request-response message exchange pattern.
- The server must validate the request message and make sure that it is compatible with one accepted by the server API.
- The response of the server and the associated impact of the execution of the request message must meet the expectations of the client regarding this response. The server must do what the client expects.
- The client must validate the eventual response message and make sure that it is accepted by the client as a response.
- The client must react appropriately to the response and fulfill the purpose of the server sending this response and the purpose of the client initiating the interaction.

This means that both request and response messages must be validated and understood (correctly interpreted and responded to) by the application that receives them. In addition, many other factors must be taken into account, e.g. performance, scalability, reliability and security. This chapter, however, deals with the coupling aspect of interoperability, which has a relevant impact on the agility of software development.

The coupling expresses interdependencies between applications. The aim is to reduce these as much as possible to avoid unnecessary limitations in the development and variability of applications. What can be achieved, however, is a balance between two contradictory goals:

- On the one hand, two uncoupled applications (with no interaction between them) can evolve freely and independently, promoting agility, adaptability, changeability, and even reliability (if one fails, it will not affect the other).
- On the other hand, applications need to interact in order to work towards common or complementary goals, which means that some degree of previously agreed mutual knowledge must exist. The more they share with each other, the easier interoperability becomes, but the greater the coupling becomes.

Figure 4. Schema sharing in symmetric message-based distributed application interaction

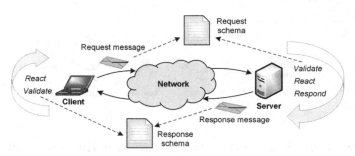

The fundamental problem of application integration is to provide the lowest (*at most*) possible coupling while ensuring minimum (*at least*) requirements for interoperability. The main goal is to make sure that each interacting application knows just enough about the others to interact with them. Unnecessary dependencies and restrictions should be avoided.

Existing data interoperability technologies, such as XML and JSON, assume that interacting applications use the same message schema as shown in figure 4. This can be called *symmetric interoperability*, reminiscent of the early days of Web and HTML documents when the client reads the document created by the server and both needed to use the same document specification. Today, data has been separated from its specification (schema), but both client and server are still working with the same information. The coupling has not been reduced.

The problem is that one server may need to serve several different clients and one client may need to send requests to several different servers. By sharing a schema, both client and server are coupled to the entire message set that the schema can describe, even if the client uses only a subset of the allowed requests and the server responds with only a subset of the allowed responses.

The net effect of this symmetry is that in many cases the client and server are more coupled than required, and changes in one application can very likely imply changes in the other, even if a change does not affect the actual messages being exchanged. Another solution is required.

A Model of Application Coupling

Given the graphical representation of all possible interactions between applications, any application that is non-initial (does not receive requests from others) or terminal (does not send requests to other) will typically inherit the roles of client and server as shown in figure 5. Both the left and the right part of this figure entail the client-server relationship shown in figure 4.

Each interaction involves some form of dependency (coupling) that results from the knowledge required to meaningfully establish that interaction. The coupling can be evaluated in terms of the fraction of features of an application (operations, messages, data types, semantic terms, etc.) that impose constraints on another application that interacts with it, and can be expressed in two slants as shown in figure 5:

- **Backward Coupling**: The subset of the features of an application on which its clients depend and must be used according to the application rules (the set of constraints an application imposes on its clients).

Figure 5. Backward and forward coupling

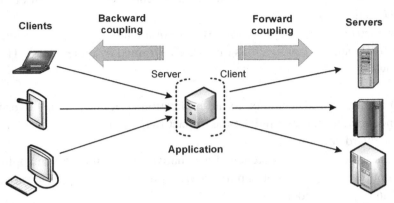

- **Forward Coupling**: The subset of the features of an application that its clients actually use, and which the application or other application that replaces it must support. In other words, the set of constraints that a client imposes on the applications it uses.

From the perspective of a particular application, these two coupling metrics can then be defined as follows:

- C_B (*backward coupling*), which indicates how much an application affects the clients:

$$C_B = \frac{\sum_{i \in C} \frac{Uc_i}{Tc \cdot M}}{|C|} \qquad (1)$$

where:

   C - Set of clients that use this application as a server, with $|C|$ as its cardinality

   Uc_i - Number of features of this application that client i uses

   Tc - Total number of features that this application has

   M - Number of known applications that are compatible with this application and can replace it, as a server

- C_F (*forward coupling*), which expresses how much a client depends on its server applications:

$$C_F = \frac{\sum_{i \in S} \frac{Us_i}{Ts_i \cdot N_i}}{|S|} \qquad (2)$$

where:

   S - Set of server applications that this client uses, with $|S|$ as its cardinality

   Us_i - Number of features that this client uses in server application i

   Ts_i - Total number of features that server application i has

N_i - Number of server applications with which this client is compatible, in all uses of features of server application i by this client

These coupling metrics give values between 0 (for completely unrelated and independent applications) and 1 (for fully dependent applications that are constrained by all features). These metrics can be interpreted as follows:

- Equation (1) means that alternatives to an application in its role as a server reduce its overall system dependency and thereby reduce the impact that the application may have on its potential clients (its backward coupling C_B).
- Equation (2) indicates that the existence of alternative servers for a given application reduces the feedforward coupling (C_F), as more applications with which this application is compatible (as a client) will dilute the dependencies.
- Both Equations (1) and (2) also express the fact that using a smaller fraction of features induces less coupling.

Not only can alternative server applications be found by intentionally designing and building them, but also by reducing the part of the features required for compatibility to the minimum required for application-to-application interaction. The smaller the number of constraints, the greater the likelihood of finding applications that meet them.

Therefore, both factors on which the coupling depends (the proportion of features used as the client and the number of available server alternatives) work in the same direction, with the first one reinforcing the second. Reducing the coupling means reducing the proportion of features used or the knowledge of one application over another. Therefore, the integration of applications developed in consideration of these aspects becomes easier.

Technologies such as Web Services (Zimmermann, Tomlinson & Peuser, 2012) and RESTful APIs (Pautasso, 2014) are poor coupling solutions because Web services are typically based on sharing a schema (a WSDL document) and RESTful APIs based on previously agreed media types. These technologies support distributed interoperability but do not solve the coupling problem.

In conventional systems, the search for an interoperable application is done by schema matching with similarity algorithms (Elshwimy, Algergawy, Sarhan & Sallam, 2014) and ontology matching and mapping (Anam, Kim, Kang & Liu, 2016). This can find similar server schemas but does not guarantee interoperability and manual adjustments are usually unavoidable.

The goal of this chapter is to integrate applications not just approximately but with accurate interoperability, even if the client and server schema are not identical, provided that certain requirements are verified. This does not mean that existing applications can be integrated, but that an application can be changed or adjusted due to normal evolution of specifications without compromising interoperability. The more specifications shared, the greater the coupling. However, less coupling means greater flexibility for changes and adjustments, with a corresponding impact on the agility of application development.

An application *adaptation* is a set of changes made to this application to accommodate changes in its specification. This implicitly assumes that the application already exists and that the changes made correspond to a solution to bridge the differences between the previous and the new specification.

Adaptations can be made at any stage of an application's lifecycle (figure 1), giving a new version of the application in practice.

The *adaptability* property expresses how easily an application can undergo a particular adaptation. As a metric, a value of 0 for adaptability means that the application cannot be adapted due to some limitations and cannot meet the new intended specification, and a value of 1 means that the cost or effort for adaptation is zero. It depends essentially on two factors:

- The *similarity S* between the specification of the application before and after the adaptation.
- The *forward coupling C_F*, the coupling between the application and its providers (the applications it uses as a server, in figure 5).

Adaptability *A* is directly proportional to these two factors:

$$A = S \cdot (1 - C_F) \tag{3}$$

Adaptability does not depend on which clients use the server- adapted application (figure 5), but only reflects adaptability (*can* it be adapted?) and cost-effectiveness. Many changes (low *S*) or high dependency on other applications (high C_F) reduce the adaptability.

Applications can be considered atomic, where only one component is either modified or unmodified or structured, and consists of several components, of which only a few are changed. The similarity between an application after adaptation and its previous specification is recursively defined by the similarity of its components as:

$$S = \begin{cases} 0 & atomic\ application\ (changed) \\ 1 & atomic\ application\ (unchanged) \\ \dfrac{\sum_{i \in T} S_i}{|T|} & structured\ application \end{cases} \tag{4}$$

where

T - set of components of the application

S_i - similarity of component *i* (recursively) of the application

A similarity of 1 means that nothing has changed, while a similarity of 0 means that all components of an application have changed.

The complementary adaptation question (*may* it be adapted?) indicates whether the change can be made without breaking interoperability. This is included in the *changeability* property *Ch* (Ross, Rhodes and Hastings, 2008), which is defined here as:

$$Ch = A \cdot (1 - C_B) \tag{5}$$

or

$$Ch = S \cdot (1 - C_F) \cdot (1 - C_B) \tag{6}$$

C_B is the backward coupling between the application to be adapted and its clients, which expresses the effects of adaptation the application. If it has low adaptability or if many of its customers are affected (high C_B), changeability becomes less than desired.

All the variables in equations (5) and (6) vary between 0 and 1. Any factor with a low value becomes dominant and sets the changeability low, resulting in a poor software architecture or implementation.

For this reason, for a given similarity expressing the degree of change made, an application is more adaptive (less likely to affect its clients and use its own servers) if it has less forward and backward coupling. This is consistent with the conclusions from the coupling model described in equations (1) and (2).

MINIMIZING COUPLING TO IMPROVE REUSABILITY, CHANGEABILITY AND AGILITY

The Concepts of Compliance and Conformance

In symmetric interoperability (figure 4), interacting applications must share the schemas of the messages they exchange. This results in a higher degree of coupling than is actually needed because applications are constrained by all the features of these schemas, although not all are used.

This chapter proposes the use of *asymmetric interoperability*, where the sender-generated schema of a message must only partially match the message schema expected by the receiver. Only the features actually used must match, and features that are not needed by the receiver but are present in the message are ignored. Optional receiver features that are not present in the message are provided with default values before the message is processed by the receiver. In addition, structured features are checked structurally and recursively component by component.

This means that a client can use different servers (send request messages to them) as long as these messages match the relevant parts of the request schema of these servers, even if they are not designed to work together.

This also means that a server can be replaced by another server with a different schema, as long as it meets all the requirements that the replaced server can fulfill. This can be caused by the evolution of the server (replaced by a new version) or by the use of a new server altogether.

It's exactly what equations (1) and (2) show that a server can interpret request messages from different clients and a server can send response messages to different clients to reduce coupling.

These *use* and *replace* relationships lead to two important schema relationships, which are central to asymmetric interoperability and are shown in Figure 6:

- **Client-Server**: *Compliance* (Czepa et al., 2017). The client must satisfy (*comply with*) the requirements set by the server to accept requests sent to it without them being validated and executed. It is important to note that any client that is compatible with a particular server can use it, regardless of whether it is designed to interact with it or not. The client and the server do not need to use the same schema. The client schema need only be compatible with the server schema in the actual features used. Because distributed applications have independent lifecycles, they cannot freely share names, and schema compliance must be checked structurally, feature by feature, between the messages sent by the client and the interface offered by the server. Note that in a response, the schema compliance roles are swapped (the server is the sender and the client is the receiver).

Figure 6. Compliance and conformance

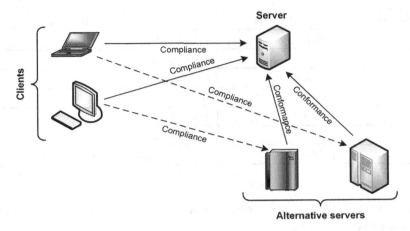

- **Server-Server**: *Conformance*. The issue is to determine whether a server S_1 serving a client can be replaced by another server S_2, such that the client-server relationship of the client is not affected, or whether the server S_2 is replacement-compatible with the server S_1. Conformance expresses the replacement compatibility between two servers. The server S_2 must have at least all the characteristics of the server S_1, thus be able to adopt the form of (*conform to*) the server S_1 and meet the expectations of the client from the server. In particular, the schema of the server S_2 must not contain any additional compulsory component with respect to the schema of the server S_1, otherwise the client would be subject to more requirements and the interoperability could be impaired. The reasons for replacing one server with another can be manifold, e.g. switching to an alternative in case of failure or capacity shortage, evolution (in this case, server S_2 would be the new version of server S_1) or simply an management decision.

For asymmetric interoperability, the server does not know the schema used by the client to generate messages. In this context, two types of schemas are considered:

- **Type Schema**: A description of the features of a message set, including the definition of each possible feature and whether it is optional or mandatory. This is typical for schema description languages like XML Schema.
- **Value Schema**: The concrete definition of a specific message with only the features that it actually has. Each message has its own value schema. This is just a self-description and, unlike type schema, does not involve variability (range of structured values). A value schema meets an unlimited number of type schemas (considering an unlimited number of optional features).

Symmetric interoperability (figure 4) uses both the client and server sharing type schemas. The server must be able to process all messages with value schemas that match its type schema, as this is also the type schema that the client uses, and therefore can send a message using one of these value schemas.

There is no such constraint on asymmetric interoperability, and as long as the value schemas of the actual messages sent match the server's type schema, interoperability is possible with less coupling. In semantic terms:

Table 2. Possible sets of built-in and structured data types

Data type category	Data type	Description
Built-in types	Integer	Integer numbers
	Float	Real numbers
	Boolean	True or false
	String	Strings
Structured types	Record	An unordered set of components
	List	An ordered set of components
Choice type	Union	A set of data types, any of which can be chosen

- Compliance means that the possible message values sent by a client are a subset of the values that match the server's type schema.
- Conformance means that the set of values that satisfies the type schema of an alternate server (figure 6) is a superset of the set of values that satisfies the type schema of the original server.

As long as compliance and conformance hold, the server can accept messages from different clients. In addition, a client can use an alternate server without noticing the difference to the original server.

A Data Schema Model as a Basis for Compliance and Conformance

Compliance and conformance start at the data level by checking whether:

- The structure of a message sent by a client satisfies to the structure of the messages that the server can accept (compliance).
- The server taking the place of another server can accept all messages that the replaced server could accept (conformance).

Because there are no common specifications, data compliance and conformance must be recursively checked structurally and component-wise until the primitive data types with predefined compliance and conformance rules are met.

A structural data interoperability mechanism must be based on:

- A set of built-in data types and the corresponding values that are considered atomic (not composed of other values).
- A set of structuring mechanisms that can be used to create arbitrarily complex (non-atomic) data types and their corresponding values.

The actual selection of these sets is not important as long as they are shared by interacting applications. They provide a basis for the interoperability of data and must be known to and shared between all interacting services. This is a principle already applied by existing interoperability approaches. The difference to the approach in this chapter is that non-atomic data must have the same structure (schema) instead of just agreeing on the structuring mechanism.

Table 3. Attributes specified for each component of the structured types

Attribute	Letter	Description
Name	N	Name of the component, possibly qualified by some ontology (just on Records)
Position	P	Ordering number of the component (on Records, position is the order by which components appear in the specification)
Type	T	Type of the component (any of the types of Table 2)
Minimum cardinality	m	Minimum number of occurrences of components with this name
Maximum cardinality	M	Maximum number of occurrences of components with this name

Table 2 shows possible sets of built-in types and structuring mechanisms loosely based on those of XML.

Union types are simply sets of types, each of which may be one of those listed in Table 2. Values belong to (satisfy) a Union type if they belong to at least one of its member types. Unlike many type systems, a value is not just a type, but anything that structurally fulfills.

The structured Record and List types consist of a number of components (which are not necessarily of the same type), each of which has the attributes described in Table 3. Tables 4 and 5 use the following attribute letters.

Structural Data Binding

A value schema is a data type in which the type attribute of each component is reduced to a single value and its cardinality is fixed (the minimum and maximum cardinalities are identical). Therefore, it just conforms to the data structure of a message with a self-description.

A type schema is as described in Tables 2 and 3 and is what a server specifies to announce the structure of the messages it can accept.

Data compliance means that the value schema of a message sent by a client must meet the minimum cardinalities of all components of a server's type schema. Those with a minimum cardinality of zero are optional.

A *data template* is a type schema that also specifies a default value for each optional component. If the message contains a component that corresponds to an optional component in the data template, it will be assigned to it. Otherwise, the default value is used.

Structural data binding is the process by which the value schema of a message is structurally assigned to the data template of a server, component by component. Each message component following the structure of the types in Table 2 looks for a match in the data template and populates the corresponding slot in the data template (replacing the default, if available). Components without a match are ignored. For structured components, this is recursive.

The data template is completely filled after the structural assignment, even if some components are missing in the message. Mandatory components (with a minimum cardinality greater than zero) must exist, without which there is no compliance and the message cannot be accepted.

The component mapping between the message and the data template is usually done by component name. However, mapping records to lists and lists to records (Table 2) allows for structural assignment

Table 4. Conditions for compliance (◄) of a structured type X with another, Y. The subscripts i and j designate component/member type and the letters designate component attributes (Table 3)

		Type Y		
		Record	**List**	**Union**
Type X	Record	For each Y_i, there is a X_j such that $X_{jN}=Y_{iN}$, $X_{jT}◄Y_{iT}$, $X_{jm}≥Y_{im}$, and $X_{jM}≤Y_{iM}$	For each Y_i, there is a X_j such that $X_{jP}=Y_{iP}$, $X_{jT}◄Y_{iT}$, $X_{jm}≥Y_{im}$, and $X_{jM}≤Y_{iM}$	X complies with at least one Y_i
	List	For each Y_i, there is a X_j such that $X_{jP}=Y_{iP}$, $X_{jT}◄Y_{iT}$, $X_{jm}≥Y_{im}$, and $X_{jM}≤Y_{iM}$	For each Y_i, there is a X_j such that $X_{jP}=Y_{iP}$, $X_{jT}◄Y_{iT}$, $X_{jm}≥Y_{im}$, and $X_{jM}≤Y_{iM}$	X complies with at least one Y_i
	Union	All X_j comply with Y_i	All X_j comply with Y_i	Each X_j complies with at least one Y_i

by position rather than name, with the position of each named component in records being specified as the position it occupies in its definition or declaration.

There is another possibility, the mapping by component type. In this case, components are assigned to those that comply with (or conform to) the other type. This has the advantage that it is not necessary to specify exactly the same name in the corresponding components. This cannot always be used because different components can have the same type but different semantics.

These mapping rules can lead to ambiguity, i.e. on match solutions that are not unique, especially when Unions are involved. In this case, the adopted solution may depend on the implementation. Types should be chosen to avoid ambiguity, or a compiler may check them and eventually generate an error.

Data Compliance

Compliance with data between a value schema and a type schema is a necessary condition to support structural data binding. There must be universal compliance rules that are not application-specific and can be defined as follows:

- Each built-in type is self-comply, except for Integer, which is complies with Float (subset).
- A Union type U corresponds to a built-in type B only if each member type U corresponds to type B.
- Table 4 describes the compliance between the more complex types of Table 2, structured and choice, and identifies the compliance between X and Y types by $X◄Y$.

Figure 7 shows a typical compliance-based client-server interaction (Czepa et al., 2017) where client and server do not need to share the same schema. The message schema of the client only has to comply the type schema of the server in the features actually used, which reduces the coupling between the client and the server.

The server publishes a request type schema that describes the type of request message values that the server can accept. When the request message arrives at the server, the value schema of the message is checked for satisfaction or compliance with the server's type schema. If compliance is met, the value of the request message is structurally bound to the data template, which is then completely populated

Figure 7. Illustrating compliance. Only the request message validation is shown

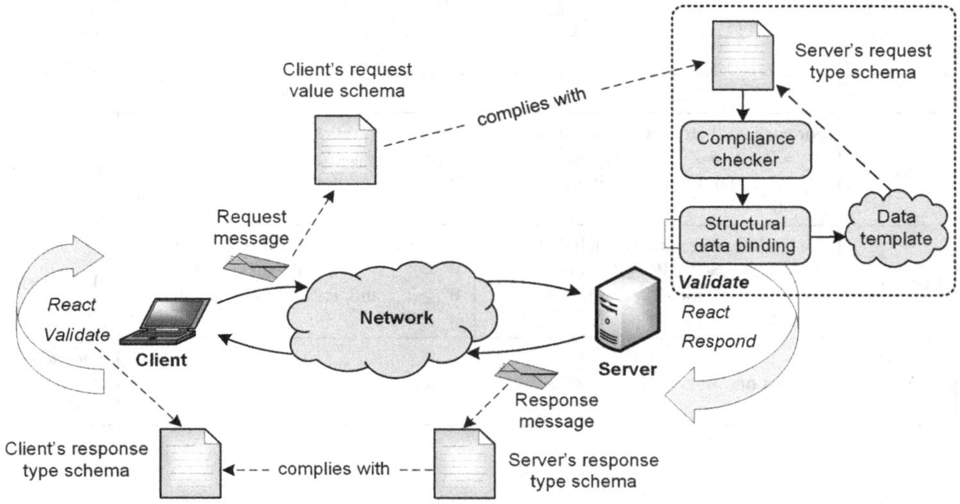

and ready for access by the server, regardless of the schema used to create the message (compliance is the only constraint).

Data Conformance

If a server application needs to take the place of another server application, it can do so as long as it matches. This can be useful in different situations, for example:

- An application is evolving (the new version replaces the old one).
- An application is being migrated to another cloud or environment, possibly with differences in the user interface.
- An alternative application is used because the original application fails or does not have sufficient capacity.
- To distribute the load of requests, distribute them across multiple (not necessarily identical) server applications.
- A management decision is made that implies the use of another application.

Conformance rules are universal and can be defined as follows:

- Each built-in type is self-contained except Float, which conforms to Integer (superset).
- A Union type V conforms to a built-in type C only if at least one member of V conforms to type C.
- Table 5 describes the conformance between the more complex types of Table 2, structured and choice, and indicates the conformance between types W and Z by W▶Z.

Table 5. Conditions for conformance ($\blacktriangleright$) of a structured type W to another, Z. The subscripts i and j designate component/member type and the letters designate component attributes (Table 3)

		Type Z		
		Record	**List**	**Union**
Type W	Record	For each Z_i, there is a W_j such that $W_{jN}=Z_{iN}$, $W_{jT}\blacktriangleright Z_{iT}$, $W_{jm}\leq Z_{im}$, and $W_{jM}\geq Z_{iM}$, and, for all remaining W_j, $W_{jm}=0$	For each Z_i, there is a W_j such that $W_{jP}=Z_{iP}$, $W_{jT}\blacktriangleright Z_{iT}$, $W_{jm}\leq Z_{im}$, and $W_{jM}\geq Z_{iM}$, and, for all remaining W_j, $W_{jm}=0$	W conforms to all Z_i
	List	For each Z_i, there is a W_j such that $W_{jP}=Z_{iP}$, $W_{jT}\blacktriangleright Z_{iT}$, $W_{jm}\leq Z_{im}$, and $W_{jM}\geq Z_{iM}$, and, for all remaining W_j, $W_{jm}=0$	For each Z_i, there is a W_j such that $W_{jP}=Z_{iP}$, $W_{jT}\blacktriangleright Z_{iT}$, $W_{jm}\leq Z_{im}$, and $W_{jM}\geq Z_{iM}$, and, for all remaining W_j, $W_{jm}=0$	W conforms to all Z_i
	Union	At least one W_j conforms to Z	At least one W_j conforms to Z	For each Z_i, there is at least one W_j that conforms to it

Figure 8. Illustrating conformance. A server application can be replaced by another, as long as it supports the features required by the clients of the original server application

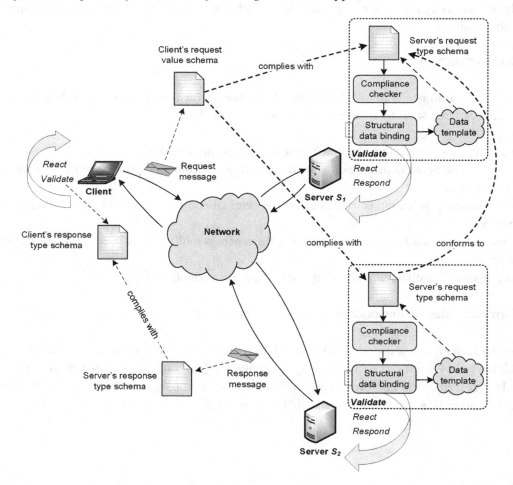

Figure 8 shows the conformance between two server applications by illustrating a situation in which a server S_1 serving a client is replaced by another server S_2, while the client-server relationship is maintained so that the client does not noticed.

The server S_2 has all the characteristics of the server S_1 (and probably more) and therefore can take the form of the server S_1 and meet the expectations of the client as to what it expects from the server. If the schema of server S_2 has additional features with respect to the server S_1, they must be optional, otherwise further demands would impose on the client and the interoperability could be impaired.

According to the definition of conformance, one client that complies to one server also complies to another server that conforms to the original server (see figure 8).

Service Compliance and Conformance

The previous sections covered data-level conformance and compliance by correlating sent-message value schemas with acceptable-message type schemas. However, applications are typically available as services that expose multiple operations. In this case, clients are typically referred to as *consumers* (of the service they use), and servers assume the role of *providers* (of the service they offer).

Each operation can have several parameters, but these can be structured into just one parameter, a record or a list as defined in Table 2. Then, the consumer must send a message (which includes at least the mandatory parameters) that complies to the argument of the request operation according to the compliance rules in Table 4. The same applies to the result returned by the operation, but now the result produced by the operation must comply what the consumer expects (sender and receiver role reversed).

A consumer can then use any server that has the required operations that the consumer is compliant and the responses meet the consumer's expectations. It is not necessary for the consumer to know the entire interface of the provider, but only what it actually uses.

In a more formal setting, consider a service C (the consumer) and a service P (the provider). C can call some of P's operations by sending request messages that trigger these calls. For each operation in P, the following definitions apply:

- Crq: The value schema of the request message, sent by the consumer.
- Prq: The type schema of the request message, expected by the provider.
- Prp: The value schema of the response message, sent by the provider.
- Crp: The type schema of the response message, expected by the consumer.

A consumer C is compliant with (can *use*) a provider P ($C \blacktriangleleft P$) if for all operations i of P that C actually calls, $Crq_i \blacktriangleleft Prq_i$ and $Prp_i \blacktriangleleft Crp_i$. Structural data binding is used to assign the value components of a received message (either request or response) to the variable components of the receiver's type schema (either provider or consumer).

Finally, a provider S is similarly conform to a provider P ($S \blacktriangleright P$) (can *replace* it) if for all operations i of P, $Srq_i \blacktriangleright Prq_i$ and $Prp_i \blacktriangleright Srp_i$.

Figure 9. An example of business-level distributed interactions

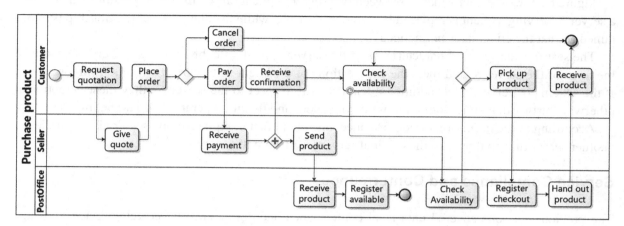

Illustrating Compliance and Conformance

Because current integration tools do not fully support compliance and conformance concepts, these concepts are simulated in this section using existing technologies, namely Web Services (Zimmermann, Tomlinson & Peuser, 2012) and XML.

Figure 9 describes a typical online product purchase scenario using the process paradigm and Business Process Modeling Notation (BPMN) (Chinosi & Trombetta, 2012) to illustrate the interactions between a customer, a seller, and a logistics company to deliver the purchased product.

A developer must independently conceive, design, and implement each of the three roles in this process choreography (Queiroz et al., 2018) as much as possible, since these roles can be performed by applications with different goals and properties. The overall goal is to minimize coupling.

Consider the interoperability between the customer and the seller as required in figure 9. For a customer this means not only finding a suitable seller, but also avoiding a lock-in to it by replacing that seller with another with a compatible interface. The partial interoperability (compliance and conformance) makes it possible to reduce the coupling to the necessary minimum.

The seller is a web service that offers multiple operations, including one called getQuote, which allows the customer to implement his RequestQuotation activity.

Listing 1 contains a fragment of a seller's WSDL file that shows only the relevant parts. A WSDL file describes the interface of a web service, including the supported operations and the corresponding parameters and results. For the sake of simplicity, listing 1 shows only the operation getQuote. It receives the specification of a product (the model and department of the seller to which it belongs), and the information returned contains a quote for each product found on that model, as well as an optional Boolean value that indicates whether this product is in stock. The customer needs a client program to handle this web service.

Listing 1. A fragment of the WSDL of one seller's web service

```
<types>
    <xs:schema xmlns:xs="http://www.w3.org/2001/XMLSchema"
            targetNamespace="http://example.com/schema/seller1"
            xmlns="http://example.com/schema/seller1"
            elementFormDefault="qualified">
        <xs:element name="product" type="Product"/>
        <xs:element name="prodInfo" type="ProdInfo"/>
        <xs:complexType name="Product">
            <xs:sequence>
                <xs:element name="model" type="xs:string"/>
                <xs:element name="department" type="xs:string"/>
            </xs:sequence>
        </xs:complexType>
        <xs:complexType name="ProdInfo">
            <xs:sequence minOccurs="0" maxOccurs="unbounded">
                <xs:element name="ID" type="xs:string"/>
                <xs:element name="cost" type="xs:decimal"/>
                <xs:element name="inStock" type="xs:boolean"
                        minOccurs="0"/>
            </xs:sequence>
        </xs:complexType>
    </xs:schema>
</types>
<interface name="Seller_1">
    <operation name="getQuote"
            pattern="http://www.w3.org/ns/wsdl/in-out">
        <input messageLabel="In" element="seller1:product"/>
        <output messageLabel="Out" element="seller1:prodInfo"/>
    </operation>
</interface>
```

Now look at listing 2 with the corresponding WSDL fragment of another seller's web service that is compatible with, but not identical to, the web service. The getQuote operation provides the same overall functionality and name, allowing syntactic interface matching. In this example, for the sake of simplicity, the semantics are not dealt with. A quote will also be obtained for the product, as indicated by a description and associated product category, and will return up to three pairs of product IDs and their respective price. The description can contain one or two strings, so that, for example, brand and model can be separated if necessary. The category is optional, but it supports two strings, for example, to indicate the division and unit of the product.

Listing 2. A fragment of the WSDL of another seller's Web Service

```
<types>
    <xs:schema xmlns:xs="http://www.w3.org/2001/XMLSchema"
            targetNamespace="http://example.com/schema/seller1"
            xmlns="http://example.com/schema/seller2"
            elementFormDefault="qualified">
        <xs:element name="productSpec" type="ProductSpec"/>
        <xs:element name="productInfo" type="ProductInfo"/>
        <xs:complexType name="ProductSpec">
            <xs:sequence>
                <xs:element name="description" type="xs:string"
                            minOccurs="1" maxOccurs="2"/>
                <xs:element name="category" type="xs:string"
                            minOccurs="0" maxOccurs="2"/>
            </xs:sequence>
        </xs:complexType>
        <xs:complexType name="ProductInfo">
            <xs:sequence minOccurs="0" maxOccurs="3">
                <xs:element name="productID" type="xs:string"/>
                <xs:element name="price" type="xs:decimal"/>
            </xs:sequence>
        </xs:complexType>
    </xs:schema>
</types>
<interface name="Seller_2">
    <operation name="getQuote"
                pattern="http://www.w3.org/ns/wsdl/in-out">
        <input messageLabel="In" element="seller2:productSpec"/>
        <output messageLabel="Out" element="seller2:productInfo"/>
    </operation>
</interface>
```

These two WSDL fragments correspond to two different schemas, and the usual way to invoke each of these services is to generate two different clients, one for each service. However, considering both WSDL fragments, it is noticeable that:

- The In element of the getQuote operation in listing 1 of type Product *complies* to the In element of the operation in Listing 2 of type ProductSpec. In other words, supplying a model and a department with one string each meets the requirements of the operation in listing 2;
- The Out element of the operation in listing 2 of type ProductInfo *conforms* to the Out element of the operation in Listing 1 of type ProdInfo. This means that all values returned by the operation in listing 2 are as valid as if the operation in listing 1 had returned them.

This means that a client that is generated to invoke the service that belongs to listing 1 can also invoke the service that listing 2 belongs to without any changes, as long as the getQuote operation in listing 2 conforms that of listing 1. This is equivalent to relaxing the constraint that both interacting parties must use the same schema (scenario in figure 4) and that they are entitled to use compliance schemas that are easily compatible based on compliance and conformance (scenario in figures 7 and 8). This increases the range of compatible services and results in less coupling.

Comparing Structural and Classic Data Binding

The most distinguishing feature of structural data binding in relation to traditional data binding in existing interoperability technologies such as Web Services (Zimmermann, Tomlinson & Peuser, 2012) and Restful APIs (Pautasso, 2014) is that the receiver of a message (the server in requests and the client in responses) does not deal with the actual schema of the message, but only with the type schema used in the data template (figures 7 and 8). Data binding is done component by component using universal structuring mechanisms and rules (Tables 4 and 5).

Therefore, no application-specific stubs need to be defined and implemented. This is a relevant contribution to increasing agility in application development. This means that the coupling is reduced compared to classical symmetric interoperability (figure 4), with the following advantages:

- The coupling is limited to the actual features of a schema, not to the entire features of that schema.
- It is more likely that a client will find suitable servers based on a smaller set of features than based on a full schema (lower forward coupling).
- A server can serve a broader base of clients as it imposes less restrictions on them (lower backward coupling).

On the other hand, the check of schema compliance is obligatory. Many applications nowadays only check the link to the schema or the media type, as the schema or the media type must be identical for current integration approaches.

The added flexibility that compliance offers has a performance disadvantage. However, recurring messages can tune their compliance checking by sending a session-unique binding token in each message, which is cached in both interacting applications (in binding caches). In this way, compliance is checked only once when the interaction is established.

Each value / type schema combination must have a binding token. Recurring messages use the same binding token again. Rather than checking whether the schema / media type of the message is the expected one, the receiver only needs to check that the token of the message exists in the binding cache, and then know how to map the incoming message to the data template (figure 7). Like most uses of caches, this is very efficient when messages repeat and the schema does not change frequently. Fortunately, this is usually the case when applications have long-standing interactions.

The great advantage of structural bonding is speed (which translates into agility), with which interactions can change. If a client uses a different server or value schemas in messages, the receiver has a binding cache fault. Full compliance is then checked. A new binding token is created if compliance is met, and subsequent interactions use that token. Of course, a message protocol still needs to be developed to support this mechanism.

Conformance is a feature that naturally fits into structural data binding and is not supported by current integration technologies.

Other aspects such as security do not differ from existing approaches. After authentication and authorization, message encryption can be done in the usual way. The structural data binding at the receiver takes place after the message decryption.

FUTURE RESEARCH DIRECTIONS

Compliance and conformance are basic concepts that can be applied to all domains and levels of abstraction and complexity. In this chapter, they were examined in the field of agile software development. However, this is a preliminary work, and the application of these concepts to this context is currently only a suggestion.

Although formal work in certain areas such as choreographies (Yang, Ma, Deng, Liao, Yan, and Zhang, 2013) is in progress, a comprehensive and systematic study needs to be conducted to formalize the meaning of compliance and conformance at various interoperability levels, namely semantics and pragmatics. Their formal definition must be more formal and systematic.

Given the current trend of increasing adoption of cloud computing, cloud interoperability (Kostoska, Gusev, & Ristov, 2016) is also a major issue with increasing relevance to the development of agile applications where compliance and conformance may play a role. A compliance and conformance assessment study must be conducted as a partial interoperability solution for cloud-based applications.

The coupling problem is also relevant to the interoperability of non-functional aspects in application development, especially in context sensitive applications and in applications where service level requirements (SLRs) are designed and managed with respect to application interactions. In order to determine how compliance and conformance can be applied in these cases, further investigation is needed.

CONCLUSION

The most common application integration technologies, Web Services (Zimmermann, Tomlinson & Peuser, 2012) and RESTful APIs (Pautasso, 2014), focus on interoperability rather than coupling. Both require prior knowledge of the types of data involved in the interaction, which means more coupling than actually required because data schemas need to be shared by the interacting applications. Web services typically require linking to the schema shared by the consumer and the provider, while REST-based technologies typically agree on a particular schema prior to application interaction. If an application changes the schema used, the users who interact with the application must be aware of these changes to avoid breaking the interaction.

This chapter considers that both aspects, interoperability and coupling, need to be balanced. The fundamental problem of application integration is to achieve the lowest possible coupling, to minimize dependencies between applications that hinder changeability, while ensuring the minimum interoperability requirements for applications to interact effectively.

Structural compliance (Tran, Zdun, Oberortner, Mulo & Dustdar, 2012) and conformance (Khalfallah, Figay, Barhamgi & Ghodous, 2014) relax the constraints on sharing messaging schemas and therefore provide an improved solution over existing integration technologies. Two applications that have at least the characteristics that are required for interoperability can work together at design, compile, or runtime, regardless of knowledge of the other characteristics, and thus minimizing coupling.

The data binding between the received messages and the receiver-supported schema is usually implemented with a schema-specific stub that is added to the application. The binding of structural data based on compliance and conformance, as proposed in this chapter, eliminates the need for stubs because the receiver only deals with its own schema, and the binding between the message and the receiver's schema is structural and universal, without the need for specific ones. This reduces application coupling and contributes to increasing application changeability and agility of application development.

REFERENCES

Agostinho, C., Ducq, Y., Zacharewicz, G., Sarraipa, J., Lampathaki, F., Poler, R., & Jardim-Goncalves, R. (2016). Towards a sustainable interoperability in networked enterprise information systems: Trends of knowledge and model-driven technology. *Computers in Industry*, *79*, 64–76. doi:10.1016/j.compind.2015.07.001

Alenezi, M., & Magel, K. (2014). Empirical evaluation of a new coupling metric: Combining structural and semantic coupling. *International Journal of Computers and Applications*, *36*(1). doi:10.2316/Journal.202.2014.1.202-3902

Anam, S., Kim, Y., Kang, B., & Liu, Q. (2016). Adapting a knowledge-based schema matching system for ontology mapping. In *Proceedings of the Australasian Computer Science Week Multiconference* (p. 27). New York, NY: ACM Press. 10.1145/2843043.2843048

Babu, D., & Darsi, M. (2013). A Survey on Service Oriented Architecture and Metrics to Measure Coupling. *International Journal on Computer Science and Engineering*, *5*(8), 726–733.

Bassett, L. (2015). *Introduction to JavaScript Object Notation: A to-the-point Guide to JSON*. Sebastopol, CA: O'Reilly Media, Inc.

Bidve, V. S., & Sarasu, P. (2016). Tool for measuring coupling in object-oriented java software. *IACSIT International Journal of Engineering and Technology*, *8*(2), 812–820.

Bohnsack, R., Hanelt, A., Marz, D., & Marante, C. (2018). Same, same, but different!? A systematic review of the literature on digital transformation. Academy of Management Proceedings, 2018(1), 16262.

Carmona, J., van Dongen, B., Solti, A., & Weidlich, M. (Eds.). (2018). *Conformance Checking: Relating Processes and Models*. Cham, Switzerland: Springer. doi:10.1007/978-3-319-99414-7

Chinosi, M., & Trombetta, A. (2012). BPMN: An introduction to the standard. *Computer Standards & Interfaces*, *34*(1), 124–134. doi:10.1016/j.csi.2011.06.002

Czepa, C., Tran, H., Zdun, U., Kim, T., Weiss, E., & Ruhsam, C. (2017). On the understandability of semantic constraints for behavioral software architecture compliance: A controlled experiment. In *Proceedings of the International Conference on Software Architecture* (pp. 155-164). Piscataway, NJ: IEEE Computer Society Press. 10.1109/ICSA.2017.10

Delgado, J. (2019). Cloud-Based Application Integration in Virtual Enterprises. In N. Raghavendra Rao (Ed.), *Global Virtual Enterprises in Cloud Computing Environments* (pp. 46–85). Hershey, PA: IGI Global. doi:10.4018/978-1-5225-3182-1.ch003

Dornberger, R. (Ed.). (2018). *Business Information Systems and Technology 4.0: New Trends in the Age of Digital Change* (Vol. 141). Cham, Switzerland: Springer. doi:10.1007/978-3-319-74322-6

Elshwimy, F., Algergawy, A., Sarhan, A., & Sallam, E. (2014). Aggregation of similarity measures in schema matching based on generalized mean. *Proceedings of the IEEE International Conference on Data Engineering Workshops* (pp. 74-79). Piscataway, NJ: IEEE Computer Society Press. 10.1109/ICDEW.2014.6818306

Erl, T., Merson, P., & Stoffers, R. (2017). *Service-oriented Architecture: Analysis and Design for Services and Microservices*. Upper Saddle River, NJ: Prentice Hall PTR.

Farid, A. (2017). Measures of reconfigurability and its key characteristics in intelligent manufacturing systems. *Journal of Intelligent Manufacturing*, *28*(2), 353–369. doi:10.100710845-014-0983-7

Fawcett, J., Ayers, D., & Quin, L. (2012). *Beginning XML*. Indianapolis, IN: John Wiley & Sons.

Fielding, R., Taylor, R., Erenkrantz, J., Gorlick, M., Whitehead, J., Khare, R., & Oreizy, P. (2017). Reflections on the REST architectural style and principled design of the modern web architecture. In *Proceedings of the 2017 11th Joint Meeting on Foundations of Software Engineering* (pp. 4-14). New York, NY: ACM Press. 10.1145/3106237.3121282

Geetika, R., & Singh, P. (2014). Dynamic coupling metrics for object oriented software systems: A survey. *Software Engineering Notes*, *39*(2), 1–8. doi:10.1145/2579281.2579296

Hinings, B., Gegenhuber, T., & Greenwood, R. (2018). Digital innovation and transformation: An institutional perspective. *Information and Organization*, *28*(1), 52–61. doi:10.1016/j.infoandorg.2018.02.004

Hoda, R., Salleh, N., & Grundy, J. (2018). The rise and evolution of agile software development. *IEEE Software*, *35*(5), 58–63. doi:10.1109/MS.2018.290111318

ISO. (2010). *Systems and software engineering – Vocabulary. ISO/IEC/IEEE 24765:2010(E) International Standard*. Geneva, Switzerland: International Organization for Standardization.

Khalfallah, M., Figay, N., Barhamgi, M., & Ghodous, P. (2014). Model driven conformance testing for standardized services. In *IEEE International Conference on Services Computing* (pp. 400–407). Piscataway, NJ: IEEE Computer Society Press. 10.1109/SCC.2014.60

Kostoska, M., Gusev, M., & Ristov, S. (2016). An overview of cloud interoperability. In *Federated Conference on Computer Science and Information Systems* (pp. 873-876). Piscataway, NJ: IEEE Computer Society Press. 10.15439/2016F463

Liao, Y., Deschamps, F., Loures, E., & Ramos, L. (2017). Past, present and future of Industry 4.0 - a systematic literature review and research agenda proposal. *International Journal of Production Research*, *55*(12), 3609–3629. doi:10.1080/00207543.2017.1308576

Panetto, H., & Whitman, L. (2016). Knowledge engineering for enterprise integration, interoperability and networking: Theory and applications. *Data & Knowledge Engineering*, *105*, 1–4. doi:10.1016/j.datak.2016.05.001

Pantiuchina, J., Lanza, M., & Bavota, G. (2018). Improving code: The (mis) perception of quality metrics. In *Proceedings of the IEEE International Conference on Software Maintenance and Evolution* (pp. 80-91). Piscataway, NJ: IEEE Computer Society Press. 10.1109/ICSME.2018.00017

Pautasso, C. (2014). RESTful web services: principles, patterns, emerging technologies. In Web Services Foundations (pp. 31-51). New York, NY: Springer. doi:10.1007/978-1-4614-7518-7_2

Popplewell, K. (2014). Enterprise interoperability science base structure. In K. Mertins, F. Bénaben, R. Poler, & J. Bourrières (Eds.), *Enterprise Interoperability VI: Interoperability for Agility, Resilience and Plasticity of Collaborations* (pp. 417–427). Cham, Switzerland: Springer International Publishing. doi:10.1007/978-3-319-04948-9_35

Pulparambil, S., Baghdadi, Y., Al-Hamdani, A., & Al-Badawi, M. (2018). Service Design Metrics to Predict IT-Based Drivers of Service Oriented Architecture Adoption. In *Proceedings of the 9th International Conference on Computing, Communication and Networking Technologies* (pp. 1-7). Piscataway, NJ: IEEE Computer Society Press. 10.1109/ICCCNT.2018.8494072

Queiroz, M., Tallon, P., Sharma, R., & Coltman, T. (2018). The role of IT application orchestration capability in improving agility and performance. *The Journal of Strategic Information Systems*, *27*(1), 4–21. doi:10.1016/j.jsis.2017.10.002

Rezaei, R., Chiew, T., & Lee, S. (2014). A review on E-business interoperability frameworks. *Journal of Systems and Software*, *93*, 199–216. doi:10.1016/j.jss.2014.02.004

Ross, A., Rhodes, D., & Hastings, D. (2008). Defining changeability: Reconciling flexibility, adaptability, scalability, modifiability, and robustness for maintaining system lifecycle value. *Systems Engineering*, *11*(3), 246–262. doi:10.1002ys.20098

Samdantsoodol, A., Cang, S., Yu, H., Eardley, A., & Buyantsogt, A. (2017). Predicting the relationships between virtual enterprises and agility in supply chains. *Expert Systems with Applications*, *84*, 58–73. doi:10.1016/j.eswa.2017.04.037

Şimşit, Z., Günay, S., & Vayvay, Ö. (2014). Theory of Constraints: A Literature Review. *Procedia: Social and Behavioral Sciences*, *150*, 930–936. doi:10.1016/j.sbspro.2014.09.104

Tooranloo, H. S., & Saghafi, S. (2018). The relationship between organisational agility and applying knowledge management. *International Journal of Agile Systems and Management*, *11*(1), 41–66. doi:10.1504/IJASM.2018.091360

Tran, H., Zdun, U., Oberortner, E., Mulo, E., & Dustdar, S. (2012). Compliance in service-oriented architectures: A model-driven and view-based approach. *Information and Software Technology*, *54*(6), 531–552. doi:10.1016/j.infsof.2012.01.001

Yang, H., Ma, K., Deng, C., Liao, H., Yan, J., & Zhang, J. (2013). Towards conformance testing of choreography based on scenario. In *Proceedings of the International Symposium on Theoretical Aspects of Software Engineering* (pp. 59-62). Piscataway, NJ: IEEE Computer Society Press. 10.1109/TASE.2013.23

Zanero, S. (2017). Cyber-physical systems. *IEEE Computer*, *50*(4), 14–16. doi:10.1109/MC.2017.105

Zimmermann, O., Tomlinson, M., & Peuser, S. (2012). *Perspectives on Web Services: Applying SOAP, WSDL and UDDI to Real-World Projects*. New York, NY: Springer Science & Business Media.

ADDITIONAL READING

Bora, A., & Bezboruah, T. (2015). A Comparative Investigation on Implementation of RESTful versus SOAP based Web Services. *International Journal of Database Theory and Application*, *8*(3), 297–312. doi:10.14257/ijdta.2015.8.3.26

Brandt, C., & Hermann, F. (2013). Conformance analysis of organizational models: A new enterprise modeling framework using algebraic graph transformation. *International Journal of Information System Modeling and Design*, *4*(1), 42–78. doi:10.4018/jismd.2013010103

Capel, M., & Mendoza, L. (2014). Choreography Modeling Compliance for Timed Business Models. In *Proceedings of the Workshop on Enterprise and Organizational Modeling and Simulation* (pp. 202-218). Berlin, Germany: Springer. 10.1007/978-3-662-44860-1_12

Chamoux, J. (Ed.). (2018). *The Digital Era 1: Big Data Stakes*. Hoboken, NJ: John Wiley & Sons. doi:10.1002/9781119102687

Dornberger, R. (Ed.). (2018). *Business Information Systems and Technology 4.0: New Trends in the Age of Digital Change* (Vol. 141). Cham, Switzerland: Springer. doi:10.1007/978-3-319-74322-6

Dragoni, N., Giallorenzo, S., Lafuente, A., Mazzara, M., Montesi, F., Mustafin, R., & Safina, L. (2017). Microservices: yesterday, today, and tomorrow. In M. Mazzara & B. Meyer (Eds.), *Present and Ulterior Software Engineering* (pp. 195–216). Cham, Switzerland: Springer. doi:10.1007/978-3-319-67425-4_12

He, W., & Da Xu, L. (2014). Integration of distributed enterprise applications: A survey. *IEEE Transactions on Industrial Informatics*, *10*(1), 35–42. doi:10.1109/TII.2012.2189221

McLay, A. (2014). Re-reengineering the dream: Agility as competitive adaptability. *International Journal of Agile Systems and Management*, *7*(2), 101–115. doi:10.1504/IJASM.2014.061430

Ritter, D., May, N., & Rinderle-Ma, S. (2017). Patterns for emerging application integration scenarios: A survey. *Information Systems*, *67*, 36–57. doi:10.1016/j.is.2017.03.003

KEY TERMS AND DEFINITIONS

Agility: The ability to adapt (reactively and/or proactively) an application to changes in its interoperability requirements with other applications, in a timely and cost-efficient manner.

Compliance: Asymmetric property between a consumer C and a provider P (C is compliant with P) that indicates that C satisfies all the requirements of P in terms of accepting requests.

Conformance: Asymmetric property between a provider P and a consumer C (P conforms to C) that indicates that P fulfills all the expectations of C in terms of the effects caused by its requests.

Consumer: A service role performed by an application A in an interaction with another B, which involves making a request to B and typically waiting for a response.

Coupling: A measurement of how much an application is dependent on the interface of another application.

Interoperability: Asymmetric property between a consumer C and a provider P (C is compatible with P) that holds if C is compliant with P.

Provider: A service role performed by an application B in an interaction with another A, which involves waiting for a request from A, honoring it and typically sending a response to A.

Service: The set of operations supported by an application that together define its behavior (the set of reactions to messages that the application is able to receive and process).

Chapter 4
Applying Software Engineering Design Principles to Agile Architecture

Chung-Yeung Pang
https://orcid.org/0000-0002-7925-4454
Seveco AG, Switzerland

ABSTRACT

Most enterprise IT systems are very complex with a combination of COBOL and Java programs running on multiple platforms. What is needed is a solid IT architecture that supports the operation and growth of a cross-platform IT system. It must enable the iterative and incremental development of applications that are foreseen in an agile development process. The design concept of such an architecture with its infrastructure and development tool is presented in this chapter. This design concept is based on the design principles and architectural patterns of software engineering. The architecture is a combination of layered, component-based, and service-oriented architectural patterns. The agile development process is based on a model-driven approach. The architecture and development approaches were first introduced in 2004. Since then, many applications have been developed on time and within budget.

INTRODUCTION

Despite advances in software engineering, software development remains a challenge for IT professionals. Statistics have shown that most software projects run too late and too expensive. The problem becomes even more apparent when a mix of legacy and modern applications in a complex IT system comes into play. In fact, IT enterprise systems typically go through a long development phase. Over the past decades, software projects have evolved into some of the most complex software systems. For large companies, mainframe applications programmed in COBOL often form the backbone of the IT structure. New applications and components are often developed using a language such as Java on a UNIX or LINUX platform. Often, business processes require collaboration between components on different platforms.

DOI: 10.4018/978-1-7998-2531-9.ch004

Maintaining and updating an IT system that combines legacy and modern platforms is one of the toughest challenges many companies are facing today. Modern businesses have high demands on IT systems to work in highly stable yet flexible and fast environments, and to introduce new features and processes to meet their steady growth. The agile software development process, which follows the evolutionary and iterative approach of software development and focuses on adapting to change (Ambler, 2010; Larman, 2003), seems to meet the requirements. However, the process alone does not guarantee the success of a software project. There are many other factors. Attempts to use only the agile approach to software development can still fail (Harlow, 2014; Ismail, 2017). Through years of evolution in software engineering, there are design principles and techniques that can help tackling the complexity involved in application development in an enterprise IT system. They must be incorporated into the agile development process.

A cross-platform enterprise IT system requires a software architecture that supports operations and growth. The architecture must enable the iterative and incremental development of applications. The purpose of this chapter is to introduce the design and implementation concept of such an architecture. The design concept is based on design principles and architectural patterns that have emerged from decades of research in software development. It is also based on years of hands-on experience of the author with an iterative incremental process and a continuous integration approach to software development.

The materials presented in this chapter focus on four areas: what, why, how and consequences. The first section covers the historical background of software engineering and the agile development process. The following section is the "what" topic that gives an introduction to the design principles that have resulted from software development and object-oriented programming, as well as the software architecture and agile development methodology. The next section discusses the "why" and explains the motivation behind the principles of software engineering, software architecture, and the agile development process. The section "how" develops agile architecture design and its use in the agile approach to enterprise application development. In the section "consequences" the applicability as well as the experiences from the practice are presented. The chapter ends with future research directions and conclusions.

BACKGROUND

As background, the following subsections introduce the disciplines of software engineering and the agile development approach.

Software Engineering

In the early days of software history, programmers tended to develop their programs without documentation in an ad-hoc style. The programs are usually not structured and organized. With the development with many new features, the underlying software becomes unmanageable and unmanageable. One result was the software crisis of the 1960s, 1970s and 1980s (Software Crisis, 2010).

Software engineering (2010) is a discipline that offers solutions to counteract the software crisis. It defines standards, disciplines, methodologies and processes for software development. In recent decades, many new programming languages, design principles and architectural patterns, and development paradigms have been developed. Programming styles such as structural programming (Yourdon & Constantine, 1979; Jackson, 1975), object-oriented programming (Booch, et al., 2007), etc. have been introduced. In addition to programming, great emphasis was placed on analysis and design with the right documentation. The waterfall model for the development process was introduced, defining the development phases with an initial requirements analysis and specification, software design, implementation, testing and deployment, and subsequent product maintenance (Royce, 1970; Bell & Thayer, 1976).

The waterfall model for software development has long been a standard. Application development had led to the belief that a complete, detailed requirement specification had to be prepared before further development activities could be undertaken. It turns out that requirements are often a moving target and change over time. Creating a complete, detailed requirement specification for complex applications is nearly impossible. Many projects did not survive the analysis phase before the budget was used up. New development models are required.

Agile Development Approach

In 2001, a group of well-known software developers came together to define a set of principles for software development. What emerged was the Agile Manifesto (Agile Manifesto Group, 2001). It triggered a new movement in the software community with an agile development process and was widely accepted. The agile development process follows the evolutionary and iterative approach of software development (Ambler, 2010; Larman, 2003) and focuses on adapting to change. Requirements and solutions result from the collaboration of self-organizing, cross-functional teams. It promotes adaptive planning, evolutionary development, early deployment and continuous improvement, and promotes a rapid and flexible response to change.

The agile approach to software development eliminates the large documents resulting from the waterfall model and thus reduces the significant effort required for the requirements specification. The process also forces the development team to stop focusing on high-level concepts that are designed to be developed with early prototypes. The approach has numerous advantages over the conventional waterfall model.

Despite its many advantages, the agile approach also has many down sides. Rakitin (2001) criticized the agile approach as an attempt to undermine the discipline of software engineering. The concept of "working across a large document" leads to "we want to spend all our time programming, remember that real programmers do not write documentation." This leads back to ad hoc programming style. While the concept of developing program elements iteratively in small trunks and continuously integrating them into the IT system is well founded, the basic structure and mechanism of how the program elements can be developed and integrated must be well understood. Applications must be structured in such a way that they can be flexibly and easily adapted to changes. In other words, an agile software architecture is needed. There are many articles in the literature on how to use an agile approach. Most examples show that it is applied to the development of Web applications with an underlying architecture behind the http protocol. Frameworks like Wordpress, Drupal, Laravel, Node.js etc. all have their architecture. For a project that requires more than simple Web elements, proper architecture is still required.

The 2015 Standish Group CHAOS report (Hastie & Wojewoda, 2015) shows that the success rate for an agile approach is more than three times higher than for a waterfall approach. An agile approach is certainly the better choice than a traditional waterfall approach. However, the report also shows a 39% overall success rate for the agile software development approach. There is further need for improvement. One should try to consider applying the principles of software engineering that have developed after so many years of experience.

BRIEFING OF SOFTWARE ENGINEERING DESIGN PRINCIPLES, ARCHITECTURE AND AGILE METHOD

This section provides a brief description of the principles of software development, architecture, and agile methods. The focus is on the "what". The chapter is divided into three subsections. The first subsection deals with the design principles of software engineering, the second with the agile enterprise software architecture and the last with the most popular agile method Scrum.

Software Engineering Design Principles

The software design derives a solution that meets the software requirements. There is no general agreement on the design principles of software so far. The main goals of the design principles are to help developers manage the complexity of the IT landscape and provide guidelines on how to easily build and maintain software. "Divide and Conquer" and "Separation of Concern" are probably the main goals behind most design principles. This section presents a number of well-known design principles from the literature (Huang, 2010). The principles contained are listed below:

- **Rigor and Formality**: The Standish Group has suggested that the formal methodology is one of the key success factors in software development (Krigsman, 2006). The software design must be strictly formal documented to avoid ambiguity. Formal design documents, such as pseudocode or UML models, can show the basic logic of a program with sequences of steps, iterations with for and while loops, and selections with if-else statements or symbols. They improve the readability of design concept and algorithm compared to text documents. The main goal of a formal design document is to explain exactly what a program should do exactly to make it easier for developers to design. It helps both programmers and analysts to understand the programs and thus serves as documentation for the software product. In industry, the approach of documentation is essential. And here a formal design document proves to be crucial.
- **Abstraction**: A software developer cannot work on more than a few concepts and their relationships at the same time. An abstraction makes it possible to suppress unimportant details and to emphasize the important information. Abstraction is the process of identifying a set of essential features of an entity without paying attention to its details. Abstraction helps manage the intellectual complexity of software. It provides a higher-level concept that ignores certain detailed properties altogether (Colburn & Shute, 2007).
- **Modularization**: "Divide and conquer" is the main approach to dealing with complexity. The idea is to first divide or subdivide the problem into small and distinct modules. This helps to treat various individual aspects of a problem and we can focus on each part separately. Modularity in software engineering refers to the extent to which an application can be divided into smaller modules (Baldwin & Clark, 2000). Modularity is also a kind of separation of concerns. A complex problem is divided into modules so that details of each module can be handled individually and separately. In a sense, modularity is a logical subdivision of software design that allows complex software to be managed for implementation and maintenance. The logic of partitioning can be based on related functions, implementation considerations, data connections, or other criteria. The modularity offers better manageability of software development.

- **Information Hiding**: The idea of information hiding was introduced in 1972 by Parnas (Parnas, 1972). It is a principle of separation of design decisions in one module that are likely to change, protecting other modules from being changed when the design decision is changed. Parnas defined hiding information as a way to shield clients from internal program flow. To achieve hiding of information, a module may disclose a stable functional contract (e.g. an interface) that other modules can access. The internal implementation would be hidden from the outside. Therefore, changing the internal design of other modules would not be affected.

- **Cohesion**: Cohesion is a measure of the relationship between elements in a module. It is the degree to which all elements being the participants to perform a single task are included in the module. Cohesion is basically the composition of the relevant elements that hold the module together. A good software design has a high cohesion that only relevant elements for performing the module specific task are included in a module. There are different types of cohesion. Their description can be found in an article by Josika (Josika 2017).

- **Coupling**: Coupling is the measure of the degree of interdependence between the modules. Strong coupling between modules can mean that a module cannot perform its specific task without the other modules. Therefore, the module is not independent. It cannot be unit tested or used independently of each other. Sagenschneider (Sagenschneider, 2019) gave an analogy that a software system with strongly coupled modules is like a puzzle. Each module is part of the puzzle and the software system can only take on the right shape if all the pieces fit together well. If changes are made, we need to rearrange the puzzle. Parts of a puzzle do not usually fit in other puzzles. In another perspective, a software system built from strong coupling modules cannot be built using an iterative incremental approach with continuous integration. The final software product is anything but agile. A good software has a low coupling. Best of all, each module is independent and autonomous.

- **Anticipation of Change**: Each software system would undergo a number of changes and improvements throughout its life cycle. It is important to recognize elements that are likely to change in the early phase of software development. When anticipated changes are identified, special care must be taken in designing so that future changes can be easily applied. The requirement of a software system or application is often a moving target. It is nearly impossible to identify the full requirements of a software system at an early-stage with every detail. The agile development approach is widely accepted as the focus is on rapid adaptation to change. The anticipation of changes is a guideline for every software design.

- **Reusability**: The reusability of software artefacts does not normally fit into the equation of the agile software development process. However, reusing existing software artefacts can significantly speed development, especially if development iteration should only take a short time. Reusable artefacts include code, software modules, test suites, designs, and documentation. Most developers would think of reusing existing modules and code. Since the publication of the book by Gamma et al. (1995), software developers have been made aware of patterns that one is constantly using. A pattern is defined as the solution to a problem in a particular context. If one encounters a similar problem as before, one can always adapt the same solution to the problem. Patterns provide a wider dimension of software reuse. Reusability is not just a concept limited to the reuse of the existing elements. It can give software developers new thinking and discipline in designing and programming. With reusability in mind, developers can begin designing and programming a module that can solve more common problems rather than a very specific problem of an application. The design is not rigidly bound to the current requirement, making it more general, flexible, extensible, and less complex.

In addition to the design principles above, there are design principles specific to an object-oriented approach to analysis, design, and programming. The specific features of the object-oriented approach include generality, encapsulation, inheritance, and polymorphism (Booch et al., 2007). In addition to these features, Martin (2000, 2017) described the SOLID design principles. SOLID is an acronym with the following meaning:

- **S Stands for SRP (Single Responsibility Principle)**: This principle states that "a class should have only one reason to change" which means every class should be responsible to a single actor and not others.
- **O Stands for OCP (Open Closed Principle)**: Originally by Meyer (1988), this principle states that "software entities (classes, modules, functions, etc.) should be open for extension, but closed for modification". Martin (2000) reformulated it that interfaces instead of super-classes should allow for various implementations that one can replace without changing the objects that use them.
- **L Stands for LSP (Liskov Substitution Principle)**: The principle was proposed by Liskov (1988), that objects in a program should be replaced by instances of their subtypes without altering the correctness of that program.
- **I Stand for ISP (Interface Segregation Principle)**: This principle states that many custom interfaces are better than a universal interface.
- **D Stands for DIP (Dependency Inversion Principle)**: This principle states that object dependencies refer only to abstractions, not to concretions.

The SOLID principle helps to reduce tight coupling and make the code more reusable, maintainable, flexible and stable.

Agile Enterprise Software Architecture

The concept of software architecture emerged in the early 1980s in response to the increasing complexity and diversity of software systems. Architecture is defined as the governing of rules, heuristics and patterns:

- Partitioning the problem and the system that is to be built into discrete pieces.
- The techniques used to create interfaces between these pieces.
- The techniques for managing overall structure and flow.
- The techniques used to interface between the system and its environment.
- Appropriate use of development and delivery approaches, techniques and tools.

An architecture contains the methods, standards, tools, frameworks, policies, and administrative statements. Over the last 30 years, many architectural patterns have evolved from this concept. Some of the most popular are listed in the following list:

- Client/server and multi-tier
- Layered architecture
- Component-based architecture
- Event-driven architecture
- Broker architecture
- Model-view-controller (MVC)
- Pipe-filter
- Service-oriented architecture (SOA)
- Message/service bus

The list shown here only gives some of the common architectural patterns. Detailed descriptions of these patterns can be found in the book by Richards (Richards 2015). Different patterns take into account of different architectural concerns. SOA and Broker architectures are communication-related patterns, while component-based and layered architecture addresses the overall structure of the system. There are also patterns for exception handling. The design of enterprise software architecture would generally combine multiple architectural patterns to cover all requirements.

Agility is essentially about moving fast and accepting change. It is a continuous improvement. The agile software architecture provides a good solution and framework for rapid development, integration, and removal of high-quality modules.

Agile Method Scrum

There are different agile methods. The most popular is probably Scrum. Scrum is based on autonomous and self-organized teams (Drumond, 2019). It relies on an iterative (usually cyclically repeated at short intervals) and incremental (gives new functions) process. In a Scrum process (Rehkopf, 2019), product owners and business analysts would involve end users to define user stories that they would include in the product backlog. User stories are short requests or requirements written from the perspective of an end user. In an enterprise application, there are usually other stories that relate to non-functional requirements. A series of related and interdependent stories would form an epic. In other words, an epic is an extensive work that can be divided into a series of smaller tasks that are recorded in stories. A collection of epics working toward a common goal is an initiative. Themes are used for large focus areas that span the organization.

In a Scrum development process, software elements are developed in iterations called sprints. A sprint has a timeframe of not more than a month and usually two weeks. For each sprint, the project team picked up one or more user stories from the product backlog and implemented the appropriate software elements or modules. The sprint is not complete until the implementation has been fully tested. Continuous integration is generally recommended that the software elements or modules be integrated into the system with an integration test. The software system will be released to the end user once all essential features have been implemented and fully tested.

MOTIVATION BEHIND DESIGN PRINCIPLES, ARCHITECTURE, AND AGILE DEVELOPMENT PROCESS

In this section, we explore the motivation behind design principles and software architectures in an agile development process. The section is divided into three subsections. The first subsection examines the reasons for using software engineering principles and architectures. The second section, why we need design principles and architecture in an agile development process, is explained. The last subsection presents the requirements for an agile enterprise architecture.

Needs for Software Engineering Design Principles and Architecture

It is not uncommon for a large company's IT system to contain hundreds of thousands of software modules interacting in a very complex way. Maintenance and enhancements to new business needs are always a nightmare. As mentioned earlier, the software engineering design principles are based on years of experience to support the production of high quality software. These are basic guidelines for creating software that is stable, functional, flexible, easy to change, and easily adaptable to new features.

To ensure business and IT flexibility, the overall complexity of the IT system must be resolved and managed. A proper software architecture is required (Babar et al., 2014). Isotta-Riches and Randell (2014) reported that architecture was a key factor in the success of an agile approach at Aviva UK. IBM's Hopkins and Hardcombe (2014) also discussed the need for a suitable architecture for the development of complex agile systems. Netherwood states that architecture is important because it (Malan & Bredemeyer, 2010):

- Controls complexity.
- Enforces best practice.
- Gives consistency and uniformity.
- Communicates skill requirements.
- Reduces risk.
- Enables reuse.

Proper architectural design with its supporting infrastructure and tools are critical to the success of an IT project. The architecture provides an overview of how software components should be structured and developed, and how continuous integration should work. It ensures the agility of the entire system, allowing the agile development approach to run throughout the software lifecycle with little or no technical debt. It must reduce, not increase, the complexity of the IT system. Software tools and standards must simplify the development process and not make it more complicated.

The Standish Group research shows that 70% of the application code is the infrastructure (Johnson et al., 2001). There should be a clear separation between the implementation of business and technical aspects. The technical infrastructure is generally stable and the same for all applications. One can develop code segments and patterns that can be parameterized as required. Application developers should focus only on the business-related aspects and include the infrastructure code segments and patterns in their programs as needed. The application developers should not have to master the infrastructure. The overhead of writing 70% of the infrastructure-related application code can also be saved.

Figure 1. Illustration of tightly coupled modules

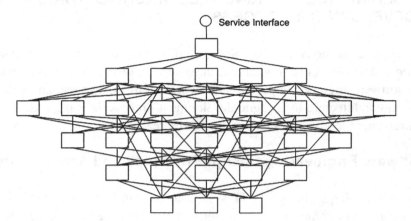

Design Principles and Architecture for Agile Development Process

It seems that the agile community is convinced that software design is generally not an issue. The design of a software architecture was considered by many to be a prime example of "great design in the foreground," which is in contrast to general agile practices. There are many examples that show implementations that are based only on user stories without architectural and modular design effort. These examples are typically simple Web applications that are already based on an event-driven architecture framework using the http protocol. Implementing an event triggered by clicking a button or simply sending the data of a web form to the web server does not require in-depth design work.

In many cases, especially complex IT systems, proper architecture and modularity are required. In fact, there are many examples of the huge problems caused by architectural debts. If one allows an ad hoc development style without proper architecture, it is easy to have a structure with tightly coupled modules, as shown in Figure 1. In fact, such a modular structure can be found in most large IT enterprise systems. Modules cannot be developed and tested individually. One may forget the flexibility, and changes are not easy.

In a Scrum process, themes, initiatives, epics and stories are fundamentally different levels of abstraction of the problems to be solved by the software system. Different themes are usually handled by different teams. There is a need for high-level abstraction with the concept of hiding information for the services or interfaces provided by different themes. Initiatives and epics contain the coherent stories and their implementation. A modular structure of the software system is indispensable if small granular modules are to be implemented in a sprint every two weeks. Modules that are heavily coupled with other modules cannot be fully implemented and tested without the dependent modules. The coupling between modules must be kept to a minimum for an iterative approach of implementation.

Ideally, one wants to develop each module independently, perform unit testing, and integrate it into the system in an iteration. This requires each module to be autonomous and to have a single responsibility. Modules seldom work independently of each other. They have to work with other modules and exchange data. So we need a mechanism for indirect interaction of modules so that data can be exchanged without one module directly accessing another. All this requires a central process control that calls the individual modules under the right conditions. Because flexibility is paramount in agile development and changes can be easily customized, anticipating change is a key principle. All the points described require an agile architecture. In fact, an agile approach like Scrum cannot be used if one has a modular structure like the one shown in Figure 1. To use an agile approach to enterprise application development, software engineering principles and agile architecture are essential.

Facilities Provided by an Agile Architecture and Development Tools

The purpose of the software architecture design is to provide a structural framework of a modular system, techniques and mechanisms for the operation and collaboration of individual parts, as well as rules and standards to which the programs should conform. The agile architecture is required to provide the following facilities:

1. Allow the integration of web-based applications.
2. Enable cross-platform application integration.
3. Enable business domain partitions and divide business domains into business components (different levels of business abstractions).
4. Ensure separation of infrastructure and application code (maximize cohesion of functions and features).
5. Enable independent development of software elements or modules (minimize coupling and promote modularity).
6. Provide mechanisms for plug-and-play and continuous integration of modules.
7. Provide style and techniques for object-oriented programming to follow SOLID principles.
8. Maximize flexibility, usability, hiding information, and reusability.

In addition to an agile architecture framework, we need development tools that provide the following capabilities:

1. Rigorously formalize the design and implementation documentation.
2. Provide a way for rapid autonomous module development.
3. Facilitate the integration of autonomous modules into the system.

HOW TO DESIGN AND BUILD AN AGILE ARCHITECTURE

In the previous sections the descriptions and motivations of the design principles, the architecture and the tools were presented together with agile methods. This section explains how to design and build an agile architecture. The first section deals with the design of an agile architecture with two subsections, one about enterprise architecture and the second about plug and play framework. The second topic deals with the use of UML modeling and code generation tools as well as the implementation of applications based on the architecture framework. The topic is also divided into three subsections. The concept of using UML models and the CASE tool for code generation is briefly explained in the first subsection. The second part deals with the implementation in a legacy platform with IBM CICS and COBOL. The third part deals with the Java implementation, which contains some open source frameworks.

Enterprise Architecture

With the advances in web technology, companies must consider integrating web-based applications into their existing applications. Integration can take place via an SOA. In the SOA, messages exchanged between the service provider and the consumer are generally XML or JSON. In addition, a client application is not tied to a single server. A service consumer can use services from different platforms. One can implement an Enterprise Service Bus (ESB) to redirect service requests to the right service providers on different platforms. Messages in XML or JSON allow interoperation between applications written in different languages. SOA, together with the use of an ESB, provides architectural patterns for communication and application integration (Chappell, 2004).

In its book Simple Architectures for Complex Enterprises, Sessions (2008) suggested that partitioning is essential for managing complexity in enterprise architectures. A structural pattern, such as a component-based architecture, can be used to provide the basic structure of business domain partitions. In this pattern, related programs are combined into a single component. Each component has one or more well-defined interfaces that provide windows for interacting with other components. Internal processing (including access to the data store) is completely encapsulated in the component.

Component-based architecture can be combined with SOA. Rather than providing interfaces in Java or COBOL, a component can provide a service interface with XML or JSON. Sessions suggested that when partitioning a corporate IT system, the services provided by each partition can be defined. In the proposed architecture, the enterprise IT system is divided into business components and components that are service providers.

Architecture patterns such as component-based architecture and SOA provide comprehensive concepts for partitioning business domains and organizing programs for an enterprise IT system. There are still many detailed problems, such as security, error handling and logging, ACID transaction processing, etc., which need to be addressed. The solutions to these problems would ultimately be the designs of the basic infrastructure framework into which the applications can be integrated.

A layered structure can be integrated into the component-based service-oriented architecture. Layering is widely used in enterprise architecture. The architecture presented here has a three layer structure. The top layer is a service and mediation layer. At this level, incoming XML or JSON messages are parsed, and the data is mapped to an input data object (such as a Java JSON object). Service requests are resolved after the security check and dispatched to the correct components. The service consumer must be authenticated and authorized to access the requested service. Control is via the standard platform infrastructure. The outputs of the components are rendered into XML or JSON. An additional feature in this layer is service transaction management. Errors can occur in all business components involved in the service. Transactions across all components would either be committed or rolled back by the transaction manager at the service and mediation level.

Another set of infrastructures is implemented at a vertical layer, providing functions such as error handling and logging. All business components can access this layer for error handling and logging. Service errors are temporarily stored in the database. They are archived after a certain time. They can be obtained from the service support team member through a standard web service.

The layered structure is shown in figure 2a. The enterprise IT system is based on a layered, component-based and service-oriented architecture. As shown in figure 2b, a business component can cut across three horizontal levels. The service interface of a business component would reside in the service and mediation layer. Business components can communicate with each other in the business processing layer.

Figure 2. Illustration of the layered, component based and service oriented architecture

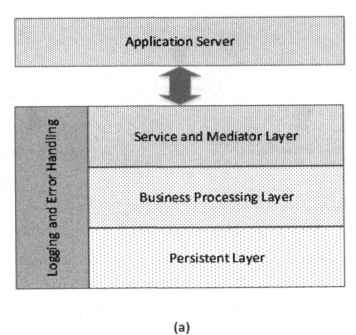

The lowest level is the persistent level where components interact with their persistent tables in the database. In this layer, modules from different business components are not allowed to interact with each other. On the other hand, they can interact with the infrastructure layer for error handling and logging.

Figure 3. Illustration of inter-platform communication with service oriented architecture

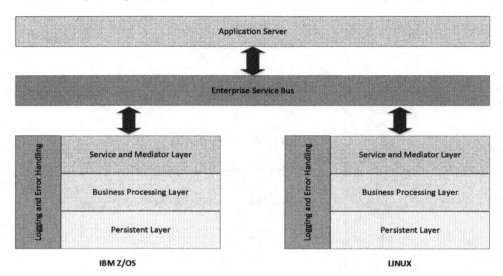

Using an Enterprise Service Bus (ESB), SOA enables cross-platform communication as seen in Figure 3. Together with the use of ESB, the enterprise architecture patterns meets the 1, 2 and 3 facilities described in the previous section.

Plug and Play Architecture

The IT architecture with its infrastructure framework helps manage the complexity of the entire enterprise business. Applications are partitioned according to their business domains. The next design is architecture in every business component or service.

Business components very rarely contain only a few modules or objects. In fact, most business components themselves are complex and consist of many modules or objects. They are usually developed by different teams for the different business areas. In the stack of layers shown in Figure 2, the modules in the lower layers are activated by the modules in the upper layers. This requires a mutual dependence between the module to be activated and the module that activates it. The module to be activated would rely on the correct data being forwarded by the module that activates it. The module that activates other modules must ensure that it has all the data needed by the enabled modules. If a new module needs to be added to the bottom level of the stack, or if a module at the bottom level needs new input data, it will ripple the changes in many modules in the stack. This structure usually results from an early implementation without architectural design. The maintenance and expansion of the final software usually requires a huge effort. It also breaks the concept of iterative development of autonomous modules with single responsibility (SOLID principles) that can be unit tested.

Modules seldom work independently of each other. They need to work with other modules and share data. So one needs a mechanism for indirect interaction of modules so that data can be exchanged without one module directly accessing another. With all this archived, a central process control is still required, which calls the individual modules under the right conditions.

The event-driven architecture pattern fits in well with the central process control and provides agility to the software. In this pattern, each module is reactive. One can use the event-driven business process flow mechanism. The process controller is basically a finite state machine. Each module must deliver an event after execution. The process controller checks the state and the event and decides on the next module to invoke. Each module is called by the process controller, which operates independently. Depending on the business logic processing and the state data, the processing of the module would lead to different events. The process controller would consider the actual state and the outbound event to determine the next process to be performed.

The process controller must not be responsible for providing input data to all modules. Therefore, a service context container is used. A module retrieves the required data by providing a logical name for the context container. The output data of the module would be assigned a logical name and placed in the context container.

In summary, the architecture design for the process of a service has the following characteristics:

- Process control is centralized using a process controller implemented in the form of a finite-state machine.
- Modules are independent autonomous units with well-defined contracts to fulfil (fulfilling SOLID principles).
- Apart from invocations of external services offered by other business components, modules are not supposed to make direct calls to other modules.
- A plug-and-play architecture is in place so that a module can be plugged in at any time for continuous integration.
- All state data will be held in a context container.
- Status data (COBOL structure in COBOL and object in Java) can be stored under a specific logical name in the context container and retrieved using this logical name.
- Each module will fetch the required state data from the context container and put new or updated state data in the context container.

The process sequence of a service is given in the following list:

1. Upon receiving a service request, the service mediator would first carry out the security and access control.
2. The service mediator parses input in XML or JSON and creates the proper input data object (COBOL structure for COBOL and Java object for Java).
3. The service mediator creates the context container and puts the input data object into the context container.
4. The service mediator identifies and activates the process-controller module, as well as setting the initial state and event.
5. The process controller determines the module to be invoked, based on the current state and event.
6. The process controller invokes the module and sets up a new state.
7. The module fetches its input data from the context container.
8. The module carries out the execution of the business. Logic.
9. The module puts output data associated with logical names, into the context container.
10. Depending on the outcome, the module sets a new event.

11.   It repeats Step 5 until the business process completes, unless an error has occurred.
12.   In the event of an error, the module would log the error message using the error handling and logging facility.
13.   The module puts the error message into the context container and sets an error event for the error case.
14.   The process controller terminates the process and returns to the service mediator when the business process is completed, or when an error occurs.
15.   The service mediator fetches the output data from the context container and renders the output into XML or JSON.
16.   The service mediator will either commit the transaction or rollback the transaction if an error has occurred.

When data needs to be processed or retrieved by an external component, a module can interact directly with the external component. Alternatively, a wrapper can be created that retrieves the input data for the external component from the context container and calls the external component. The output data of the external component is put into a context container by the wrapper. The wrapper also sets a new event for process control.

For business components that need to work with the main service component of a service, their processing steps are very similar to the list above. However, they do not provide a service interface, only interfaces for calls. In these cases, one needs process dispatchers to perform the tasks of the service mediator. Tasks such as security and access control, XML or JSON analysis, and transaction management are not required in a process dispatcher.

Plug-and-play, along with the enterprise architecture described in the previous subsection, meets all the agile architecture requirements discussed in the previous section.

Design Model and CASE Tools

A rigorous formal approach to document design (one of the principles of software engineering) is the use of UML models. Service message interfaces can be well documented by business analysts in UML class diagrams. The process flow can be modeled in UML state diagrams. The state diagrams can be further refined and each state activity converted into a program module. The state machine is constructed with a fixed algorithm and is controlled by a state transition table. The state table can be easily created or automatically generated from the process flow model.

A CASE tool that supports UML modeling can be used. The CASE tool must support code generation so that software artifacts can be generated directly from models. Code templates and patterns can be used for code generation. They offer a high degree of reusability, which will be shown in the next two subsections.

Model and Implementation in Legacy Platform

The design of the architecture presented in this chapter is not limited to implementation in specific languages. This subsection introduces the architecture implementation and module programming in COBOL.

IBM provides an infrastructure for processing TCP / IP and HTTP protocols as well as the message queue (MQ). It also facilitates XML parsing in COBOL. This allows us to build the basic infrastructure required for SOA.

The main elements of our applications are the following:

- A service mediator.
- A context container.
- Application components and their modules.
- A process controller and process-control descriptor.
- An XML parser and data-object descriptors.

The service mediator in the first layer of our architecture contains a generic module that handles security and access control, transaction management, and resource creation including the context container, and so on. It is part of the SOA infrastructure. The service mediator module uses the IBM infrastructure to retrieve the input message from our service client. The input is in XML format with a standard SOAP (Simple Object Access Protocol). After identifying the requested service and resolving the main process control module, a module is called to parse the XML data, map the XML data into COBOL record structures (copy books), and place the record structures in the context container. The mapping is based on a data object descriptor for a particular service. This data object descriptor contains meta-information for the mapping between the native COBOL data structure to / from the XML data structure. When the business process is completed, the service mediator also calls a module to retrieve the COBOL output record structures from the context container and uses the metadata in the data object descriptors to render the output XML. To develop a service, the data object descriptors must be created along with the process control descriptors and configured to allow the service mediator to perform its functions.

As already mentioned, the service interface is modelled in the UML class diagram. UML classes are used with extended attributes properties to capture both COBOL and XML data structures and their mappings. Data object descriptors and other artefacts are generated from UML class diagrams. An illustration of the UML class model and generated software artefacts is shown in Figure 4.

Figure 5 shows the state chart with a code segment of a process controller. In this illustration, the process is quite simple, as each activity leads to a single event. Normally, an activity can lead to a number of different events that branch out in different process flows. The technical error handling uses a standard flow pattern that does not need to be included in the process flow model. In the event of an error, an exception is thrown and the process terminates with error messages returned to the service consumer.

An activity in the state chart represents a COBOL module. Each module is programmed as a separate unit. It is activated by the process controller with the transfer of the context container. The required data is retrieved from the context container, without knowing where and how this data is made available. The output data is stored in the context container. An event is generated by the module depending on the result of its action. When modelling the process flow, it must be ensured that each module finds its required data in the context container. For early testing of the process, dummy modules can be inserted that just generate the events and updated the state data in the context container. These dummy modules can be successively replaced by real modules in the iterative process.

All usages of the infrastructure can be put into a number of code patterns that can be parameterized. Therefore, developers can easily use these patterns in the model and set the parameters without worrying about the code behind the infrastructure. There are also many repeatable business patterns that

Figure 4. Class model and software artifacts generation

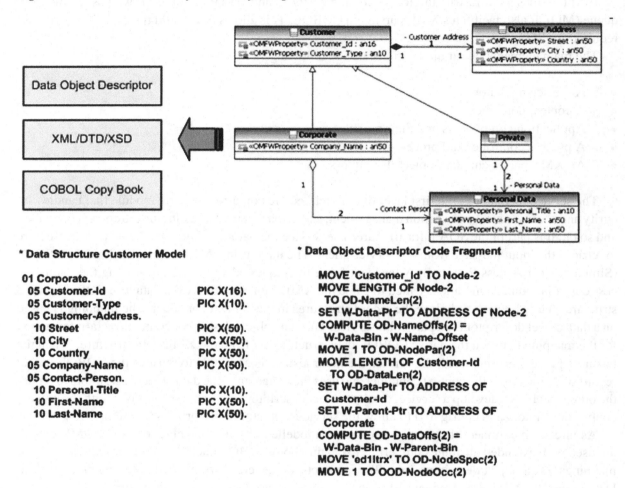

* Data Structure Customer Model

```
01 Corporate.
   05 Customer-Id             PIC X(16).
   05 Customer-Type           PIC X(10).
   05 Customer-Address.
      10 Street               PIC X(50).
      10 City                 PIC X(50).
      10 Country              PIC X(50).
   05 Company-Name            PIC X(50).
   05 Contact-Person.
      10 Personal-Title       PIC X(10).
      10 First-Name           PIC X(50).
      10 Last-Name            PIC X(50).
```

* Data Object Descriptor Code Fragment

```
MOVE 'Customer_Id' TO Node-2
MOVE LENGTH OF Node-2
   TO OD-NameLen(2)
SET W-Data-Ptr TO ADDRESS OF Node-2
COMPUTE OD-NameOffs(2) =
   W-Data-Bin - W-Name-Offset
MOVE 1 TO OD-NodePar(2)
MOVE LENGTH OF Customer-Id
   TO OD-DataLen(2)
SET W-Data-Ptr TO ADDRESS OF
   Customer-Id
SET W-Parent-Ptr TO ADDRESS OF
   Corporate
COMPUTE OD-DataOffs(2) =
   W-Data-Bin - W-Parent-Bin
MOVE 'ed1ltrx' TO OD-NodeSpec(2)
MOVE 1 TO OOD-NodeOcc(2)
```

can be integrated into reusable code patterns using parameters. Along with reusable code templates, reuse can be significantly increased. Reusable code segments are generally well tested. This reduced the effort for troubleshooting and testing. As mentioned above, 70% of the code usually refers to the infrastructure. The expense of writing this code portion can be significantly reduced if reusable code patterns are included in the model.

Figure 6 shows an example of the activity diagram and the generated code. The activity model has the following characteristics:

- Program rules and logic are modelled in the UML activity diagram.
- Each action in the model can contain code or a link to a code pattern with parameters.
- The code generator uses different structures for different actions with different stereotypes.
- Different code templates are also used to generate COBOL modules for different purposes.

Figure 5. State model and code generation of a process controller

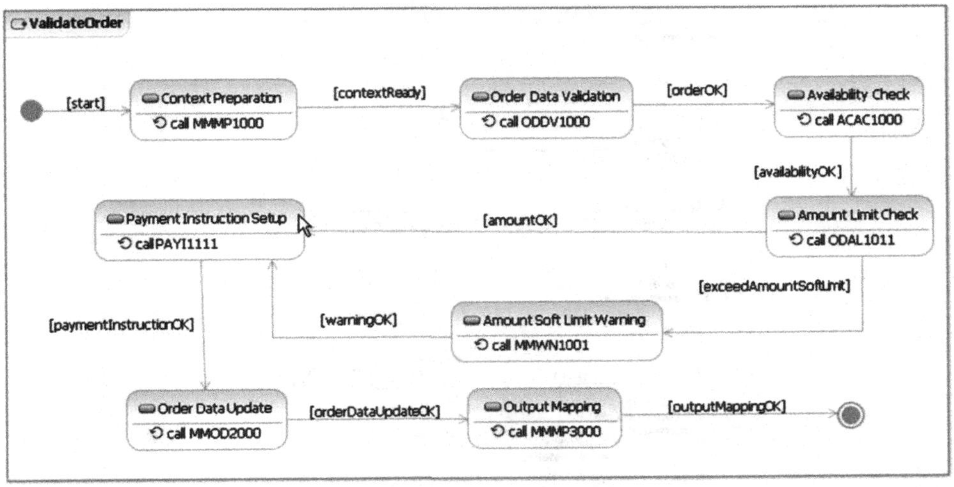

```
* Process Control Descriptor Code Segment:

  MOVE "OrderOK" TO CP-Event(3)
  MOVE "Order Data Validation" TO CP-State(3)
  MOVE "ACAC1000" TO CP-Activity-Name(3)
  MOVE "Availability Check" TO CP-Next-State(3)
```

To create a service, one must use UML class diagrams to create the data object descriptors. Process control descriptors for process control can be generated based on state charts. COBOL modules can be developed using activity diagrams.

Model and Implementation in Java With Frameworks

Many tools and standards for service-oriented development in Java are available. For example, standards such as Simple Object Access Protocol (SOAP) and Web Services Description Languages (WSDLs) are defined by W3C. There are many open source tools support these standards. Services can be implemented as Web-service servlets or endpoint of message-oriented middleware (MOM) using components such as ActiveMQ. Enterprise Service Buses (ESB), such as Mule ESB, can be used as a service integration platform to provide services creation and hosting, message brokering, message forwarding, data transformation, transaction management, security control, and security Database access etc.

The high-level architecture presented in this chapter combines the patterns of SOA, component-based, and layered architecture. The basic design concept of the component-based architecture is listed below:

Figure 6. Activity modeling of module logic and code generation

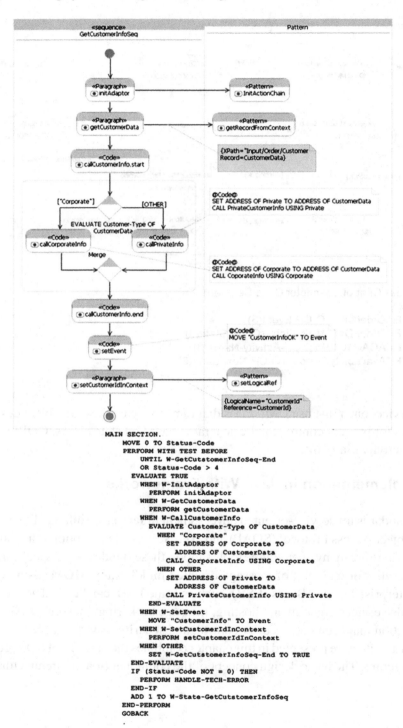

```
MAIN SECTION.
    MOVE 0 TO Status-Code
    PERFORM WITH TEST BEFORE
        UNTIL W-GetCutstomerInfoSeq-End
        OR Status-Code > 4
    EVALUATE TRUE
        WHEN W-InitAdaptor
            PERFORM initAdaptor
        WHEN W-GetCustomerData
            PERFORM getCustomerData
        WHEN W-CallCustomerInfo
            EVALUATE Customer-Type OF CustomerData
                WHEN "Corporate"
                    SET ADDRESS OF Corporate TO
                        ADDRESS OF CustomerData
                    CALL CorporateInfo USING Corporate
                WHEN OTHER
                    SET ADDRESS OF Private TO
                        ADDRESS OF CustomerData
                    CALL PrivateCustomerInfo USING Private
            END-EVALUATE
        WHEN W-SetEvent
            MOVE "CustomerInfo" TO Event
        WHEN W-SetCustomerIdInContext
            PERFORM setCustomerIdInContext
        WHEN OTHER
            SET W-GetCutstomerInfoSeq-End TO TRUE
    END-EVALUATE
    IF (Status-Code NOT = 0) THEN
        PERFORM HANDLE-TECH-ERROR
    END-IF
    ADD 1 TO W-State-GetCutstomerInfoSeq
    END-PERFORM
    GOBACK
```

Figure 7. Service design using Mule ESB design tool

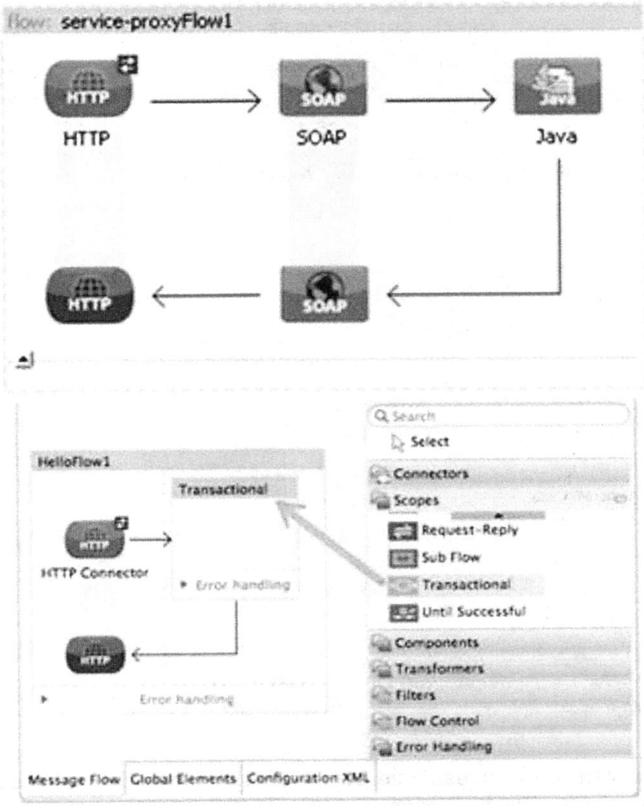

- Business Service components should be autonomous, pluggable and application-specific objects.
- Objects of a component can be plain old Java objects (POJOs) or Enterprise Java Beans (EJBs) with a single responsibility.
- Objects and / or beans of a component are packed together in a JAR, EAR or WAR file (for web services).
- Each component has a well-defined interface and contract to fulfill independently of the other components (that is, they are completely decoupled from the other components).
- To access objects across packages, one should always use the interfaces with dependency injections provided by frameworks such as Spring framework. In this way, the coupling and dependencies of objects across different components can be reduced.

The first layer of the layer architecture pattern shown in Figure 2 is primarily a structural and logical concept. Framework like Mule ESB already provides the infrastructure needed for service dispatching, transaction management, security control, and more. Figure 7 shows how to use the Mule ESB design tool. Services and components contain objects for business processing and data persistence. Error handling and event logging components must be accessible through their interfaces for all objects and beans.

Figure 8. Service design using Mule ESB design tool

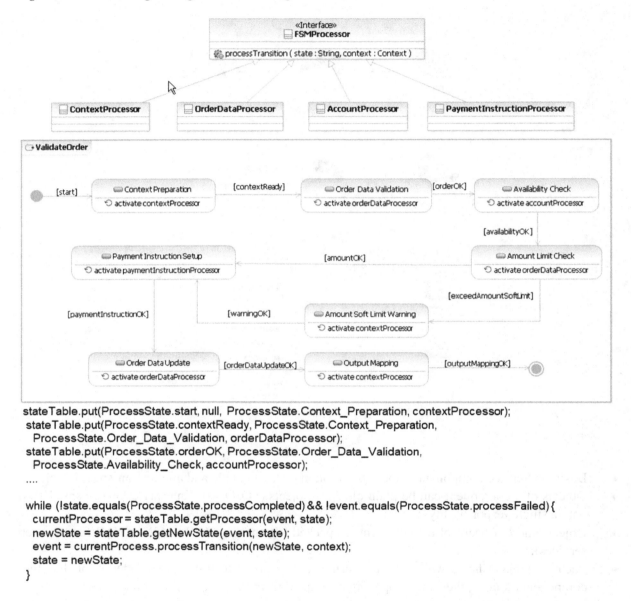

```
stateTable.put(ProcessState.start, null, ProcessState.Context_Preparation, contextProcessor);
stateTable.put(ProcessState.contextReady, ProcessState.Context_Preparation,
  ProcessState.Order_Data_Validation, orderDataProcessor);
stateTable.put(ProcessState.orderOK, ProcessState.Order_Data_Validation,
  ProcessState.Availability_Check, accountProcessor);
....

while (!state.equals(ProcessState.processCompleted) && !event.equals(ProcessState.processFailed) {
  currentProcessor = stateTable.getProcessor(event, state);
  newState = stateTable.getNewState(event, state);
  event = currentProcess.processTransition(newState, context);
  state = newState;
}
```

Error and log messages must be easily accessible, traceable, and understandable to support teams (that is, no print stack or long log files). One may need to archive error and log messages.

In the proposed architecture, the processing of the business logic of a service is performed by a central process controller. This process control separates the detailed data processing from the process flow. It helps to free the business components from handling application-specific processes and improve their reusability. The process flow is modeled using UML state charts as shown in Figure 8. The process controller is basically a finite state machine. This finite state machine is driven by a state transition table. The state machine can be implemented on a template for generating the process controller. Therefore, the code for the process controller class can be generated with its state transition table based on the state model shown in Figure 8. For each component, a processor interface is implemented, as shown in figure 8. Action for each state in the state diagram is associated with activating the processor of the component.

The context container in the architecture uses the application context from the Spring Framework. Data beans, which mainly contain business data, are used for communication between objects and components. These beans are implementations of their interfaces. They are instantiated by Spring Framework and injected into the objects and components when they are need. Only the interfaces of the data beans are exposed to the objects and components that use them.

CONSEQUENCES AND APPLICABILITY

Many IT projects still fail even when the agile development approach is used. The author has observed a lot of project failure is due to the lack of proper architecture. As mentioned before, an application cannot be developed incrementally and iteratively without an architecture and mechanism that allow the development of autonomous modules. A key to success in software projects is to master complexity and have an agile IT architecture. The development of loosely coupled services, components and autonomous modules is relatively simple. With continuous, iterative system integration, it is unlikely that a project will go awry. The design and implementation approach of an architecture presented in this chapter can fulfil these purposes. It be used in any enterprise IT system. It takes accounts of software engineering design principles and help to manage IT complexity through different levels of abstractions and modularity. The proposed plug and play mechanism also demonstrate how modules can be developed independently and iteratively.

The architecture with tools has been used since 2004 in a large financial institution for application development (Pang, 2015; Pang, 2016). The infrastructure of the layered, component-based service-oriented architecture was in place. Since then, many applications using this approach have been successfully developed and delivered on time and within budget. It has been shown that the total development costs can be reduced by a factor of four. No project has failed.

VISION FOR THE FUTURE

A code-centric approach to software development has persisted for the past 50 years. Most programmers and project managers, even in the community with agile approaches, still believe that this is the way to develop software. A vision for the future is that coding, while still needed, should not be the main task in the development of quantitative and qualitative applications. The new development of low-code and no-code software platforms has aroused great interest among IT managers. This should be the future and deserve more attention and research.

Business processes in different business areas of a large company typically have very similar patterns. For example, all payment and trade transactions in a financial institution require the retrieval of customer and account information, availability and credit checks, generation of customer position movements, debiting and / or crediting of accounts, posting the transaction in the general ledger, and so forth. The future is to develop standard model templates for the high-level abstractions of business applications and create rigorous patterns for business process models. These model patterns can be tailored to different infrastructures and business components by providing the code segments and wrappers. Programs can then be generated from these models. Thus, one can have standard models for business processes that can be used for different business areas.

CONCLUSION

In this chapter, description and motivation of software engineering design principles and architecture are presented. It is shown that the agile development approach with successive increment and iteration of modules cannot be done without a proper architecture. The chapter presents an architectural blueprint for an agile and model-driven approach to software development. The design of the architecture is based on software engineering principles.

Patterns like layered, component-based and service-oriented architecture form the basis of the architectural design. The architecture has been further refined to provide centralized process control in the form of a finite state machine, context container, and autonomous module development. Infrastructure and modelling tools have been developed to support application development through architecture. Major modelling artefacts include UML class diagrams, state charts, and activity diagrams. Codes are generated from these models for both COBOL and Java. With a centralized process control software architecture proposed in this chapter, software components or modules can be developed as autonomous units and tested for units. The architecture also provides a plug-and-play mechanism for components and modules. The software architecture forms a basis for the rapid development of individual software components and continuous integration. It makes changes and extensions rather uncomplicated tasks.

An agile approach combined with a model-driven approach enables the implementation of an iterative and incremental development process with rapid delivery of useful software. It eliminates the heavy documents, but also provides useful documentation of the models. In addition to the requirement specifications, programming can also begin at an earlier point in time. The approach was applied to many projects, all of which were successfully completed on time and on budget.

REFERENCES

Agile Manifesto Group. (2001). Manifesto for Agile Software Development. *Agile Manifesto*. Retrieved July 26, 2010, from http://agilemanifesto.org

Ambler, S. W. (2010). Agile Modeling. *Ambysoft*. Retrieved July 26, 2010, from http://www.agilemodeling.com/

Babar, M. A., Brown, A. W., & Mistrik, I. (2014). *Agile Software Architecture*. Waltham, MA: Morgan Kaufmann.

Baldwin, C. Y., & Clark, K. B. (2000). *Design Rules: The power of modularity*. Cambridge, MA: MIT Press. doi:10.7551/mitpress/2366.001.0001

Bell, T. E., & Thayer, T. A. (1976). Software Requirements: Are They Really a Problem? In *Proceedings of the 2nd International Conference on Software Engineering*, (pp. 61-68). IEEE Computer Society Press.

Booch, G., Maksimchuk, R. A., Engle, M. W., Young, B. J., Conallen, J., & Houston, K. A. (2007). *Object-Oriented Analysis and Design with Applications* (3rd ed.). Upper Saddle River, NJ: Addison-Wesley.

Chappell, D. A. (2004). *Enterprise Service Bus*. Sebastopol, CA: O'Reilly.

Colburn, T., & Shute, G. (2007). Abstraction in Computer Science. *Minds and Machines*, *17*(2), 169–184. doi:10.100711023-007-9061-7

Drumond, C. (2019). What is Scrum? *Atlassian*. Retrieved July 11, 2019, from https://www.atlassian.com/agile/scrum

Fowler, M. (2006). *Patterns of Enterprise Application Architecture*. Boston, MA: Addison-Wesley.

Gamma, E., Helm, R., Johnson, R., & Vlissides, L. (1995). *Design Patterns: Elements of Reusable Object-Oriented Software*. Reading, MA: Addison-Wesley.

Harlow, M. (2014). Coconut Headphones: Why Agile Has Failed. *Code Rant*. Retrieved December 11, 2014, from http://mikehadlow.blogspot.ch/2014/03/coconut-headphones-why-agile-has-failed.html

Hastie, S., & Wojewoda, S. (2015). Standish Group 2015 Chaos Report - Q&A with Jennifer Lynch. *InfoQ*. Retrieved from May 26, 2019, from https://www.infoq.com/articles/standish-chaos-2015

Hopkins, R., & Harcombe, S. (2014). Agile Architecting: Enabling the Delivery of Complex Agile Systems Development Projects. In M. A. Babar, A. W. Brown, & I. Mistrik (Eds.), *Agile Software Architecture*. Waltham, MA: Morgan Kaufmann. doi:10.1016/B978-0-12-407772-0.00011-3

Huang, M. (2010) Software Engineering Principles. *Lecture Note from University of Arkansas*. Retrieved May 26, 2019, from http://www.csce.uark.edu/~mqhuang/courses/3513/s2010/lectures/SE_Lecture_3.pdf

Ismail, N. (2017). UK wasting 37 billion a year on failed agile IT projects. *Information Age*. Retrieved May 26, 2019, from https://www.information-age.com/uk-wasting-37-billion-year-failed-agile-it-projects-123466089/

Isotta-Riches, B., & Randell, J. (2014). Architecture as a Key Driver for Agile Success. In M. A. Babar, A. W. Brown, & I. Mistrik (Eds.), *Agile Software Architecture*. Waltham, MA: Morgan Kaufmann. doi:10.1016/B978-0-12-407772-0.00014-9

Jackson, M. A. (1975). *Principles of Program Design*. Cambridge, MA: Academic Press.

Johnson, J., Boucher, K. D., Connors, K., & Robinson, J. (2001). Collaborating on Project Success. *SOFTWAREMAG*. Retrieved July 26, 2010, from http://www.softwaremag.com/archive/2001feb/collaborativemgt.html

Josika, K. (2017) Software Engineering | Coupling and Cohesion. *GeeksForGreeks*. Retrieved June 6, 2019, from https://www.geeksforgeeks.org/software-engineering-coupling-and-cohesion/

Krigsman, M. (2006). Success Factors. *ZDNet*. Retrieved July 26, 2010, from http://www.zdnet.com/blog/projectfailures/success-factors/183

Larman, C. (2003). *Agile and Iterative Development: A Manager's Guide*. Reading, MA: Addison-Wesley.

Liskov, B. (1988). Keynote address - data abstraction and hierarchy. *ACM SIGPLAN Notices*, *23*(5), 17–34. doi:10.1145/62139.62141

Malan, R., & Bredemeyer, D. (2010). Software Architecture and Related Concerns. *Resources for Software Architects*. Retrieved July 26, 2010, from http://www.bredemeyer.com/whatis.htm

Martin, R. (2000). *Design Principles and Design Patterns*. Retrieved July 12, 2017, from https://web.archive.org/web/20150906155800/http://www.objectmentor.com/resources/articles/Principles_and_Patterns.pdf

Martin, R. (2017). *Clean Architecture: A Craftsman's Guide to Software Structure and Design*. Upper Saddle River, NJ: Prentice Hall PTR.

Meyer, B. (1988). *Object-oriented Software Construction*. Upper Saddle River, NJ: Prentice Hall PTR.

Pang, C. Y. (2015). Ten Years of Experience with Agile and Model Driven Software Development in a Legacy Platform. In A. Singh (Ed.), *Emerging Innovations in Agile Software Development*. Hershey, PA: IGI Global.

Pang, C. Y. (2016). An Agile Architecture for a Legacy Enterprise IT System. *International Journal of Organizational and Collective Intelligence*, *6*(4), 65–97. doi:10.4018/IJOCI.2016100104

Parnas, D. L. (1972). On the Criteria To Be Used in Decomposing Systems into Modules. *Communications of the ACM*, *15*(12), 1053–1058. doi:10.1145/361598.361623

Rakitin, S. R. (2001). Manifesto Elicits Cynicism: Reader's Letter to the Editor by Steven R. Rakitin. *IEEE Computer*, (34), 4.

Rehkopf, M. (2019). User Stories. *Atlassian Agile Guide*. Retrieved May 22, 2019, from https://www.atlassian.com/agile/project-management/user-stories

Richards, M. (2015). *Software Architecture Patterns*. Sebastopol, CA: O'Reilly.

Royce, W. (1970). Managing the Development of Large Software Systems. *Proceedings of IEEE WESON*, (28) 1-9.

Sagenschneider, D. (2019). Local Microservices: Object Orientation Behavior Coupling Problem. *DZone*. Retrieved June 6, 2019, from https://dzone.com/articles/local-microservices-object-orientation-behaviour-c

Sessions, R. (2008). *Simple Architectures for Complex Enterprises*. Redmond, WA: Microsoft Press.

Software Crisis. (2010). Software Crisis. *Wikipedia*. Retrieved July 26, 2010, from http://en.wikipedia.org/wiki/Software_crisis

Software Engineering. (2010). Software Engineering. *Wikipedia*. Retrieved July 26, 2010, from http://en.wikipedia.org/wiki/Software_engineering

Yourdon, E., & Constantine, L. L. (1979). *Structure Design: Fundamentals of a Discipline of Computer Program and System Design*. Upper Saddle River, NJ: Yourdon Press.

ADDITIONAL READING

Agile Software Development Process, & the Agile Manifesto Group. (2001). Manifesto for Agile Software Development. *Agile Manifesto*. http://agilemanifesto.org

Ambler, S. W. (2010). Agile Modeling. *Ambysoft*. Retrieved July 26, 2010, from http://www.agilemodeling.com/

Bass, L., Clements, P., & Kazman, R. (2003). *Software Architecture in Practice* (2nd ed.). Reading, MA: Addison-Wesley.

Coplien, J., & Bjornvig, G. (2010). *Lean Architecture for Agile Software Development*. West Sussex, UK: John Wiley & Son.

Erl, T. (2009). *SOA Design Patterns*. Upper Saddle River, NJ: Prentice Hall PTR.

Fowler, M. (1997). *Analysis Patterns: Reusable Object Models*. Reading, MA: Addison-Wesley.

Fowler, M. (2006). *Patterns of Enterprise Application Architecture*. Reading, MA: Addison-Wesley.

Gamma, E., Helm, R., Johnson, R., & Vlissides, L. (1995). *Design Patterns: Elements of Reusable Object-Oriented Software*. Reading, MA: Addison-Wesley.

Garland, J., & Anthony, R. (2003). *Large-Scale Software Architecture: A Practical Guide using UML*. West Sussex, UK: John Wiley & Son.

Geetha, C., Subramanian, C., & Dutt, S. (2015). *Software Engineering*. Delhi, India: Pearson Education India.

Hohpe, G., & Woolfe, B. (2004). *Enterprise Integration Patterns: Designing, Building, and Deploying Messaging Solutions*. Reading, MA: Addison-Wesley.

Hunt, J. (2006). *Agile Software Construct*. London, UK: Springer.

Larman, C. (2003). *Agile and Iterative Development: A Manager's Guide*. Reading, MA: Addison-Wesley.

Martin, R. (2017). *Clean Architecture: A Craftsman's Guide to Software Structure and Design*. Upper Saddle River, NJ: Prentice Hall PTR.

McGovern, J., Ambler, S. W., Stevens, M. E., Linn, J., Sharan, V., & Jo, E. K. (2003). *A Practical Guide To Enterprise Architecture*. Upper Saddle River, NJ: Prentice Hall PTR.

Mellor, S. J., Scott, K., Uhl, A., & Weise, D. (2004). *MDA Distilled: Principles of Model-Driven Architecture*. Reading, MA: Addison-Wesley.

Model-Driven Approach to Software Development. Arlow, J. & Neustadt, I. (2004). Enterprise Patterns and MDA: Building Better Software with Archetype Patterns and UML. Reading, MA: Addison-Wesley.

Sommerville, I. (2015). *Software Engineering* (10th ed.). Essex, UK: Pearson Education Limited.

KEY TERMS AND DEFINITIONS

Agile Software Architecture: A software architecture that lays out blueprints of the organization and structure of software components as well as well-defined mechanism on how components can be tested and integrated into the system that would sustain the agile approach throughout the software development life cycle.

Agile Software Development Process: An evolutionary and iterative approach to software development with focuses on adaptation to changes.

COBOL: The programming language designed for commercial business data processing used for applications that often form the backbone of the IT structure in many corporations since 1960.

Component-Based Architecture: A software architecture that breaks down the application design into reusable functional or logical components that expose well-defined communication interfaces.

Enterprise Service Bus (ESB): A software architecture model used for designing and implementing the interaction and communication between mutually interacting software applications in service-oriented architecture (SOA).

JSON (JavaScript Object Notation): An open-standard file format that uses human-readable text to transmit data objects consisting of attribute–value pairs and array data type.

Layered Architecture: A software architecture from which the concerns of the application are divided into stacked groups (layers). Each level would interact only with the levels above and below.

Mainframe: Mainframe computer systems like IBM z/OS.

Model-Driven Approach to Software Development: A model centric rather than a code centric approach to software development with code generated from models.

Service-Oriented Architecture (SOA): A technical software architecture that allows client applications to request services from service provider type applications in a host system.

SOAP: Simple Object Access Protocol, a standard from W3C.

Software Component: A software unit of functionality that manages a single abstraction.

Software Crisis: A term used in the early days when software projects were notoriously behind schedule and over budget and maintenance costs were exploding.

Software Engineering: The application of engineering to the development of software in a systematic method.

SOLID: An acronym for object-oriented design principles proposed by R. Martin in 2000.

Spring Framework: An application framework and inversion of control container for the Java platform.

Waterfall Model: A sequential design, used in software development processes, in which progress is seen as flowing steadily downwards (like a waterfall) through the phases of Conception, Initiation, Analysis, Design, Construction, Testing, Deployment, and Maintenance.

WSDL: Web Service Description Language, a standard from W3C.

XML (Extensible Markup Language): A markup language that defines a set of rules for encoding documents in a format that is both human-readable and machine-readable.

Chapter 5
Analyzing GraphQL Performance:
A Case Study

Mafalda Isabel Landeiro
ⓘD https://orcid.org/0000-0002-8005-6746
Instituto Superior de Engenharia do Porto, Instituto Politécnico do Porto, Portugal

Isabel Azevedo
Instituto Superior de Engenharia do Porto, Instituto Politécnico do Porto, Portugal

ABSTRACT

Web applications today play a significant role, with a large number of devices connected to the internet, and data is transmitted across disparate platforms at an unprecedented rate. Many systems and platforms require applications to adapt quickly and efficiently to the needs of consumers. In 2000, the Representation State Transfer (REST) was introduced, and the developers quickly adopted it. However, due to the growth of consumers and the different needs, this architectural style, in the way it is used, revealed some weaknesses related to the performance and flexibility of the applications. These are or can be addressed with GraphQL. In this chapter several alternatives to use GraphQL are explained and their benefits in terms of performance and flexibility. Some prototypes were implemented in an organization, and the results of some experiments were analyzed in light of possible gains in performance.

INTRODUCTION

Web applications are becoming more common and there is a growing need to respond quickly to deliver the best possible experience for consumers. Data management service architectures are common because the application core must be centralized and connected to multiple systems and a variety of platform types.

Once introduced, Representational State Transfer (REST) was quickly adopted by developers because of its main features: scalability, interoperability, simplicity, and extensibility (Fielding & Taylor, 2000).

DOI: 10.4018/978-1-7998-2531-9.ch005

However, in large organizations that deal with complex entities and requests, this architectural style has begun to reveal some drawbacks.

In 2015, Facebook introduced GraphQL, a technology that can improve application flexibility, performance and memory utilization. Since multiple access to an endpoint is no longer required and it is no longer necessary to specify what data the client wants to receive, it was quickly adopted. With GraphQL, one can reduce the number of requests needed to get the desired data.

Since GraphQL was developed to optimize a REST API, it is easy to point out some aspects where this query language surpasses this architectural style. Some studies have compared their use according to various criteria. Some similarities and the lack of maturity of GraphQL were identified at this time (Stubailo, 2017). Several quality attributes were analyzed, and it was concluded that REST has superior performance in atomic calls, while GraphQL handles better overfetching and underfetching (Guillen-Drija, Quintero & Kleiman, 2018). Another study showed the best network response times with GraphQL (Vázquez-Ingelmo, Cruz-Benito & García-Peñalvo, 2017).

Other companies such as Netflix (Shtatnov & Ranganathan, 2018), GitHub (Torikian et al., 2016) and Paypal (Stuart, 2018) have also introduced GraphQL as an alternative to REST APIs and presented their conclusions highlighting the benefits.

The Institute of Systems and Computer Technology, Technology and Science (INESC TEC) has a one-year web platform called INESC TEC Research Information System (IRIS), which essentially manages research and human resources.

This application handles queries of varying complexity, mainly in the area of project management, and the actual solution has some performance issues. When the response time is longer than ten seconds, users are known to lose their attention (Möller, 2010). This web application has a backend that follows the REST architecture, and the frontend is one of the main consumers of the available REST APIs.

IRIS has been enhanced with many new features, and the need for integration with different platforms has increased, especially for the project management module. Using REST APIs raises some data query issues, such as:

- The necessity to call more than one endpoint to obtain the necessary data;
- Consumers receive more data than necessary;
- The performance started to degrade.

Some temporary solutions have been considered, e.g., customizing the server response to provide the most data needed in just one request. However, an increase in response size was observed with only a slight improvement in performance.

In addition, some studies show that REST APIs were used to meet the needs of different consumers. However, this solution is not optimally resilient, even if best practices are followed, as in some cases many endpoint requests may be required or additional data may need to be received (Vázquez-Ingelmo et al., 2017). Therefore, a more flexible and efficient solution is sought.

Despite recent developments with GraphQL, there is a lack of understanding about the possibility to conjugate its flexibility with performance.

In terms of data query, several architecture solutions using GraphQL have been explored to understand the alternatives for improving IRIS performance and flexibility. The following hypotheses were formulated with IRIS as the basis for our study:

- **H01:** REST API allows the same performance as a GraphQL API;
- **H02:** REST API allows the same performance as a solution that uses REST with GraphQL;
- **H1:** REST API allows better performance in atomic calls than GraphQL API;
- **H2:** GraphQL API offers better performance than REST API when multiple endpoints are consulted;
- **H3:** The integration of GraphQL with a REST API allows better performance than a REST API standalone.

The hypotheses H01 and H02 are conservative.

The performance and achievable results of GraphQL were at the heart of the work presented in this chapter. The research question of this study, which is closely related to the case study, was:

- Can GraphQL improve searching performance when compared to the existing solution?

The evaluation experience therefore took into account the following measures, taking into account tests of varying complexity:

- **Time:** The API response times need to be improved. By examining them, one can find the solution that gives better results.
- **Size:** Request size can also affect performance because there are solutions that can handle short and simple API responses better than more complex and larger responses.

The main purpose of this chapter is to present a set of architectural solutions, using GraphQL, that can improve data fetch performance. The study was done using a real case of a REST API that needed to be improved, in order to provide the optimal response times for its consumers. Using the measurements mention earlier, this chapter will show how each solution can improve a web API by taking into account distinct scenarios. All the steps from the decision of considering GraphQL to the outcome of the best solution will be described, giving the possibility to replicate the same process to other web applications.

BACKGROUND

This section provides an overview of REST and GraphQL, but also highlights the main characteristcs.

REST

Representational State Transfer (REST) is an architectural style used in distributed hypermedia systems (Stubailo, 2017). According to Fielding and Taylor (2000), the following restrictions apply to this style:

- **Client-Server:** The principle of separation of concerns is presented. The client knows the available services and sends requests to the server that can be executed or rejected. In this way, applications that follow this style can be portable and evolve the components separately.

- **Stateless:** The communication between client and server must have all the required information. State data is not stored on the server side. The client is the one who has to control all information in order to be understood by the server. This feature increases the transparency, reliability, and scalability of REST.
- **Cache:** It is possible to reuse data from similar previous requests.
- **Uniform Interface:** A key feature of the REST architectural style (Fielding & Taylor, 2000) that defines the client-server connection by identifying resources, their manipulation, self-describing messages, and hypermedia as the application state system.
- **Layered System:** Another feature is that multi-layer systems consist of different layers to isolate the units according to their responsibilities, thereby improving scalability.
- **Code-On-Demand:** Clients can download and run the code on the client side. This is an optional feature of this style.

Nowadays, web services are often used to exchange data between different web systems.

A RESTful web service is a web service implementation that follows the constraints that REST applies to. Requests for this type of web service are made through Hypertext Transfer Protocol (HTTP) methods, and the client-server information exchange can be done in JavaScript Object Notation (JSON), HTTP, or eXtensible Markup Language (XML).

The main principles of a REST API are the following:

- **Resource addressability:** Each resource is identified by a Uniform Resource Identifier (URI) and represents a domain concept.
- **Resource representations:** Clients work with resource representations.
- **Uniform interface:** To manage the resources, the methods defined by the HTTP protocol are used.
- **Statelessness:** Every client-server interaction is unique.
- **Hypermedia As The Engine Of Application State (HATEOAS):** Resources are related to each other together so the client needs to know the links between them.

GraphQL

In 2012, Facebook was struggling with some performance issues with its mobile applications and realized that it needed to optimize how data was sent to client applications, which led to the development of GraphQL. It was only ready for mass production outside the company in 2016 and has been used by, among others, Facebook, Netflix, GitHub, PayPal and Airbnb (Porcello & Banks, 2018). Figure 1 shows a timeline that shows the history of GraphQL.

GraphQL is a query language for API and its execution mechanism in a backend service. This makes it possible to reduce the number of requests required to obtain the desired data. Clients can define the data requests and expected responses because GraphQL aims to fulfill data by focusing on the product but consuming what is acceptable.

This query language in the application layer is transport-independent, although it is generally HTTP-based (Porcello & Banks, 2018), and compatible with any backend that follows the protocol specification (Vázquez-Ingelmo et al., 2017).,

Figure 1. GraphQL timeline

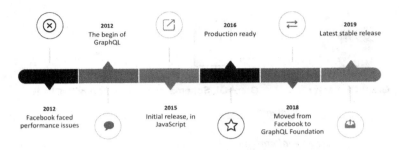

Figure 2. Advantages and disadvantages of GraphQL

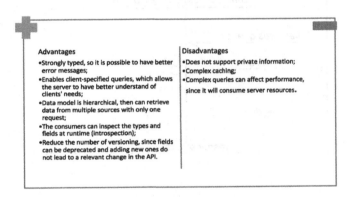

It is also considered a specification for client-server communication (Porcello & Banks, 2018). Figure 2 shows some of its characteristics (Brito, Mombach & Marco Tulio Valente, 2019; Porcello & Banks, 2018; Wittern, Cha & Laredo, 2018).

A GraphQL schema must be specified to characterize the types, relationships, and operations that may be performed on the data. In this way, the GraphQL server knows how and what data is exposed to the GraphQL client. Figure 3 shows the basic interactions when using GraphQL (Wittern et al., 2018).

The GraphQL client can examine the schema to gain knowledge of the types of data exposed and possible operations. It then sends queries in JSON to the server that already specify what operations must be performed and what data should be returned. To retrieve data for a particular field, there is a function called resolver that returns the information in the type and format specified by the schema. They are asynchronous and can be used to retrieve data from different providers: REST APIs, databases, or others.

Upon receiving this request, GraphQL Server will check to see if the request conforms the GraphQL schema and, if necessary, execute it and return the data to the client or with an error.

Figure 3. Interactions when using GraphQL

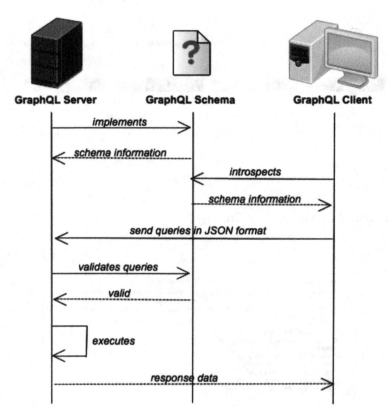

Schema

The GraphQL schema is important because neither the client nor the server knows how to communicate without this schema. Therefore, this schema design is one of the first steps in implementing a GraphQL API. It is necessary to use the Schema Definition Language (SDL), which is language and frame independent, so it does not matter which technologies are used to develop the applications. These schemas are text documents that list the types available and their relationships, entry points, queries, and mutations. Code 1 shows an example of a GraphQL schema.

Code 1. Example of a GraphQL schema

```
schema {
        query: Query
        mutation: Mutation
}

type User {
        id:          ID!
```

```
        userName: String
        name:          String
        projects: [Project]!
}

type Project {
        id: ID!
        name:          String
        responsible: User
        subProjects: [Project]
        team: [User]!
}

type Query {
        listProjects(of: String): [Project]!
        user(userName: String): User
        projectTeam(name: String): [User]!
        users: [User]!
}

type Mutation {
        createProject(responsible: String, name: String): Project
        createUser(userName: String, name: String): User
        addUserToTeam(name: String, userName: String): Project
}
```

The root of the document describes how the schema is divided into:

- **Query:** This is a GraphQL root type because this type maps the available data fetching operations defined in the schema.
- **Mutation:** The definition is the same as Query, but data would be written according to the types described in the schema.

Each GraphQL schema must have a Query type, but it is optional to have a Mutation type. In queries and mutations, the input parameters are named so that the order of a request is not important because the system can automatically match them by specifying the parameter name.

Queries are used to retrieve data from a GraphQL API. They describe the data that a client requests to a GraphQL server and also specify the data units after the field that should return the JSON response. If a query is successful, the return contains the key "data". In case of failure, it contains the "error" key and details about the error.

To simplify defining the expected data format and making it reusable for other queries, fragments are used. Code 2 displays a request to retrieve all users, expecting only their identifiers (ID and username) that are in the fragment.

Code 2. Example of query and fragment

```
query {
        users {
                userIdentification
        }
}

fragment userIdentification on User {
        id
        username
}
```

Mutations are defined in a similar way to queries, but can have side effects because they can change data on the server.

Code 3 reflects the call for a mutation that creates a project and expects the username of the person responsible as the return data.

Code 3. Mutation example

```
mutation {
        createProject(responsible: "someone", name: "project 1") {
                responsible {
                        username
                }
        }
}
```

The declared types User and Project are GraphQL Object Types. This means that some fields are defined for them. Each type has its fields like id, userName, and name from User, indicating that they can be part of any GraphQL Query that uses the User type. In the sample schema, there is also String, which is classified as a scalar type, so that sub-selections are not possible for queries. Fields whose type contains an exclamation mark must not be null. Therefore, the GraphQL service should always return a value when querying these fields. Finally, those with square brackets represent an array of the type specified between them; for example, the projects of Users field is a list of Project objects.

Adoptions Overview

As mentioned at the beginning of the GraphQL subsection, some companies use GraphQL, and some of them have shared the conclusions that have been made since the introduction of this technology. This project highlights the experiences of Netflix, GitHub and PayPal.

Netflix has an internal application called Monet that manages the creation and assembly of ads to reach external platforms such as the New York Times and YouTube (Shtatnov & Ranganathan, 2018).

Figure 4. Architecture of Monet before and after GraphQL, from (Shtatnov & Ranganathan, 2018)

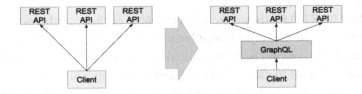

Monet was developed with a React User Interface (UI) layer that can be accessed through REST APIs. As application development began, use cases became more complex and there were some problems, such as: bottlenecks in the network bandwidth. After some consideration to address these issues, an intermediate layer of GraphQL proves to be the best solution because of its robust ecosystem and powerful third-party tools (see Figure 4).

The following benefits were found after using this solution for about six months:

- **Main Problem Solution:** Address the network bandwidth bottleneck.
- **Redistributing Load and Payload Optimization:** Server-to-server calls have very low latency and high bandwidth, which improves performance eightfold compared to client-to-server calls. With the ability for the client to define the data required for each request, the pages began to receive 200 KB instead of 10 MB of data.
- **Reusable Abstractions:** GraphQL allows data to be defined and how it relates to the system so it does not have to worry about business logic related to data join operations.
- **Chaining Type Systems:** Defining entities on the GraphQL server makes it easy to generate the TypeScript types, which can incorporate the checks into the build process and avoid problems before incorrect code is deployed.
- **Developer Interface (DI) / Developer Experience (DX):** With the GraphQL Query Wrapper, components implemented in the UI must only describe the required data, and the wrapper takes care of everything.
- **Handling Failures:** If a GraphQL Query Resolver fails, the successful ones would still return data to the client.
- **Simplify Backend End Data Model:** Modeling for the client is irrelevant. Typically, the backend provides a CRUD interface (Create, Read, Update, and Delete) for raw entities.
- **Testing Components:** Because GraphQL queries can be translated into stubs for testing purposes, resolvers can be tested from React components.

Even though the reported benefits, there were some problems during the transition, such as GraphQL resolvers running in isolation, so the network requests were being duplicated. This issue was solved to recur to a cache layer between resolvers and REST APIs. Another problem was that GraphQL did not allow debugging ib the browser network tab.

Another problem was that GraphQL did not allow debugging on the browser network tab. The solution was to add logs to GraphQL response payloads and make that information available to the client. The last difficulty report concerned the casting of objects. However, because TypeScript was used, customizing the methods to require object properties was smooth.

GitHub has completely migrated its REST API to GraphQL to improve API scalability and API specification (Torikian et al., 2016).

When analyzing their REST API, they concluded that 60% of their database-tier requests come from their API, mainly due to most of the requests needed to navigate through the hypermedia to retrieve all the information they need. The second issue was found when auditing their endpoints in preparation for an APIv4 because it was difficult to gather some meta-information about their endpoints.

The transition started in the GitHub backend team, especially in the implementation of emoji reactions in comments. After this initial investigation, the front-end team was also interested in GraphQL. They managed to have a better way to access user data and improve the website's presentation efficiency.

The main advantages pointed out by GitHub are the type of safety, introspection, the generated documentation and predictable reactions.

PayPal was another company that introduced GraphQL to its technology stack (Stuart, 2018). PayPal Checkout initially had REST APIs that caused problems because the web, mobile apps, and their users were not considered in the REST principles. Increasing client-to-server round-trips to get all the basic data results in increased processing and rendering time.

Therefore, developers have created an Orchestration API that returns the required data. However, this solution also has performance issues. After that, they tried to create a bulk REST API, which is a real-time orchestration that allows clients to set the size and shape of the response. However, this solution was not perfect because the client needs to have detailed knowledge of how the APIs work.

Then they tried out GraphQL and went "all-in" and it brought developers productivity, better app performance, and user satisfaction. The specific aspects considered to be the best part of the GraphQL implementation are the following:

- **Performance:** With a single roundtrip, it is possible to retrieve exactly the required data.
- **Flexibility:** Clients define the shape and size of the data.
- **Developer Productivity:** The learning process of this technology is simple and useful tools are available.
- **Evolution:** It allows them to make better decisions when developers reject or refine their APIs because they know which fields their clients use.

In conclusion, these three examples illustrate how GraphQL, as a middle layer or standalone, can optimize the performance of APIs.

COMPARISON BETWEEN REST AND GRAPHQL

The first version of GraphQL was received with great enthusiasm, leading to some studies on what it looks like compared to REST and in which cases could be a better choice.

Three features are obvious (Porcello & Banks, 2018) as REST disadvantages when the comparison is performed:

- **Overfetching:** The client does not specify the responses of a REST API, but with the information available that may be useful to certain consumers, it results in unnecessary data.

- **Underfetching:** Although the response may contain a lot of data, the details of some fields sometimes require calling other endpoints, etc., which slows down the user experience.
- **Managing REST Endpoints:** In general, what the customer wants changes and this results in an adaptation of the endpoints between the backend and the frontend teams.

Nevertheless, it is necessary to go deeper to compare them.

For this case study, several studies have been analyzed that aim to compare GraphQL with REST and consider different aspects. These three studies were selected on the basis of their relationship to the project context and the way in which they could support the evaluated hypotheses. Stubailo focuses on some properties of an API as resources, on Uniform Resource Locator (URL) routes compared to GraphQL schemas and route handlers versus resolvers (Stubailo, 2017), while Guillen-Drija focuses on some quality attributes such as time behavior and memory usage, overfetching, and others (Guillen-Drija et al., 2018). Vázquez-Ingelmo controls the size of requests and network response times (Vázquez-Ingelmo et al., 2017).

Table 1 shows the similarities and differences found by Stubailo. It has been concluded that they share many universal concepts, but some key aspects may dictate the use of one instead of the other.

GraphQL looks great to quickly implement an API that can return complex data, reducing the time it takes to deploy multiple endpoints to respond to client demands. On the other hand, REST is already mature with many tools and integrations. The results of the study by Guillen-Drija are shown in Table 2.

Table 1. Similarities and differences between REST and GraphQL found by Stubailo

		REST	GraphQL
Resources	Identification	Yes	Yes
	HTTP Usage	Yes	Yes
	JSON Response	Yes	Yes
	Object Identify	Endpoint	Separate from how is fetch
	Determination of Shape and Size	Server	Client
URL routes vs. GraphQL schemas	List of Operations	List of Endpoints	List of fields (at Query and Mutation)
	The distinction between Reading and Writing	Yes	Yes
	Multiple Calls to Relate Resources	Yes	No
	First-class Concept	No	Yes
	Modify Reading into Writing/ Writing into Reading	HTTP verbs	Keyword in the query
Route handlers vs. resolvers	Function Call	Endpoints	Fields
	Handle Networking Boilerplate	Using frameworks or libraries	Using frameworks or libraries
	Number of Handler/ Resolver Calls	One by each request	Many by each query
	Response Build	By developer	By GraphQL execution library

Table 2. Similarities and differences between REST and GraphQL found by Guillen-Drija

Sub characteristic	Metric	REST			GraphQL		
		Average	Standard deviation	Error	Average	Standard deviation	Error
Temporal behavior	Response time	11.13	3.77	0.69	16.23	4.22	0.77
	Throughput (calls)	149.63	11.05	2.02	190.7	7.01	1.28
Resources usage	Memory usage (bytes)	588.6	65.69	11.99	156.33	5.37	0.98
	Cache usage						
	Overfetching (bytes)	688.67	116.28	21.23	79.33	15.49	2.83
	Underfetching (made calls)	4	0.68	0.12	1	0	0
Capacity of software	Capacity (answered calls/made calls)	1			1		
	Speed under stress (ms)	970.17	123.36	22.52	1138.97	88.74	16.20

The main conclusions are:

- Due to the use of caching in REST, this style usually has a better response time than GraphQL.
- With the details that the GraphQL requests can have, this language offers an advantage in under- and overfetching.
- For atomic calls, REST provides better response speed.
- GraphQL handles memory usage better.

Given the network response time shown in Figure 5, where REST has longer network response times than GraphQL, and the overall size of 13.90 KB (GraphQL) versus 26.66 KB (REST), implementing the GraphQL API improves system performance and reduces memory usage.

In summary, according to the studies discussed in this section, GraphQL has better flexibility, response times, and memory utilization compared to REST, although the two technologies share some similar aspects and cannot be considered substitutes.

Case Study

The Institute of Systems and Computer Engineering, Technology and Science (INESC TEC) is a private institution that is classified as an interface between science and industry (INESC TEC, 2017) and focuses on four areas:

- Scientific research and technological development;
- Technology transfer;
- Advanced consulting and training;
- Pre-incubation of new technology-based companies.

Figure 5. Graphic with network performance results obtain by Vázquez-Ingelmo

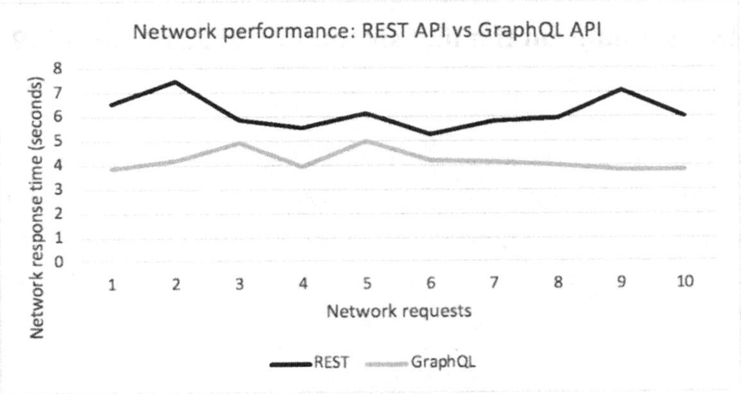

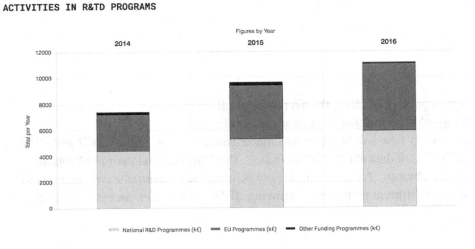

It has thirteen Research and Development (R&D) centers divided into four areas: Computer Science, Industry and Innovation, Networked Intelligent Systems and Power and Energy. Activities in Research and Technological Development (R&TF) programs are steadily growing (see Figure 6).

The growth in activities led to the creation of a new web platform, IRIS, to manage scientific data, as well as others that have an indirect impact on scientific activities, such as researchers' personal information.

This platform is available to all of the institution's integrated researchers (approximately 842 researchers) and is not integrated with exclusive access (approximately 253 researchers) so that currently 1095 users can access IRIS. From November 2017 to June 2019, 8155 different sessions were created. Between November and December 2017, 923 sessions were held. In comparison to the first half of 2018 with the first half of 2019 (see Figure 7), sessions grew. There were a large number of sessions in January 2018, as IRIS was presented to the researchers, but the monthly sessions in 2018 were between 250

Figure 6. Activities in R&TD programs of INESC TEC, from ('INESC TEC', 2017)

Figure 7. IRIS sessions on the first six months of 2018 and 2019

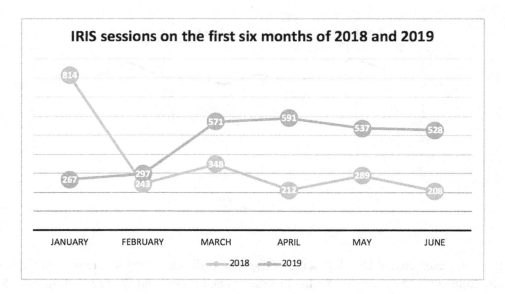

Figure 8. IRIS integration with different platforms

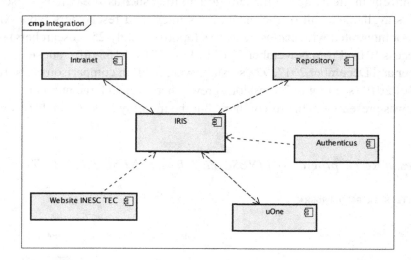

and 300. At the beginning of 2019, the average was still in place, but with the completion of the project management module, the number of sessions has increased.

IRIS is a relatively new solution that was made available at the end of 2017 and allows for the management and retrieval of data about the researchers, their projects and their publications. However, some problems became obvious. As shown in Figure 8, many new features have been added, and the need for integration into different platforms is growing. IRIS has taken on an essential role as an integrative platform.

Figure 9. Component diagram of IRIS

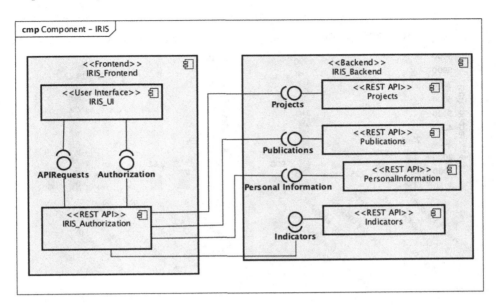

The architecture used in IRIS (see Figure 9) has a backend that uses Spring implemented REST APIs, and a frontend that uses them, that was developed with Angular (User Interface), and an authorization module that also has a REST API (Spring).

Problem

One of the latest application modules presented in the previous section is project management, which includes several user profiles, such as: project controllers, human resources technicians, project managers, research units coordinators, project team members, and others. This module also integrates with:

- **uOne:** It is a platform that supports daily project task management to support the management of teamwork.
- **Intranet:** It contains information about the project proposal.
- **Website:** It uses information about the projects to be shown to the public.
- **Repository:** All project documentation is stored here.

In IRIS, data queries vary in complexity. The use of REST APIs has raised some issues, such as: the need to use more than one endpoint to retrieve the required data, the fact that every consumer has its needs and receives excess data, as well as the impact on the performance of the process.

The actual solution has some performance issues, as shown in the case in Figure 10. The sum of the response times is greater than ten seconds, a value that is associated with attention loss even in simple queries (Möller, 2010).

Figure 10. Response time and size of a simple search on IRIS

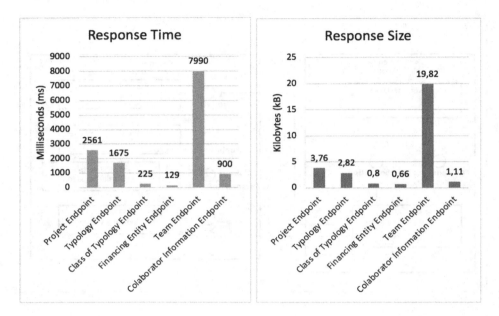

Some possible solutions have been investigated, e.g., customizing the server response to provide the most required data in just one request. However, the response size increased and the performance improved only marginally.

In addition, some studies show that REST APIs were used to meet the needs of different consumers. However, this solution does not provide the ideal elasticity even by best practices, as in some cases many requests for different endpoints are required or unnecessary data are received (Vázquez-Ingelmo et al., 2017). Therefore, a more flexible and efficient solution was sought.

Why GraphQL?

The Analytic Hierarchy Process (AHP) (Saaty, 1980) is a method to make complex decisions based on meaningful attributes and to consider different alternatives. This method was used to select the idea for this project. Three different attributes were considered:

- **Knowledge:** The ability to apply a particular solution.
- **Efficiency:** To what extent can this solution improve the problems of the current solution?
- **Costs:** Implementing this alternative incurs higher costs such as licenses, special hardware, and training needs.

Therefore, the hierarchy shown in Figure 11 was considered.

Thereafter, priorities for each attribute were defined with the development team (Table 4), with efficiency rated as the most critical, followed by knowledge and cost at the end. The comparative scale used is shown in Table 3, which is adapted to (Saaty & Vargas, 1991).

Figure 11. AHP tree of idea selection

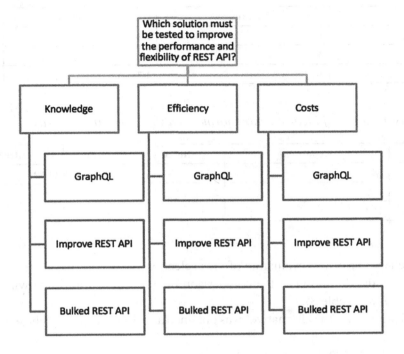

The next step is to normalize the matrix of Table 4 and calculate the relative priority of each attribute (consult Table 5).

Then, it should evaluate the consistency of the relative priorities (see Equation 1).

$$\lambda_{max} = \frac{21}{5} \times (0.2828) + \frac{31}{21} \times (0.6434) + 13 \times (0.0738) = 3.0967$$

$$IC = (\lambda_{max} - n) \div (n-1) = (3.0967 - 3) \div (3-1) = 0.0484$$

$$RC = IC \div 0.58 = 0.0484 \div 0.58 = 0.08 < 0.1, so\, the\, values\, are\, consistent.$$

Table 3. Scale for Comparison on AHP

Scale	Degree of preference
1	Equal importance
3	Moderate importance of one factor over another
5	Strong or essential importance
7	Very strong importance
9	Extreme importance
2,4,6,8	Values for inverse comparison

Table 4. Comparison matrix of idea selection

	Knowledge	Efficiency	Costs
Knowledge	1	1/3	5
Efficiency	3	1	7
Costs	1/5	1/7	1

Table 5. Comparison matrix of idea selection normalized with a relative priority

	Knowledge	Efficiency	Costs	Relative Priority
Knowledge	5/21	7/31	5/13	0.2828
Efficiency	15/21	21/31	7/13	0.6434
Costs	1/21	3/31	1/13	0.0738

Equation 1. Relative priorities evaluation of idea selection

The next phase is the definition of the comparison matrix for each attribute with each alternative (see Table 6, Table 7 and Table 8).

The composed priority for the alternatives was obtained and the best one was chosen (see Equation 2).

Equation 2. Calculation of the best alternative

$$\begin{pmatrix} 0.5371 & 0.7791 & 0.5 \\ 0.2314 & 0.1610 & 0.25 \\ 0.2314 & 0.0599 & 0.25 \end{pmatrix} \times \begin{pmatrix} 0.2828 \\ 0.6434 \\ 0.0738 \end{pmatrix} = \begin{pmatrix} 0.6901 \\ 0.1875 \\ 0.1224 \end{pmatrix}$$

The idea was to explore GraphQL, which can improve the performance and flexibility of APIs, and study the best integration of this technology into the current architecture.

Table 6. Comparison matrix of idea selection for knowledge

	GraphQL	Improve REST API	Bulked REST API	Priority Vector
GraphQL	1	1/2	1/2	0.5371
Improve REST API	2	1	1	0.2314
Bulked REST API	2	1	1	0.2314

Table 7. Comparison matrix of idea selection for efficiency

	GraphQL	Improve REST API	Bulked REST API	Priority Vector
GraphQL	1	9	7	**0.7791**
Improve REST API	1/9	1	5	**0.1610**
Bulked REST API	1/7	1/5	1	**0.0599**

Table 8. Comparison matrix of idea selection for costs

	GraphQL	Improve REST API	Bulked REST API	Priority Vector
GraphQL	1	2	2	0.5
Improve REST API	1/2	1	1	0.25
Bulked REST API	1/2	1	1	0.25

For the analysis of this key element, the use of anchored scales based on the likelihood of technical success probability and strategic adaptation can also be considered.

Design and Implementation

Prototype 1: GraphQL Standalone

Prototype 1 is the solution that aims to replace the use of the REST API with a GraphQL API when the data search is performed. Since the current solution complies with the OpenAPI specification ("OpenAPI", 2017), this file can be used to convert the existing API to a GraphQL schema using the Swagger2GraphQL tool (Krivtsov, 2016 / 2019b).

This solution has three components (see Figure 12):

- **Projects (GraphQL-Spring API):** This is the API that is responsible for accepting requests from data consumers, processing them, and authenticating the clients.
- **Security (Spring Security):** This is the module responsible for API authentication and access control.

Figure 12. Component diagram of Prototype 1

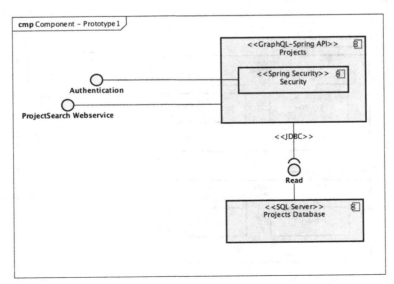

- **SQL Server Database (Database):** This is the database that contains the information available. This component already exists. It is used for the data query.

These three components are on separate servers. The Projects API has different layers (see Figure 13):

- **Service:** It is responsible for receiving a response to HTTP requests. It consists of two segments:
  - **Resolver:** It defines which query should be executed and what data is required. For this reason, it communicates with the Repository segment.
  - **Exception Handler:** It controls any exceptions that might occur and handles them so that resolvers can use them to answer some requests.
- **Data:** It controls the entire data management and presents the next segments:
  - **Entity:** It has the types defined in the GraphQL schema and associated with Java objects.
  - **Repository:** It carries out database operations to retrieve all required data in the formats defined in Entity.
- **Security:** It is responsible for managing authentication and access control.

Database access used Spring Data to create CRUD repositories that automatically provide search, save, count, and delete methods for each entity. Thus, the implementation of resolvers is easy; only need to call the repositories of each entity. The Spring Data module has been adopted because it is a layer that already exists in the current solution and can be reused.

The data layer specified all the entities required to query the database and the corresponding type in the GraphQL schema. It also contains the repositories.

Exceptions have been defined at the service layer. Furthermore, this layer contains the resolver. The resolver type can be divided into two types:

Figure 13. Module layer of Prototype 1

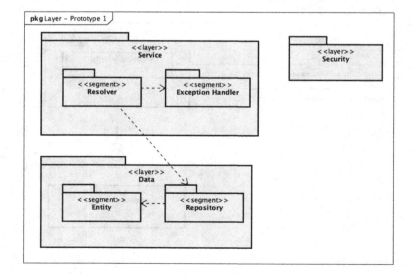

- **The Main Resolver:** Here, the behavior of all queries defined in the schema is translated into a Java method. This class must implement GraphQLQueryResolver. With the prefix get and the name of the query, an association between the method and the query is automatically established. For this prototype, the implemented behavior is to query the information in the database using the repositories, and then return the information, if any, or the exception.
- **The Auxiliary Resolvers:** This defines how a given type from the schema receives the value of an attribute. The type is declared in the schema.

Figure 14 shows the process of a data query request in Prototype 1. The consumer sends a POST request with the query to be executed and the expected output. This is done by the QueryResolver, which acts as the main resolver, and the information is searched for in the database through the repository. After receiving the information, the resolver checks whether data should be returned or not. If it should, it will go through all the necessary auxiliary turnbuckles to retrieve all the necessary information and forward it to the consumer, even if they are not shown in the sequence diagram. If no data needs to be returned, the main resolver returns the exception to the consumer.

In summary, Prototype 1 uses the database-directly connected GraphQL for data query.

Prototype 2: REST With GraphQL

Prototype 2 uses a middle layer between the REST API and the consumer, along with a GraphQL API, when the data search is performed. As with prototype 1, Swagger2GraphQL (Krivtsov, 2016 / 2019b) was used to build the GraphQL schema without any further customization. Swagger2GraphQL is a tool that can be used to convert an existing Swagger schema into GraphQL types. The resolvers are set with HTTP calls to the endpoints of the REST API. By querying the GraphQL API, the GraphQL schema generated from the conversion can be extracted (Krivtsov, 2016 / 2019a).

This API acts as an intermediary between the REST API and the client. The solution consisted of three components (see Figure 15):

Figure 14. Sequence diagram of a query in Prototype 1

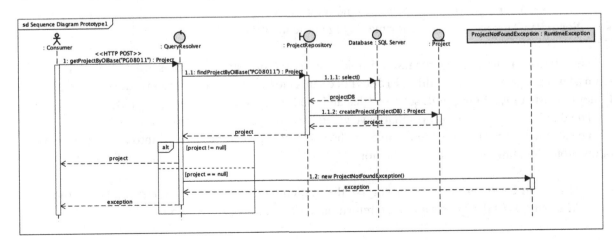

Figure 15. Component diagram of Prototype 2

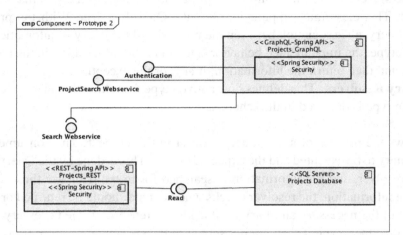

- **Projects_GraphQL (GraphQL-Spring API):** This is the API responsible for receiving requests from data consumers and requesting data to Projects_REST. It also authenticates the clients.
- **Projects_REST (REST-Spring API):** This is the current solution that responds to Project_GraphQL requests.
- **Security (Spring Security):** This is the module responsible for authentication and access control of each API.
- **SQL Server Database (Database):** This is the database that contains the information available.

These three components are located on different servers. The Projects_GraphQL API consists of two layers (see Figure 16), as this API is only an intermediate:

- **Service:** This is responsible for receiving a response to HTTP requests and consists of two segments:
  - **Resolver:** This defines which query to run and which endpoint to call from Projects_REST
  - **Exception Handler:** This controls any exceptions that might occur and handles them so that Resolver can use them to answer the requests.
- **Security:** This is responsible for managing authentication and access control.

The libraries that are fundamental to implementing the prototype are the same as prototype 1 apart from a few exceptions, because this API does not connect to the database. Therefore, the solution resource folder consists only of GraphQL schema files and the Spring integration with GraphQL.

The data layer specifies entities that have an equivalent type in the GraphQL schema.

The service layer contains the resolvers. The resolver type can be divided into two types, as in the other prototype, but with different behavior:

- **The Main Resolver:** For this prototype, the implemented behavior is to retrieve data in the REST API using HTTP requests and then return the data, if any, or the exception.

Figure 16. Module layer of Prototype 2

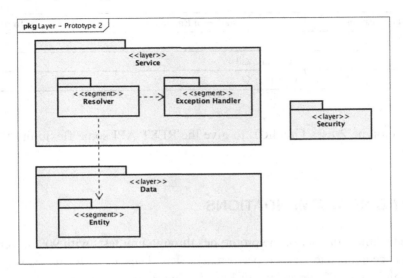

- **The Auxiliary Resolvers:** They have the same responsibility as defined in Prototype 1, but the query is made through a REST web service.

The process flow of a data query request in Prototype 2 is shown in Figure 17. The consumer sends a POST request with the query to be executed and the expected output, as in Prototype 1. This request is processed by the QueryResolver, the main resolver. The information is searched for in the REST API via an HTTP request. After the information is available, the QueryResolver checks whether data should be returned or not. If nothing to return, the main resolver returns the exception to the consumer. If there is data, even though it is not shown in the sequence diagram, the application will go through any necessary auxiliary resolvers to fetch all the necessary data, send more requests to the REST API, and retrieve them to the consumer.

Figure 17. Sequence diagram of a query in Prototype 2

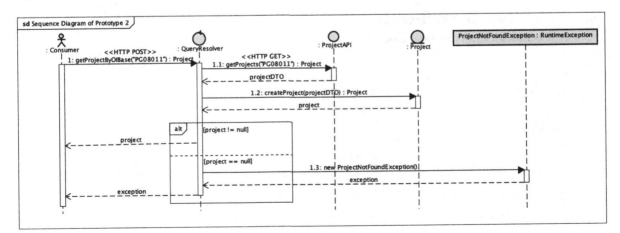

Table 9. Classification of different levels of complexity

Complexity Classification	Number of Endpoints/Entities to Achieve all the Information
Low	1
Normal	Between 2 and 4
High	More than 5

In summary, Prototype 2 uses GraphQL to give the REST API some flexibility that increases the size of the request.

SOLUTIONS AND RECOMMENDATIONS

After ensuring the technical quality of the prototypes through unit tests with 90% coverage, integration tests, load tests and acceptance tests, their performance was checked. Performance was measured using various request complexities (Table 9) and evaluated using time and size metrics.

To get the necessary information, the PRTG tool was used to create sensors. Assigned to these sensors is a specific configuration that periodically requests an API and records the response time and response size.

To create a table with a sample of results using different complexities, the following query requests were used on the GraphQL APIs (prototypes 1 and 2):

- Complexity low (see Code 4)

```
query {
    financingEntityById(financingEntityId:4) {
        entityName
        entityAcronym
    }
}
```

Code 4. Query request for complexity low
  ◦ Complexity normal (see Code 5)

```
query {
    projectByOIBase(OIBase:"PG08011") {
        OIBase
        shortName
        typology {
            typologyId
        }
        beginDate
        expectedEndDate
```

```
    title
    description
    proposalId
}
```

Code 5. Query request for complexity normal

    ◦   Complexity high (see Code 6)

```
query {
    projectByOIBase(OIBase:"PG08011") {
        OIBase
        beginDate
        expectedEndDate
        contractReference
        teams {
                coordinator
                oi
                coordinate
                structure {
                        sigla
                    }
            }
        typology {
                typologyDescription
                typologyClass {
                        designation
                }
                financingEntity {
                        entityAcronym
                }
            }
        }
    }
```

Code 6. Query request for complexity high

```
query {
projectByOIBase(OIBase:"PG08011") {
OIBase
beginDate
expectedEndDate
contractReference
teams {
 coordinator
 oi
```

```
coordinate
structure {
 sigla
}
}
typology {
typologyDescription
typologyClass {
 designation
 }
 financingEntity {
 entityAcronym
 }
}
}
}
```

PGRT generates a report containing the information needed for the current solution. It generates tables 10, 11 and 12 with the average time and size of requests for each API according to the complexity of the requests.

- Complexity low (consult Table 10)
- Complexity normal (consult Table 11)
- Complexity high (consult Table 12)

Based on this information, it can be seen that an API does not have the same response time or size in cases of varying complexity. In Figure 18, prototypes generally have a better response time than the current solution, with the exception of the low complexity where prototype 1 achieves the worst result

Table 10. Mean results for requests with complexity low

	Time (ms)	Size (kB)
Current solution	129	0.66
Prototype 1	203	0.13
Prototype 2	195	0.07

Table 11. Mean results for requests with complexity normal

	Time (ms)	Size (kB)
Current solution	4236	6.58
Prototype 1	255	0.98
Prototype 2	480	1.15

Table 12. Mean results for requests with complexity high

	Time (ms)	Size (kB)
Current solution	13480	28.97
Prototype 1	2070	0.77
Prototype 2	830	1.51

than the others. In Figure 19, it can be concluded that the prototypes significantly improve the response size compared to the current solution.

Based on the results of the experiment and the application of the ANOVA test, the hypotheses given in the section INTRODUCTION may be considered correct or false:

H_{01}: REST API allows the same performance as a GraphQL API;

This hypothesis is false because neither the response time nor the response size between the current solution and the prototype 1 are the same. With a 95% confidence interval and Tukey's Honestly Significantly Different (HSD) test (Dubitzky, Wolkenhauer, Cho, & Yokota, 2013), they differ significantly in response time and response size (see Table 13).

H_{02}: REST API allows the same performance as a solution that uses REST with GraphQL;

This hypothesis is also false, since neither the response time nor the response size between the current solution and the prototype 2 are the same. Compared to the previous test, they differ considerably in response time and size (see Table 14).

Figure 18. Average of response time by API

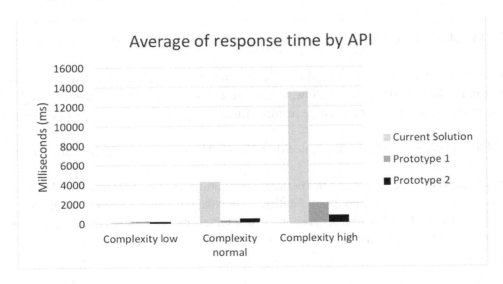

Figure 19. Average of response size by API

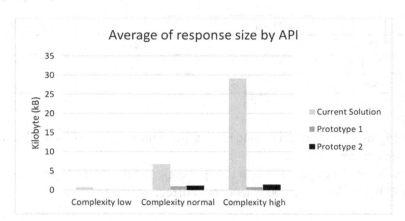

Table 13. Differences' analysis between the current solution and Prototype 1 (Tukey's HSD test)

Measure	Difference	Standardized difference	Critical value	Pr > Diff	Significant	Lower bound (95%)	Upper bound (95%)
Time	5710	4	2	0	Yes		|||||||||||||||||
Size	11	3	2	0	Yes		|||||||||||||||||

Table 14. Differences' analysis between the current solution and Prototype 2 (Tukey's HSD test)

Measure	Difference	Standardized difference	Critical value	Pr > Diff	Significant	Lower bound (95%)	Upper bound (95%)
Time	5520	3	2	0	Yes		|||||||||||||||||
Size	11	3	2	0	Yes		|||||||||||||||||

H1: REST API allows better performance in atomic calls than GraphQL API;

The hypothesis can only be considered valid if we assign more weight to the time measure. The response time in the REST API is better. However, the response size is better in the GraphQL API. This can be concluded by observing the average results of low complexity experiments as outlined above.

H2: GraphQL API allows better performance than REST API when multiple endpoints are consulted;

This hypothesis is correct because it has better response time and size for normal and high complexity requests involving more than one endpoint / entity. At normal complexity, the GraphQL API has a 93% faster response time and a 85% smaller response size. Given its high complexity, Prototype 1 is 84% faster in time and 97% smaller in size.

H3: The integration of GraphQL with a REST API allows better performance than a REST API standalone.

As with H1, this condition can have different classifications, depending on the weight given for time and size measurements. At normal and high complexities Prototype 2 is better. At low complexity, however, the response time is 33% better.

Since prototypes have better overall performance than the current solution, comparison is difficult because they do not differ significantly (see Figure 20). The average response size is the same. However, to give an answer to a possible implementation to resolve the IRIS performance problem, the result of the ANOVA tests is clear: Prototype 1 performs best (see Figure 21), taking into account all the complexities.

Figure 20. Comparison between the solutions, based on the combination of meantime and mean size

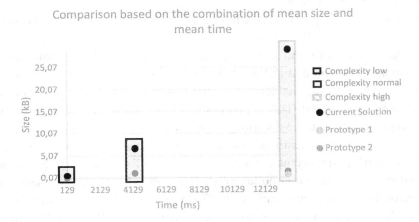

Figure 21. Summary of means - time and size

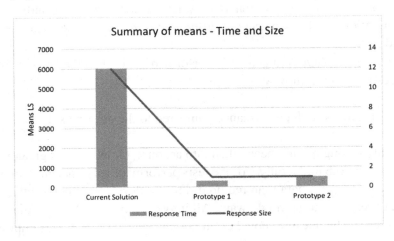

FUTURE RESEARCH DIRECTIONS AND CONCLUSION

GraphQL is a new technology, so there are many details to explore. Regarding the case, the performance analysis should be tested on more APIs, and the unimplemented alternative of the design should also be investigated. The evaluation revealed that REST APIs have a better response time on atomic calls than GraphQL APIs. Therefore, the alternative can be an integrative solution that brings together the best of each solution.

Performance was examined using specific technologies (Java and Spring Boot). In order to validate the overall performance, their influence should be discarded. It is also necessary to examine the performance with different types of complexities. In this study, the complexity was related to the endpoints / entities to be queried. However, it is also possible, for example, to examine the size of requests. The other major threat to validity is the use of just one case study and all its peculiarities so as not to generalize the results. Further studies are required.

In summary, this is another step towards the implications of using GraphQL. However, much remains to be explored.

This chapter introduced how to find a solution to a performance problem related to a REST API.

First, the performance problem that INESC TEC had in a platform called IRIS, which is responsible for research data management, was analyzed. The REST API response time was incorrect, and the response size was larger than required. Then a process was followed to find a solution. There were three possible solutions on the table, and the decision was to take a step into GraphQL.

This technology was new to the team. It took some time to learn how it works, what principles and best practices they have. It was important to understand how REST and GraphQL can improve the performance when used in certain situations simultaneously. There are also some documented customizations of GraphQL by well-known companies such as Netflix, GitHub and PayPal, which help to understand the process that would be required for a possible transformation from REST to GraphQL.

One of the major difficulties with this adoption case was the lack of related scientific work, and the way to get around it was to explore the gray literature and always look for new articles that could be published during the project's implementation. However, the prior art has been understood and described with sufficient information to take into account different design alternatives and to establish some hypotheses to be validated.

Both prototypes used GraphQL and generally performed better than the current solution.

The research question of this study was:

- Can GraphQL improve search performance compared to the existing solution?

Although flexibility testing has not been taken into account, GraphQL has greater flexibility in API requests, as evidenced by Stubailo's study. For the tests performed, only one endpoint was requested for all GraphQL APIs without more data than required. From a developer's perspective, there is no need to worry about what every consumer might want. All information is available so they can manage their requirements themselves. The question now has an answer: yes, GraphQL can improve search performance by taking time and size measurements into account.

In conclusion, GraphQL performance analysis responded to the integration of GraphQL into REST and the adoption of GraphQL, highlighting the performance benefits that could be achieved.

INESC TEC analyzes all results and prototype 1 is analyzed carefully to be applied to IRIS.

ACKNOWLEDGMENT

This research was supported by INESC TEC.

REFERENCES

Brito, G., Mombach, T., & Valente, M. T. (2019). Migrating to GraphQL: A Practical Assessment. *2019 IEEE 26th International Conference on Software Analysis, Evolution and Reengineering (SANER)*, 140–150. 10.1109/SANER.2019.8667986

Dubitzky, W., Wolkenhauer, O., Cho, K.-H., & Yokota, H. (Eds.). (2013). Tukey's Honestly Significant Difference Test. In Encyclopedia of Systems Biology (pp. 2303–2303). doi:10.1007/978-1-4419-9863-7_101572

Fielding, R. T., & Taylor, R. N. (2000). Principled design of the modern Web architecture. *Proceedings of the 2000 International Conference on Software Engineering. ICSE 2000 the New Millennium*, 407–416. 10.1145/337180.337228

Guillen-Drija, C., Quintero, R., & Kleiman, A. (2018). GraphQL vs REST: una comparación desde la perspectiva de eficiencia de desempeño. Retrieved November 20, 2019, from doi:10.13140/RG.2.2.25221.19680

INESC TEC. (2017). Retrieved 22 February 2019, from INESC TEC. Retrieved November 20, 2019, from https://www.inesctec.pt/en/institution

Krivtsov, R. (2019a). *Swagger to GraphQL API adapter. Contribute to yarax/swagger-to-graphql development by creating an account on GitHub* [JavaScript]. Retrieved November 20, 2019, from https://github.com/yarax/swagger-to-graphql (Original work published 2016)

Krivtsov, R. (2019b). *Yarax/swagger-to-graphql* [TypeScript]. Retrieved November 20, 2019, from https://github.com/yarax/swagger-to-graphql (Original work published 2016)

Möller, S. (2010). Usability Engineering. In S. Möller (Ed.), Quality Engineering: Qualität kommunikationstechnischer Systeme (pp. 57–74). doi:10.1007/978-3-642-11548-6_4

OpenAPI. (2017, December 26). Retrieved 26 December 2017, from Open API Initiative. Retrieved November 20, 2019, from https://www.openapis.org/

Porcello, E., & Banks, A. (2018). *Learning GraphQL - Declarative Data Fetching for Modern Web Apps* (1st ed.). Retrieved November 20, 2019, from http://shop.oreilly.com/product/0636920137269.do

Saaty, T. L. (1980). *The Analytic Hierarchy Process: Planning, Priority Setting, Resource Allocation.* New York, NY: McGraw-Hill.

Saaty, T. L., & Vargas, L. G. (1991). *Prediction, Projection and Forecasting: Applications of the Analytic Hierarchy Process in Economics, Finance, Politics, Games and Sports*. Retrieved November 20, 2019, from https://www.springer.com/kr/book/9789401579544

Shtatnov, A., & Ranganathan, R. S. (2018, December 10). *Our learnings from adopting GraphQL*. Retrieved 9 February 2019, from Netflix TechBlog. Retrieved November 20, 2019, from https://medium. com/netflix-techblog/our-learnings-from-adopting-graphql-f099de39ae5f

Stuart, M. (2018, October 16). *GraphQL: A success story for PayPal Checkout*. Retrieved 17 January 2019, from PayPal Engineering. Retrieved November 20, 2019, from https://medium.com/paypal-engineering/ graphql-a-success-story-for-paypal-checkout-3482f724fb53

Stubailo, S. (2017, June 27). *GraphQL vs. REST*. Retrieved 3 December 2018, from Apollo GraphQL. Retrieved November 20, 2019, from https://blog.apollographql.com/graphql-vs-rest-5d425123e34b

Torikian, G., Black, B., Swinnerton, B., Somerville, C., Celis, D., & Daigle, K. (2016, September 14). *The GitHub GraphQL API*. Retrieved 17 January 2019, from GitHub Engineering. Retrieved November 20, 2019, from https://githubengineering.com/the-github-graphql-api/

Vázquez-Ingelmo, A., Cruz-Benito, J., & García-Peñalvo, F. J. (2017). Improving the OEEU's Data-driven Technological Ecosystem's Interoperability with GraphQL. *Proceedings of the 5th International Conference on Technological Ecosystems for Enhancing Multiculturality*, 89:1–89:8. 10.1145/3144826.3145437

Wittern, E., Cha, A., & Laredo, J. A. (2018). Generating GraphQL-Wrappers for REST(-like) APIs. In T. Mikkonen, R. Klamma, & J. Hernández (Eds.), *Web Engineering* (pp. 65–83). London, UK: Springer International Publishing. doi:10.1007/978-3-319-91662-0_5

KEY TERMS AND DEFINITIONS

Data: All the information that is available for querying.

Flexibility: Facility how the application adapts to new consumers necessities.

GraphQL: Query language created by Facebook to mitigate performance issues.

Performance: API fulfillment based on time and size.

Query: Search with criteria to obtain specific data.

Response Size: The size of the response that the consumer receives.

Response Time: The time between the request accepted by the API until the consumer receives a response.

REST: The architectural style that allows communication by HTTP.

Chapter 6
Gamification:
Model–Driven Engineering Approaches

Pedro Aguiar

Ⓘ https://orcid.org/0000-0003-1356-0210

Instituto Superior de Engenharia do Porto, Instituto Politécnico do Porto, Portugal

Isabel Azevedo

Instituto Superior de Engenharia do Porto, Instituto Politécnico do Porto, Portugal

ABSTRACT

Gamification has been applied in diverse areas to encourage participation, improve engagement, and even modify behaviors. However, many gamified applications have failed to meet their objectives, and poor gamification design has been pointed out as a recurrent problem, despite a growing number of gamification frameworks and their valuable guidelines. Model-driven engineering approaches have been proposed as possible solutions to the deficient, and incoherent, inclusion of several dynamics and mechanics. They allow achieving a formalism that can avoid many errors and inconsistencies in the process. Moreover, these efforts are necessary to achieve a conceptualization of gamification that facilitates its inclusion in applications. Three proposals are analyzed, all based on domain-specific languages (DSL), which allows users to design complex gamification strategies without requiring programming skills. The MDE approach can be used to enrich gamification design by providing a platform that involves various concepts and the necessary connections between them to ensure harmonious designs.

INTRODUCTION

Games are not just about entertainment, not now, nor over the years. America's Army game series, for instance, included the AA game (Land & Wilson, 2006). It was designed to increase recruiting and values such as loyalty, and honor, and was "the first successful and well-executed serious game that gained total public awareness" (Djaouti, Alvarez, Jessel, & Rampnoux, 2011). Soon game aspects attracted the attention of developers in an attempt to have its benefits in other applications as well. The classic

DOI: 10.4018/978-1-7998-2531-9.ch006

definition of gamification is the use of design elements characteristic of games in non-game contexts (Deterding, Dixon, Khaled, & Nacke, 2011).

This chapter addresses gamification, introducing its various definitions provided by different authors, as well as comparing and contrasting the views reflected in each of them. The problem of gamification not achieving certain established goals due to poor design is also analyzed along with some possibilities to address it, such as gamification-related guidelines provided by many frameworks.

The solutions present in this chapter follow a Model-Driven Engineering (MDE) approach in combination with Domain-Specific Languages (DSLs), providing domain experts a platform to develop gamification strategies. The following section contains background information about what gamification is, relevant frameworks for the development of gamification in systems, and an introduction to MDE and DSL.

The main objective of this chapter is to discuss and disseminate an alternative, and less widely used, method of formalizing gamification strategies. Through this method, domain experts can aggregate various factors present in a DSL to develop harmonious solutions that can later be integrated into the desired system.

In the remainder of this chapter, gamification concepts and applications are explored in its second section ("Background"). In the third section, an analysis is performed on some of the researched frameworks, followed by a section dedicated to MDE approaches in gamification. The final section explores the future of gamified applications and the role of MDE.

BACKGROUND

Gamification has been explored by various authors, and thus different definitions have been provided. These definitions are presented and compared in this section. Furthermore, to showcase what gamification can offer, some examples of successful applications are analyzed within this section, as well as examples of applications that did not produce the expected results.

DEFINITIONS

The first definition to be analyzed is: "Gamification is the use of game design elements in non-game contexts" (Deterding et al., 2011). The authors justify their definition by emphasizing the following words:

- Game.
- Element.
- Design.
- Non-game contexts.

For the keyword "game", the authors began by clarifying that gamification was related to games, but not related to "play". The concept of games being a subcategory of the broader category "play". Then the authors proceed to explain that games are defined by explicit rule systems and competition between actors of those systems towards goals or outcomes. The concept of gamefulness is described as a "systematic complement" to playfulness. Furthermore, this is due to gamefulness relating to the qualities of gaming over the qualities of playing.

As for the keyword "element", the authors point out the difference between a serious game and a gamified application. The design of the former is of a full-fledged game, while the latter aggregates game elements. Game elements were defined as features that are characteristic of games, as in features that are common and significant when it comes to gameplay.

When it comes to the keyword "design", it was first stated that, in this context, the concept of "gamification" is reserved for the usage of game design and not the usage of game-based technologies. As a result of their research, game design elements were categorized through different levels of abstraction:

1. **Game Interface Design Patterns:** Effective interaction of design components/solutions, through common or prototypical implementations, for a specific problem (e.g., Badge, Leaderboard).
2. **Game Design Patterns and Mechanics:** Common gameplay elements of game design (e.g., Time constraint, Turns).
3. **Game Design Principles and Heuristics:** Guidelines to evaluate either an approach to a design problem or to analyze a design solution (e.g., Enduring play, Clear goals).
4. **Game Models:** Conceptual game design models that break down the various components of games (e.g., (Brathwaite & Schreiber, 2008; Hunicke, Leblanc, & Zubek, 2004)).
5. **Game Design Methods:** Practices and methods related to game design (e.g., Playtesting, Play-centric design).

Lastly, for "non-game contexts" the authors consider that the overall context is what separates gamification from a meta-game. Gamification makes use of game design elements that do not follow a specific game dynamic, while the meta-game maintains the context, consequentially remaining game design.

A second definition for gamification considers gamification as "a process of enhancing a service with affordances for gameful experiences in order to support user's overall value creation" (Huotari & Hamari, 2012). This definition focuses on the goal of gamification and not the methods used. Furthermore, this is due to what the authors concluded in their research about game elements and how they do not implicitly create gameful experiences. As such, gamification was defined as a process of enhancing a service with specific qualities to provide gameful experiences. The list below contains both systemic and experiential conditions the authors found necessary when defining games or gamification, each condition belonging to a specific level of abstraction:

- **1st level:** Contains conditions common to all games:
  - **Systemic Condition:** A game is a system.
  - **Experiential Condition:** A game requires the involvement of users.
- **2nd level:** Consists of conditions characteristic to most games:
  - **Systemic Conditions:** Rules, conflicting goals, and uncertain outcomes.
  - **Experiential Conditions:** Offers suspense, gamefulness, and/or hedonic pleasure.
- **3rd level:** Contains conditions that are unique to games, therefore they cannot be converted to general terms.

Lastly, the author of a gamification framework known as Octalysis proposed the following definition for gamification: "the craft of deriving all the fun and engaging elements found in games and applying them to real-world or productive activities" (Chou, 2015). Furthermore, the author defines gamification as a type of design designated as "Human-Focused Design", which optimizes human motivation in a system. However, "Function-Focused Design" focuses on optimizing system efficiency. This definition of gamification emphasizes fun and engagement factors.

Each of the analyzed definitions focuses on different aspects of gamification, although they all seem to have in common that it provides a game-like experience. In sum, gamification can augment user interactions (Deterding, 2015). Moreover, to produce gameful experiences, design elements that can be found within the game industry are used to motivate users to perform specific actions. These game design elements consist of every feature that is both common and impactful within the game context. For instance, the use of rewards is standard in most (if not all) designs of gamification due to its effect of motivating users to keep performing a requested action. However, the reward needs to be meaningful for the user in question.

APPLICATIONS

The following are two examples of companies who have successfully deployed gamified services:

- **Fitocracy:** Aims to motivate users to uphold a healthier lifestyle, using game mechanics present in roleplaying games (RPG), rewarding users with in-game experience and levels should they work out or eat healthy (Hamari & Koivisto, 2015). Fitocracy is based on a traditional form of gamification providing rewards, as well as social features, granting the user a means to find online fitness groups who will encourage each other to stay healthy.
- **Duolingo:** Helps users learn new languages through gamified lessons. More than 30 are available with free lessons in this language-learning platform. It allows their users to assess their progress, customize their profile, socialize through language, play through learning lessons using a retainable but limited life pool, which restrains the user from taking a lesson should they run out of lives. Due to badges having a decreasing effect over time, winning streaks are used to keep users motivated (Huynh, Zuo, & Iida, 2018).

Not well-defined objectives are among the usual explanations for failure in gamification design (Mora, Riera, González, & Arnedo-Moreno, 2017). An inadequate understanding of what motivates target users can also cause some problems. Some companies failed to meet their business objectives, for instance:

- **My Marriott Hotels:** To attract new employees, this gamified application had its users take different positions as employees of a hotel (Robson, Plangger, Kietzmann, McCarthy, & Pitt, 2016). Users would fulfill several hotel-related activities, providing a realistic experience as an employee. Depending on how successful the users were in keeping their customers happy, they would either gain or lose points. After a year, this application was removed from its host due to the failure to attract employees. The main culprit of this failure was the application's overall design, as the points players would collect had no real purpose, as well as the lack of social elements to keep people motivated.
- **Google News:** The goal was to encourage users to read news through the Google platform by rewarding users with badges related to the news topic that would appear on the user's profile page. Users were not attracted to the concept of earning unusable badges, neither to sharing information about the news they have read through the badges they earned. The gamification strategy in ques-

tion did not consider the target users and their interests. And thus, the platform failed to motivate users as was intended.

In summary, many companies attempted to implement gamification on their services, with varied outcomes. In 2012, Gartner predicted that, by 2014, 80% of gamified applications would fail to meet business objectives due to poor design (Burke, 2014) and since then, there have been many attempts to mitigate the issue presented (Morschheuser, Hamari, Werder, & Abe, 2017; Morschheuser, Hassan, Werder, & Hamari, 2018; Walz & Deterding, 2015).

A study about the gamification effects on systems was performed to assess the overall value a gamified system can offer (Hamari, Koivisto, & Sarsa, 2014). This research was conducted around the definition proposed by Huotari & Hamari (2012) regarding gamification. Furthermore, this definition consists of a three-step process starting with the implemented motivational affordances causing psychological outcomes, which will, in turn, produce the desired behavioral outcomes. The results about gamification usefulness varied depending on the motivational affordances used and the expected psychological outcomes which would develop behavior changes on the target audience.

The study revealed that points, leaderboards, and badges were the most prominent types of motivational affordances used in gamified systems, as well as the prominence of behavioral analysis over psychological analysis about the effects of gamified applications on its respective user base. The overall result of the research conducted is that gamification does provide benefits, should it be implemented under the correct circumstances, two of the main factors to consider before adding a gamified application would be the role of the context to be gamified and the types of users who would engage with the application.

FRAMEWORKS

A recent study examined 40 frameworks (Mora et al., 2017). It is beyond the purpose of this chapter to perform such extensive analysis. This section introduces some frameworks widely used in gamification design. They are all broadly recognized, but they also have detailed descriptions and available support. Moreover, they do not only provide guidelines but align them to users and their possible motivations.

The Mechanics, Dynamics, and Aesthetics framework is not directly related to gamification, but the information it provides regarding game elements and strategies should not be neglected.

Octalysis

According to Yu-Kai Chou, who proposed Octalysis (Chou, 2015), a game's purpose is only to please the individual playing it by appealing to several specific "Core Drives", which, in turn, motivate them to continue playing (see Table 1). Yu-kai Chou defines "White Hat Gamification" and "Black Hat Gamification", the former encompasses positive motivators, while the latter includes the negative motivators. However, Chou (2015) reassures that "Black Hat Gamification" is not necessarily bad since it can motivate people to take either beneficial or harmful actions.

The Octalysis framework is visually divided vertically, having the drives on the left associated with logic, calculations, and ownership, and on the right associated with creativity, self-expression, and social aspects.

The following list contains detailed information about the 8 Core Drives:

Table 1. The Octalysis framework adapted by Chou (2015)

Core Drive	Examples	Associated Side	Gamification Type
Epic Meaning and Calling	• Narrative • Elitism • Creationist • Destiny Child	• Left Brain • Right Brain	• White Hat
Development and Accomplishment	• Quest Lists • Progress Bar • Status Points • Boss Fights	• Left Brain	• White Hat
Empowerment of Creativity and Feedback	• Milestone Unlocks • Instant Feedback • Boosters • Real-Time Control	• Right Brain	• White Hat
Ownership and Possession	• Exchangeable Points • Virtual Goods • Collection Sets • Avatar	• Left Brain	• Black Hat • White Hat
Social Influence and Relatedness	• Friending • Gifting • Mentorship • Brag Button	• Right Brain	• Black Hat • White Hat
Scarcity and Impatience	• Prize Pacing • Countdown Timer • Appointment Dynamics • Options Pacing	• Left Brain	• Black Hat
Unpredictability and Curiosity	• Random Rewards • Easter Egg • Sudden Rewards • Rolling Rewards	• Right Brain	• Black Hat
Loss and Avoidance	• Progress Loss • Rightful Heritage • Status Quo Sloth • Visual Grave	• Left Brain • Right Brain	• Black Hat

- **Epic Meaning and Calling:** This first Core Drive affects the individuals who believe that their actions are contributing to something greater than themselves. These players tend to work on projects which benefit the entire community in question. This Core Drive also includes players who have been lucky in the earlier stages of the game, whether they have completed a difficult task earlier than expected, or they were gifted with a particularly rare item.
- **Development and Accomplishment:** This Core Drive is focused on personal progress, challenges, and developing skills. The use of badges or leaderboards is important to represent which challenges the user overcame. The more challenging it is to attain a particular achievement, the more meaningful it feels.
- **Empowerment of Creativity and Feedback:** Whenever users find themselves repeatedly trying different combination, in an attempt of discovering the best possible combination, in a system that provides instant feedback to the decisions made and, ultimately, rewards users for being successful in their endeavor, the "Empowerment of Creativity and Feedback" is the Core Drive that appeals these types of users. These kinds of game dynamics also allow the game developers to

have longer development periods before adding new content due to the large amounts of existing combinations.

- **Ownership and Possession:** This is the drive containing the type of users who have their possessions as one of their main types of motivation. As such, these users search for ways to improve the items already in their possession or ways to own more valuable items.

- **Social Influence and Relatedness:** The Core Drive "Social Influence and Relatedness" contains the users that are motivated by social elements such as companionship, mentorship, and competition. These users tend to become encouraged whenever one of their friends reaches a higher level, driving them to reach the same level as they have.

- **Scarcity and Impatience:** This drive takes advantage of people desiring the unattainable, having people thinking about obtaining a significant reward during an entire day because they can't have it at that specific moment.

- **Unpredictability and Curiosity:** This Core Drive enlists the users that find the suspense, or randomness, to be its own reward. These users wonder about all the possible positive outcomes whenever they perform a specific action, which maintains their motivation should they not obtain the outcome they desire.

- **Loss and Avoidance:** This final drive contains the users who avoid negative repercussions, which motivates them to act accordingly so that they do not lose anything significant. Temporary opportunities to obtain unique rewards fit into this drive since it compels these types of users to act quickly before they lose their opportunity to be rewarded.

Six Steps to Gamification

The "Six steps to gamification" (Werbach & Hunter, 2012), or 6D Framework, is based on six different steps:

- **Define Business Objectives:** The first step consists in the establishment of a list with concrete system performance objectives (e.g., Increasing customer retention, improving employee productivity), which are not to be confused with the mission objectives set by the organization. Following the conclusion of the initial list of objectives, a process regarding the removal of every non-important achievement should begin. Once the process is complete, objectives that are mere means to an end should no longer be present within the list. Lastly, each objective needs to have a description explaining how its completion can affect the company's growth.

- **Delineate Target Behaviors:** The second step consists in specifying the various tasks to be executed by the users. Users should attain rewards by performing tasks. However, it is essential to avoid "all-or-nothing" situations because they do not promote user progression. Then success metrics should also be defined for each key performance indicator of the gamified system in question. The ratio of monthly active users, or the number of rewards that users have collected, are two examples of possible key performance indicators to be considered when analyzing the system's overall performance.

- **Describe Your Players:** This step requires an in-depth understanding of the targeted user-base. As such, establishing whether or not the player-base will consist of employees or customers is necessary, since employees and customers may not have the same kind of motivators.

- **Devise Your Activity Cycles:** Unlike various games, gamified systems cannot rely on linear and limited progression systems. This is due to the necessity of maintaining users performing activities for extended periods. Thus, the usage of cycles is crucial to keep users motivated.
- There are two types of cycles: engagement loops, and progression stairs. Engagement loops contain three components. Each of these components holds different descriptions related to what players can do, why they do it, the system's feedback, respectively. Figure 1 shows how these components are connected.
- The progression stairs are used to affect the user's experience as the more the user progresses. This can be developed by presenting different challenges or increasingly more difficult scenarios as the user becomes more experienced. However, users should always receive rewards that are fit for the current stage of progression.
- **Don't Forget the Fun:** After all the design choices made until this step, it is necessary to ensure that the system in development will grant its users a fun experience. If the users are performing actions that are, subjectively, fun, the more likely it is that they will keep performing said actions.
- **Deploy the Appropriate Tools:** Lastly, utilizing all the work developed in each previous step, the implementation step begins. Through the usage of the most appropriate tools, all the gamified system's mechanics and dynamics should be implemented to provide a better user experience.

Related to the step "Describe your players", it is relevant to know who the system's users are, since what can motivate one user, may not motivate another, and if the developed motivators are not fit for the current user-base, the gamified system will fail. Thus, creating several different groups of users, and using various kinds of motivators, can be efficient in dealing with the issue. Furthermore, to assist with what may motivate specific player-bases, Werbach & Hunter (2012) refer to the taxonomy of player types introduced by Bartle (1996), consequently presenting the following player categories: achievers, explorers, socializers, and killers.

Achievers are interested in rewards such as badges, explorers look for new content to enjoy, socializers tend to engage with friends, and lastly, killers desire to overwhelm others. Each specific individual has elements of the previously mentioned archetypes. As such, it is essential not only to identify these archetypes within the player-base but also to have a system prepared for changes since the players may have a shift in their motivations over time.

Mechanics, Dynamics, Aesthetics

The Mechanics, Dynamics, and Aesthetics (MDA) framework is an approach to related to understanding games, instead of gamification, which attempts to connect game design with development, game criticism, and technical game research (Hunicke et al., 2004).

This framework is not directly related to gamification, but it is essential in the current context due to the information it provides regarding game design strategies, which in turn enhances the overall understanding of gamification strategies by breaking down the consumption of games and game design into concrete components.

A game is consumed like any other entertainment product, but its consumption is comparatively unpredictable. To better assist designers with design decisions regarding a specific game, this framework considers games as artifacts. Thus, indicating "that the content of a game is its behavior - not the media that streams out of it towards the player" (Hunicke et al., 2004).

Figure 1. Activity cycle adapted from Werbach & Hunter (2012)

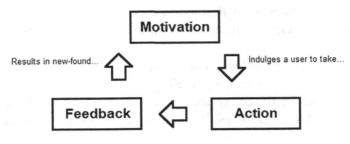

Figure 2. Game consumption components and their respective design counterparts Adapted from Hunicke et al. (2004)

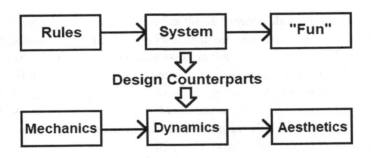

To clarify the consumption process of games, the MDA framework formalizes it through a sequence of distinct components as represented in Figure 2 as well as their respective design counterparts.

The design components can be described by the following:

- **Mechanics:** Contains information about game components, such as data representation and algorithms (e.g., shoot, jump, collect).
- **Dynamics:** The behavior of the mechanics behind a player's input and overall outputs are defined within this component (e.g., puzzle, survival, tower defense).
- **Aesthetics:** This last component represents the expected emotional responses whenever a player interacts with the system (e.g., challenge, fellowship, fantasy).

Problems With Current Frameworks

Deterding (2015) reviewed some of the current gamification frameworks (Burke, 2014; Kapp, 2012; Kumar, 2013; Paharia, 2013; Werbach & Hunter, 2012; Zichermann & Cunningham, 2011), analyzing specific characteristics. The following list consists of the common issues found in the study:

- **Little Formative Research:** General lack of specification on formative research, commonly disregarding data collection methods (with some exceptions).
- **Reliance on Player Typologies:** Overuse and misuse of the taxonomy introduced by Richard Bartle (Bartle, 1996).
- **Appeals to Motivational Psychology:** Use of untested motivation models based on the Self-Determination Theory (SDT) (Deci & Ryan, 2012).
- **Inherent-Additive, Pattern-Based Approach:** Misunderstanding of both how game elements should be used, and of MDA taxonomy. Recommend a pattern-based approach when developing gamification concepts.
- **Lacking Guidance in Game Design Pattern Choice:** A small amount of guidance regarding which design pattern to use, and how to customize it, within a specific context. It is suggested to apply mechanics that are appropriate to a type of user, but there is no indication of what mechanics are suitable for each of the player types.
- **No Iterative Prototyping:** Lack of methods to evaluate alternative design decisions.
- **Data-Driven Design:** It is recommended to monitor and track user engagement after deploying the gamification instance, neglecting data of user behaviors on prototype stages of development.

Mora et al. (2017) analyzed a wide array of gamification frameworks, categorizing each one of them (and their respective issues) regarding their main sectors of application: business, generic, health, and learning. The study revealed the most common context for gamification frameworks was the business environment, as well as the predominance of user-centered designs, along with the overall disregard of business-related issues, such as risk, feasibility, and investment. Deterding (2015) stated that the psychological factor is recognized in most frameworks, but the respective preferences of each user type are generally not considered. Further details regarding the frameworks reviewed can be consulted in both of the presented studies (Deterding, 2015; Mora et al., 2017).

MODEL-DRIVEN ENGINEERING

Model-Driven Engineering is an approach that uses models as the main artifacts for the software development process (Brambilla, Cabot, & Wimmer, 2017). It avoids the implicit complexity of application development (Schmidt, 2006). A Domain-Specific Language facilitates the use of the concepts in question.

In this context, models implement, at least, two roles through abstraction:

- **Mapping Feature:** Models are based on the original system.
- **Reduction Feature:** Models only contain a relevant selection of the original system's properties.

Models additionally attend to different purposes when developing software through an MDE approach. They can be used for descriptive purposes, such as describing a system or a context. Models can also be used for prescriptive purposes, permitting the development of a method to study a problem, and lastly, to specify how the system should be implemented.

To follow the MDE approach, appropriate tools are necessary to define both models and transformations during the implementation phase. Suitable compilers or interpreters are also required to execute and produce the desired software artifacts. As MDE is based around models, the specification of the modeling language is realized through a model. This procedure is designated as metamodeling, and it can have different levels of abstraction. A meta-metamodel is the result of specifying a modeling language using a metamodel.

A DSL is a possible approach when it is required for a language to efficiently define a specific set of tasks (Gronback, 2009).

A DSL determines the base structure, behavior, and requirements related to a particular domain. Metamodels can be used to set relationships between concepts in a domain and to specify the key semantics/constraints related to each of these concepts. DSLs are typically used to simplify development processes, but they can also be used to validate what has been specified within the domain context. Once the design of the DSL is complete, code generators can be used to produce source code or other artifacts, such as model representations.

Figure 3 represents several significant steps when developing a gamification instance for a system. It contains both the traditional and the MDE approach. It is essential to recognize that the step "Gamification instance" (see Figure 3) is not final and that it is always necessary the assistance of an IT expert to link the generated gamification application with the system to be gamified as well as providing required increments. For instance, authentication services may be one of the increments to be considered. However, by having the gamification expert formalizing the gamification design through an MDE approach, the application's code is directly connected to the model. Thus, there is no loss of information between the gamification expert and the IT professional in the implementation phase.

Solutions that use the MDE approach have emerged to ease the inclusion of game elements in non-game applications. Three solutions are described in detail in the following sections: GaML, MEdit4CEP, and Gamify. However, even though these solutions are intended to assist with the development of successful gamification strategies, they do not bypass the need to define concrete business objectives, nor they are means to disregard valuable information regarding the user base of the system to be gamified. Each of the solutions to be analyzed follows a similar design process to the MDE approach shown in Figure 3.

GAML

GaML is a "language for modeling gamification concepts" (Herzig, Jugel, Momm, Ameling, & Schill, 2013) with the primary objective of developing a readable language to non-technical gamification experts.

To develop the intended language, the developers of GaML structured gamification concepts using the taxonomy of game design elements provided by Deterding et al. (2011), classifying the concepts as game design elements with five different levels of abstraction, as previously described. The language itself focuses only on the first two levels (what "visual concepts exist and how these elements relate to each other" (Herzig et al., 2013)), while the other levels are related to the creation of a compelling gamification design, which is associated with the conceptualization of a specific design and not with the language.

For the first level of abstraction (game design patterns), basic visual gamification elements are pointed out, as well as possible synonyms in the specific context instance and its subtypes.

The second level of abstraction in the taxonomy of game design elements, defined as "Game Design patterns and mechanics" (Deterding et al., 2011), determines the gameplay factors of gamification, for instance, rules and conditions, since these elements insert logic into the gamification context. Further

Figure 3. Usual and MDE approach

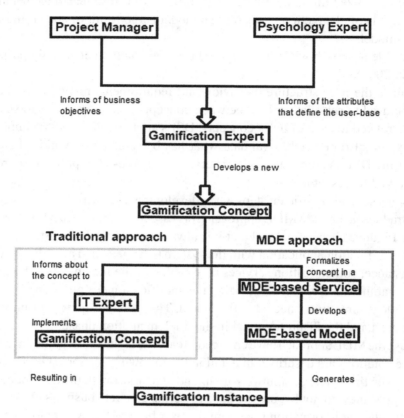

information about the approach adopted and the game design elements chosen for each level of abstraction can be consulted on the paper in question (Herzig et al., 2013).

The next step in developing GaML was the language specification, which was distributed into the three following phases:

- **Design Objectives:** Four primary design objectives are defined for the language:
  - ○ Domain experts should be capable of formalizing previously developed gamification concepts in GaML.
  - ○ It should be possible to deploy an automatically compilable, valid instance of GaML into gamification platforms.
  - ○ Trivial IT knowledge should be necessary to make GaML understood by domain experts.
  - ○ IT experts should be fully capable of developing strategies in GaML, while domain experts should only be partially capable of doing so.
- **Model and Syntax:** Describes the higher-level aspects of GaML's grammar, such as how to define the model, the game mechanics, for instance.
- **Semantics:** Explains how static semantics were defined in the language, and in which aspects they can be found, to assist the user with designing their gamification instance.

In short, GaML assists with both the conceptualization and implementation of gamification. "Stop Smoking" (Matallaoui, Herzig, & Zarnekow, 2015) is a serious game developed in the Unity Engine with an achievement system implemented by GaML. Its users are rewarded with badges by performing the system's designated actions. Further information regarding the case studies developed to showcase the language in question can be found in both of the examined papers (Herzig et al., 2013; Matallaoui et al., 2015). Even though one of the primary objectives was to create a language that could be partially writable by domain experts, it was stated that domain experts could not develop a model with complicated gamification strategies.

MEdit4CEP-Gam

MEdit4CEP-Gam (Calderón, Boubeta-Puig, & Ruiz, 2018) is a model-driven solution that can also be used by non-technical gamification experts, but unlike GaML (Herzig et al., 2013), graphical DSLs are used to allow gamification design graphically. This approach can successfully hide the implementation details when defining the desired model, which will later be transformed into the code to be executed by their system, designed with an Event-Driven Service-Oriented Architecture.

The procedure of MEdit4CEP-Gam approach can be described by the following:

1. The gamification expert develops a graphical gamification domain by defining its event types and event properties.
2. Should the finished gamification domain model be invalid, the gamification expert is warned to fix the detected problems. Once the model is valid, it will be saved, so it is ready for import/export.
3. Using the previously defined model, "the strategy expert will create the gamification strategy models describing the activities the participants can perform, the awards they can receive and the analytics that need be monitored".
4. Like the domain model, the previously developed strategy model will also be automatically validated, and the user should correct any error so that this model can also be saved and ready to be imported/exported.
5. The strategy models will then be "automatically transformed into code, which consists of both the code implementing the conditions that must be met so that the Complex Event Processing (CEP) engine can detect situations of interest, and code of actions to be performed in the Enterprise Service Bus (ESB) when detecting such situations".
6. The first part of the generated code will be added to the Complex Event Processing (CEP) engine at runtime.
7. The second part of the generated code is added to the ESB at runtime.
8. Lastly, the ESB sends both simple events and previously defined event patterns, so that the CEP engine may create new complex events, which will be sent back to the ESB, in order to broadcast this new event information to each user of the platform in question, and the designers in question.

To define the domain-specific elements of the gamification context, the developers of MEdit3CEP (Calderón et al., 2018) used the first level of abstraction in the taxonomy of game design elements (Deterding et al., 2011) and proposed the definition of its domain to be separated by the components category and the mechanics category. The following list contains a small description of each category and its elements:

- **Components:** Contains the concepts which identify the context, as well as both the elements related to gamified systems and the game elements involved with gamification strategies.
  - **Application:** Identifies the system to be gamified.
  - **Course:** Represents relevant information about the course (educational context) to be gamified, within a said application.
  - **ActivityType:** Identifies possible user actions within the Application element (e.g., pressing a button/link).
  - **Event:** Defines a feature of an ActivityType. The feature can be monitored, evaluated, and measured.
  - **RewardType:** Establishes the types of rewards that can be obtained by the users. The proposed rewards are as follows: Points; Level; Badge; Leaderboard; Status; Prize; Certificate; Good (virtual goods).
- **Mechanics:** Embraces concepts "involved in the design of a gamification strategy". Its elements are used to define interactions between game components and the system.
  - **Strategy:** It's the main element in defining a gamification strategy. It consists of three different elements: Activity; Criterion; Reward.
  - **Activity:** Identifies an ActivityType element in a gamified Application, involved in the gamification strategy.
  - **Reward:** Identifies a RewardType element, which has a weight attribute attached to it, that allows a designer to set the value of each reward of the strategy in question. The rewards can assist with measuring each user's performance.
  - **Criterion:** Sets the conditions to accomplish for the Event element, depending on each user's performance. It also sets the Reward elements a user should receive, would the criterion be satisfied.

With these categories and elements in mind, Calderón et al. (2018) proceeded to develop the metamodel through the usage of software such as the Eclipse Modeling Framework (EMF). The finished result of the metamodel in question is an extended version of the Model4CEP metamodel with both the gamification elements previously described and the components related to the CEP engine.

More information about how the gamification components interact with the CEP setup, as well as the evaluation involving the user's experience regarding the modeling editor, can be consulted in the article by Calderón et al. (2018).

This solution provides a reliable tool for conceptualizing and implementing gamification while being user-friendly for domain-experts. Moreover, due to the usage of an MDE approach, it can transform the models developed by domain-experts into code, to later be monitored and controlled by their event-driven service-oriented architecture system. But, due to it having such a high-level graphical design, it fails to assist with the development of intricate gamification strategies.

Gamify

Gamify (Aguiar, 2019) provides a textual-based DSL like GaML, but it can also generate guidelines depending on the domain expert's choices while designing the gamification strategies. Figure 4 represents the base metamodel, which includes various entities:

- **Gamify:** Serves as the main element for the development of gamification strategies.
- **System:** This entity allows the domain-experts to specify the state of their system to be gamified and to describe its user base. Once defined, the information saved in this entity will be used to assist the domain-expert with the gamification design to be developed (based on the book by Werbach & Hunter (2012)).
- **GameDynamic:** Referring to the information provided by Hunicke et al. (2004), this entity's main purpose is to guide users when developing their gamification design. It is used to define the overall dynamics of the gamification design desired, which can later be used to generate DSL presets, automatically creating a set of game mechanics and achievements depending on the dynamics defined by the user. A certain dynamic may be recommended depending on the user base attributes set in the entity "System".
- **GameMechanic:** Allows the specification of mechanics, events and rules, following guidelines provided by the MDA framework (Hunicke et al., 2004).
- **Event:** Can be used to define user actions, or events, existent within a previously defined game mechanic, specifying its name and type of event.
- **Restriction:** Applies additional restrictions to a previously defined event, such as time limits or action limits.
- **Achievement:** Consists of a set of conditions and rewards, which can be obtained should the user perform the necessary actions which would satisfy the previously set conditions. An achievement can be hidden from the view of the users until its conditions are completed so that its rewards can be bestowed upon the user (Octalysis' sudden rewards strategy (Chou, 2015)).
- **Condition:** Contains the threshold required to satiate a game mechanic's condition, as well as requirements necessary for the condition to be active.
- **Reward:** Sets the rewards acquired within the list of available items whenever a user completes a set of conditions, such as badges, prizes, or points that can be used to complete another set of conditions.
- **Item:** Contains information about possible user rewards, such as prizes, badges, or points.

General details about the various types and presets available to the user when designing a gamification strategy are the following (see Figure 5):

- **SystemAttributes:** Contains different possible states of the system to be gamified.
- **UserTypes:** Used to specify who will be the users of the gamified system (based on the book by Werbach & Hunter (2012)).
- **UserBaseAttributes:** Contains different user types based on the basic player types introduced by Bartle (1996).
- **DynamicTypes:** List of available preset dynamics (based on the paper by Hunicke et al. (2004)), with the option to be generated into DSL text. The custom option does not provide any text generation.
- **GameMechanicsTypes:** List of game mechanics to be chosen by the user, which can generate text related to the option selected.
- **EventTypes:** Contains both possible events and user actions that can affect conditions.
- **PrizeTypes:** Type of goods that can be obtained by users.
- **RestrictionTypes:** Type of limits to be added to a specific event.

Figure 4. Gamify metamodel

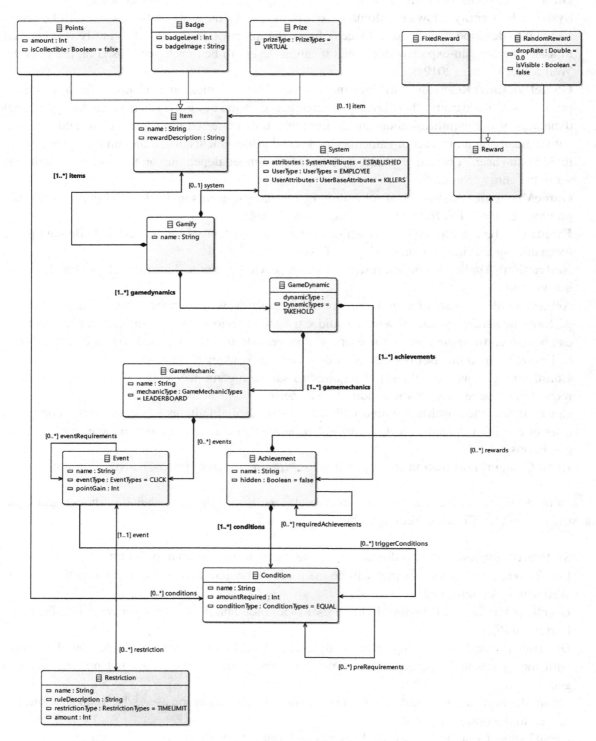

Figure 5. Other gamify concepts

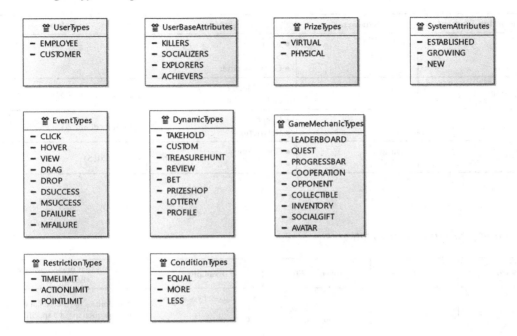

Table 2. Basic visual game mechanics

Game Design Element	Synonyms	Subtypes	References
System	• Service • Application	-	(Chou, 2015; Werbach & Hunter, 2012)
Event	• Dynamic Event • Mechanic Event • User Action	-	(Hunicke et al., 2004)
Condition	• Requirement	-	(Chou, 2015; Werbach & Hunter, 2012)
Restriction	• Regulation • Limit	-	(Deterding et al., 2011; Hunicke et al., 2004)
Item	• Goods • Collectible • Currency	• Badge • Points • Prize	(Chou, 2015; Deterding et al., 2011)
Reward	Earned: • Goods • Collectible • Currency	• Random Reward • Fixed Reward	(Chou, 2015; Deterding et al., 2011)

- **ConditionTypes:** Defines how will a condition be satiated.

Tables 2 and 3 contain information about each of the elements that reside in the metamodel. However, Table 4 provides information about the various reward strategies that the metamodel is prepared to replicate. The strategies in question are based on the Octalysis Framework (Chou, 2015).

Table 3. Aggregated visual game mechanics

Game Design Element	Synonyms	Aggregates	References
Gamify	• Context	• Item • System • GameDynamic	-
GameDynamic	-	• GameMechanic • Achievement	(Hunicke et al., 2004)
GameMechanic	-	• Event • Restriction	(Hunicke et al., 2004)
Achievement	• Quest • Mission	• Condition • Reward	(Chou, 2015)

Table 4. Gamification reward strategies

Strategies	Core Drives	Experiential Effects	Examples	Situations that make rewards visible	Major Findings
Fixed Action Rewards	2;4;6	• Increases engagement • Builds loyalty	• Virtual or physical goods • Points • Collectibles • Currency	System notifies the user about the actions required to get a specific reward.	(1)
Random Rewards	2;4;6;7	• Builds loyalty • Can enhance engagement of veteran users	Randomized: • Virtual or physical goods • Collectibles • Amount of currency	After successfully overcoming a previously set challenge or spending currency on a box of random goods.	(2)
Sudden Rewards	1;3;4;5;7	• Augments socialization within user base • Increases engagement	• Virtual or physical goods • Points • Collectibles • Currency	Completing a hidden set of actions, or by finding an Easter Egg.	(3)
Rolling Rewards	1;2;4;5;6;7	• Can enhance user engagement substantially	All types of rewards are eligible, from minimum to significant value.	Interacting with a lottery-like mechanic.	(4)
Social Treasure	3;4;5;6	• Augments socialization	Points, currency, collectibles which cannot be obtained by other means.	Sending in-game gifts to friends; Inviting friends to join the platform.	(5)
Prize Pacing	2;4;5;6;7;8	• Augments engagement	Collection of categorized shards, which turn into specific rewards once all shards are collected.	System informs the user about the obtainable reward after collecting a full set of shards.	(6)

The following list contains information related to the column "Major Findings" of Table 4:

- **(1):** The usage of this strategy is particularly relevant in competitive scenarios between companies/shops. Users are more likely to buy items in a certain shop that will eventually reward them in doing so.
- **(2):** Random rewards are often more effective in later stages of play, once all the non-repeatable fixed rewards have been collected. An exception to the previous affirmation is companies that specialize in providing random items to customers who find the surprise to be its own reward.

- **(3):** Depending on how the sudden reward is implemented, it can either cause users to share their experience, allowing other users the chance to replicate said experience or, should the sudden reward seem random, it can cause speculation within the community, having the users creating theories on how to obtain the reward in question.
- **(4):** This strategy allows users to have a chance of gaining very valuable goods, with relatively small effort. By maintaining the possible rewards visible, and by making this mechanic available in the early stages of play, it can attract new users to try their luck.
- **(5):** Social treasures often require a special type of point or currency that can only be obtained through interaction with other users. As such, this mechanic usually stimulates users to invite their friends to join them, or to socialize with other users, which helps both with solidifying a sense of community, and with increasing the general user base.
- **(6):** This last strategy rewards dedicated users by providing them with collectibles that have no value until all the pieces regarding a specific category are collected. Once a user gathers a full set, they receive a fitting reward, depending on the category of the pieces.

When designing the reward strategies for a gamification design, the variables "requiredAchievements" (Achievement) and "preRequirements" (Condition) can be used to either create a sequence of achievements (e.g., To obtain a level 2 badge, it is necessary to obtain the level 1 badge), each having their specific reward, or to create a complex condition for a particular achievement, effectively developing a challenge (e.g., a user needs to succeed on a set dynamic 10 times while using less than 10 total actions).

This current solution aims to succeed in being user-friendly for domain-experts, even when developing complex gamification strategies, due to the use of guidelines that adapt to the domain expert's choices. However, the solution currently lacks in available game dynamics, game mechanics and events, possibly hindering specific designs.

Solutions Comparison

This section focuses on relating various details of the analyzed solutions. Table 5 contains several benefits from each of the solutions examined. Benefits implicitly provided through the MDE approach are not included.

FUTURE RESEARCH DIRECTIONS AND CONCLUSIONS

MDE is an approach to software development that is especially useful when the problem in question envelops complex domain concepts (Schmidt, 2006). Through the usage of the appropriate tools, DSLs, transformations, and code generation, MDE can effectively address platform complexity.

Gamification is a moderately new concept, and thus the appearance of new strategies for gamified applications and new tools to implement them are bound to happen in the future.

Though flawed, each of the proposed solutions is in the right direction of addressing the problem of poor gamification design. And this is due to the implicit guidance provided by these solutions to domain-experts whenever they design new gamification strategies. The added assistance provided results in the avoidance of common design pitfalls. Even so, domain-experts will require knowledge about developing appropriate gamification strategies before utilizing any of the previously analyzed solutions, though

Table 5. Solutions specifics

Solution	DSL Type	Benefits	Limits
GaML	• Textual	• Provides a mature achievement-based system	• Readable but only partially writable by domain experts
MEdit4CEP	• Graphical	• User-friendly • Controls and monitors gamification strategies through the CEP engine	• Does not allow complex gamification strategies
Gamify	• Textual	• Provides design guidelines • Allows complex gamification strategies • User-friendly • Can generate text	• Limited number of available mechanics, and dynamics

both MEdit4CEP-Gam and Gamify attempt to assist with the strategy design. The studied frameworks provide invaluable information about the subject. Even though the Octalysis Framework and the Six Steps to Gamification were intended to assist with gamification, the MDA framework presents general information about games that can augment a domain expert's overall understanding of game elements. Nonetheless, these gamification frameworks are not flawless. Although they supply general information about how to implement gamification, they do not assist domain-experts with specific situations. The following list of actions consist of suggestions to mitigate some of the issues previously discussed regarding the studied frameworks:

- Performing a study regarding player typologies in a gamification environment. The data used for this study would be from both employees and customers.
- Development of a new model of player typologies using the data gathered from the study. The conclusions obtained during the development of the model can allow the establishment of new motivational strategies.
- Develop a detailed design strategy model using all the information obtained, replacing the MDA framework's taxonomy and the use of all-purpose patterns.
- Incentivize an iterative approach for the development of gamification strategies, implementing changes depending on user activity.

MDE is a suitable approach when dealing with several problems, including the introduction to gamification and the model-code gap (Fairbanks, 2010), ultimately simplifying the development process and preventing inadvertent introduction of errors. In this context, MDE can also encourage Agile software development since, should the need arise to change or add entities to the gamification strategy, it is possible to quickly implement these changes to the respective DSL resulting in newly generated code that can be easily integrated into the desired system. By performing this process, both the model representing the strategy adopted remains updated, as well as its corresponding generated code.

Regardless of how gamification design is achieved, a formal gathering of user necessities is imperative to avoid problems that would otherwise remain undetected. Additionally, no gamification approach will succeed without the proper identification of the objectives, or without knowledge about the user base in question.

REFERENCES

AguiarP. (2019, March 22). *Gamify*. Retrieved from: https://bitbucket.org/1140459/gamify/src/master/

Bartle, R. (1996). Hearts, clubs, diamonds, spades: Players who suit MUDs. *Journal of MUD Research*, *1*(1), 19. Retrieved from https://www.researchgate.net/directory/publications

Brambilla, M., Cabot, J., & Wimmer, M. (2017). *Model-Driven Software Engineering in Practice* (2nd ed.). San Rafael, CA: Morgan & Claypool Publishers.

Brathwaite, B., & Schreiber, I. (2008). *Challenges for Game Designers* (1st ed.). Rockland, MA: Charles River Media, Inc.

Burke, B. (2014). *Gamify: How Gamification Motivates People to Do Extraordinary Things*. Abingdon, UK: Routledge.

Calderón, A., Boubeta-Puig, J., & Ruiz, M. (2018). MEdit4CEP-Gam: A model-driven approach for user-friendly gamification design, monitoring and code generation in CEP-based systems. *Information and Software Technology*, *95*, 238–264. doi:10.1016/j.infsof.2017.11.009

Chou, Y. (2015). *Actionable gamification: Beyond points, badges, and leaderboards*. Fremont, CA: Octalysis Media.

Deci, E. L., & Ryan, R. M. (2012). Motivation, personality, and development within embedded social contexts: An overview of self-determination theory. The Oxford Handbook of Human Motivation, 85–107. doi:10.1093/oxfordhb/9780195399820.013.0006

Deterding, S. (2015). The Lens of Intrinsic Skill Atoms: A Method for Gameful Design. *Human-Computer Interaction*, *30*(3-4), 294–335. doi:10.1080/07370024.2014.993471

Deterding, S., Dixon, D., Khaled, R., & Nacke, L. (2011, September 28). From Game Design Elements to Gamefulness. *Defining Gamification, 11*, 9–15.

Djaouti, D., Alvarez, J., Jessel, J.-P., & Rampnoux, O. (2011). Origins of serious games. In *Serious games and edutainment applications* (pp. 25–43). New York, NY: Springer. doi:10.1007/978-1-4471-2161-9_3

Fairbanks, G. (2010). *Just enough software architecture: A risk-driven approach*. Boulder, CO: Marshall & Brainerd.

Gronback, R. C. (2009). *Eclipse modeling project: A domain-specific language (DSL) toolkit*. London, UK: Pearson Education.

Hamari, J., & Koivisto, J. (2015). Why do people use gamification services? *International Journal of Information Management*, *35*(4), 419–431. doi:10.1016/j.ijinfomgt.2015.04.006

Hamari, J., Koivisto, J., & Sarsa, H. (2014). Does Gamification Work? - A Literature Review of Empirical Studies on Gamification. *Proceedings of the Annual Hawaii International Conference on System Sciences*, *14*, 3025–3034. 10.1109/HICSS.2014.377

Herzig, P., Jugel, K., Momm, C., Ameling, M., & Schill, A. (2013). GaML-A modeling language for gamification. *2013 IEEE/ACM 6th International Conference on Utility and Cloud Computing*, 494–499.

Hunicke, R., Leblanc, M., & Zubek, R. (2004). MDA: A Formal Approach to Game Design and Game Research. *AAAI Workshop - Technical Report, 1.*

Huotari, K., & Hamari, J. (2012). Defining gamification: A service marketing perspective. In *Proceeding of the 16th International Academic MindTrek Conference*, (pp. 17–22). New York, NY: ACM. 10.1145/2393132.2393137

Huynh, D., Zuo, L., & Iida, H. (2018). An Assessment of Game Elements in Language-Learning Platform Duolingo. In *2018 4th International Conference on Computer and Information Sciences (ICCOINS)*, (pp. 1–4). Piscataway, NJ: IEEE.

Kapp, K. M. (2012). *The gamification of learning and instruction*. San Francisco, CA: Wiley.

Kumar, J. (2013). Gamification at work: Designing engaging business software. In *International Conference of Design, User Experience, and Usability*, (pp. 528–537). New York, NY: Springer. 10.1007/978-3-642-39241-2_58

Land, S. K., & Wilson, B. (2006). Using IEEE standards to support America's Army gaming development. *Computer*, *39*(11), 105–107. doi:10.1109/MC.2006.405

Matallaoui, A., Herzig, P., & Zarnekow, R. (2015). Model-Driven Serious Game Development Integration of the Gamification Modeling Language GaML with Unity. 2015 48th Hawaii International Conference on System Sciences, 643–651. 10.1109/HICSS.2015.84

Mora, A., Riera, D., González, C., & Arnedo-Moreno, J. (2017). Gamification: A systematic review of design frameworks. *Journal of Computing in Higher Education*, *29*(3), 516–548. doi:10.100712528-017-9150-4

Morschheuser, B., Hamari, J., Werder, K., & Abe, J. (2017). How to gamify? A method for designing gamification. *Proceedings of the 50th Hawaii International Conference on System Sciences 2017.* 10.24251/HICSS.2017.155

Morschheuser, B., Hassan, L., Werder, K., & Hamari, J. (2018). How to design gamification? A method for engineering gamified software. *Information and Software Technology*, *95*, 219–237. doi:10.1016/j.infsof.2017.10.015

Paharia, R. (2013). *Loyalty 3.0: How to revolutionize customer and employee engagement with big data and gamification*. New York, NY: McGraw Hill Professional.

Robson, K., Plangger, K., Kietzmann, J. H., McCarthy, I., & Pitt, L. (2016). Game on: Engaging customers and employees through gamification. *Business Horizons*, *59*(1), 29–36. doi:10.1016/j.bushor.2015.08.002

Schmidt, D. C. (2006). Model-Driven Engineering. *IEEE Computer, 39*(2), 9. Retrieved from https://citeseerx.ist.psu.edu/

Walz, S. P., & Deterding, S. (2015). *The gameful world: Approaches, issues, applications*. Cambridge, MA: MIT Press. doi:10.7551/mitpress/9788.001.0001

Werbach, K., & Hunter, D. (2012). *For the Win: How Game Thinking can Revolutionize your Business*. Philadelphia, PA: Wharton School Press.

Zichermann, G., & Cunningham, C. (2011). *Gamification by design: Implementing game mechanics in web and mobile apps.* ⌈O'Reilly Media, Inc.

KEY TERMS AND DEFINITIONS

Domain-Specific Language (DSL): A custom computer language specialized to a particular application domain.

Gamification: Concept with different definitions, but it is generally known as the use of game design elements in non-game contexts.

Gamify: An MDE solution based on a textual DSL that provides both gamification strategy guidelines, as well as language-related guidelines to assist domain experts in developing successful gamification strategies.

GaML: MDE solution based on a textual DSL that provides a structure for modeling gamification concepts.

Mechanics, Dynamics, and Aesthetics (MDA): A framework related to game development, seeking to combine game design with development, game critique, and technical game research to achieve a better general understanding of games.

MEdit4CEP-Gam: MDE solution with a graphical DSL that is appropriate for non-technical gamification experts to formalize their gamification designs.

Model-Driven Engineering (MDE): An approach that uses models as the main artifacts for the software development process. Furthermore, it relies on both code transformations and code generation to successfully produce software.

Chapter 7
Reuse in Agile Development Process

Chung-Yeung Pang
https://orcid.org/0000-0002-7925-4454
Seveco AG, Switzerland

ABSTRACT

Reusability is a clear principle in software development. However, systematic reuse of software elements is not common in most organizations. Application programmers rarely design and create software elements for possible future reuse. In many agile software development processes, the project teams believe that the development of reusable software elements can slow down the project. This can be a misconception. This chapter examines various ways to reuse software. Three approaches to developing reusable software artifacts from 15 years of experience in the agile development process are presented. The first approach is to create generic programs or configurable frameworks that support similar solutions for a variety of use cases and environments. The reuse of patterns is the second approach presented. Another effective way is to use a model-driven approach with model patterns. These approaches help to speed deployment software. The final product is flexible and can easily be adapted to changes. This is one of the main goals of an agile approach.

INTRODUCTION

An experienced programmer would reuse his / her code written for another project whenever a similar function is needed. In fact, people always use the same solution for similar problems. That is why experience can be very valuable. When implementing a new module, a veteran programmer, after years of observation by the author, often cuts out code fragments from old modules that he / she has written and inserts them into the new module. He / she is usually more efficient and productive as he / she already has experience solving similar problems. Transforming this experience into a set of reusable elements that anyone can use would bring great benefits to overall software development. That's what software reuse is all about.

DOI: 10.4018/978-1-7998-2531-9.ch007

With advances of software technologies, there are many packages and libraries containing reusable software elements available commercially or open sources. Different business or system units from large organizations usually provide business domain specific or infrastructure related software components and functions (e.g. a function to retrieve customer data, etc.) for application development. Using these software elements in application development forms the common practice of reuse. With decades of experience working for many large organizations, the author finds that it is not a common practice for application programmers to design and build software elements for possible future. When developers have to meet deadlines and provide functionality, building software elements that can be reused is never a priority. In fact, often one can find programs with hard coded values and algorithm that prevent them from being reused in different context without code changes.

In recent years, the agile software development process has become very popular in the software industry (Ambler, 2010; Larman, 2003). In this approach, the emphasis is on providing working software with the highest business values as a measure of the progress of a software project. It prefers functioning software over documentation and customer collaboration over contract negotiation. As a result, so many developers are simply write ad hoc-style code, even though the agile approach does not exclude the value of analysis and design. For many agile development teams, designing and building reusable software elements are out of the question.

Although agile development practice has great advantages in software development, many projects are still failing (Harlow, 2014; Ismail, 2017). When a software element has high reuse potential through configuration and extension, it is flexible and easily adapt to changes. This actually fulfil the motivation of agile software approach that the end system should be flexible and easy to change. The purpose of this chapter to describe the techniques to design and build reusable software artefacts and demonstrate that they bring many benefits. The development process to provide working software can be speeded up. The end product is flexible and easily adaptable to changes, which is one of the main goals in using an agile approach.

The chapter gives a brief survey of software reuse. It presents the general reusable software artefacts with their motivation, implementation concept, consequences and applicability. Specific approaches to develop reusable software artefacts that evolved out of 15 years of experience of agile development practice are described. The approaches include those for "generic programming and configurable framework", "pattern based reuse" and "model driven approach". The chapter is organized with a first section on the background of agile software development and reusing software. It is followed by a section on reusable software elements. The three approaches mentioned before will be described in three different sections. The chapter ends with sections on the vision for the future and a final conclusion.

BACKGROUND

In the background, the first subsection deals with the history of software development and the agile approach. Following is a subsection on reuse based software engineering.

History of Software Development and Agile Approach

In the early days of software history, programmers tended to develop their programs without documentation in an ad-hoc style. As software systems evolved with features over the years, they were no longer serviceable (Software Crisis, 2010). Software engineers argued that software development should not just be coding. Analysis and design with the right documentation are as important as writing code (Software Engineering, 2010). It has gone the extra mile that much effort has been put into requirements specification and design work, resulting in a tremendous amount of documentation. The author has experienced that a number of projects did not survive the requirement specification analysis phase before the budget was exhausted and no single working software was created.

In 2001, a number of prominent software engineers joined forces to create a Manifesto for Agile Software Development (Agile Manifesto Group, 2001). They were not satisfied with the usual software development practices, especially with the extensive documents nobody would read. They came up with 12 principles. Four main principles related to the context of this chapter are:

- Individuals and interactions over processes and tools.
- Working software over comprehensive documentation.
- Customer collaboration over contract negotiation.
- Responding to change over following a plan.

The agile approach to software development is widespread in the software community. Many agile development methods have been introduced. The most popular are Scrum, Kanban and extreme programming (Stellman & Greene, 2015). In particular, these methods divide the product development work into small increments that minimize the planning and design effort. Iterations are short periods, which usually take one to four weeks. Work software is the primary measure of progress. Program elements from each iteration should be continuously integrated into the system.

The Agile Software Development Manifesto provides only principles for software development. There is no framework for how the development should be done. An agile development method like Scrum provides the blue print of a software development process. However, there is no suggestion on the mechanism how program elements should be developed in each iteration and how they can be continuously integrated into the system.

The 2015 CHAOS report (Hastie & Wojewoda2015) shows that the statistical success rate in agile software development is three times higher than traditional approaches. However, the report also shows that the overall success rate of an agile approach project is only 39%. Despite using the agile approach many projects still fail. This chapter proposes techniques for improving the situation.

Reuse Based Software Engineering

Reuse is a distinct field of study in software engineering. It started with the concept of reusable software components. Early developments in reuse research include the idea of program families and domain analysis concepts (Biggerstaff & Perlis, 1989). Other areas of reuse research include function libraries, methods and tools for domain engineering, design patterns, domain-specific software architecture, components, generators, measurements and experiments, and business and finance (Soora, 2014; Jacobson, et al., 1997). There are also areas of computer science research that are central to reuse: abstract data types and object-oriented methods, programming language theory, software architectures, compilers, models for software development processes, metrics and experiments, and organization theory (Krueger, 1992; Frakes & Kang, 2005; 2015). Reuse can also be applied in the different phases of the software lifecycle, e.g., requirements analysis and specification, software design, implementation, testing and deployment, and product maintenance (Leach, 2011).

There are many approaches to the software reuse concept. In order to organize and place different concepts and models of reuse, a set of conceptual frameworks for the reuse of software has been proposed. Biggerstaff and Richter (1989) propose a framework that divides available reusability technologies into two main groups: composition technologies and generation technologies. Krueger (1992) proposed a framework with four taxonomies for reusable artifacts. The four taxonomies are abstraction, selection, specialization and integration. Another framework developed by Freeman (1987) asked questions such as "what is reused?", "How should it be reused?" and "What is required to enable a successful reuse?". His framework defines five levels of reusable information code fragments, logical structure, functional architecture, external knowledge (e.g. knowledge of application domains and software development), and environmental knowledge related to organizational and psychological issues. Other frameworks are based on forms of reuse such as data, code, and design (Horowitz & Munson, 1984; Jones, 1984). Reusable software artifacts include application systems, subsystems or frameworks, components, modules, objects and functions or procedures.

Reusability is a key principle of software engineering. However, as mentioned earlier, application programmers rarely create their programs considering reuse. For reusable software artifacts to be widely reusable, they must be properly documented so that the software project members can use these software artifacts during development. This type of task rarely has priority in the development process. In an agile approach to software development, such a task does not seem to have business value. The project team could assume that reuse would slow down the deployment of working software. As shown in this chapter, it's a mistake to make reusable software artifacts slow down project progress. Rather, it can accelerate. The final product would be flexible and easy to adapt to changes.

REUSABLE SOFTWARE ELEMENTS

Nobody would start a software project from scratch these days. Reuse happens all the time, though the development team may not even notice it. Business concepts, architectures and experiences are used repeatedly. Reusable software elements include application systems, subsystems or frameworks, components, modules, objects and functions or procedures (Sommerville, 2015, Leach, 2011). This section explains how to reuse these reusable elements in the following subsections. Each subsection would contain description, motivation, implementation approach, consequence and applicability of the various reusable elements.

Function and Object Libraries

The simplest reusable software items are libraries that contain callable functions or procedures. Throughout software development history, there are many libraries that provide system-related issues such as input and output (IO), scientific and mathematical calculations, and more.

With the development of object-oriented programming we have libraries with application interfaces (API). When we code with Java, the SDK provides the most basic classes for many functions. The functions are constantly being improved and expanded. For legacy programming languages like COBOL, system vendors like IBM would provide a variety of features for their infrastructure, such as security, communications, and database.

Apart from the libraries provided by vendors or open sources, it is always advisable to develop features that are used repeatedly within an organization. A good example is a Java function that is constantly used to read a file within the project class paths with a specific filename. It was noted that there were a dozen implementations in a financial institution to resolve and validate an International Bank Account Number (IBAN). The same functions but different approaches have been found in different programs. The functions are usually hard-coded within the module that needs them. For a developer to implement such a feature, he / she must first understand the structure and validation algorithm of IBAN. This usually takes longer than coding the function. Functions like these examples should be placed in reusable function libraries.

In general, a function in libraries performs exactly one function and requires one or more input parameters. Normally only one output is provided. Such a function is relatively easy to implement. Most programming languages, such as Javascript, support the development of callable functions. In Java, a class can contain a list of static methods. Each of these methods would perform a single function. In COBOL, a function would be a callable module. Reusable libraries in COBOL are basically a collection of modules. A callable COBOL module can contain COBOL structures for its input and output. Libraries in object-oriented languages usually contain object classes. Each object (instant of a class) would represent a distinct entity, and it would contain methods for operating its properties. For example, a list object has list properties and methods to handle list items. For programmers to use functions or objects from a reusable library, documentation must be provided. The minimum documentation for a function contains a description of the operation and a description of the input and output parameters. Descriptions of the object and all its public methods are required for a class.

In an agile development approach, creating reusable object or function libraries does not contribute to immediate business value. Such an activity appears to burden the project and not bring the benefit of enterprise-wide software development. Often this is a mistake. Similar functions and objects can be used repeatedly in an application. The multiple development of the same function or object, especially from different developers, would require much more effort than documenting and storing in a reusable library. The document would also help the QA team to test the object or feature. A QA team can test a function, object, or module as a black box. It helps to improve the quality of the software system.

System and Application

Objects and functions are small reusable elements. Systems and applications can be reused to a greater extent. For example, an achieving system can be integrated when documents are needed to be achieved in an application.

The development of a new system may involve the reuse of a number of applications. For example, the integration of an Enterprise Resource Planning (ERP) system, a Management Information System (MIS), a Customer Relationship Management (CRM) system, and financial applications can be a new general-purpose system for a business. Thus, users do not have to enter the same data for each application. It is also more user-friendly to have a unique system than a number of independent applications.

Such integration would require changes and extensions to individual applications. Independent applications usually have their own data structure and database. In an integrated environment, data such as that for customers, sales, bookings, etc. must be exchanged or shared between applications. An author's suggested approach is to provide APIs to transfer shared data to and from each application. It should be avoided to extend an application so that it can access data from another application. An agent can be used for this purpose. The agent can provide a communication channel between applications. In addition, a new GUI may need to be developed to ensure a consistent style and navigation for the various applications. Again, the front-end GUI can communicate with the agent, which sends the requests to the applications and sends the output of the applications back to the front-end GUI.

For more examples such as Software Product Lines, Commercial Off-the-shelf (COTS), and ERP systems, see Sommerville's (2015) book. Many systems and applications are available commercially or in open source. There are also companies that develop their own systems.

Component

In most organizations, there is a development team that is responsible for the software of a particular business domain. The team usually provides a set of software components that can be invoked by any application as needed. Components are reusable elements. They have a higher granularity than functions or objects in a function library and are sometimes considered as subsystems. Typically, they provide a set of services or interfaces through which they can be activated. They would perform most if not all activities related to their business domain. A business architecture typically includes a component model. This model shows the components available from various business units with the services or interfaces they provide. The technical architecture provides mechanisms for calling business components.

All classes of a Java programmed component are usually packaged in a JAR, WAR, or EAR file. In a legacy environment with COBOL, modules of a component are packaged together. In a service-oriented system, components can provide services to consumers. This allows components to work together in a cross-platform environment in an application.

Architecture and Framework

Any working software has an architecture, although it may not have been designed by the development team. When we create a simple website, we use the HTML framework with the HTTP protocol. Designing architectures is not an issue for many agile development teams, especially when building web applications using frameworks like Node.js, Lavavel, Vue.js or CMS frameworks like Drupal and Wordpress. All of these frameworks have a solid architecture. Developers must follow the style, structure, and mechanism that the architectures of these frameworks dictate for the integration of their program elements.

Architecture is very important for a corporate IT system. The architecture must set standards and mechanisms for executing specific actions in an application. Logging and exception handling are a good example. Imagine, with a sales order something goes awry and it has been processed by different components in different systems. It would be a nightmare if customer support helpdesk staff had to investigate the problem based on the different types of logs from different systems.

One big mistake that a project can make is that application programmers need to have a deep understanding of the technical infrastructure. Application programmers should focus on business logic that brings business benefits. A set of reusable infrastructure components should be developed separately.

They are usually programmed by system programmers. If application programmers can focus only on business logic without having to worry about the infrastructure, they are much more efficient, ultimately increasing the agility to make changes to the final application.

Software architectures are generally associated with frameworks. A software framework is an abstraction in which software that provides generic functions can be selectively changed by additional user-written code, thereby providing application-specific software. It is a standard method of creating and deploying applications and is a universal, reusable software environment that provides certain functionality as part of a larger software platform to facilitate the development of software applications, products and solutions. Software frameworks may include support programs, compilers, code libraries, tool sets, and Application Programming Interfaces (APIs) that merge all the different components to enable the development of a project or system.

Following an agile development practice, application programmers should be able to create individual program elements and integrate them into the system in small, time-limited iterations. Therefore, the architecture or framework would have to provide a plug-and-play mechanism for integrating program elements. When the application programmers finish a module, the module must be integrated into the business process. This must be possible without having to modify existing modules to forward data and invoke the new module. In fact, without a plug-and-play architecture framework, it is very difficult to perform the agile incremental and iterative development process.

An example of a plug-and-play architecture was presented by Pang (2016) for a legacy IT system with COBOL programs. A Java implementation of an architecture framework is presented in the next section.

GENERIC PROGRAMMING AND CONFIGURABLE FRAMEWORK

The original concept of generic programming is the implementation of an algorithm with elements that have more than one interpretation, depending on parameters that represent types (Meyer, 1988). In the Cambridge dictionary, generic is defined as "relating to a whole group of similar things, not a specific thing." Generic programming deals with the using abstract representations of efficient algorithms, data structures and other software concepts as well as their systematic organization. The goal of generic programming is to express algorithms and data structures in a broad, interoperable form that allows their direct use in software construction.

Generic programming can be applied to all reusable software elements (Kramer & Finkelstein, 1991; Jazayeri et al., 1998). We can have generic systems, applications, architectures and frameworks, services and components, down to generic functions and procedures. In this chapter, generic programming is considered a flexible, monolithic solution that can be used in a variety of applications and environments. It improves extensibility, reusability and compatibility. An in-depth discussion of the full spectrum of generic programming would go beyond the scope of this chapter. This section introduces some general programming techniques that are suitable for agile development. Topics covered are configurable algorithm and framework as well as scripting languages and generic database schema.

Configurable Algorithm and Framework

Generic programming was first supported in programming languages such as ADA. For a function like swapping two elements you can have the following function declaration:

generic type Element_T is private; -- Generic formal type parameter

procedure Swap (X, Y: in out Element_T);

This function can be applied to elements of all kinds. The type is defined dynamically at runtime when the function is used. The generic type is also supported in Java, as shown below for an ArrayList class:

public class ArrayList<E>;

Generic programming is not limited to what a programming language supports in application development. It is also not limited to primitive functions like swap or base class like a list. You can develop an algorithm for one or more activities that require multiple elements and components to work together. The involved elements or components can be configured in a context.

As discussed in the previous section, an agile development process requires a plug-and-play architecture framework. The example presented here is a framework that is based on a finite-state machine in the form of a Java-programmed process control. The steps and processes of the process controller are configured externally. The implementation of such a process controller is shown in the code segment in Figure 1.

The finite-state machine (i.e. the process controller) calls an object based on the actual state and event. An object must provide an event for the transition after completing its task. This event usually depends on the result of the process. If everything is ok, the default event is an "OK" event. This event, along with the status of the process, is used by process control to determine the next object to invoke. This implementation uses the Spring framework. The configuration of the process controller is specified in a text file in JSON (see Figure 2).

For an object to perform its task, input data is always required. The process controller should be generic and not responsible for transferring data to the objects. A data transfer mechanism can be achieved using a data object container. Each object retrieves data objects that provide the input from that container and fills the output data with the output objects that are eventually stored in the container. The application context of Spring framework can be used as a data object container. Figure 3 shows an example of the Java implementation of an object and the retrieval of data objects from the Application Context of the Spring framework.

After implementing an object for a step in the business process in an iteration, the object can be inserted into the configuration of the process controller in the process descriptor file. The design of the business process must ensure that the required data objects are available at runtime when the object is activated by the process controller.

The example above shows the power of generic programming. It shows how a continuous integration of iteratively developed program elements can be achieved. The implementation of the process controller can be used in any business process in any application.

Script Language and Generic Database Schema

In an agile development process, application programmers develop program elements iteratively. Each iteration has a short timeframe and therefore the program elements should be kept rather small. It may happen that the functionality of a program element is small, but the development of the required infrastructure is rather a big task, e.g., designing a database to store persistent data. An application program-

Figure 1. Implementation of generic process controller using finite state pattern

```java
public void build() throws Exception {
  if (applicationContext == null) {
        applicationContext = new ClassPathXmlApplicationContext("/applicationContext.xml");
  }
  InputStream stream = new ClassPathResource(configName).getInputStream();
  String configData = IOUtils.toString(stream, StandardCharsets.UTF_8);
  JSONParser parser = new JSONParser();
  JSONObject processObj = (JSONObject) parser.parse(configData);
  JSONArray arr = (JSONArray) processObj.get("process");
  String stateEvent = "start";
  if (arr != null) {
    for (Object proc : arr) {
      String state = ((JSONObject) proc).get("state").toString();
      if (stateEvent.equals("start")) {
        startState = state;
      }
      if (processTable == null) {
        processTable = new HashMap<String, BusinessProcess>();
        nextStateTable = new HashMap<String, String>();
      }
      BusinessProcess process = processTable.get(state);
      if (process == null) {
        String name = ((JSONObject) proc).get("name").toString();
        process = (BusinessProcess) applicationContext.getBean(name);
        processTable.put(state, process);
      }
      if (stateEvent.equals("start")) {
        nextStateTable.put(stateEvent, state);
      }
      String event = ((JSONObject) proc).get("event").toString();
      stateEvent = state + " : " + event;
      String nextState = ((JSONObject) proc).get("next state").toString();
      nextStateTable.put(stateEvent, nextState);
    }
  }
}

public String start() throws Exception {
  String stateEvent = "start";
  String state = startState;
  while (!state.equals("exit")) {
    BusinessProcess process = processTable.get(state);
    String event = process.execute(stateEvent);
    if (!state.equals("exit")) {
      state = nextStateTable.get(stateEvent);
      stateEvent = state + " : " + event;
    }
  }
  return stateEvent;
}
```

Figure 2. Process descriptor in JSON

```
{"process": [
  {"state": "validate input", "name": "validate_input", "event": "OK", "next state": "check eligibility"},
  {"state": "validate input", "name": "validate_input", "event": "Invalid Input", "next state": "handle error"},
  {"state": "check eligibility", "name": "check_eligibility", "event": "OK", "next state": "check availability"},
  {"state": "check eligibility", "name": "check_eligibility", "event": "Not Eligible", "next state": "handle error"},
  {"state": "check availability", "name": "check_availability", "event": "OK", "next state": "exit"},
  {"state": "check availability", "name": "check_availability", "event": "Not Available", "next state": "handle error"},
  {"state": "handle error", "name": "handle_error", "event": "OK", "next state": "exit"}
]}
```

Figure 3. Example of data object and its retrieval from spring framework application context

```
public interface OrderCurrData {
    void setISOCode(String iso);
    void setAccount(String account);
    void setAmount(double amount);
    void setBookingText(String bookingText);
    void setCreditDebitFlag(int flag);

    String getISOCode();
    String getAccount();
    double getAmount();
    String getBookingText();
    int getCreditDebitFlag();
}

// Object that sets the data
OrderCurrData outCurrData = (OrderCurrData) applicationContext.getBean("Order Curr Data");
outCurrData.setISOCode(isoCode);
outCurrData.setAccount(accountNo);
...

// Object that gets the data
OrderCurrData inCurrData = (OrderCurrData) applicationContext.getBean("Order Curr Data");
String isoCode = inCurrData.getISOCode();
String accountNo = inCurrData.getAccount();
...
```

mer may feel that designing a well-structured database has no business value. Therefore, he / she would save the data in some files without a suitable format. In this case, it would be a nightmare for the other developer who needs to create a search engine for the data.

Most applications require a proper database design. This task would require a detailed analysis of the affected persistent data and the required search mechanisms. Many modules to be developed in later iterations depend on this design. Therefore, the project requires a pre-defined detail design task that does not conform to the concept of an agile development process. One possible solution is a generic database schema.

Figure 4. Generic Java persistent object interface

```java
public interface SmfwPersistentManager {
    void init();
    void close() throws Exception;
    String startTransaction() throws Exception;
    void commit(String transName) throws Exception;
    void rollback(String transName) throws Exception;
    void close(String transName) throws Exception;

    void setCurrentSchema(String schemaName) throws Exception;
    void createNewDataStructure(String dataStructureName) throws Exception;
    void createIndex(String dataStructureName,
        String indexName, String[] fields) throws Exception;

    void add(String dataStructureName, Object pojo) throws Exception;
    Object find(String dataStructureName, Object pojo) throws Exception;
    void modify(String dataStructureName, Object searchPojo, Object newPojo) throws Exception;
    void delete(String dataStructureName, Object searchPojo) throws Exception;
    List<Object> search(String dataStructureName, String searchCriteria) throws Exception;
}
```

In a normal database schema, a table is created for each data structure, whose columns are mapped to the fields of the data structure. This would not work for a generic database schema because it has to process different data structures. One solution to this problem is to use a scripting language such as XML or JSON. Instead of storing each field in a separate column, each entry stores a single text in XML or JSON that contains the entire data structure. In other words, the table-based database effectively becomes a document-based database. Document-based databases are a feature of NoSQL. However, most organizations prefer to use mature and stable relational SQL databases, such as IBM DB2, Oracle, MySQL, etc. instead of NoSQL.

The most common SQL relational databases support the storage and indexing of documents. IBM DB2 provides support for XML and JSON documents. MySQL offers Document Store with X DevAPI for JSON documents. They also support transaction processing for documents. It is possible to create a generic module to handle both basic CRUD operations and transactions for various data structures.

An example with Java is worked out here. This example uses simple old Java objects (POJO) to represent data structures. The persistent data processing capabilities provided by the generic Java object are shown in Figure 4. The basic mechanism includes the following. The data structure represented by the POJO is resolved using Java Reflection. Depending on the requested function, a corresponding JSON document is generated using the data structure as well as the data of the POJO. The metadata such as the name of the data structure and the indexed fields are needed to create a new data structure. The function search allows search criteria written in a script such as "age <30 and gender = m". Other features shown in Figure 4 are quite transparent.

The use of a document-based database has advantages and disadvantages compared to a table-based database. There are a considerable number of articles that explain the two types of database styles (Chan, 2019; Shiff & Rowe, 2018). The main advantage of the document-based database is that the data schema can be flexibly changed without having to change existing data. With the implementation of a generic module (see Figure 4), application programmers do not need to create individual schemas for their data structures. Programmers do not have to worry about database connection and writing SQL statements to their program elements. It is more suitable for agile development processes.

PATTERN BASED REUSE

We live in a world full of patterns. Our habits are nothing more than repeatedly following a series of behavioral patterns. Since the publication of the book by Gamma et al. (1995), software developers have been made aware of patterns that we are constantly using and should be used in software development. A pattern is defined as the solution to a problem in a particular context. A pattern-driven approach would be to identify the problem to be solved and look up the pattern that provides the solution to the problem in the given context.

In software development, there are patterns for the development process, patterns for architectural, structural and behavioral designs, as well as code patterns for implementation and so on. Usage patterns provide a general overview of the use of applications. They help identify the information a business component should deliver and the expected interactions with other components. The pattern-driven approach complements the agile approach to software development in a way that accelerates developmental iterations by avoiding reinventing the wheel at every stage of development.

Patterns can accelerate the development process by providing proven and proven development paradigms. They should be stored in a repository and published so that every developer in the enterprise can access them. This section explains various types of patterns for analysis and business process, architecture and design, and usage and code in the subsections.

Analysis and Business Patterns

In his classic book, Martin Fowler defines a pattern as an "idea that was useful in one practical context and is likely to be useful in others" (Fowler, 1996). He also discusses the analysis paradigm that reflects "conceptual structures of business processes, not actual software implementations." Analysis patterns are conceptual models that capture an abstraction of a typical situation in modeling. They focus on the organizational, social and economic aspects of a system, as these aspects are central to the requirements analysis and the acceptability and usability of the final system (Geyer-Schulz & Hahsler, 2001).

In addition to business processes, under certain circumstances there may be patterns for conducting analysis. An example is the pattern described by Wake (Wake, 2018) for writing and sharing user stories. The Scrum model can also be viewed as a model for an agile software development process.

Identifying reusable patterns in an IT system can be of great value. Business processes, rules, algorithms and data structures are generally refined and proven over the years. They can be very useful for the future development and improvement of applications. They also provide documentation of the system in operation and materials for training business analysts and developers. In fact, the way companies do business always follows certain patterns. They rarely change, though there may be variations in the details. For example, the business process of a customer business order always includes the following four processes, regardless of the product type for the business:

1. Trade order entry.
2. Validation of the trade order after accounts have been selected for settlement and booking.
3. Making an offer with quote and pricing information.
4. Acceptance of the offer for the trade by the client and start of the trade settlement process.

There are also standard patterns for dealing with errors and exceptions when the validation fails or the time for an offer has expired, etc. The trade validation process also includes standard checks for entitlement, availability, credit and amount limits, and so on. When developing a customer order application for a new product, business analysts can follow these patterns to identify the detail requirements of business process steps and include them as tasks in the product backlog in the Scrum development process.

Architectural and Design Patterns

The concept of the design pattern in software development was first described by Gamma et al. al. (Gamma, 1995). It focuses on finding a reusable solution to a common problem in a particular software design context. It is not intended as a ready-made design that application programmers convert directly to source code. It is more a description of how to solve a problem that can be used in many different situations. Developers still have to adapt the design to their specific requirements.

In the classic book by Gamma et al. there are a number of examples of categories such as creation patterns, texture patterns, and patterns of behavior. The use of delegation, aggregation and consultation concepts is well described. In general, you cannot simply pick up one of these examples with source code and use it as it is. For example, consider a design pattern for facet and decor type enhancements presented by Pang (Pang, 2001). In the example he tries to solve the problem that a university member can be a student or an employee. The member can also be both a student and an employee. Depending on the client's use of the college member object, it may be a student or a co-worker. The exact problem does not occur in most business cases. However, presenting a business partner who is both a customer and a supplier is a similar problem. The solution and much of the featured base code can be used after the solution has been tailored to the problem of each business partner.

Patterns presented in the literature are usually for general purposes. In a corporation for a particular business, there are many design patterns that can be reused in multiple applications. They are domain-specific patterns. An example of a domain-specific pattern is a series of activities involved in the booking process of an order (see below):

1. Get the amount decimal places for the respective product from the financial instrument component.
2. Convert the booking amount for the order into a format with the correct decimal places.
3. If the order amount unit is the currency unit of the ledger, use the same amount to post the ledger.
4. If the order amount unit is not the currency unit of the ledger, proceed as follows:
   a. Get the exchange rate from the financial instrument component.
   b. Convert the booking amount to the amount in ledger currency.
   c. Use the converted amount for ledger booking.

Design patterns can also be applied in the software architecture. In fact, there are many well-structured architectural patterns. Some of the most popular are client / server, layer architecture, component-based architecture, event-driven architecture, model-view-controller (MVC), service-oriented architecture

Figure 5. Code pattern of booking process

```
FinancialInstrument finInst = (FinancialInstrument)
  applicationContext.getBean("FinancialInstrument");
ISOData bookingISOData = finInst.getISOData(${BookingISO});
double bookingAmountDouble = ${OrigAmount} * bookingISOData.getDecimal();
int bookingAmount = (int) Math.round(bookingAmountDouble);

BookingManager bookingManager = (BookingManager)
  applicationContext.getBean(${BookingManager});
bookingManager.setNewBooking();
bookingManager.setAccount(${AccountNo});
bookingManager.setAmount(bookingAmount, bookingISOData.getDecimal());
bookingManager.setBookingText(${BookingText});
bookingManager.setCreditDebitFlag(${CreditDebitFlag});

if (${BookingISO}.equals(bookingISOData.getLedgerISOCode())) {
        bookingManager.setLedgerAmount(bookingAmount, bookingISOData.getDecimal());
} else {
        double ledgerAmountDouble = ${OrigAmount} *
         finInst.getLedgerExchangeRate(${BookingISO}) *
         bookingISOData.getLedgerDecimal();
        int ledgerAmount = (int) Math.round(ledgerAmountDouble);
        bookingManager.setLedgerAmount(ledgerAmount, bookingISOData.getLedgerDecimal());
}
bookingManager.book();
```

(SOA), etc. (Richards 2015). In his book, Fowler presented many patterns for enterprise application architecture (Fowler, 2006). Patterns include object relational mapping, web presentation, concurrency, session state, etc. To design an architecture for an enterprise IT system, it is usually necessary to identify the combination of architectural patterns that meet the requirements (Pang, 2015; Pang, 2016).

Developers should be encouraged to use patterns. They should also be trained to identify the theme and variations of their design and implementation in order to derive patterns that developers can reuse for other applications with similar problems.

Code Patterns and Template

A pattern is usually associated with templates in the form of models or snippets of code. Developers can complete the design or implementation with context-specific elements based on these templates. Note the domain-specific pattern of activities involved in the posting process of a purchase order example in the previous subsection. We can have a code segment as shown in Figure 5.

The code segment in Figure 5 uses the symbols $ {xxx} as wildcards. With this code segment, developers can replace all placeholders with correct variable names. With available code segments and reusable templates, developers can finish the code with little effort.

REUSE IN MODEL DRIVEN APPROACH

Software development usually starts with modeling. Models provide abstractions of high-level design concepts and enable communication between software users that code alone cannot. These models are drawn on a flipchart or graphically displayed in a CASE tool. After all, these models become programs in one way or another.

The Object Management Group (OMG) attempts to standardize modeling techniques in software development in a Model Driven Architecture (MDA) (MDA, 2010; Mellor, 2004). MDA is seen as a way to organize and manage enterprise architectures that are supported by automated tools and services to both define the models and facilitate the transformation between different model types. MDA should provide a blueprint for rapid software development. The focus is on rigorous software modeling and code generation from models.

In this section, the first subsection introduces an approach that combines agile practice and model-driven software development. This is followed by a subsection on reusable model patterns. As demonstrated later in this section, the model-driven approach to rapidly deploying workable software is very effective. The final product is flexible and can easily be adapted to changes. This is exactly the goal of an agile development process.

Agile and Model Driven Approach to Software Development

In a recent article titled "no developers required: Why this company chose no-code over software devs" (Clark, 2019), Clark reported:

- A Dutch insurer has decided no-code development lets it create new services faster.
- Univé turned to the no-code platform from Betty Blocks to help business experts develop software. It offers a graphical approach to building software, instead of requiring developers to key in lines of code.
- Univé innovation manager Bas Wit commented that normal development simply takes too much time and one never gets exactly what one wants the first time around.

Agile development process Scrum does not really define how analysis and development should be done. Scrum promoters generally recommend a Product Backlog with a list of all requirements in the form of user stories (Rehkopf, 2019). User stories are selected according to their business value priorities and programmed in consecutive sprint iterations. The question now is how to ensure that user stories can capture all the needs of a complex application, especially if they are small enough to be implemented in a sprint. The second question is how to get a complete overview of business workflow and processes from user stories. User stories are not detailed requirements specifications. Therefore, many negotiations between customers, business analysts and developers are expected to be required. Interestingly enough, many models are being eradicated during these negotiations. Converting the scratched models into formal models that can be converted into codes would be a very effective and fast way to build working software. Converting models to code requires more detailed information and possibly some code segments. This approach has proven to be very successful (Pang, 2016).

Unfortunately, there are only a few modeling tools that can do a complete model code transformation. However, the meta-information of the models can be extracted from most models. In addition to code templates and patterns, domain-specific code generators can be easily created (Pang, 2016). Experience has shown that many application programmers write spaghetti code. Code verification is a tedious and time-consuming task. With a short sprint time frame and an urgent delivery of program elements, this task is often omitted. As a result, the program may be of poor quality and difficult to maintain. On the other hand, you can create spaghetti code, but it would be difficult to create a spaghetti model. Model are easy to change and improve. They are perfect for the documentation. Generated code usually has the same structure and pattern, so it's easy to follow. The construction of code generators initially seems to bring no business benefits. However, measured against the experience of graphical and model-driven approaches, this can bring enormous economic benefits in the long term.

Reusable Model Patterns

Patterns can be abstracted in models. Frequently, code patterns and templates are assigned to the patterns. The domain-specific pattern example shows a number of activities involved in the booking process of an order. An action with parameters symbol can be used to represent this pattern. In a UML activity diagram, an action that should use this pattern may have a link to the pattern icon with constraints indicating the association of the program variables with the parameters. Figure 6 shows the action link to the pattern. The link is also associated with a UML constraint that provides the mapping information of program variables for the placeholders of the example code segment shown in Figure 5.

Figure 6 shows the model of a simple order process. Most of the code is actually provided by the patterns. There is only one action with the stereotype << code >>, which contains a small piece of code. The {thrown exception} constraint for the process indicates that the generated code for the OrderBooking class involves throwing an exception. Based on the model, a complete code for the OrderBooking class can be generated.

Business Process Pattern

Patterns can be fine-grained and cover only the design and / or implementation of a particular data or architectural structure, algorithms such as account verification or error logging, or the use of certain elements of software components. It can also cover the entire process of a business process. Take the example of a model for the order validation process in a financial institution. The model can represent an abstraction applied to various order validation such as foreign exchange orders, payment orders, security orders, etc. with some differences. The collaborative business components in the process flow, such as customer information, employee information, product, contract, financial instrument, pricing engine, etc., are similar in different order types. In this way, reusable patterns in the form of models, templates and code snippets can be created, which can be parameterized. Once these patterns exist for a business process, repeating the implementation for another business case can be greatly simplified.

A model for the order validation process is shown in figure 7. From this model, the JSON process descriptor shown in figure 2 can be generated. For the program to work, the implementation of each step of the process flow must follow a specific pattern. For example, it must retrieve input data from the context container and place output data in the context container, as previously described. It must return

Figure 6. Order booking process model

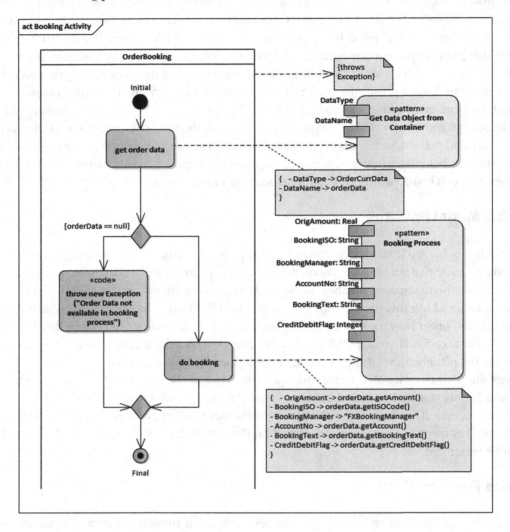

an event after completion. If an error occurs, an error object must be placed in the context container for the error handler to retrieve it.

As shown in figure 7, the model is pretty simple. Adding new process steps or removing existing process steps is a simple task. It provides a plug-and-play mechanism for continuously integrating new process steps that are developed iteratively.

Consequences and Project Experience

Creating generic programs and code generators requires development effort. They have no business benefit. However, experience has shown that projects that focus on architecture and reuse are typically completed successfully and quickly (Pang, 2015; Pang, 2016). The code generators and generic programs described in this chapter are actually quite simple to create. They do not require a sophisticated mecha-

Figure 7. Order validation process flow model

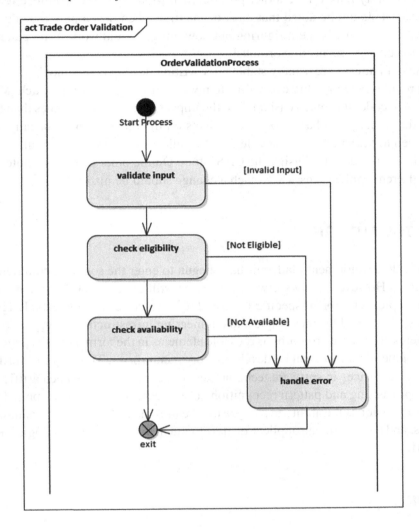

nism. In fact, in one of the first projects where the modeling approach was used, the code was created manually in the same way that a code generator should. This step has shown that the approach is feasible when applied to real projects. The first experience with this approach was a project that initially started with a normal programming approach. After one and three-quarter years of development, progress was too slow and there was no sign of completion. Modeling and generic programming approach were introduced to rebuild the project from scratch. It only took four months to complete the project with some primitive code generators installed. When completed, there were 800 change requests. All of them were easy to integrate into the application. Since then, many new applications have been created using the same approach for 15 years. They were all completed on time and within budget.

Many programmers would say that they can write modules and JSON scripts just as fast as modeling and code generation. One key difference is that you can present a model in a meeting with users, business analysts, and stakeholders, and change it immediately. This is not possible with a code. Models are also great for documentation. They give an overview of how the application works. Code written by one programmer is rarely reused by another programmer. Model patterns optimize reuse. In terms of development speed, it should be noted that most of the time when developing a module is not writing the code. Rather, a lot of time is spent figuring out how things should work. With patterns and generic programs, this effort can be reduced enormously.

Code segments of patterns are usually stable after writing, testing and deploying. The reuse of these code segments provides better quality every time to rewrite similar code from scratch. Models are much easier to change than code. It is much easier to see the impact of the model changes than the code. Often, changing the code in one place has unexpected effects on the others. This is usually not the case for models. If you need to set a new business rule for all applications in this pattern, all programs that use this pattern can be easily identified using the CASE tool. On the other hand, it is quite difficult to find all the code in different applications where such a change should be made.

VISION FOR THE FUTURE

Low-code or no-code development platforms have begun to enter the software community trend. They hold many promises. However, many software developers still believe that they are not suitable for applications with complex, enterprise-specific logic and infrastructure requirements. Large organizations have the most basic logic and business logic and engineering infrastructure components. If they can be identified together with generic programs as reusable elements in the form of model patterns, a low-code or no-code development platform can be developed for an enterprise. This requires further research.

Other important advances in software technologies in recent years have been artificial intelligence, natural language processing and pattern recognition. These technologies can be applied to software development. A future vision is the ability to analyze user requirements, create new business rules, identify program patterns, and then automate application development using these technologies. Research in this area is paying off.

CONCLUSION

Do not get stuck by reinventing the wheel, but go ahead and build on what has been done. If something has already been done, try reusing it as often as possible. Reuse is an important topic in software development. Because design patterns have been introduced, reuse is not limited to code. It has been extended to analysis and design concepts as well as the way things are to be done.

Despite the benefits of reuse in application development, it is not common for application programmers to develop classes or modules that are reusable. Reuse is always restricted to developers who reuse their own previous works. The popularity of the agile software development approach does not really encourage building reusable software elements. More emphasis has been put on the rapid coding and development of program elements that seem to have the highest business value for end users. Systematic reuse requires engineering and support tools. It has no obvious business value and therefore is not even be considered. This chapter has shown that this is a mistake. The systematic reuse of software elements can improve the software development process, enabling fast delivery of high quality software and easy adaptation to changes.

The main reusable software elements including application systems, subsystems or frameworks, components, modules, objects, and functions or procedures with their motivation, implementation concept, consequences and applicability in agile development process are described in this chapter. Three approaches to develop reusable software artefacts that evolved out of 15 years of experience in agile development process are presented. The first approach is to create generic programs or configurable frameworks that support similar solutions for a variety of use cases and environments. Reuse of pattern is the second approach presented. Another effective way, not just for reuse but for general software development, is to use a model-driven approach with model patterns. These approaches can pave the way for a corporation to have a low-code development platform.

This chapter describes the key reusable software elements, including application systems, subsystems or frameworks, components, modules, objects, and functions or procedures, with their motivation, implementation concept, consequences, and applicability in the agile development process. Three approaches to the development of reusable software artifacts, resulting from 15 years of experience in the agile development process, are presented. The first approach is to create generic programs or configurable frameworks that support similar solutions for a variety of use cases and environments. The reuse of patterns is the second approach presented. Another effective way, not just for reuse but for general software development, is to use a model-driven approach with model patterns. These approaches can pave the way for a corporation to develop a low-code development platform.

To encourage reuse, the development teams must build a culture. It does not come automatically. Development teams need to recognize and enforce the benefits. By training the development team, providing tools and infrastructure for reusable libraries, creating configurable frameworks, adapting the model-driven approach to code generation, and so on, the reuse culture of the development team can evolve.

REFERENCES

Agile Manifesto Group. (2001). Manifesto for Agile Software Development. *Agile Manifesto*. Retrieved July 26, 2010, from http://agilemanifesto.org

Ambler, S. W. (2010). Agile Modeling. *Ambysoft*. Retrieved July 26, 2010, from http://www.agilemodeling.com/

Biggerstaff, T. J., & Perlis, A. J. (1989). *Frontier Series: Software Reusability* (Vols. 1-2). New York, N.Y.: ACM Press.

Biggerstaff, T. J., & Richter, C. (1989). Reusability Framework, Assessment, and Directions. Frontier Series: Software Reusability: Vol. I. *Concepts and Models*. ACM Press.

Chan, M. (2019). SQL vs. NoSQL – what's the best option for your database needs? *Thorn Technologies*. Retrieved July 19, 2019, from https://www.thorntech.com/2019/03/sql-vs-nosql

Clark, L. (2019). No developers required: Why this company chose no-code over software devs. *ZDNet*. Retrieved June 26, 2019, from https://www.zdnet.com/google-amp/article/no-developers-required-why-this-company-chose-no-code-over-software-devs/

Fowler, M. (1996). *Analysis Patterns: Reusable Object Models*. Boston, MA: Addison-Wesley.

Fowler, M. (2006). *Patterns of Enterprise Application Architecture*. Boston, MA: Addison-Wesley.

Frakes, W. B., & Kang, K. (2005). Software Reuse Research: Status and Future. *IEEE Transactions on Software Engineering, 13*(7), 529–536. doi:10.1109/TSE.2005.85

Freeman, P. (1987). *Tutorial: Software Reusability*. Los Alamitos, CA: IEEE Computer Society Press.

Gamma, E., Helm, R., Johnson, R., & Vlissides, L. (1995). *Design Patterns: Elements of Reusable Object-Oriented Software*. Reading, MA: Addison-Wesley.

Geyer-Schulz, A., & Hahsler, M. (2001). Software Engineering with Analysis Patterns. *CiteSeerX*. Retrieved May 26, 2019, from http://citeseerx.ist.psu.edu/viewdoc/summary?doi=10.1.1.70.8415

Harlow, M. (2014). Coconut Headphones: Why Agile Has Failed. *Code Rant*. Retrieved December 11, 2014, from http://mikehadlow.blogspot.ch/2014/03/coconut-headphones-why-agile-has-failed.html

Hastie, S., & Wojewoda, S. (2015). Standish Group 2015 Chaos Report - Q&A with Jennifer Lynch. *InfoQ*. Retrieved from May 26, 2019, from https://www.infoq.com/articles/standish-chaos-2015

Horowitz, E., & Munson, J. B. (1984, September). An Expansive View of Reusable Software. *IEEE Transaction on Software Engineering SE, 10*(5), 477–487. doi:10.1109/TSE.1984.5010270

Ismail, N. (2017). UK wasting 37 billion a year on failed agile IT projects. *Information Age*. Retrieved May 26, 2019, from https://www.information-age.com/uk-wasting-37-billion-year-failed-agile-it-projects-123466089/

Jacobson, I., Griss, M., & Jonsson, P. (1997). *Software Reuse. Architecture, Process and Organization for Business Success*. Reading, MA: Addison Wesley.

Jazayeri, M., Loos, R. G. K., & Musser, D. R. (1998). Generic Programming. In *International Seminar on Generic Programming Dagstuhl Castle, Germany*. Berlin, Germany: Springer.

Jones, C. (1984). Reusability in programming: A survey of the state of the art. *IEEE Transactions on Software Engineering, 10*(5), 488–494. doi:10.1109/TSE.1984.5010271

Kramer, J., & Finkelstein, A. (1991). A Configurable Framework for Method and Tool Integration. *European Symposium on Software Development Environments and CASE Technology*. Retrieved May 26, 2019, from http://citeseerx.ist.psu.edu/viewdoc/download?doi=10.1.1.129.7971&rep=rep1&type=pdf

Krueger, C. W. (1992). Software Reuse. *ACM Computing Surveys, 24*(2), 131–183. doi:10.1145/130844.130856

Larman, C. (2003). *Agile and Iterative Development: A Manager's Guide*. Reading, MA: Addison-Wesley.

Leach, R. J. (2011). *Software Reuse: Methods, Models, and Costs*. Retrieved May 26, 2019, from https://pdfs.semanticscholar.org/700b/83bc8d4a2e4c1d1f4395a4c8fb78462c9f5a.pdf

MDA. (2010). MDA – The Architecture of Choice for a Changing World. *OMG*. Retrieved July 12, 2017, from https://www.omg.org/mda/

Mellor, S. J., Scott, K., Uhl, A., & Weise, D. (2004). *MDA Distilled: Principles of Model-Driven Architecture*. Reading, MA: Addison-Wesley.

Meyer, B. (1988). Genericity Versus Inheritance. *Journal of Pascal, Ada, & Modula-2, 7*(2), 13-30.

Pang, C. Y. (2001). A Design Pattern Type Extension with Facets and Decorators. *Journal of Object-Oriented Programming, 13*(13), 14–18.

Pang, C. Y. (2015). Ten Years of Experience with Agile and Model Driven Software Development in a Legacy Platform. In A. Singh (Ed.), *Emerging Innovations in Agile Software Development*. Hershey, PA: IGI Global.

Pang, C. Y. (2016). An Agile Architecture for a Legacy Enterprise IT System. *International Journal of Organizational and Collective Intelligence, 6*(4), 65–97. doi:10.4018/IJOCI.2016100104

Rehkopf, M. (2019). User Stories. *Atlassian Agile Guide*. Retrieved May 22, 2019, from https://www.atlassian.com/agile/project-management/user-stories

Richards, M. (2015). *Software Architecture Patterns*. Sebastopol, CA: O'Reilly.

Shiff, L., & Rowe, W. (2018). NoSQL vs SQL: Examining the Differences and Deciding Which to Choose. *Bmc*. Retrieved July 11, 2019, from https://www.bmc.com/blogs/sql-vs-nosql

Software Crisis. (2010). Software Crisis. *Wikipedia*. Retrieved July 26, 2010, from http://en.wikipedia.org/wiki/Software_crisis

Software Engineering. (2010). Software Engineering. Wikipedia. Retrieved July 26, 2010, from http://en.wikipedia.org/wiki/Software_engineering

Sommerville, I. (2015). *Software Engineering* (10th ed.). Essex, UK: Pearson Education Limited.

Soora, S. K. (2014). A Framework for Software Reuse and Research *Challenges. International Journal of Advanced Research in Computer Science and Software Engineering, 4*(8), 441–448.

Stellman, A., & Greene, J. (2015). *Learning Agile: Understand SCRUM, XP, Lean, and Kanban*. Sebastopol, CA: O'Reilly.

Wake, B. (2018). Back to basics: Writing and splitting user stories. *Medium.com*. Retrieved May 25, 2019, from https://medium.com/agile-outside-the-box/back-to-basics-writing-and-splitting-user-stories-8903a931499c

ADDITIONAL READING

Agile Software Development Process, & the Agile Manifesto Group. (2001). Manifesto for Agile Software Development. *Agile Manifesto*. http://agilemanifesto.org

Ambler, S. W. (2010). Agile Modeling. *Ambysoft*. Retrieved July 26, 2010, from http://www.agilemodeling.com/

Bass, L., Clements, P., & Kazman, R. (2003). *Software Architecture in Practice* (2nd ed.). Reading, MA: Addison-Wesley.

Erl, T. (2009). *SOA Design Patterns*. Upper Saddle River, NJ: Prentice Hall PTR.

Ezran, M., Morisio, M., & Tully, C. (2002). *Practical Software Reuse*. London, UK: Springer. doi:10.1007/978-1-4471-0141-3

Fowler, M. (1997). *Analysis Patterns: Reusable Object Models*. Reading, MA: Addison-Wesley.

Fowler, M. (2006). *Patterns of Enterprise Application Architecture*. Reading, MA: Addison-Wesley.

Gamma, E., Helm, R., Johnson, R., & Vlissides, L. (1995). *Design Patterns: Elements of Reusable Object-Oriented Software*. Reading, MA: Addison-Wesley.

Garland, J., & Anthony, R. (2003). *Large-Scale Software Architecture: A Practical Guide using UML*. West Sussex, UK: John Wiley & Son.

Geetha, C., Subramanian, C., & Dutt, S. (2015). *Software Engineering*. Delhi, India: Pearson Education India.

Hohpe, G., & Woolfe, B. (2004). *Enterprise Integration Patterns: Designing, Building, and Deploying Messaging Solutions*. Reading, MA: Addison-Wesley.

Hunt, J. (2006). *Agile Software Construct*. London, UK: Springer.

Larman, C. (2003). *Agile and Iterative Development: A Manager's Guide*. Reading, MA: Addison-Wesley.

McGovern, J., Ambler, S. W., Stevens, M. E., Linn, J., Sharan, V., & Jo, E. K. (2003). *A Practical Guide To Enterprise Architecture*. Upper Saddle River, NJ: Prentice Hall PTR.

Mellor, S. J., Scott, K., Uhl, A., & Weise, D. (2004). *MDA Distilled: Principles of Model-Driven Architecture*. Reading, MA: Addison-Wesley.

Model-Driven Approach to Software Development. Arlow, J. & Neustadt, I. (2004). Enterprise Patterns and MDA: Building Better Software with Archetype Patterns and UML. Reading, MA: Addison-Wesley.

Shamil, F. R. (2019). Software reuse and software reuse oriented software engineering. T4 Tutorials. Retrieved July 11, 2019, from https://t4tutorials.com/software-reuse-and-software-reuse-oriented-software-engineering/

Sommerville, I. (2015). *Software Engineering* (10th ed.). Essex, UK: Pearson Education Limited.

KEY TERMS AND DEFINITIONS

Agile Software Development Process: An evolutionary and iterative approach to software development with focuses on adaptation to changes.

COBOL: The programming language designed for commercial business data processing used for applications that often form the backbone of the IT structure in many corporations since 1960.

CRUD (Create, Read, Update, and Delete): Basic functions of a computer database.

Design Pattern: A reusable solution to a common problem in a particular software design context.

Document-Oriented Database: A database designed for storing, retrieving and managing document-oriented information, also known as semi-structured data.

Generic Programming: An implementation of an algorithm with elements that have more than one interpretation, depending on parameters representing types.

JSON (JavaScript Object Notation): An open-standard file format that uses human-readable text to transmit data objects consisting of attribute–value pairs and array data type.

MDA (Model-Driven Architecture): An approach to structuring software specifications that are expressed as models for software design, development, and implementation.

Model-Driven Approach to Software Development: A model centric rather than a code centric approach to software development with code generated from models.

NoSQL: A non-SQL database that provides a mechanism for storage and retrieval of data that is modeled in means other than the tabular relations used in relational databases.

Plain Old Java Object (POJO): An ordinary Java object, not bound by any special restriction and not requiring any class path.

Service-Oriented Architecture (SOA): A technical software architecture that allows client applications to request services from service provider type applications in a host system.

Software Component: A software unit of functionality that manages a single abstraction.

Software Engineering: The application of engineering to the development of software in a systematic method.

Software Reuse: The process of creating software systems from predefined software components.

Spring Framework: An application framework and inversion of control container for the Java platform.

UML (Unified Modeling Language): A general-purpose, developmental, modeling language in the field of software engineering that is intended to provide a standard way to visualize the design of a system.

XML (Extensible Markup Language): A markup language that defines a set of rules for encoding documents in a format that is both human-readable and machine-readable.

Section 3
Testing and Maintenance

This section covers testing and maintenance.

Chapter 8
Software Testing

Pooja Kaplesh
Chandigarh University, India

Severin K. Y. Pang
Cognitive Solutions and Innovation AG, Switzerland

ABSTRACT

Testing software is a process of program execution with the intent to find errors. For this purpose, various testing techniques have been used over time. Testing software is an intensive field of research in which much development work has been done. This field will become increasingly important in the future. There are many techniques for software testing. This chapter gives an overview of the entire range of software testing with suggestions for their implementation. One focus is on testing in an agile development process why the different types of software tests are important, and their cycle and methodology are described. In addition, different levels, types, and a comparative study on different types of tests are presented. The chapter also includes suggestions for performing the various tests and an effective approach to testing a software system.

INTRODUCTION

Software testing is an activity to test whether a software system provides the expected functionality and performance and to ensure that it is error free as far as possible. In doing so, a software or system component is executed to evaluate one or more characteristics of interest. Test software also helps to find errors, gaps or missing requirements as opposed to actual requirements. This can be done either manually or with automated tools. Some refer to software testing as white box or black box testing. In simple terms, software testing is a process for verifying and validating the tested application.

Software testing is an important activity as it is designed to ensure the quality of a software system. All software systems must function properly and reliably. Unrecognized software defects or errors can cause a software system to behave unexpectedly. Unreliable software can lead to a loss of customer business, which can cause huge losses for the company, as in the case of the MP3 player from Microsoft - the crash of Zune. Failures of software systems cause not only financial losses, but also the reputation of

DOI: 10.4018/978-1-7998-2531-9.ch008

the company. Well-tested software systems usually pay off. An early detection of errors and deficiencies would require less effort to fix than if they were discovered at a late stage. Software testing should therefore not be late to start in development.

This chapter explains various aspects of software testing and how they should be carried out. The purpose of this chapter is to give an overview of the entire test spectrum with suggestions for their implementation. A main focus is on testing in an agile development process. The chapter begins with a section on the background software testing. The first aspect that is discussed concerns the lifecycle of software testing. There are different types and levels of tests. They are explained in the following sections. Subsequently, test cases will be discussed with an example. The following are topics about software testing techniques and alpha versus beta testing. After that, an effective test approach is presented. The last topic concerns the skills of the testers and the quality assurance (QA) team. The chapter ends with a conclusion.

BACKGROUND

Software tests are used to determine the correctness of software assuming some specific hypotheses. In the early days of software development, debugging was the primary form of software testing. It was mainly done by the programmer who wrote the code, and the goal was to get the application up and running without causing the system to crash. Myers (1979) first introduced the separation of debugging and testing. Since then software testing has become an important field of research, and much has been developed in this area. Information on software test research can be found in the articles by Bertolino (2007), Chauhan & Singh (2014), Pettichord et al. (2008) and Sneha & Malle (2017).

The main objectives of the software test are summarized below (Myers, 1979; Chauhan & Singh, 2014):

- Detection: Various errors, defects and deficiencies are detected. The system capabilities and various limitations, the quality of all components, the work products, and the overall system are evaluated.
- Prevention: This information is used to prevent or reduce errors, clarify system specifications, and measure system performance. Different ways are shown to avoid risks and solve future problems.
- Demonstration: It shows how the system can be used with various acceptable risks. It also shows that functions with special conditions are ready for integration and how the product can be used.
- Improving quality: Effective software testing minimizes errors and improves the quality of the software.
- Verification: Verify that the system behaves as specified. It checks and tests elements for software compliance and consistency by evaluating the results against predefined requirements. In verification, we ask a question: Are we building the product properly?
- Validation: Check the correctness of the system by checking what users have specified and what they actually want. In validation, we ask the question: are we building the right system?

There are many approaches to testing software. Reviews, walkthroughs, or inspections are referred to as static testing, while the execution of programmed code with a particular set of test cases is called dynamic testing. Static testing includes verification, while dynamic tests include validation. In this chapter we focus more on dynamic testing.

Figure 1. STLC phases

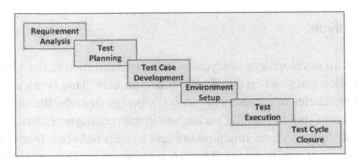

In a traditional software lifecycle with the waterfall model (Royce, 1970, Bell & Thayer, 1976), the final stage of a software development process is verification when performing various tests such as final integration, acceptance tests, performance tests, and so on. This type of development process with successive stages of development has been considered ineffective in the software community. In 2001, a group of prominent software developers came together to define a set of principles for software development. What emerged was the Agile Manifesto (Agile Manifesto Group, 2001). It triggered a new movement in the software community with an agile development process and was widely accepted. The agile development process follows the evolutionary and iterative approach of software development (Ambler, 2010; Larman, 2003) and focuses on adapting to change. Agile tests have emerged. This topic is also covered in this chapter.

SOFTWARE TESTING LIFE CYCLE (STLC) AND AGILE TESTING PROCESS

The Software Testing Life Cycle (STLC) is a set of activities performed by a QA team to methodically test the software product. The term "testing" not only includes testers in STLC but also, in some cases, business analysts, developers and stakeholders. In STLC, test cases are executed. This section develops the STLC model with a concluding section on agility testing.

Different Phases of the STLC Model

Figure 1 shows the phases involved in the STLC. Each of these phases is linked to a specific entry and exit criterion as well as to activities and services. The entry criteria contain the required elements that must be executed before starting the test process. The exit criteria define the items that must be completed before the test can be completed.

Entry and exit criteria must be defined for all levels in the STLC. Theoretically, the subsequent phase would not begin until the exit criteria for the previous phase are met. In practice this is not always possible. In this section, we therefore focus on activities and deliverables for the specific phases of the STLC lifecycle.

STLC Phases

1. Requirement Analysis:

In the traditional software development lifecycle with a waterfall model, the QA team would only be involved in the verification phase when development is complete. This is not effective. As mentioned earlier, the later the deficiencies in requirement analysis, design or code, the more difficult the corrections become. The QA team should actually participate in the requirements analysis. During this phase, the QA team must analyze the system functionality and system behavior from a test point of view to become aware of the testable requirements. The QA team must work with various stakeholders such as customers, business analysts, technical managers, systems architects, etc. to understand the requirements in detail. The requirements can be both functional (what the software program should do) and non-functional (which defines the overall performance, security, availability, etc. of the system). At this stage, the feasibility of automation for the given test mission should also be explored.

Activities in this phase are:

- Study and analyze the types of tests to be carried out
- Gather details on testing priorities
- Create a Requirement Traceability Matrix (RTM)
- Identify details about the test environment where testing is carried out
- Feasibility assessment of automation (if needed)
- Create usage scenario simulations with wire frame and mock-ups to review requirements with stakeholders
  Deliverables in this phase include:
- RTM report
- Report on the feasibility assessment of automation (if planned)

2. Test Planning:

In this phase the test strategy or the test plan is defined. A senior QA manager would identify the required effort and cost estimate for the project and then create and complete the test plan that needs to be executed.

Activities in this phase are:

- Preparation of test plan/strategy document for different types of testing
- Training requirement
- Estimation of the test effort
- Test tool selection
- Resource planning and definition of roles and responsibilities

Deliverables in this phase include:

- Test plan / strategy document
- Effort estimation document

3. Test Case Development:

The creation, verification and revision of test cases and test scripts are done in this phase of the STLC. Test data must be identified, verified and then transformed.

Activities in this phase are:

- Create test cases, automation scripts (if required)
- Analyze, review and align test cases and scripts
- Design test data (if test environment is set up)

Deliverables in this phase include:

- Test data
- Test cases / scripts

4. Test Environment Setup:

The test environment addresses the hardware and software conditions under which a project is tested. Setting up the test environment is an important phase in the testing process. Setting up the test environment can be done in parallel with the test case development. The test team may not participate in this task if the customer or the development team provides the test environment. In this case, the test team must perform a readiness check (smoke test) of the given environment.

Activities in this phase are:

- Prepare hardware and software requirement list and analyze required architecture and environment setup for the test environment
- Make a list of hardware and software requirements and analyze the required architecture and environment setup for the test environment
- Set up test data and test environment
- Perform smoke test

Deliverables in this case include:

- Smoke test results
- Standby environment with test data

5. Test Execution:

The testers would run tests based on the test plans and the test cases created in an earlier phase. The test results will be reported to the development team. In case of defect detection, the development team must fix the error and redeploy the code. After the correction, re-test is performed.

Activities in this phase are:

- Run tests and document test results
- Log defects for failed cases
- Assign defect to test cases and retest the fixes
- Track the defects to completion

Deliverables in this phase include:

- RTM completed with the execution status
- Defect reports
- Updated test cases with results

6. Test Cycle Closure:

The test team would meet, discuss and analyze test artifacts to identify methods that need to be enforced in the future. The process is similar to the sprint retrospective of a Scrum development process (Scrum, 2019). It is an opportunity for the QA team to inspect themselves and make a plan for improvements to be implemented in the next cycle. The team members learn from the lessons of the current cycle. The idea is to eliminate the method bottlenecks and implement best practices for similar cases in the future.
Activities in this phase are:

- Measure cycle completion criteria, time, coverage, cost, software quality, and key business goals
- Prepare metrics for test support with higher parameters
- Document the lessons learn from the project
- Create final report
- Report qualitatively and quantitatively on the quality of the work product for the customer
- Analyze the result to sort the defect distribution by severity

Deliverables in this phase include:

- Test closure report
- Test metrics

Agile Testing

Agile testing (Crispin & Gregory, 2009) is a software testing practice that follows the principles of agile software development. Unlike the traditional waterfall approach, the agile development process follows the evolutionary and iterative approach of software development (Ambler, 2010, Larman, 2003) and focuses on adapting to change. In an agile approach, the development process is divided into small parts of iterations. In each iteration, requirements analysis, design, coding and testing of a software element are performed. The iteration is not completed until the software element has been fully tested. If the process also supports continuous integration, an integration test must also be performed in the software system.

In the traditional software development approach, we have a separate QA team responsible for testing in the verification phase of the development process. Agile testing, on the other hand, involves all members of a cross-functional, agile team with specialist in testing to ensure that the business value desired by the customer is achieved. The STLC model can actually be applied to an iteration. The test planning is part of the development planning in the iteration. Part of the design of the software element is actually the design of the test cases for the software element. In fact, Test Driven Development (TDD) (Beck, 2002; Astels, 2003) suggests writing a test before writing a production code. It is based on coding guided by tests. The iteration is completed when the test cycle is complete. The entire STLC must fit within the timeframe of an iteration, which is usually two weeks to a month.

Inspired by the agile manifesto, some software developers have devised a version of the test manifesto (Laing, 2015). The test manifesto includes:

1. Testing throughout over testing at the end.
2. Preventing bugs over finding bugs.
3. Testing understanding over checking functionality.
4. Building the best system over breaking the system.
5. Team responsibility for quality over tester responsibility.

This manifesto defines the direction in which agile testing moves.

TYPES OF TESTING

There are mainly two types of testing, namely manual testing and automated testing. They are described in the following subsections.

Manual Testing

Manual testing is a type of test where testers run test cases manually without automation tools. Manual testing is a simple test method that can pinpoint bugs in the code. Each new application should be manually tested before machine-controlled testing. Manual testing requires a lot of effort. However, it is important to confirm the feasibility of automation testing. Manual testing does not require a sophisticated testing tool. As a rule, 100% automation is not possible. Manual tests are always required.

The following list shows how manual testing should be done by the QA team:

- Read the guidelines in the Software Requirement Specification (SRS) and understand the documentation of the software project
- Design test cases that cover all requirements in the documentation
- Review and discuss the test cases with the team leader and, if necessary, with the customer
- Execute the test cases on the AUT
- Report bugs
- If bugs are resolved, rerun the failed test cases to see if they have passed

There are different kinds of tests that can be done manually. They are listed below, and further elaboration of the test types will be presented later in this chapter:

1. Black Box Testing
2. White Box Testing
3. Grey Box Testing
4. Unit Testing
5. System Testing
6. Integration Testing
7. Acceptance Testing

Here are some common myths and facts about manual testing:

Myth: Everyone can test manually
Fact: Testing requires many technical or non-technical skills
Myth: Testing guarantees 100% error-free product
Fact: Testing ensures that as many defects as possible are detected. Identifying and correcting all possible defects is difficult or impossible.
Myth: Automated testing is more powerful than manual testing
Fact: 100% automation tests cannot be performed. Manual tests are also mandatory
Myth: Testing is simple and easy
Fact: Testing is considered a challenging task. Testing an application with minimal test cases requires high analytical capabilities

Automated Testing and Test Automation

Manual testing is performed by a person or tester who sits in front of a computer system and carefully performs the test cases or steps. Automated testing and test automation use software to run a test case suite. The automation software can also review the test statistics of the system being tested, compare predicted and actual results, and produce specific test reports (Bhaggan, 2009).

Automated testing and test automation are different. Automated testing is the process of performing specific tests through automation (that is, a series of regression tests) as opposed to manual execution, while test automation refers to automating the process of tracking and managing the various tests (McMeekin, 2017). In this chapter, the authors use the term automation testing to capture both cases.

Why Automation Testing?

Successive development cycles require repeated execution of identical test suites. With a test automation tool, it is possible to store this test suite and play it again if necessary. Once the test suite is automated, no human intervention is required. This increased the return of investment (ROI) of automation testing. The goal of automation is to limit the number of test cases to be executed manually. The motivation behind automation in testing include the following points (Hayes, 2004):

- Manually testing all fields, all workflows, and all negative scenarios is costly, time-consuming, and automation testing can bring huge savings, especially if the test cases need to be repeated many times
- Manual testing can become boring and therefore error prone
- It is difficult to test multilingual websites manually
- No human intervention is required for automation. One can run machine driven test unattended (overnight)
- Automation can increase test coverage
- Automation testing speeds up the test execution
- For load or performance tests that send thousands of input data to the system, it is not possible to do it manually

Automated Testing Variations

There are several types of automated testing. The most common ones are described below:

- Automated Unit Testing: For this type of testing, test programs must normally be written at the code level. The test programs are usually written in test functions, methods, and routines programmed by the developers. Typical tools for automated component testing are JUNIT for Java programs and NUNIT for .NET programs. JUNIT offers a test suite that bundles a number of test cases. The suite can be expanded with new unit tests. It can be executed each time the software is extended or changed to ensure that all units continue to function properly.
- Component API Testing: Software components provide a set of well-defined APIs. Scripts can be written to test the components to automate the API calls. The API allows testers to verify component requirements regardless of their GUI implementation.
- Web Services Testing: What is tested here are usually the functional, compliance, and security issues. In web applications, one can test the request and response of the applications, whether they are secure and encrypted or not, and the correct response to the request. The most popular tool for testing web services is SoapUI.
- GUI testing: Many test automation tools provide recording and playback capabilities that allow users to interactively record user actions and play them as often as they like, comparing actual results with expected ones. The advantage of this approach is that little or no software development is required. This approach can be applied to any application that has a graphical user interface.

Automated Testing Approaches

For automated testing, software is required to carry out the testing process. This test software is usually created as follows:

- Creation of test modules:
  JUNIT is mentioned as a unit test tool for testing Java classes and methods. To use JUNIT, one has to write a test class with methods to build the class and call the method one wants to test. The determination of whether the test was successful or not can be based on the methods to be tested yielding the expected results. The component test classes and methods can be combined into a suite that can be used for future repeated testing of application classes and methods. A test module

(or test method) should not be complicated and perform many other functions than performing a particular test. Otherwise, the test module must also be tested.

- Scripts Programming:

Programming scripts involves writing test scripts (Milad et al., 2014). Test Script is a series of commands or events stored in a script language file to run a test case and report the results. It can contain logical decisions that affect the execution of the script, as well as several possible paths, constant values, and variables. The advantage of test scripts is that scripts can repeat the same statement several times in loops of different data. Test scripts can be written in scripting languages such as Javascript, Perl, Python, Ruby, Tcl, Unix shell scripts, and so on. It is easy to write test scripts in Perl that send XML or JSON messages to a web application and validate the response messages (Sawyer, 2014). The script can send thousands of messages to the web application to test the workload or performance.

There are several test automation frameworks that provide rule sets for writing scripts that result in "less maintenance." The most popular are the following (Saad, 2019):

- Linear - Simplest form of creating a test, possibly generated by tools like those that use record and playback. Just write one single program without modularity in sequential steps.
- Structured - Test script uses control structures - typically 'if-else', 'switch', 'for', 'while' conditions / statements.
- Modularity - Objects (e.g. button, menu) are created together with small and precise methods (e.g. clickButton (), selectMenuItem ()) so that individual functions are defined once and reusable in all test methods. The test script is the collection of these small methods and reusable objects.
- Data driven - Test data (input and output values) are separated from the script and stored in external files. When the script is run, these values are selected from external files, stored in variables, and replace the hard-coded values, if any.
- Keyword driven - Different keywords are created for different data and actions in the main script, which can only be referenced. Both data and actions are defined outside the script. The functionality to be tested is written in tabular form using the keywords. This table is stored in external files. The script analyzes this table and performs the appropriate actions (Rashmi & Bajpai, 2012; Rantanen, 2007).
- Hybrid - Two or more of the above patterns are used.

- Tools:

Instead of modules or scripts for building automation tests, open source or commercial tools can also be used. For example, SoapUI is an open source test tool that allows testers to set up automation tests. Naveen (2015) provides a step-by-step example of using SoapUI to set up automation tests. As mentioned earlier, many test automation tools provide recording and playback capabilities that allow users to interactively record user actions and play them as often as they like, comparing the actual results with the expected ones. Most of them are commercial products. For an overview of some test tools and techniques, see the article by Chaudhary (2017). In his review one will find various tools for test management, functional tests and load tests.

Agile Development and Automated Testing

The agile development process typically involves continuous deployment with a series of short iterations in a development and deployment pipeline. The main focus of an agile system is on the flexibility and easy adaptation of changes throughout the development lifecycle. Continuous integration and continuous provision require continuous testing (Sadiq, 2019). Regression testing is required to ensure that code changes do not break the existing code base. Therefore, automated testing is essential for agile development. Writing automated test scripts should be part of the development process. The test suite should be incrementally built in each development iteration. In other words, continuous integration of test cases into the test suite is required. The agile concept should also be applied to testing.

Strategies for automating agile testing can be found in the article by Collins et al. (2012). Various automation testing tools can also be found in Agile Testing by Tutorials Point (2016).

Testing Approach

Developers should never deploy software elements without first testing them themselves. The first tests refer to software units and are usually performed manually. Developers typically use debuggers to go through the code they write and see if they work as intended. After the initial manual tests, the unit test cases can be grouped together in a test-suite for future testing. The test-suit should ensure that all units continue to function as the existing code is changed, expanded, and extended with new features. This would start the process of the automation testing. In fact, automation testing should only be done after manual testing. Manual tests should always be performed first, especially if the software system is not yet stable. Applying automation tests too early can cause the test programs and scripts to be rewritten or new settings made when extensive explorations, changes, or corrections are required. If certain parts of the software system are stable, automation tests should be set up, especially as the system starts to grow. Without automation testing, maintenance costs can skyrocket as the system grows large, and regression testing would be very costly if performed manually. The larger the system, the greater the need for automation testing. Load and performance tests can normally only be performed with automated tests. They should only be done if the system is stable enough for such tests.

In an agile development process, software elements are developed step-by-step in small iterations. At each iteration, the product must be stable and well tested. The TDD Approach suggests designing test cases together with the software module before coding is started. After the requirements analysis test scripts can be written and test data can be created. These scripts and data would be part of the automation test. The developers creating the software modules still had to do manual tests. The development iteration will not complete until the test with these scripts and data is completed successfully. If continuous integration into the development process is required, test scripts and data for the new features must also be included in the automation testing of the integrated system. Thus automation tests are constructed iteratively. Because the agile approach to software development focuses on flexibility and adaptability to change, the software for automation testing must also be agile and flexible. They go hand in hand.

LEVELS OF TESTING

This section describes various levels of testing in the following subsections.

Unit Testing

Unit testing is a very important type of software testing that tests individual software components. Unit testing of software applications are performed during the development (encoding) of an application. The goal of unit testing is to isolate part of the code and verify its correctness. In procedural programming, a unit can also be a single function or procedure. Unit tests are usually done by the developer.

In the STLC cycle, unit testing is the first test that is performed before the integration test. Unit tests are a type of white box testing performed by the developer. Due to the time constraints or the lack of willingness of the developers to test, testers can perform the correct component tests during the development phase to save time and money. There are several tools that can be used to test units. As is already mentioned, JUNIT is typical. In order to use JUNIT, the unit test class must be written. This is usually done by the developer. If a tester is to test with JUNIT, the tester must either be able to write the unit test code or modify the existing code with new data to test the other scenario.

Specific reasons for performing unit tests are as follows:

- Unit testing fix bugs / errors at the beginning of the development cycle and reduce costs.
- It helps developers to understand the code base so they can quickly make the necessary changes

The advantages of unit testing are:

- Unit testing allows a developer to revise the code at a later date to ensure the module continues to function properly. The method is to write down test cases for all functions and features so that any change that causes a defect can quickly locate and correct the cause. As already mentioned, a test-suite containing a bundle of unit tests can be built. The test suite can be run after modifying or extending the software to ensure that all units behave properly.
- Unit tests provide insights into the Unit API for better understanding.
- The tester can test parts of the software without having to wait for development to complete.

Unit tests also have the following disadvantages:

- Testing cannot capture every single defect in an application.
- It is impossible to evaluate every execution path in a software application. The same applies to unit tests.
- The number of scenarios and test data that the developer can use to verify the source code is limited. After all the options have been tried, the component test is stopped and the code is integrated into the system.

Integration Testing

Integration testing is a level of software testing where individual units are combined and tested as a group. The purpose of this level of testing is to expose faults in the interaction between integrated units. A typical software package project consists of multiple software modules, coded by different programmers. Integration Testing focuses on checking interactions amongst these modules. Therefore it is conjointly termed as 'I & T' (Integration and Testing), 'String Testing' and 'Thread Testing'.

The reason for integration testing is that although each software module is unit tested, defects still exist for various reasons like:

Integration testing is software testing that combines individual units and test them as a group. The purpose of this level of testing is to uncover defects in the interaction between integrated units. A typical software package project consists of software modules that are coded by different programmers. Integration testing focuses on verifying the interactions between these modules. Therefore, it is collectively referred to as "I & T" (integration and testing), "string testing" and "thread testing".

Although each software module has been unit tested, there are reasons for integration test, such as:

- Ensures that the software modules work together properly and according to the expectations of the test team, if they are integrated with each other.
- Because modules work together, a change in one module can affect others and cause errors in the system even though the modified module has been unit tested. During development, customer requirements may change at any time. It must be ensured that all modules still work together as expected. In such cases, integration tests must be performed.
- The interfaces of the software modules to the database should be tested.
- Any external hardware interfaces must be tested with software.
- A module is generally designed by a single developer whose perception and programming may be different from other programmers' common sense. Integration testing is required to verify the consistency of the software modules.

System Testing

System Testing is the testing of a complete and fully integrated software product. It is being tested as part of black box testing, that is, during these tests only external work functions of the software are evaluated. It does not require any internal knowledge of code, design, architecture, etc., and is entirely based on the user perspective. It is a method to monitor and evaluate the behavior of the complete and fully integrated software product or system. System testing involves the external view of how the software works from the user's perspective.

System tests are required for the following reasons:

- Test fully integrated applications, including external peripherals, to see how components interact with each other and with the system as a whole. This is also referred to as an end-to-end testing scenario.
- Thoroughly verify all inputs in the application to determine the desired outputs.
- Testing of the user experience with the application.

This is a very basic description of what should be considered in the system test. One needs to create detailed test cases and test-suites that test every aspect of the application from the outside, ignoring the actual source code.

There are several types of system testing. The types of system testing that are commonly used in a large software development company are listed below:

1. Usability Testing - Usability testing is a non-functional testing methodology that checks how easy the system can be used by end users. The focus is on application usability, control flexibility, and the ability of the system to achieve its goals.
2. Load Testing - Load testing is a type of performance testing that determines the performance of a system under real load conditions. It is important to know that a software solution provides the performance required under real load.
3. Regression Testing - The regression testing is a type of software testing that confirms that a recent program or code change did not affect existing functionality. It also ensures that over time no old errors occur by adding new software modules.
4. Recovery Testing - Recovery tests are performed to demonstrate that a software solution is reliable, trustworthy and can successfully resolve possible crashes.
5. Migration Testing - Migration testing ensures that software can be easily transferred from legacy system infrastructures to current system infrastructures.
6. Function Testing - Function testing, also known as the function completeness testing, tests all functions that the system should provide and identifies possible missing functions. Testers may compile a list of additional features that a product needs to improve the system during the functional testing.
7. Hardware / Software Testing - "HW / SW Testing" is performed when the tester focuses on the hardware-software interaction during the system test.

Acceptance Testing

User acceptance testing is defined as a type of test performed by the customer to certify the system in relation to the agreed requirements. This test takes place during the final testing phase before the software application is moved to the market or production environment. The main purpose of this test is to validate the end-to-end business flow. It does NOT focus on cosmetic errors, spelling mistakes or system tests. This kind of testing is performed in a separate test environment with production-like data buildup. It is a kind of black box (explain later) testing involving two or more end users.

Once the software has undergone unit, integration and system testing, the need for acceptance tests may seem superfluous. The acceptance test is still required for the following reasons:

- Developers write code based on a requirements document that matches their "own" understanding of the requirements and may not meet the requirements that the client places on the software.
- Changes to requirements throughout the project may not be effectively communicated to developers.

The sequence of the different test levels is shown in Figure 2. It begins with unit testing, followed by integration testing, system testing, and finally acceptance testing.

Figure 2. Levels of testing

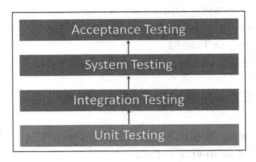

Table 1. Steps of a login page test case

Sr. No.	Functional Test Cases	Type- Negative/ Positive Test Case
1	Verify that a user can log in with a valid username and password.	Positive
2	Verify that a user cannot log in with a valid username but invalid password.	Negative
3	Verify the login page when both fields are blank and the Submit button is clicked.	Negative
4	Verify the 'Forgot Password' functionality.	Positive
5	Verify the messages for invalid login.	Positive
6	Verify the 'Remember Me' functionality.	Positive
7	Verify that the data appears in the password field as either asterisks or bullets.	Positive
8	Verify if a user can log in with a new password after changing the password.	Positive
9	Verify that the login page allows concurrent login with different credentials in a different browser.	Positive
10	On the login page, verify that the keypad 'Enter' key is working properly.	Positive

TEST CASES

A test case is a specification of the inputs, execution conditions, test methods, and expected results that define a single test to be performed to achieve a particular software test goal, for example, to exercise a particular program path or to verify compliance with a specific requirement. It is defined as a series of actions that are performed to validate a particular feature or functionality of the software application. For some tips on writing test cases, see the article by Balamurugan (2019).

A test case should include a title, a description, a precondition, an assumption, expected results, and test steps. An example of a login page test case is given below:

Title: Login page - Authenticating the user to the web application.
Description: A registered user should be able to successfully log in to the web application if the correct username and password are provided. Otherwise, the login should be rejected.
Prerequisite: The user must already be registered with username and password.
Assumption: The user interacts with the web application through a standard browser.

Expected Result: The user can work with the web application after successfully logging in by entering the correct username and password. Otherwise, a pop-up dialog will be displayed with an invalid user and password message.

Test steps: The test steps are given in Table 1.

SOFTWARE TESTING TECHNIQUES

In general, there are three types of testing techniques: black box testing, white box testing, and gray box testing. They are described in the following subsections.

Black Box Testing

Black box testing is a testing technique that tests the functionality of the application under test (AUT) without knowledge of the internal code structure, implementation details, and internal paths of the software. This type of testing is based solely on the software requirements and specifications. Black box testing focuses only on the input and output of the software system.

There are many types of black box tests. The following are the celebrities:

- Functional testing - This type of black box testing is related to the functional requirements of a system. This is usually done by software testers.
- Non-functional testing - This type of black box testing does not relate to testing specific features, but to non-functional requirements such as performance, scalability, usability, etc.
- Regression testing - Regression tests are performed after code fixes, upgrades, or other system maintenance to validate the new code do not affect the existing code adversely.

The black box testing techniques are listed below:

- Equivalence Class Testing: This technique reduces the number of possible test cases to an optimal level while maintaining adequate test coverage. Test items are grouped into classes where all items in each class should behave exactly the same. For example, infants are 0-4 years old. If you create a test case with a 0-year-old infant, you should cover system behavior for all infants. The idea is that you only have to test one of each element to make sure the system works.
- Boundary Value Testing: Boundary value testing concentrates on the values at the limits. This technique determines whether a certain range of values is accepted by the system or not. Using the infant as an example, the limits to be tested are infants aged 0 and 4 years. This is useful to reduce the number of test cases. It is best for systems where input is within certain ranges.
- Decision Table Testing: This testing technique tests system behavior for various input combinations. This is a systematic approach in which the various input combinations and their corresponding system behavior (output) are recorded in tabular form (i.e. decision table). A decision table inserts causes and their effects into a matrix. There is a unique combination in each column.

White Box Testing

White box testing is testing the internal structure, design and coding of a software solution. In this type of testing, the code is visible to the tester. The focus is on checking the flow of input and output through the application, improving the design and usability, and increasing security. White box tests are also referred to as clear box testing, open box testing, structural testing, transparent box testing, code-based testing and glass box testing. It is usually done by developers.

An important white box testing method is code coverage analysis. The code coverage analysis eliminates gaps in a test case suite. It identifies areas of a program that are not exercised by a series of test cases. Once gaps are identified, test cases are created to verify untested parts of the code, thereby increasing the quality of the software product.

For the code coverage analysis, automated tools are available. Here are some coverage analysis techniques:

- Statement Coverage - This technique requires every possible statement in the code to be tested at least once during the software development testing process.
- Branch Coverage - This technique checks every possible path (if-else and other conditional loops) of a software application.

Apart from the above techniques, there are many types of coverage such as condition coverage, multi-condition coverage, path coverage, function coverage, etc. Each technique has its own merits and attempts to test (cover) all portions of the software code. With statement and branch coverage, one can usually achieve 80-90% code coverage, which is sufficient in most cases.

Gray Box Testing

Gray box testing is similar to black box testing. However, designing tests requires knowledge of internal data structures and algorithms. It uses internal data structures and algorithms to design test cases more than black box testing, but much less than white box testing. This method is important when performing integration tests between two or more code modules written by different developers, with only their interfaces exposed for testing. It may also be necessary to set up a specific test environment and provide the database with test data.

ALPHA TESTING VS BETA TESTING (ACCEPTANCE TESTING)

This section explains the alpha and beta tests of the acceptance tests. The testing sequence is shown in figure 3.

Alpha Testing

Alpha testing is a type of acceptance testing that is performed to identify any potential problems / errors before the product is released to everyday users or the public. The goal is to perform the tasks that a typical user might perform. Alpha tests are conducted in a lab environment and usually the testers

Figure 3. Acceptance testing

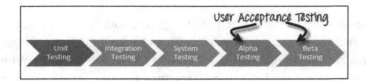

are internal to the organization. To make it as easy as possible, this type of testing is called alpha only because it is done early, toward the end of software development, and before the beta test. The features of the alpha test include:

- It is carried out at the developer's site by testing professionals.
- Both black-box and white-box testing techniques are used.
- It is performed in a well-controlled test environment.
- The test cycle is longer compared to the beta testing.

Beta Testing

Beta testing is another type of acceptance testing. Beta testing of a product is done according to the result of the alpha test by "real users" of the software application in a "real environment". The beta version of the software is released to a limited number of end users of the product for feedback on product quality. Beta testing reduces the risk of product failure and enhances product quality through customer validation. This is the last test before a product is shipped to customers. Direct feedback from customers is a key benefit of the beta testing. These tests allow you to test the product in the customer's environment. Other features of the beta test are:

- Beta testing is a kind of black box testing that is performed in the user's real environment.
- Testing is done by end users, customers and stakeholders.
- This is done after the alpha tests and before the actual release of the software product.
- Generally, software products such as utilities, applications, operating systems, etc. are tested.
- Beta testing is also referred to as field testing and pre-release testing.

EFFECTIVE TESTING APPROACH

Each software project must ensure that the following two aspects apply:

1. The right product is built.
2. The product is built right.

In most cases, the QA team only cares about the quality of the product being built, but does not care about building the right product. The business analysts are responsible for building the right product. If the product being built is not the right product, all the effort to build it properly would be in vain. Redesigning the product after it is built would require much more effort and expense. The QA team should also actively participate in the development of the right product. As mentioned in the STLC section, the QA team should participate in the requirements analysis phase in determining the use of wire frames, and in developing mock-ups for business functions and test data. Simulations of usage scenarios with modeling of system functions and behavior as well as test data can help the stakeholders to validate the requirements of the system. They can illustrate the data that needs to be fed into the system and the outcome of the business processes. The QA team can define the final acceptance criteria together with the stakeholders. This provides better overview of the requirements to the developers.

During the development phase, the QA team should work with business analysts and developers to break down functions and identify their behavior. The QA team should create test cases and data to test each feature and behavior. It should set up automated tests and procedures for test automation. The white box tests should continue to be performed manually by the developers for the code they developed. Code quality can be further enhanced through pair programming, code review and complete code walkthrough, and more. The QA team would do the gray box and black box tests. For Gray Box testing, the QA team would need to design the test data and maintain the database with the developers. The QA team is also responsible for integrating the test cases into the test automation process. Based on the tests performed on the functions, the business analysts should verify that the implemented functions meet the requirements.

In common agile development practice, user stories are generally used to define requirements (User Story, 2019). User stories are usually written by stakeholders and business analysts based on interviews with the end users of the software system. A user story should contain acceptance criteria. The QA team should deal with acceptance criteria for user stories. These criteria form the basis for the design of test cases. In TDD, test cases are also elements of user stories. The test cases of a user story must be executed successfully before the development of this particular user story is considered done.

A correction of the code is required if defects are detected during testing. Similar tests are generally performed to check if the defects are resolved. However, if enhancements or extensions are required, design and implementation must be reworked. This would lead to the development of new test cases that the QA team has to create.

Upon completion of the software system, the QA team would continue to be engaged in acceptance testing, performance and stress testing, designing smoke testing for operations, security testing, etc. The QA team should be heavily involved in the entire development lifecycle of the software system to perform effective testing, regardless of which software development method (e.g., Waterfall or Agile) is used.

SOFTWARE TESTER SKILLS AND TESTING TEAM

Testing is not that easy. Testing requires highly qualified people to understand the program flow and then test it. A software tester requires both technical and non-technical skills.

Non-technical skill required by the software tester include:

- Analytical skills: A good software system tester should have good analytical skills to analyze the features and behavior of the software system, break it down into small test units, and build effective test cases.
- Communication skills: A software tester must have both verbal and written communication skills. Test artefacts such as test cases / plans, validation strategies, test reports, etc. should be easy to follow and understand. Interacting with developers, especially when troubleshooting or other problems, requires discretion and diplomacy of the testers.
- Time management and organizational skills: Testing can sometimes be a tedious and uninteresting task, especially during the code development process, when the same tests must be repeated several times before the code is defect free. The testing must be very efficient and must not cause any delay in the overall development. A tester must organize the tasks with appropriate time management to increase the efficiency and productivity of the entire project.
- Nice attitude: A tester must have a great attitude. He / she has to check for breakage, orientate himself / herself to details, prepare himself / herself for the analysis and propose system improvements. Software technology is developing at an overwhelming pace. A good tester must constantly improve his / her technical skills with advanced technologies. He / she should prepare to work independently for tasks without too much supervision.
- Passion: To be outstanding in a career or a job, one has to have a tremendous passion for it. A software tester should have a passion for his / her field. Although some testing tasks can be cumbersome with many repetitions, the work of the testers in a QA team can be interesting, creative and challenging. For example, designing and creating business scenarios with mockups and wire frame can be creative and challenging. Analyzing the functionality and behavior of the software system, planning the test process and creating test cases are anything but boring. If a tester considers the work to be uninteresting after trying it, he / she should switch to another job.

The skills required for a tester are summarized in figure 4.

Figure 4. Testing skills

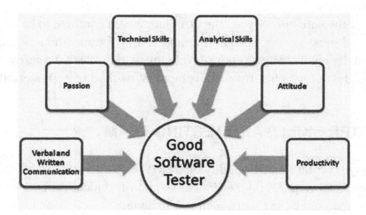

CONCLUSION

This chapter gives an overview of various aspects of the software testing. It starts with STLC. Contrary to the concept that testing by the QA team should start only in the verification phase of a software development cycle when development is complete, the authors suggested that the QA team be actively involved in the requirements analysis phase. The QA team can design and conduct business scenario simulations with mockups and wire frames to validate business requirements with stakeholders. The QA team should be active throughout the software development lifecycle, analyzing, verifying and validating all functions and behaviors of the software system.

This chapter also covers manual testing and automation testing. The concept of these two types of testing is presented along with the way they can be performed. The test levels including unit, integration, acceptance and system testing are explained. The characteristics of a test case are explained and illustrated by means of an example. Key software testing techniques are discussed for black box testing, white box testing, and gray box testing. The differences between alpha and beta tests for acceptance testing are described. A proposal for effective testing is also given. The chapter concludes with the topic software tester skills. The chapter gives an overview of the entire range of testing with suggestions for their implementation.

REFERENCES

Agile Manifesto Group. (2001). Manifesto for Agile Software Development. *Agile Manifesto*. Retrieved July 26, 2010, from http://agilemanifesto.org

Agile Testing. (2016). Agile Testing Tutorial. *Tutorials Point*. Retrieved September 09, 2019, from https://www.tutorialspoint.com/agile_testing/index.htm

Ambler, S. W. (2010). Agile Modeling. *Ambysoft*. Retrieved July 26, 2010, from http://www.agilemodeling.com/

Ambler, S. W., & Astels, D. (2003). *Test Driven development: A Practical Guide*. Upper Saddle River, NJ: Prentice Hall PTR.

Balamurugan, M. (2019). 17 Best Tips to Write Effective Test Cases. *Java Code Greeks*. Retrieved September 09, 2019, from https://www.javacodegeeks.com/2019/09/17-best-tips-to-write-effective-test-cases.html

Beck, B. (2002). *Test Driven Development: By Example*. Reading, MA: Addison-Wesley.

Bell, T. E., & Thayer, T. A. (1976). Software Requirements: Are They Really a Problem? In *Proceedings of the 2nd International Conference on Software Engineering*, (pp. 61-68). IEEE Computer Society Press.

Bertolino, A. (2007). *Software Testing Research: Achievements, Challenges, Dreams*. Software Verification and Validation Lab, University of Kentucky. Retrieved May 26, 2019, from http://selab.netlab.uky.edu/homepage/sw-test-roadmap-bertolino.pdf

Bhaggan, K. (2009). *Test Automation in Practice*. Delft University of Technology.

Chaudhary, S. (2017). Latest Software Testing Tools and Techniques: A Review. *International Journal of Advanced Research in Computer Science and Software Engineering*. Retrieved May 26, 2019, from https://pdfs.semanticscholar.org/87eb/9a3d22bca4397e8b5e53a5e852457f18ccfd.pdf

Chauhan, R., & Singh, I. (2014). Latest Research and Development on Software Testing Techniques and Tools. *International Journal of Current Engineering and Technology*, *4*(4), 2368–2372.

Collins, E., Dias-Neto, A., & de Lucena, V. F., Jr. (2012). Strategies for Agile Software Testing Automation: An Industrial Experience. In *IEEE 36th Annual Computer Software and Applications Conference Workshops* (440-445). IEEE.

Crispin, L., & Gregory, J. (2009). *Agile Testing: A Practical Guide for Testers and Agile Teams*. Reading, MA: Addison-Wesley.

Hayes, L. (2004). *The Automated Testing Handbook*. Automated Testing Institute.

Laing, S. (2015). The Testing Manifesto. *Growing Agile Coaches*. Retrieved May 26, 2019, from http://www.growingagile.co.nz/2015/04/the-testing-manifesto

Larman, C. (2003). *Agile and Iterative Development: A Manager's Guide*. Reading, MA: Addison-Wesley.

McMeekin, K. (2017). Test Automation vs. Automated Testing. *DZone*. Retrieved May 26, 2019, from https://dzone.com/articles/test-automation-vs-automated-testing-the-differenc

Milad, H., Nahla, E., & Mostafa, S. (2014). A Review of Scripting Techniques Used in Automated Software Testing. *International Journal of Advanced Computer Science and Applications*, *5*(1), 194–202.

Myers, G. (1979). *The Art of Software Testing. IBM Systems Research Institute, Lecturer in Computer Science, Polytechnic Institute of New York*. John Wiley & Sons.

Naveen, K. (2015). Step by Step Process to Perform Automation Test using SoapUI. *TESTINGFREAK*. Retrieved May 26, 2019, from http://testingfreak.com/step-by-step-process-to-perform-automation-test-using-soapui

Pettichord, B., Kaner, C., & Bach, J. (2008). *Lessons Learned in Software Testing: A Context-Driven Approach* (1st ed.). John Wiley & Sons.

Rantanen, J. (2007). *Acceptance Test-Driven Development with KeywordDriven Test Automation Framework in an Agile Software Project*. Helsinki University of Technology, Software Business and Engineering Institute.

Rashmi & Bajpai, N. (2012). A Keyword Driven Framework for Testing Web Applications. *International Journal of Advanced Computer Science and Applications*, *3*(3), 8–14.

Royce, W. (1970). Managing the Development of Large Software Systems. *Proceedings of IEEE WESON*, (28), 1-9.

Saad, M. (2019). How to Develop Test Scripts Using Top 5 Most Popular Test Automation Frameworks. *Software Testing Help*. Retrieved September 09, 2019, from https://www.softwaretestinghelp.com/automation-testing-tutorial-5

Sadiq, S. (2019). 7 Ways to Make Test Automation Effective in Agile Development. *DZone*. Retrieved November 07, 2019, from https://dzone.com/articles/7-ways-to-make-test-automation-effective-in-agile

Sawyer, X. (2014). A Test to Remember: Testing Your Web Application. *Perl Dancer Advent Calendar*. Retrieved May 26, 2019, from http://advent.perldancer.org/2014/12

Scrum. (2019). Scrum (software development). *Wikipedia*. Retrieved July 20, 2019 from https://en.wikipedia.org/wiki/Scrum_(software_development)

Sneha, K., & Malle, G. (2014). Research on software testing techniques and software automation testing tools. *IEEE Xplore*. Retrieved May 26, 2019, from https://ieeexplore.ieee.org/document/8389562

User Story. (2019). User Story. *Wikipedia*. Retrieved July 26, 2019, from https://en.wikipedia.org/wiki/User_story

KEY TERMS AND DEFINITIONS

Acceptance Testing: A type of test performed by the customer to certify the system in relation to the agreed requirements.

Agile Software Development Process: An evolutionary and iterative approach to software development with focuses on adaptation to changes.

Agile Testing: A software testing practice that follows the principles of agile software development.

Alpha Testing: A type of acceptance testing that is performed to identify any potential problems/errors before the product is released to everyday users or the public.

Automated Testing: The process of performing specific tests through automation.

Beta Testing: A type of acceptance testing that the testing of a product is done by "real users" of the software application in a "real environment."

Black Box Testing: A testing technique that tests the functionality of the application under test without knowledge of the internal code structure, implementation details, and internal paths of the software.

Gray Box Testing: Similar to black box testing but designing tests requires knowledge of internal data structures and algorithms.

Integration Testing: A level of software testing where individual units are combined and tested as a group.

Manual Testing: A type of test where testers run test cases manually without automation tools.

Software Testing Life Cycle (STLC): A series of step-by-step activities performed by a QA team to methodically test the software product.

System Testing: The testing of a complete and fully integrated software product.

Test Automation: Automating the process of tracking and managing the various tests.

Test Case: A specification of the inputs, execution conditions, test methods, and expected results that define a single test to be performed to achieve a particular software test goal.

Unit Testing: A type of software testing that tests individual software components.

White Box Testing: A testing technique to test the internal structure, design and coding of a software solution.

Chapter 9
Framework for Reusable Test Case Generation in Software Systems Testing

Kamalendu Pal

City, University of London, UK

ABSTRACT

Agile methodologies have become the preferred choice for modern software development. These methods focus on iterative and incremental development, where both requirements and solutions develop through collaboration among cross-functional software development teams. The success of a software system is based on the quality result of each stage of development with proper test practice. A software test ontology should represent the required software test knowledge in the context of the software tester. Reusing test cases is an effective way to improve the testing of software. The workload of a software tester for test-case generation can be improved, previous software testing experience can be shared, and test efficiency can be increased by automating software testing. In this chapter, the authors introduce a software testing framework (STF) that uses rule-based reasoning (RBR), case-based reasoning (CBR), and ontology-based semantic similarity assessment to retrieve the test cases from the case library. Finally, experimental results are used to illustrate some of the features of the framework.

INTRODUCTION

The strategic importance of software has long been understood by professionals and policymakers around the world (Dutta, Wassenhove & Kulandaiswamy, 1998). Software has become an indispensable part of every industry, from mobile phone manufacturers to the safe landing of spaceships. The advancement of software design and development is always an open topic for researchers to address complex systems with numerous domain-specific requirements. The success of a system is based on the quality result at every stage of development, and therefore, superior software development is an essential element of success. These quality-enhancing features become more important as the transition from hardware to software-enabled products accelerates. Today's technological innovation in the software industry is similar to the

DOI: 10.4018/978-1-7998-2531-9.ch009

early 1970s, when digital electronics began to replace the mechanical and analogue technologies that underpinned the products of attractive desktop calculators to black-and-white televisions.

The landscape of the top software dependent product and service companies is changing rapidly. The value is evolving fast as hardware features are mostly standardized and differentiate software between high and low end products. At the same time, more miniaturized computing power provides the value of embedded software in products is expected to continue its market demand. In fact, software enables an estimated *high percentage* of automotive product innovations, from entertainment to fatal accident avoidance systems (Charette, 2005; Charette, 2009). These new-generation, software-based touch-and-feel-sensitive systems are highly dependent on human-computer interactions. Computer interfaces are becoming more and more sensitive and demanding as the number of products increases, from biometrically detectable automotive unlocking systems to sophisticated automotive dashboards that design and use *intelligent software* displays. As software-based user interactions become the operational norm, software-driven automation of the design and development of these software systems promise a new degree of quality while reducing production costs. A company with consistently high-performing software has less downtime in operation and develops products with fewer disruptions that impact the end-user experience.

The automotive manufacturing industry is witnessing a new era of software-driven innovative products and processes. Particularly, using the Internet of Things (IoT) technologies and enhanced computing power in solving operational problems. For example, self-driven cars are slowly becoming a reality with high hope of commercialization for public transportation soon. The world would now have self-driven cars if the automotive industry could model very accurately the randomness of human-drivers and pedestrians on public roads. One solution to this problem would be restricted lanes for autonomous vehicles only. Self-driving cars can communicate and coordinate with each other that human drivers often fail to do. It should be noted that operational data analysis and error-free software systems are the main driving forces of these self-driven cars.

The road traffic and observation data of the self-driven car can reveal interesting patterns and correlations in the collected data set. The important mechanism for finding causal relationships is often guided by intelligent data analysis software controlled by artificial intelligent (AI) techniques. For example, algorithmic sorting, searching and data clustering are often used to analyze the observation data. In this way, the introduction of AI-based software applications improves human performance in using these automated systems.

Academics and practitioners (Holcombe, 2008) are pushing for innovations in software design and development based on artificial intelligence. At the same time, technological innovations and their applications are transforming information and communication technology (Prahalad & Mashelkar, 2010). The world of software design and development also focuses on technological innovation to enable efficient software design and development processes. True, innovative technologies and techniques are now shaping everything, from capturing software requirements to delivering software, and as new perspectives emerge, fully automated customer service in software development processes are on the horizon. The technologies that enable global software design and development, such as software development platforms and tremendous computing power, data storage, and innovative software testing techniques are rapidly advancing and becoming increasingly possible.

Software being developed in the industry requires careful operational planning and the coordination of required resources. The inception, design, implementation, testing and maintenance of a software product requires team effort and is organized and executed in such a way that the product customers are satisfied. Software lifecycle models distinguish between different phases or activities when creating software using feed-forward and feed-back loops according to the principle of separation of interests. This separation reduces the complexity of each phase or activity, but at the same time requires efficient and effective coordination.

Researchers (Shepperd & Schofield, 1997; Mair, Martincova & Shepperd, 2012) have also highlighted the critical importance of software testing and the appropriate use of relevant resources (e.g. time and cost) for the purpose of the software development are very important. Ultimately, the development costs for test cases are reduced and the quality of the implemented software systems improved (Nikolik, 2012). It is predicted that mathematically distorted information spent nearly sixty percent of the total software testing time designing test cases (Myers, Badgett & Sandler, 1997). As a result, the effective design and use of software test cases has become an attractive topic in software engineering research to automate software testing practice.

A case-based reasoning (CBR) is based on using information from previous situations to determine the results for new problems or cases (Pal, 1997) (Pal, 2017). This problem-solving strategy mimics human problem-solving activities to plan a decision based on past experience. A CBR system consists of a *case base*, which is the set of all cases known to the system. The case database can be considered as a particular kind of knowledge base containing only cases. When a new case is presented to the system, it will look at the case base in a *selection process* for similar cases that are most relevant to the present case. If a similar case is found, the system retrieves this case and tries to change it (if necessary) to find a potential solution to the new case. This process is called *adaptation*. The method of selecting and retrieving cases is referred to as "*similarity assessment*." The similarity assessment is based on the best matching cases, ordered by some *similarity metrics* (Pal & Parmer, 2000). This case-similarity matching approach differs from a deductive rule-based approach in which problems are solved by chaining the inference rules (Pal & Campbell, 1997).

The knowledge intensive software test decision-making process, specialized software testers are often referred to as the "*previous test situation*". To aid this process, an automated software engineering CBR system should find cases that are most similar to a new test case and thus act as a base-case, and its solution can provide guidance for a new test case. However, this choice, which is cognitively a complex activity, is usually approximated by a simple metric scheme in case-based computing. Such a similarity assessment scheme for the present research will be described later in this chapter.

To deduce from past experience with software testing to interpret a new test case (as do software testers in the industry) or to find an equitable solution to a new problem (as the software test case generator does) is case-based analogical reasoning (or CBR) software testing. Often this test case generation is guided by RBR (Rule Based Reasoning). This hybrid knowledge-driven framework (i.e., CBR and RBR) is just right for reusable test case requirements. On the other hand, although there are many test cases that can be reused in the application of software tests, the testing process differs due to the different operating system, operating environment, hardware type, network conditions and end-user characteristics, and so on. This undoubtedly increases the complexity of the software test case, which determines the need to reuse test cases to account for various factors and to find the best solution based on the use of previous test cases. This makes CBR useful and highly appreciated.

This chapter examines three important aspects of software development, agile software development methods, the use of knowledge-based techniques, and software testing that benefit most from efficient software delivery. Customers are demanding rapidly developed software products, which is why software development companies are moving to agile methods to deliver high-quality applications in a short time.

The programmers write and automate units of software systems and integration tests that provide good code coverage. They are disciplined in handling source code control and code integration. Qualified testers are involved from the beginning of the development cycle and given time and resources to adequately perform all required test forms. An automated software test suite that covers system functionality at a higher level is run and reviewed on a regular basis.

The rest of this chapter is structured as follows. Section 2 describes the background information of the software development and the agile methodologies. Section 3 provides an overview of the software unite testing deployment in the proposed framework. Section 4 deals with related research. Section 5 explains how to use the ontology in the software test case library. Section 6 contains information about retrieving and adaptation of test cases. Section 7 contains an experimental description of the reuse of test cases. Finally, section 8 gives a conclusion of research issues.

SOFTWARE DEVELOPMENT AND AGILE METHODOLOGY

Software is a series of instructions for the computer that perform a task, called a program. Simply software can be classified into two main categories: system software, and application software. The system software is made up of control programs. The application software is any program that processes data for the software system's user; and often it uses different mathematical models to automate the operational decision making (Pal, 2019).

Software development consists of transitions of system concept, requirements specification, analysis and design, implementation as well as testing and maintenance (Laplante, 2007). This abstraction applies both to the plan-driven process model (e.g. spiral (Boehm, 1988), the evolutionary model (Nauman & Jenkins, 1982), the unified process model (Kruchten, 2000), and, to a lesser extent, Agile models in which activities can be mixed, which completely eliminating transitions (e.g. in eXtreme Programming (Beck, 1999)).

About the V-Modell, which originates from the system technology (Forsberg & Mooz, 1991) and has been taken over into the software development (Pfleeger & Atlee, 2009), testing on a high level is often presented as quality assurance of the final product. As such, this link between software quality assurance and testing is an integral part of industry-specific problem analysis, solution design, and implementation. Many software companies have introduced agile development techniques to increase productivity. The main reason for adopting agile development methods throughout the project lifecycle is to produce higher-quality software in less time while reducing development costs.

In this way, the software industry has moved from traditional software development models to agile development to respond to ever-more-complex software and dynamic user demands. In contrast to traditional models, agile methodologies are characterized by shorter production times and intensive customer interaction. This customer-focused design and redesign practice accommodates the changes required by dynamic customer requirements. Although different software development methods use the same agile principles that are formulated in the *agile manifesto* (Beck et al., 2001), they differ in several parameters.

Agile software development became popular in the early years of this century when a group of developers met to discuss ways in which software development was considered a craft. After announcing the manifesto for agile software development, many different approaches, heuristics, tools, and techniques came to the fore. Excellent tests adapt to all these different contextual factors.

Agile development practice requires multi-functional teams that follow the principles of iterative and incremental development practice. The testing process should be well prepared for efficiency and testing should be done early and frequently. There must be a detailed agenda and specification of which test results should be available at the end of each iteration (or sprint).

The agile methodology, a conceptual framework for software development with face to face customer interaction, promotes the iterative development method throughout the project lifecycle. The agile software development team produces very few written documents compared to traditional software development models (e.g. Waterfall or V model). Agile methods focus on working software as a primary measure of progress. In addition, testing is always testing - the process of evaluating something by learning it through exploration and experimentation.

A BRIEF REVIEW OF SOFTWARE TESTING

Software companies are investing in quality assurance to reduce the cost of software development and maintenance and increase revenue and profit margins. To help increase net income, a quality assurance organization must consider the cost and value of the test-ware required for quality assurance of software artifacts such as requirements, specifications, designs, test case generation, and code.

In addition, modern software development is a knowledge-intensive activity. The number of resources available to modern software development is amazing. Process models, development methods, technologies, and development tools are part of the toolbox of the modern software designer, which includes several toolkits, configuration management tools, test suites, standards, and intelligent compilers with sophisticated debugging capabilities, just to name a few. The software engineer's vision of carefully crafting language statements into a work program is outdated and gives way to the use of a variety of tools and techniques that support the coordination of work and the creation of systems that conform to the complexity of the concept demanded by users of modern software, While it is unclear whether these tools had the impact expected from Computer Aided Software Engineering (CASE) providers, the burden on tool mastery (Brooks, 1987) for software developers has increased.

Much of the development cycle is spent on debugging, where the programmer performs a long, failure trace and tries to locate the problem in a few lines of source code to clarify the cause of the problem. In this way, testing among software quality assurance techniques is one of the most commonly used techniques in practice. Consequently, testing is also extensively studied in research. An important aspect of testing that is receiving a lot of attention in the issue of generating reusable test cases.

Software testing has been the most widely used software quality assurance technology for many decades. Due to its successful practical application, considerable research effort has been made to improve the effectiveness of tests and to scale the techniques for dealing with increasingly complex software systems. Therefore, automation of test activities is the key factor for improving test effectiveness. Automation involves four main activities: (i) generating tests, (ii) performing these tests on the system under test, (iii) evaluating the results of test procedures, and (iv) managing the results of test executions.

Comparison of Traditional and Agile Software Testing

It pays to understand the differences between traditional software testing and agile testing, as shown in Figure 1. Traditional software development uses a phased approach (e.g. requirement elicitation, specifi-

Figure 1. The difference between traditional software development model and agile model

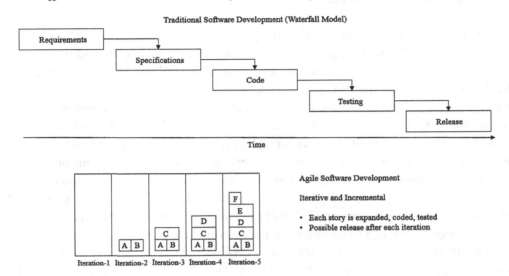

cation, coding, testing, and release). Testing takes place at the end of the software development, shortly before the release. This is shown schematically in the upper part of Figure 1. The diagram is idealistic because it gives the impression that there is just as much time for testing as for coding. However, this is not the case with many software developments projects. Testing is 'squished' because coding takes longer than expected and the teams end up going through a code-and-fix cycle.

Agile is iterative and incremental. This means that the testers test each code increment as soon as it is complete. An iteration can only take a week or a month. The team builds and tests a bit of code to make sure it's working properly, and then proceeds to the next part that needs to be created. The agile software development is shown in the lower part of Figure 1.

The approaches to projects that agile teams pursue are diverse. A team can be dedicated to a single project or be part of another larger project. Every project, every team and sometimes every iteration is different. How a software development team solves problems depends on the problem, the people involved, and the software tools that the team will use.

The fact that knowledge in software development settings is both dynamic and situation-specific has led the research community to apply a CBR decision-support approach (Pal, 1999). The general CBR paradigm postulates that much of the human problem solving is to apply past experiences to analogously related situations. In this way, CBR-driven actions are based on past experience, and to the extent that one can remember the similarities and differences between current and past circumstances, successful, defective, and failed actions can be repeated, modified, or avoided. Early case-based systems focused on how this type of reasoning can be mimicked in artificial intelligence (AI) systems. Recent systems, however, have begun to examine how case-based technology can be used to support human decision-making by providing external memory for cases and effectively expanding one's own knowledge to incorporate the experiences of others (Kolodners, 1993; Goel & Diaz-Agudo, 2017; Pal & Palmer, 2000; Watson, 2003; Pal, 2017).

RELATED RESEARCH WORKS

In software testing, a program with well-designed input data is run to observe errors (Ipate & Holcombe, 1997; Mall, 2006; Jalote, 2006; Myers, 2004). In other words, software testing addresses the problem of effectively finding the difference between the expected behavior given by the system models and the observed behavior of the implemented system (Binder, 1999).

Software testing, on average, account for a large percentage of total development costs and would increase even further with the rapid growth in the size and complexity of software (Mall, 2008; Myers, 2004; Owterweil, 1996). As systems grow larger and more complex, testing time and effort is expected to increase. Therefore, the automation of software testing has become an urgent practical necessity to reduce test cost and time. In addition, the test case plays an important role in software testing, and the generation of test cases has generally been identified as an important research challenge. In recent years, a research group (Orso & Rothermel, 2014) presented the results of an informal survey in which researchers in testing were asked to comment on the most notable achievements of the research effort and the open challenges in the field. The most common keywords in the experts' answers are the word "generation", which, together with a few other terms such as "tools" and "practice". This observation confirms the importance of the topic of test generation approaches, which must be accompanied by good tool support to cover practical needs.

The recent survey (Anand et al., 2013) covers test-case and test data generation techniques that include various techniques like symbolic execution, model-based testing, combinatorial interaction testing, adaptive random testing, and search-based testing. Relevant work includes that of Mayrhauser's research project (Mayrhauser, 1994), which is a presumptive attempt to design a system that can use the idea of test case generation. In his work, he introduced a new method of test case generation to improve the reuse of test cases through domain analysis and domain modeling. After that, a lot of research was put into the reuse of the test case. It can mainly be divided into two aspects: the generation of reusable test-cases and the management of reusable test cases.

Xu and colleagues (Xu et al., 2003) advocated a theoretical model for generating and executing patterns, making the test cases independent of the software under test and achieving the goal of reusing tests. Wang has focused on a test-case generation approach based on ontology (Wang et al., 2007). To precisely and accurately describe the test case, Guo and his colleague (Guo et al., 2011) pointed to an ontology-based method widely used as the basis for the sharing and reuse of knowledge in information science. Researchers (Xiao-Li et al., 2006) developed a test case library and discussed the model of test case management. To aid effective reuse of tests, academics (Shao, Bai & Zhao, 2006) proposed a software test design model based on the analysis of reusable test assets and their relationships.

There are many outstanding researchers who focus on generating or managing test cases. However, there are only a few studies that focus on how reusable test cases can be efficiently retrieved from the test library. In recent years, CBR has been seen as an effective approach to improving this problem and the associated research is just beginning. As we know, CBR for test case generation involves the following steps: (1) retrieving relevant test cases from the test case library; (2) selecting a set of the most suitable test cases; (3) modify and evaluate the set of test cases in the test process; (4) storing the new test cases in the test case library as a valuable and reusable resource for future applications or systems. Throughout the process, it is a central issue to describe and retrieve the appropriate test cases. The biggest drawback of CBR is that the case is not easy to adapt and often requires artificial adjustment. However, if one uses ontology to describe the test case, the test case has a semantic capability that is easily modified. Therefore, the following section describes the ontology-based test case library and the retrieval of the reusable test case from this library by computing the semantic similarity between the test case and the test request.

USE OF ONTOLOGY IN SOFTWARE TEST CASE LIBRARY

Planning and running software tests require, among other things, specialized knowledge of testing techniques, criteria, artifacts, and tools (Ipate & Holcombe, 1997). This diversity of concepts and relationships makes it necessary to build a common understanding. Ontology is a technique for collecting domain knowledge and therefore offers great potential for the knowledge-rich testing process. Ontologies have acquired important roles in information systems, knowledge management and information exchange systems, and in the development of fields such as semantic technologies (Vasanthapriyan et al., 2017). When testing software, ontologies can provide a precise selection of terms for communication between testers, developers, managers, and users. Ontologies therefore reveal the hidden assumptions about this practice (Cai et al., 2009) and support the acquisition, organization, reuse, and exchange of knowledge in the domain.

Software test is a technique to obtain information about software systems quality. Performance test is a type of software test that aims at evaluating software performance at a given scenario, but it requires specialized knowledge about tools, activities and metrics of the domain. For example, in software engineering – the specification is described in natural language at first. The test requirements and the test cases are no exception. For the machine, there is no link between two different sentences with similar meaning which described by natural language. However, ontology can establish a semantic association between these two different sentences which can be understood by machine. There, this research project uses ontology to build the test-case library and model the test requirements.

Software testing is a technique for obtaining information about the quality of software systems. The performance test is a type of software test that aims to evaluate software performance in a given scenario. However, it requires specialized knowledge of domain tools, activities, and metrics. For example, in software engineering - the specification is first described in natural language. The test requirements and the test cases are no exception. For the machine, there is no connection between two different sets of similar meaning, which are described by the natural language. However, the ontology can produce a semantic association between these two different sets that can be understood by the machine. There, this research project uses the ontology to build the test case library and model the test requirements.

Ontology-Based Test Case Library

Ontology is a technique for representing and manipulating knowledge in a area of application (e.g., software testing). This chapter describes the definition of ontology-based test case and test case library as follows:

Definition 1. *An ontology is a structure*

$$O := (\ C,\ \leqslant_C,\ R, \sigma,\ \leqslant_R)$$

consisting of (i) two disjoint sets C and R whose elements are called concept identifiers and relation identifiers respectively, (ii) a partial order $\leq_c$ on C, called concept hierarchy or taxonomy, (iii) a function $\sigma : R \rightarrow C^+$ called signature, and (iv) a partial order $\leq_R$ on R, called relation hierarchy, where $r_1 \leq_R r_2$ implies $|\sigma(r_1)| = |\sigma(r_2)|$ and $\pi_i(\sigma(r_1)) \leq_c \pi_i(\sigma(r_2))$, for each $1 \leq i \leq |\sigma(r_1)|$.

Often researchers call concept identifiers and relation identifiers just *concepts* and *relations*, respectively for sake of simplicity.

Definition 2. *For a relation $r \in R$ with $|\sigma(r)| = 2$, one can define its domain and its range by* $\mathrm{dom}(r) := \pi_1(\sigma(r))$ *and range$(r) := \pi_2(\sigma(r))$.*

If $c_1 \leq_c c_2$, for $c_1, c_2 \in C$, then c_1 is a subconcept of c_2, and c_2 is a subconcept of c_1. If $r_1 \leq_R r_2$, for $r_1, r_2 \in R$, then r_1 is a subrelation of r_2, and r_2 is a sub-relation of r_1.

If $c_1 \leq_c c_2$ and there is no $c_3 \in C$ with $c_1 <_c c_3 <_c c_2$, then c_1 is a direct subconcept of c_2, and c_2 is a direct super-concept of c_1. One can note this by $c_1 \prec c_2$. Direct superrelations, and direct subrelations are defined analogously.

Definition 3. *Let $\wr$ be a logical language. A $\wr$-axiom system for an ontology $O := (C, \leq_c, R, \sigma, \leq_R)$ is a pair $A 6 = (AI, \alpha)$ where (i) AI is a set whose elements are called axiom identifiers and (ii) $\alpha : AI \rightarrow \blacklozenge$ is a mapping. The elements of $A 6 = \alpha(AI)$ are called axioms.*

An ontology with $\wr$-axiom is a pair (O, A) where O is an ontology and A is a $\wr$-axiom system for $\blacklozenge$.

Definition 4. *An ontology with $\wr$-axiom is a pair (O, A) is consistent, if*
$$A \cup \{\forall x : x \in c_1 \rightarrow x \in c_2 | c_1 \leq c_2\} \cup \{\forall x : x \in r_1 \rightarrow x \in r_2 | r_1 \leq r_2\} \quad is \quad consistent.$$

Definition 5. Test Case Ontology (TCO): TCO *consists of two sets – test case concepts (TCC) and relations (R), and these sets don't intersect with each other.*

For convenience, following basic relations of ontology are used in the rest of this chapter:

Theorem 1: P(x) relation. if the type of concept " is P, then it can be described as "P(For example: has (means that is exist.

Theorem 2: R(x, y) relation. if the type of relationship between concept " and " is "R" then the relation can be described as R(For example: instance (describes the instance relationship between two concepts, it means that concept " is the instance of ".

Definition 6. Test Case Library (TCL): TCL = {TCO, Rules}. Rules represent a set of inference rules, which is explained in detail below. Rule are used to modify the test case.

A test-case when testing software consists of a series of inputs, execution conditions, and expected results for a particular purpose. In the ontology-based test case library, the exact definition of terms can be represented by a set of description logic formulas. To clearly illustrate the process of reusing test cases, a test case is defined as a seven-tuple: {TID, TP, PR, TE, TI, TO, ER}, and the tuples are shown in Table 1.

Table 1. The properties of a test case

Property	Name of Property	Description
TID	Test Identification	Unique identifier of a test case
TP	Test Purpose	The indivisible purpose of the testing
PR	Precondition	The condition needs to meet before testing
TE	Test Environment	The environment needed in the testing
TI	Test Input	The input data
TO	Test Operation	The process of testing
ER	Expected Result	The expected result

Definition 7. Test Case Sequence (TCS): *The test case sequence is composed of the least one test case. And there is a certain sequence existed between the test cases. It can be defined as follows:*

TCS: ^{3} 1has (TOC) ^ Pre (tco$_i$, tco$_j$) ^ instance (tco$_i$, TCO) ^ instance (tco$_j$, TCO)

For a better description, number restrictions and an R (x, y) relation are used in the formal expression of TCS.

- ^{3} n R: at least number restrictions, the number of relationship "R" is at least n.
- £ n R: at most number restrictions, the number of relationship "R" is at most n.
- Pre (x, y): sequence relationship, it means that x is prior to y.

Ontology-Based Test Task

At the beginning of software testing, the testers must determine the test target. A test target can be represented as a set of test requirements. For example, for functional coverage testing, each function of the application or system awaiting a test corresponds to a test requirement. In addition, testers must also determine the test environment. Therefore, a test task can be defined as a 2-tuple (TT, TE) and TT refers to the test target while TE is the test environment. If TR represents the test requirement that cannot be subdivided into smaller requirements, TT can be defined as follows:

TT: ^{3} 1has (TR) ^ Pre (tr$_i$, trj$_j$) ^ instance (tr$_i$, TR) ^ instance (tr$_j$, TR)

This definition is very similar to the definition of TCS. It also shows that at least one test case sequence is required to complete a test target.

Here is a simple example to illustrate the relationship between them. For example, suppose a test requirement set R = {tr$_1$, tr$_2$, tr$_3$, tr$_4$}, and there exists an order between them, such as tr$_{1 \circledR}$ tr$_{2 \circledR}$ tr$_{3 \circledR}$ tr$_4$. One tries to find test case set {tc$_{31}$, tc$_{32}$ ... tc$_{3n}$} for tr$_3$, and test case set {tc$_{41}$, tc$_{42}$ ... tc$_{4n}$} for tr$_4$. In the actual testing, the number of test cases in each test case set for each test requirement is not equal. If the output of tc$_{11}$ meets the precondition of tc$_{22}$, then one can add them into a same test case sequence. The rest can be done in the same way. Finally, the test case sequence for the specific test target can be found.

Figure 2. The proposed software framework

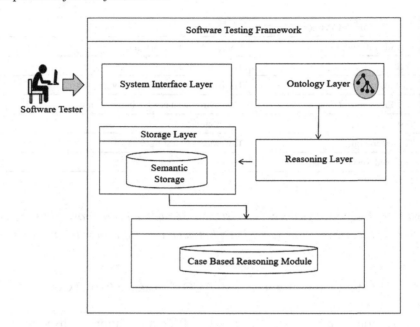

Test Case Retrieval Mechanism

If the test requirement (TR) is regarded as query case, and the test case library is viewed as case base, the reusable test case generation might be considered as searching the cases that has the highest degree of matching with query-case from case base. These analyze and rewrite the cases according to the actual conditions. This section will discuss these issues.

The software system framework shown in Figure 2 consists of three layers: system interface and ontology layer, storage and reasoning layer, and the last layer is a case-based reasoning layer. The process of the framework is summarized as follows. Via the interface for the sharing of experiences, software testers can comment on their testing knowledge with the aid of software testing variables. The semantic data is expressed in triplicate structures according to the concepts and relationships of the software testing ontology.

WordNet-Based Test Case Retrieval

The test case retrieval process consists of finding the test case whose TP matches the TR from the test case library. Since different people in software engineering have different expressions for the same requirement, the string comparison method, which only judges if all strings are the same, is not applicable here. In this chapter, the ontology similarity calculation method is used to obtain a test set of cases in which the TPs of each test case semantically match the TR to varying degrees. The calculation of the ontology similarity is based on the WordNet, a large lexical database for English. Nouns, verbs, adjectives, and adverbs are grouped into groups of cognitive synonyms (synsets), each of which expresses a particular concept. Synsets are interlinked by conceptual-semantic and lexical relationships (Miller, 1995; Fellbaum, 1998). The approach of this chapter distinguishes the part of the language to which the word belongs. Different parts of speech have different weights in the calculation. As mentioned above, TP refers to the indivisible purpose of the test. Each test case can be modeled as a node in the ontology diagram. TP, which should contain a verb and multiple nouns, is a property of the node.

There are many methods to measure the semantic similarity of ontology based on WordNet (Budanitsky & Hirst, 2001). In general, these methods can be divided into the following categories: (1) based on the path length of the concept; (2) based on information; (3) based on features; (4) other comprehensive calculation method. Because one has to find as many test cases as possible to account for in the retrieval phase for reusable test cases, when calculating the similarity of two concepts, only two basic factors are considered: the concept path length (h_w) and the coincide path length (h); and they are defined as follows:

Definition 8. Concept Path Length (h_w): The path length from concept to the root.
Definition 9. Coincide Path Length (h): The length of the overlap path from two concept to the root.

This path calculation technique is used to retrieve a similar test case from the test case library. Suppose that there are two concepts W_i and W_j. The concept path length of W_i is h_{wi}, and the concept path length of W_j is h_{wj}. The length of coincide path between them is h. The definition of contact ratio (cr) is as follows:

Then the similarity between W_i and W_j can be calculated as follows:
And the similarity between TP and TR can be obtained by the following formula:
$+$
In the above formula, α and β are the factor parameters whose value ranges in (0, 1), and $\alpha + \beta = 1; \alpha^3 \beta$.

For the two concepts W_1 and W_2, their location relation in WordNet can be classified into two categories: (1) the coincide path length is 0 (h = 0); (2) the coincide path length is greater than 0 (h > 0). According to information theory, in the first case there is almost no similarity between W_1 and W_2. In the second case, the greater the ratio of the coincide path length in the concept path length, the less the similarity between W_1 and W_2.

Take for example, {mammal, bird, dog, cat} to prove the validity of the formula suggested in this chapter above. Figure 3 shows the part of the hierarchical semantic structure in WordNet that contains the four nouns. The results of the similarity calculation are shown in Table 2.

The results show that the similarity between mammal and dog is greater than in mammal and bird. And the similarity between dog and bird is the lowest in the results. This not only corresponds to the facts, but also to information theory. Therefore, the formula can be used to retrieve similar test cases from the test case library.

Rule-Based Test Case Adaptation

In this framework, rule-based techniques are used to adopt the previous test-cases for the present case. There are three types of situations in this framework: rewriting, modifying the script execution command, and changing environment variables.

Figure 3. The part of the hierarchical semantic structure in WordNet

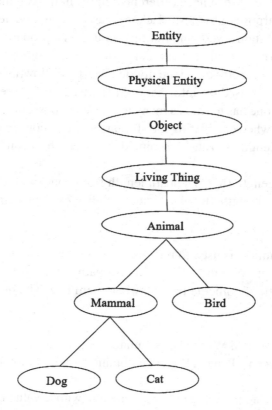

Table 2. The similarity calculation results of the four nouns

(W_1, W_2)	h	h_{w1}	h_{w2}	cr	Sim (w_1, w_2)
(mammal, bird)	4	5	5	4/5	0.6640
(mammal, dog)	5	5	7	5/6	0.6823
(dog, cat)	5	7	7	5/7	0.6134
(dog, bird)	4	7	5	4/7	0.5164

In different test environments, the execution command of the test case and the environment variables of the test case are different. However, the system has a robust function implementation and business logic that does not change with the environment. Therefore, the system must change the related information of test cases retrieved from the test case library according to the test environment specified in the test task using the case selection algorithm.

The operating system is an important element in the test environment. For example, the following rewrite rules for test cases apply to Windows and Unix:

Rewrite the operating system running the test case if the operating system information of the test case differs from that of the test task.

testTask(?tt) ^ hasOS(?x, ?tt) ^ testcase(?c) ^ hasOS(?y, ?tc)^ different(?x, ?y) -> transoms(?x, ?c)

$$(1)$$

Modify the script execution command.

Is-OS(?x, Windows) ^ script(?file) -> execute("cmd" + ?systemDrive + ?file) Is-OS(?x, Linux) ^ script(?file) -> execute("./" + ?file)

$$(2)$$

Other changes caused by changing the test environment can be written to similar rule types.

TEST CASE REUSE EXPERIMENT

The implemented system uses a test case library consisting of 155 test cases and 16 rules. The system uses OWL to describe the test case and SWRL to describe the rewrite rules. In one experiment, the test task was broken down into six test requirements. The experimental results are shown in Table 3.

CONCLUSION

This chapter describes how to generate reusable test cases from a test library based on the ontology. Here, the knowledge base is the case library, which depicts what can be learned from a test case and defines the rules that were used to adapt the retrieved test case. In addition, it was argued that each test case in the case library differs from the others, but the semantic similarity between the test cases can be calculated using a particular calculation approach. The results of the presented experimental calculation show that the approach proposed in this chapter can significantly reduce the time required to generate reusable test cases and reduce the workload of the software testing process.

The chapter also suggested an approach to calculate the ontological semantic similarity between test case and test request based on the specific algorithm. However, this approach is too crude at this time and more appropriate approaches need to be identified in future research. Moreover, the presented approach did not consider coverage of the generated test case sequence, and the test case sequence generation process still requires manual intervention. It also fails to create a fully machine-generated test case. In the future, more test cases would be used for experimental exercises, and research plans to validate the proposed technique in practice.

Table 3. Results of the experiment

No	Test Cases	Sim (TP, TR) ^{3} 0.6	Percentage	Time
01	16	10	0.625	4.01
02	14	8	0.571	3.87
03	10	7	0.7	3.73
04	10	6	0.6	3.73
05	15	9	0.6	3.88
06	23	11	0.478	4.13

REFERENCES

Anand, S., Burke, E. K., Chen, T. Y., Clark, J. A., Cohen, M. B., Grieskamp, W., ... McMinn, P. (2013). An orchestrated survey of methodologies for automated software test case generation. *Journal of Systems and Software*, *86*(8), 1978–2001. doi:10.1016/j.jss.2013.02.061

Beck, K. (1999). Embracing change with extreme programming. *Computer*, *32*(10), 70–77. doi:10.1109/2.796139

Beck, K., Beedle, M., Bennekum, A. V., Cockburn, A., & Cunningham, W. (2001). *The Agile Manifesto*. Software Development.

Binder, R. V., Legeard, B., & Kramer, A. (2015). Model-based testing: Where does it stand? *Communications of the ACM*, *58*(2), 52–56. doi:10.1145/2697399

Boehm, B. W. (1988). A spiral model of software development and enhancement. *Computer*, *21*(5), 61–72. doi:10.1109/2.59

Brooks, F. P. (1987). No Silver Bullet: Essence and Accidents of Software Engineering. *Computer*, *20*(4), 10–19. doi:10.1109/MC.1987.1663532

Budanitsky, A., & Hirst, G. (2001). Semantic Distance in WordNet: An Experimental Application-Oriented Evaluation of Five Measure. *Proceeding Workshop WordNet and Other Lexical Resources, Second Meeting of the North American Chapter of the Association for Computational Linguistics*.

Cai, L., Rensing, C., Li, X., & Wang, G. (2009). Novel gene clusters involved in arsenite oxidation and resistance in two arsenite oxidizers: Achromobacter sp. SY8 and Pseudomonas sp. TS44. *Applied Microbiology and Biotechnology*, *83*(4), 715–725. doi:10.100700253-009-1929-4 PMID:19283378

Charette, R. N. (2005). Why Software Fails. *IEEE Spectrum*, *2*.

Charette, R. N. (2009). This Car Runs on Code. *IEEE Spectrum*, *1*.

Dutta, S., Wassenhove, L. N. V., & Kulandaiswamy, S. (1998). Benchmarking European Software Management Practices. *Communications of the ACM*, *41*(6), 77–86. doi:10.1145/276609.276623

Fellbaum, C. (1998). *WordNet: An Electronic Lexical Database*. Cambridge, MA: MIT Press. doi:10.7551/mitpress/7287.001.0001

Forsberg, K., & Mooz, H. (1991). The relationship of system engineering to the project cycle. In *Proceedings of Annual Conference of the National Council on System Engineering*. National Council on Systems Engineering. 10.1002/j.2334-5837.1991.tb01484.x

Goel, A. K., & Diaz-Agudo, B. (2017). *What's hot in case-based reasoning?* AAAI.

Guo, S., Tong, W., Zhang, J., & Liu, Z. (2011). An Application of Ontology to Test Case Reuse. *International Conference on Mechatronic Science, Electrical Engineering and Computer*, Jilin, China.

Holcombe, M. (2008). *Running an Agile Software Development Project*. Hoboken, NJ: John Wiley & Sons; doi:10.1109/MEC.2011.6025579.

Ipate, F., & Holcombe, M. (1997). An integration testing method that is proved to find all faults. *International Journal of Computer Mathematics*, *63*(3-4), 159–178. doi:10.1080/00207169708804559

Jalote, P., & Jain, G. (2006). Assigning tasks in a 24-h software development model. *Journal of Systems and Software*, *79*(7), 904–911. doi:10.1016/j.jss.2005.06.040

Kolodner, J. (1993). *Case Based Reasoning*. Morgan Kaufmann. doi:10.1016/B978-1-55860-237-3.50005-4

Kruchten, P. (2000). *The Rational Unified Process: An Introduction* (2nd ed.). Boston, MA: Addision Wesley Longman Publishing.

Laplante, P. A. (2007). *What Every Engineer Should Know about Software Engineering* (1st ed.). CRC Press. doi:10.1201/9781420006742

Mair, C., Martincova, M., & Shepperd, M. (2012). An Empirical Study of Software Project Managers Using a Case-Based Reasoner. In *Proceedings of 45th Hawaii International Conference on System Science*, (pp. 1030-1039). IEEE Computer Society. 10.1109/HICSS.2012.96

Mall, R. (2006). *Fundamentals of Software Engineering* (2nd ed.). Prentice Hall.

Mayrhauser, A. v., Walls, J., & Mraz, R. (1994). Sleuth: A Domain Based Testing Toll. In *IEEE International Test Conference* (pp. 840-849). 10.1109/TEST.1994.528031

Miller, G. A. (1995). WordNet: A Lexical Database for English. *Communications of the ACM*, *38*(11), 39–41. doi:10.1145/219717.219748

Myers, G. J. (2004). *The Art of Software Testing* (2nd ed.). Hoboken, NJ: John Wiley & Sons.

Nauman, J. D., & Jenkins, A. M. (1982). Prototyping: The New Paradigm for System Development. *Management Information Systems Quarterly*, *6*(3), 29–44. doi:10.2307/248654

Nikolik, B. (2012). Software quality assurance economics. *Information and Software Technology*, *54*(11), 1229–1238. doi:10.1016/j.infsof.2012.06.003

Orso, A., & Rothermel, G. (2014). Software testing: a research travelogue (2000–2014). *Proceedings of the on Future of Software Engineering*, 117-132.

Owterweil, L. (1996). Strategic directions in software quality. *ACM Computing Surveys*, *28*(4).

Pal, K. (1999). An approach to legal reasoning based on a hybrids decision-support system. *Expert Systems with Applications*, *1*(1), 1–12. doi:10.1016/S0957-4174(99)00015-9

Pal, K. (2017). Supply Chain Coordination Based on web Service. In H. K. Chan, N. Subramanian, & M. D. Abdulrahman (Eds.), *Supply Chain Management in Big Data Era* (pp. 137–170). Hershey, PA: IGI Publication. doi:10.4018/978-1-5225-0956-1.ch009

Pal, K. (2019). Markov Decision Theory-Based Crowdsourcing Software Process Model. In V. Gupta (Ed.), *Crowdsourcing and Probabilistic Decision-Making in Software Engineering: Emerging Research and Opportunities* (pp. 1–22). Hershey, PA: IGI Global Publishing.

Pal, K. & Campbell, J.A. (1997). An application of rule-based and case-based reasoning within a single legal knowledge-based system. *ACM SIGMIS Database: the DATABASE for Advances in Information Systems, 28*(4), 48-63.

Pal, K., & Palmer, O. (2000). A decision-support system for business acquisition. *Decision Support Systems, 27*(4), 411–429. doi:10.1016/S0167-9236(99)00083-4

Pfleeger, S. L., & Atlee, J. M. (2006). *Software Engineering: Theory and Practice*. London, UK: Pearson.

Prahalad, C. K., & Mashelkar, R. A. (2010). Innovation's Holy Grail. *Harvard Business Review, 88*(7/8), 132–141.

Shao, Z. L., Bai, X, Y., & Zhao, C.C. (2006). Research and implementation of a reuse-oriented test design model. *Journal of Mini-Micro Systems, 27*, 2150-2155.

Shepperd, M., & Schofield, C. (1997). Estimating software project effort using analogies. *IEEE Transactions on Software Engineering, 23*(11), 736–743. doi:10.1109/32.637387

Vasanthapriyan, S., Tan, J., Zhao, D., Xiong, S., & Xiang, J. (2017). An Ontology-based Knowledge Sharing Portal for Software Testing. *IEEE International Conference on Software Quality, Reliability and Security*, 472-479. 10.1109/QRS-C.2017.82

Wang, H., Xing, J., Yang, Q., Song, W., & Zhang, X. (2016). Generating effective test cases based on satisfiability modulo theory solvers for service-oriented workflow applications. *Software Testing, Verification & Reliability, 26*(2), 149–169. doi:10.1002tvr.1592

Watson, I. (2003). *Applying Knowledge Management: techniques for building corporate memories*. San Francisco, CA: Morgan Kaufmann Publishers.

Xiao-Li, L., Wei, G., Xin-Li, C., & Ke-Gang, H. (2006). Designing a test case library system of supporting sharing and reusing. *Journal of Computational Science, 33*, 290–291.

Xu, R., Chen, B., & Chen, B., Wu, M., & Xiong Z. (2003). Investigation on the pattern for Construction of Reusable Test Cases in Object-oriented Software. *Journal of Wuhan University, 49*(5), 592–596.

KEY TERMS AND DEFINITIONS

Case-Based Reasoning: The main idea of case-based reasoning (CBR) is to adapt solutions that were used to solve previous problems and use them for solving latest problems (cases). A CBR system consists of a case base (which is the set of all cases that are known to the system) and an inferencing mechanism to drive a solution from the stored cases.

Critical Software Systems: Software whose failure would impact safety or cause large financial or social losses.

Ontology: Information sharing among business partners using information system is an important enabler for business operations management. There are different types of data to be shared across business operations, namely – order, demand, inventory, shipment, and customer service. Consequently, information about these issues needs to be shared in order to achieve efficiency and effectiveness. In this way, information-sharing activities require that human and/or machine agents agree on common and explicit business related concepts (the shared conceptualizations among hardware/software agents, customers, and service providers) are known as explicit ontologies; and these help to exchange data and derived knowledge out of the data to achieve collaborative goals of business operations.

Rule-Based Reasoning: In conventional rule-based reasoning, both common sense knowledge and domain specific domain expertise (i.e. software testing) are represented in the forms of plausible rules (e.g. IF <precondition(s)> THEN <conclusion(s)>. For example, an instance of a rule in common law: IF {(Jo has a driving license) AND (Jo is drunk) AND (Jo is stopped by police)} THEN {(Jo's driving license will be revoked by the transport authority)}. Moreover, rule-based reasoning requires an exact match on the precondition(s) to predict the conclusion(s). This is very restrictive, as real-world situations are often fuzzy and do not match exactly with rule preconditions. Thus, there are some extensions to the basic approach that can accommodate partial degrees of matching in rule preconditions.

Software Life Cycle Processes: It provides a framework for the sequence of activities to be performed for software projects.

Software Process Standards: It presents fundamental standards that describe activities performed as part of the software life cycle. In some cases, these standards also describe documents, but these represent plans for conducting activities.

Software Quality: Software engineering standards, if sufficiently comprehensive and if properly enforced, establish a *quality system*, a systematic approach to ensuring software quality, which is defined as (1) the degree to which a system, component, or process meets specified requirements and (2) the degree to which a system, component, or process meets customer or user needs or expectations.

Software Quality Assurance: Software quality assurance is defined as follows (1) a planned and systematic pattern of all actions necessary to provide adequate confidence that an item or product conforms to established technical requirements and (2) a set of activities designed to evaluate the process by which products are developed or manufactured.

Software Testing: Software testing provides the mechanism for verifying that the requirements identified during the initial phases of the project were properly implemented and that the system performs as expected. The test scenarios developed through these competitions ensures that the requirements are met end-to-end.

Verification and Validation: The process of determining whether the requirements for a system or component are complete and correct, the products of each development phase fulfill the requirements or conditions imposed by the previous phase, and the final system or component complies with specified requirements.

Chapter 10
Teaching Property–Based Testing:
Why and How

Isabel Azevedo

Instituto Superior de Engenharia do Porto, Instituto Politécnico do Porto, Portugal

Nuno Malheiro

ⓘ https://orcid.org/0000-0002-6686-9038

Instituto Superior de Engenharia do Porto, Instituto Politécnico do Porto, Portugal

ABSTRACT

Given the large dimensions of software algorithms, the creation of unit test sets is both very difficult to use as an assurance of software quality and also very resource consuming. Some of the industry has already focused on this issue, and several methods are being used to cope with traditional testing shortcomings. Property-based testing has been one of these techniques and has been gaining traction, mainly due to the shift to functional programming techniques which can be seen in most of the popular languages and platforms. To give students tools that can increase the quality of their production as software developers, property-based testing has been taught in the Advanced Programming Techniques course of the master's program in Informatics Engineering of the Instituto Superior de Engenharia do Porto.

INTRODUCTION

Compared to other engineering, software engineering is a relatively new area. It has matured over the years as new trends and concerns have emerged. Testing, which is considered an essential activity to ensure software quality, is a reasonably established software development practice. However, not all testing methods are taught and, hence, known and used. For instance, model-based mutation and testing (MBT) approaches appear to be more popular in academia than in industry, where it is less widespread (Garousi & Felderer, 2017).

DOI: 10.4018/978-1-7998-2531-9.ch010

Model-based testing is a technique where test cases are generated from the requirements (Dalal et al., 1999). Property-based testing (PBT) is a type of MBT in which properties play a dominant role, and they are related to requirements that the system is expected to satisfy. Moreover, there are some other characteristics:

- Random data is used to evaluate the previously defined properties.
- The first property that encounters an error is returned by the PBT tool, or a simplified one (identified by shrinking).
- Generators are used to produce input data. However, their writing may not be straightforward.

PBT acts as a complement to the software engineering lifecycle, preventing the introduction of defects in the code (Fink & Bishop, 1997). It is related to a tool developed to formulate and test properties expressed in Haskel programs, launched in 1999, which brought visibility to the approach: QuickCheck (Claessen & Hughes, 2000).

Agile methods are designed to ensure that software components are created quickly and respond to changing requirements without neglecting their quality. Testing is a noticeable quality assurance approach to decrease software defects. However, as software systems are becoming increasingly complex and interconnected, their proper testing is becoming more difficult and challenging, leading to an increase in the number and complexity of software defects.

One way to mitigate the undesired effects is to include PBT in the development life cycle (Derrick et al., 2009). Its adoption in the software development industry can reduce the cost of defects in software. Defects have associated costs, namely:

- They have a visible cost related to the time taken to prevent and correct them.
- There is also an invisible cost related to customer abandonment.

Thus, the time invested in testing properties and writing generators can be translated into a higher level of confidence of the source code reliability (Labuschagne, Inozemtseva, & Holmes, 2017) and can help detecting bugs, as happened for Ericsson (Arts, Hughes, Johansson, & Wiger, 2006), Klarna (Hughes, 2016), and Volvo Cars (Arts, Hughes, Norell, & Svensson, 2015).

Software engineering research has impacted industrial practice, such as the REST architectural style (Fielding, 2000) and its high usage. However, despite some notorious examples, the collaboration between industry and academy has not always been so fruitful (Basili et al., 2018). This gap seems to be even more pronounced in software testing (Beszédes & Vidács, 2016; Garousi, & Felderer, 2017).

PBT has not yet have been largely adopted by software developers. Developers will be inclined to use what they have learned about in subjects that have been introduced in their formal education. PBT has been integrated into bachelor's and master's courses and used to test functional code (Page, 2011; Waldmann, 2017). Lars Brünjes, Director of Education at IOHK, emphasized the importance of property-based testing for the company, especially for complex systems, to ensure their quality, but also the importance of learning the approach (Brünjes, 2018).

This chapter has a two-fold objective, namely:

- It aims to show how the subject has been approached in a master's course and the results found, after a contextualization of the subject and its scope, and relevance outside its more traditional use with functional programming.
- The chapter intends to enhance PBT usage in agile development. Tests represent a key concern in agile software development, and PBT has captured the attention of the community, even in some relatively new areas as blockchain software engineering (Chepurnoy & Rathee, 2018). For instance, last year a workshop about property-based testing for Java was organized at the Agile Testing Days (Agile Testing Days, 2018), and the European Testing Conference 2019 (Moura, 2019) had a presentation devoted to PBT, especially its ability to reduce test-debt, with smaller, more readable and fewer tests.

In the remainder of this chapter, property-based testing will be explored, especially in the next section, which describes tools that support the approach and its usage in the academy and enterprises. A third section is dedicated to introducing a variation of PBT, Property-Based State Machine Testing, that allows complete workflows to be tested. The experience in teaching PBT in a master course of Instituto Superior de Engenharia do Porto is contextualized and explained in the fourth section. The concluding section summarizes the main points of this chapter, also providing some overview of what the future of the approach in our course can be, but in other programs as well, and what is expected for its large adoption.

PROPERTY-BASED TESTING

Unlike example-based testing, no expected input and output is provided when using property-based testing. Properties are defined and, based on them, test cases are automatically generated. PBT is a "generative test". Because test data are generated, it is possible to have a very large number of tests, which is quite infeasible to achieve when tests are written manually.

PBT does not intend to prove the correctness of the code under testing, but to find problems signaled by properties that are falsified. When an issue is detected, it must be analyzed to figure out its cause. The problem may be related to (1) the generator, (2) the specifications model that was used for the properties, or (3) the code, which is supposed to be following the specifications.

The idea behind PBT is not new. The first applications date back at least to 1994 (Fink & Levitt, 1994; Fink, Ko, Archer, & Levitt, 1994), but, after some initial popularity, the results provided by Google Trends may indicate some recovery (see Figure 1). Using data about searches mainly submitted to the Google search engine that goes back to January 1, 2004, Google Trends provides a timely index of the volume of queries submitted by users in different geographic areas. Worldwide data was considered for the graph shown in Figure 1.

The results shown in Figure 1 include searches containing the terms "property-based testing" or "property-based testing". The numbers in the graph vary from 0 to 100, where 100 indicates the highest popularity for the search term. A score of 0 does not mean that zero queries were submitted, but simply that there was not enough data to compute its popularity. A value of 50 indicates that the term has half of its popularity compared to its recorded peak. For the same period, the United States of America was the country where the search query was most popular in accordance with data provided by Google Trends.

Figure 1. Internet search behavior for terms related to PBT (from 2004-01 to 2019-06)

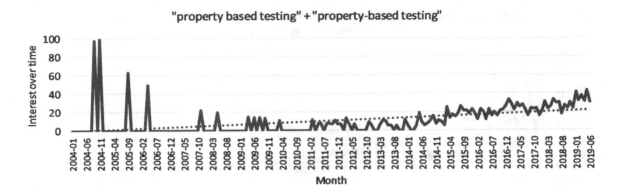

Figure 2 uses data from Google Trends. The trend in popularity for model and property-based testing seems to go in opposite directions. In fact, in June 2018, for the first time, the indicative value of interest over time for PBT was greater than this value for MBT.

The same tendency is not verified in the number of scientific works published as provided by Google Scholar as can be seen in Table 1. The in MBT seems to be growing, also in PBT, but at a substantially slower pace. The search queries used were "model-based testing" and "property-based testing", respectively.

A wide range of applications of PBT is described in the literature. Automatic grading of applications is a possibility explored in (Stahlbauer, Kreis & Fraser, 2019). The author found a strong correlation between the manual grades and the number of properties violated in an experiment with 37 implementations of a certain game. Metamorphic Testing (MT) is a PBT approach that uses properties of the system to identify metamorphic relations with long tradition in testing machine-learning systems (Chen et al., 2018), but also in other areas with detection of faults in embedded systems (Kuo, Chen, & Tam, 2011) and C compilers (Le, Afshari, & Su, 2014; Tao, Wu, Zhao, & Shen, 2010), among others. However, MT uses techniques different from those covered in this chapter, and one of its core aspects is the Metamorphic Relation (MR): "an expected relationship among the inputs and outputs of multiple executions of the target program" (Chen, Kuo, Tse, & Zhou, 2003).

Some difficulties related to the usage and adoption of property-based testing:

- To obtain a measurement of test coverage it is necessary a careful choice of the distribution of the generated test cases and the analysis of the data used.
- The abstract nature of PBT might make the approach more difficult to learn than simple unit tests. An experiment with a small number of participants (13) where one morning was dedicated to introducing the tools for both approaches (property-based testing and unit testing) reveled some difficulties in writing PBT tests (Claessen, Hughes, Pałka, Smallbone, & Svensson, 2010).

Figure 2. Internet search behavior for terms related to MBT (from 2004-01 to 2019-06)

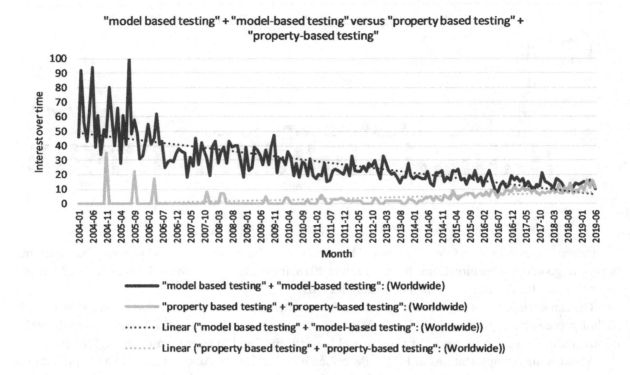

Table 1. Research related to MBT and PBT

Initial year	End year	Property-based testing(number of results)	Model-based testing (number of results)
-	1980	0	8
1981	1990	1	14
1991	2000	29	194
2001	2010	226	4980
2011	-	786	11500

Properties

Properties are specified from functional requirements, and they are important to the test cases to be used but properties and tests are different concepts (Nilsson, 2014a): properties are defined in the abstract, while real values are used in tests. Properties act as specifications.

The exact notation depends on the tool in use, but a property can be something as simple as:

For all integers x, the result of adding 1 to x should be greater than x.

Notice that abstract parameters are used, x in the example, and not concrete values.

However, properties are easy to write but a useful property need to be related to relevant requirements, and this is more difficult to achieve quickly and substantially more complex. A good understanding of the problem and its domain is mandatory.

A question with more than 20 years remains relevant: "How is it determined that the properties represent a complete model of a program's possible failures?" (Fink & Bishop, 1997). Some program properties closely related to the specifications should be at the heart of the testing effort since they capture the most relevant requirements.

Some patterns have been proposed to make easy the definition of properties (Laucher, 2015; O'Farrell, 2015; Wlaschin, 2015):

- **Relations**: Known two functions and their behaviors, and how they relate, a property can be established that clarifies this relationship in terms of their results:
- For all x obtained by GenX, the result of f1(x)is greater/less than f2(x).
- GenX here is just a generator that allows obtaining values to be tested.
- **Reference Implementation or "The Test Oracle"**: There is a base implementation of a given function, f_1, and another one, f_2, was developed for a given reason, but it is known that both should provide the same results:
- For all x obtained by GenX, the result of f_1(x)is equal to f_2(x).
- **Round Trip, Symmetry, or "There and back again"**: Some operations can be undone because of the existence of a corresponding operation that allows getting the original values when applied. Considering fToY(x) and fFromY as examples of those operations, one can have this property:
- For all x obtained by GenX, the result of fToY(x)is equal to fFromY(x).
- However, the transformations provided by these operations cannot be lossy. For instance, an operation that returns 1 for all positive numbers, does not allow to obtain the original value.
- **Idempotent or "The more things change, the more they stay the same"**: Applying certain operations multiple times does not change the result. If f is an example of such functions, a property can be written as:
- For all x obtained by GenX, the result of f (x)is equal to f(f(x)).
- **Different paths, same destination**: The order of some operations or how they are associated does not impact the final result. Considering the case of commutative operations f_1 and f_2, for instance, the following property can be then defined:
- For all x obtained by GenX, the result of f1(f2(x)) is equal to f2(f1(x));
- **Some things never change or Invariants**: some properties are not affected by some operations. If p and f are examples of such properties and operations, respectively, the following property is valid:
- For all x obtained by GenX, the result of p(f(x))is equal to p(x).
- A usual example is the size of a list that remains the same after a map operation.
- **Fuzzing:** For any given input the result of some functions should be true. Being f an example of such function, one can have the following property:
- For all x obtained by GenX, the result of f(x) is true.
- What needs to always be true, depends on the problem in hand. For instance, the result must be always valid, or the time to get a result should be less to 1 second, among other characteristics that need to be reinforced and properly tested.

Fuzzing has been viewed doubtfully by the author of a tool that is introduced later in this chapter, namely the possibility of "fuzzing can just be applied to arbitrary programs with minimal understanding of their behaviour" (MacIver, 2016) and the imperative necessity to reason about the properties and what is been done when using PBT, otherwise it is not PBT.

Generators

Generators are used by the properties to generate random cases. PBT libraries make available generators for simple types and sets, typically including extreme cases, such as the maximum integer, for instance. It is usually easy to create numbers from an interval or chars from a set of possibilities. Standard generators can accept parameters that condition or restrict the values to be generated.

Complex data structures require the definition of a custom generator. It is not uncommon to have a generator using another generator.

Analysis of the generated dataset is usually made straightforward by the PBT tools. It may reveal the need to rebalance the distribution of data without compromising their variability.

Shrinking

When a failing case occurs, the shrinking process starts, to simplify the understanding of what happened, a strategy that is adopted in PBT tools. The input is reduced to the smallest input, i.e. the minimum failure example, that would still produce an error. This is important to simplify and speed debugging, as many test failures, all of which have the same cause, do not need to be manually verified. Shrinking can be seen as "extracting the signal from the noise" (Hughes, 2016).

Tools

QuickCheck, a tool for testing Haskell application already introduced, was the forerunner of several others that followed. PBT has been widely used in the context of functional programming, where QuickCheck was born, but tools have been also made available for other styles and languages. Table 2 provides an overview of different solutions without the concern of complete coverage of all alternatives. However, from the list provided by Wikipedia (2019), maintained or active tools were included for some commonly used languages, and some others were added, such as Whisker, which is probably the first PBT tool for blocks-based programs. On the other hand, QuickCheck for Java (Jung, 2012) and JCheck (2013), for instance, were excluded as their last update was in 2012 and 2013, respectively. Others were excluded because still in a very early stage after some years of the first release.

Hebert (2019) considers the commercial product QuickCheck for Erlang and Elixir, provided by QuviQ, as the most complete implementation of QuickCheck. QuviQ, a Swedish company, is described as "the leading supplier of services and tools in the area of property-based testing" (QuviQ, 2019a). The author very positively sees the implementations available for Erlang, Haskell, and Scala. Hypothesis framework is highlighted by its unique features to property-based testing.

Figure 3 uses data from Google Trends using "ScalaCheck" as a search term. The interest by region using the same service are: Switzerland (100), United Kingdom (72), Sweden (62), Australia (59), Finland (58), Germany (52), Poland (43), United States (41), Russia (30), Spain (27), France (26), Canada (25). These values vary from 0 to 100, where 0 only means the inexistence of enough data and 100

Table 2. Some open-source tools

Tool	Language/ platform	Release year	Current version	Documentation
FsCheck	.Net	2013	2.14.0	(FsCheck, 2019)
CurryCheck	Curry	2016 (included in Curry PAKCS since version 1.14.0 and KiCS2 since version 0.5.0)	-	(Hanus, 2016)
PropEr	Erlang	2011	1.3.0	(PropEr, 2018).
QuickCheck	Haskell	1999	2.13.2	(QuickCheck, 2019)
SmallCheck	Haskell	2011	1.1.5	(Runciman, Naylor, & Lindblad, 2008)
jqwik	Java	2017	1.2.0	(jqwik, 2019).
fast-check	JavaScript	2017	1.16.0	(Fast-check, 2019)
PrologCheck	Prolog	2014	-	(Amaral, Florido, & Costa, 2014)
Hypothesis	Python	2013	4.32.3	(MacIver, 2019a).
ScalaCheck	Scala	2008	1.14.0	(Nilsson, 2018).
Whisker	Scratch	2018	0.2	(Stahlbauer, Kreis, & Fraser, 2019)

Figure 3. Internet search behavior for terms related to ScalaCheck. Source: GoogleTrends (from 2007-01 to 2019-06)

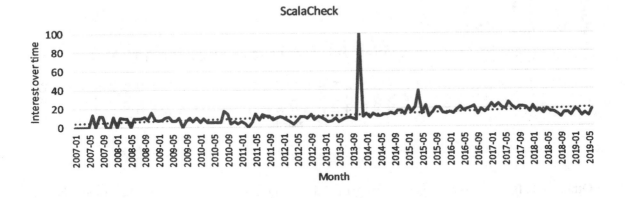

signals the location with the most popularity when considered the total searches. Despite some peaks, the interest in the tool may be rising.

Since its release in March 2017, jqwik has been capturing some attention (see Figure 4). The interest seems to be increasing, but no data is available for any specific country (interest by region).

Quickcheck has other meanings besides PBT, and two terms were used at Google Trends as shown in Figure 5. The number of searches has been decreasing, but using both words, quickcheck and Haskell. The interest by region, as provided by Google Trends, is only different from 0 for Germany.

Figure 4. Internet search behavior for terms related to jqwik (past 5 years)

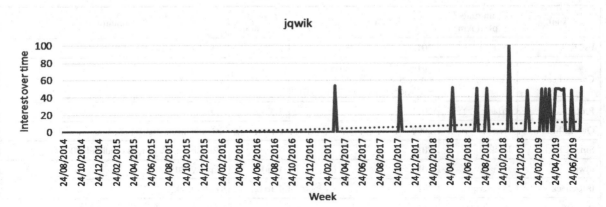

Figure 5. Internet search behavior for two terms: Quickcheck and Haskell (from 2004-01 to 2019-06)

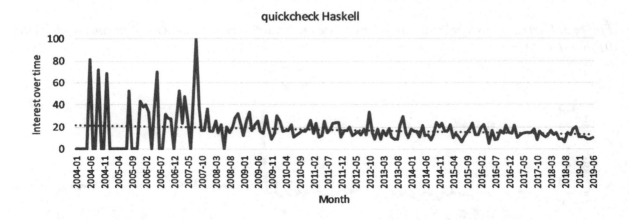

Other tools have names too generic to get results using the Google service, while others have also other meanings as their usage started much before any release. However, figures 1 to 5 only shows possible interest for the terms provided, without a guarantee that the searches were related to PBT.

Returning to commercial tools, QuviQ provides some products (QuviQ, 2019a) that implement approaches to PBT having different targets and characteristics that represent commercial versions of QuickCheck: QuickCheck for Erlang and Elixir, QuickCheck for C and C++, QuickCheck Automotive, QuickCheck for Web Services, and QuickCheck for other languages and APIs. QuickCheck Automotive is related to AUTomotive Open System Architecture (AUTOSAR) and the compliance with some standards already developed under this initiative.

Property-Based State Machine Testing

Stateful testing of command sequences with evaluation of a condition after each command (Nilsson, 2014b) uses the idea of state machines to test more complex situations.

Property-Based State Machine Testing (PBSMT) is PBT but at the level of application behavior, not only functions and data structures that matter. The inputs are generated but also the combination of steps. When a failure is detected, the input and the workflow are shrunk to have the smallest input and set of steps needed to break the code. Shrinking is now even more valuable.

Stateful property tests are especially useful when the implementation is complex and integration and system tests are applicable (Hebert, 2019), not unit tests. The author highlights that "most of the amazing stories of property-based testing [...] involves large and complex stateful systems where tricky bugs are found with a relatively tiny test. Those usually turn out to be stateful properties".

ScalaCheck (2019) and Hypothesis (MacIver, 2019b) are two tools that use similar approaches to PBSMT. However, other mature tools also support Property-Based State Machine Testing.

PBT in the Software Development Industry

Even though PBT is not yet widely used in the software industry, some motivating examples are already known, such as the use of QuickCheck in project FIFO, to uncover 25 important defects of several types including timing errors, race conditions, incorrect use of library API's, etc. or even the use of QuickCheck on Google's levelDB to find sequences of calls that could corrupt databases (Hebert, 2019).

Some applications of PBT have been reported for software testing in the automotive industry. Over 3.000 pages of textual specifications of the AUTOSAR standard were translated into QuickCheck models and a large volume of generated tests was used. Over 200 issues were exposed (Arts, Hughes, Norell, & Svensson, 2015).

In (Castro, 2015) there is a use of PBT in the risk management information system ARMISTICE (Gulías, Abalde, Castro, & Varela, 2006) for systematic, effective, and efficient testing of business rules. This led to an increase in the confidence of the validation of business concepts and domain rules while coping with the problem of developing good test sets.

PBT has also been used in the industry to test telecoms software (Arts, Hughes, Norell, & Svensson, 2015), and specifically an industrial implementation of the H.248 protocol (Media Gateway Controller) composed of 212 pages. The protocol defines several commands that a media gateway controller can send to a media gateway, how they should be interpreted, and the possible responses. As a result, five errors were found, including one that represented an incoherence in the protocol specification.

An Experience in Teaching PBT

The authors have been teaching the course of Advanced Programming Techniques (APT), included in the master's program in Informatics Engineering from the Instituto Superior de Engenharia do Porto, for four years. It aims at introducing students to novel or underused programming techniques which can increase software quality. The course uses the language Scala and the PBT tool Scalacheck (Nilsson, 2014a).

The Course

The course's program consists of an initial series of lectures and consolidation exercises, followed by a capstone project.

The lectures usually include the exposition of the theory quickly followed by interactive problem solving to both maintain high levels of attention and also begin the consolidation of the subject matter. In the interactive problem solving, the teacher presents a problem and tries to create a solution from the inputs given by the students. The inputs from the students can be iteratively improved by the proposing student or other students to create a better solution. The consolidation exercises are to be performed by the students on their own and, even though they can discuss the problem with the teacher, any proposed solution must come from the student.

The capstone project starts with a warmup phase in which the complete project environment is created, including the project building tool, the linter, and the libraries to be used in the project for both development and testing. After the warmup, three milestone phases follow:

- MS1 in which a minimum viable product is to be developed, usually using very naïve algorithms and simple unit tests.
- MS2 in which property-based tests are to be created for the project.
- MS3 in which the algorithms are required to be at their full complexity, while still being able to pass all the tests.

The capstone project usually includes at least one complex algorithm, for which the number of unit tests, required to have a good confidence degree in its implementation, would be prohibitively high. In the last two years, PBT has been introduced as a means of dealing with the issue.

In each of the milestones, students are given feedback, which can be used to produce a more satisfactory solution to the milestone and resubmitted in the final submission. In the final submission (MS3), it is expected that the previous milestones are fully understood and developed.

Therefore, it is expected that, by the end of the course, students can find properties in software and develop property-based tests for these properties.

Consolidation Exercises

The consolidation exercises for the PBT part of the course start with familiarization with properties and generators using very simple exercises and are complemented with a major exercise which is based on a buggy implementation of a previous capstone project, for which the students must find and implement properties and generators. Given the lack of experience of the students at that time, the project contains a TODO list and commentaries to try to steer the students' resolutions in the right direction.

Simple Exercises

These exercises consist, initially, on the development of properties using already developed generators, included in the library. These include generators for simple types such as numbers, characters, sets, etc. Examples and exercises are given for set properties; string properties; mathematical properties, etc.

Figure 6. Simple generator exercise

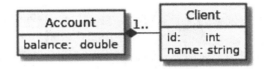

Once the knowledge of how to properly develop a property is well established, the creation of generators can be exercised. The development of custom generators is usually based on simple generators used together to accomplish the task. As an example, suppose the simple domain diagram exposed in Figure 6.

The objective of the exercise is to create a generator of accounts, with a random balance and set of clients. To generate an account it is, therefore, mandatory that a client can be generated, so the first generator to be developed will be a client generator.

To develop a client generator, since the client contains only simple types, the existing generators for integers and strings are used to generate random clients. The developed generator can then be sampled by the students to ensure its correct implementation. Once the client generator is concluded, an account generator can be created. It will be created using both the numerical and non-empty container generators, which already exist in the framework. The numerical generator will create instances of the balance attribute (which can be positive or negative). The non-empty container generator will use the previously created client generator to instantiate a non-empty set of clients.

Major Exercise

The major exercise brings together the creation of properties with custom generators. Students are given an already developed project, for which they must create property-based tests. In the test area of the project, there are some unit tests and a prototyped property-based test with the definition (but not implementation) of some of the generators needed and a TODO statement for each. The student must read the problem and identify all the generators needed. The relation between generators is also an issue to be dealt with. The first part of the major exercise ends with simple property-based tests. In the next part, students who could not find the bugs in the project (due to poorly developed generators), are given a generation strategy, which will necessarily find a bug. Once bugs are found, students must submit to the teacher:

- What bugs were found and their significance for the project.
- Why did the unit test fail to find the bugs?
- How the bugs could be corrected.

THE CAPSTONE PROJECT

The capstone project consisted of a solution to the Aircraft Scheduling Problem (ASP) (Lieder & Stolletz, 2016). This problem's domain can be defined as is shown in Figure 7.

Figure 7. Aircraft scheduling problem domain diagram

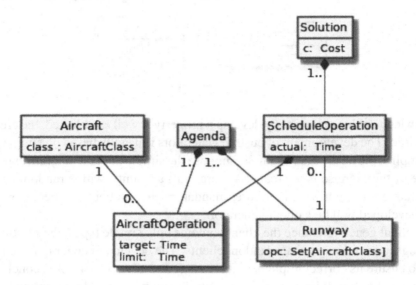

Problem Definition

An aircraft belongs to a class based on its size, weight and type of operation it is trying to perform (landing or take-off). Figure 7 highlights the main domain concepts. An aircraft operation (AircraftOperation) is an association between an aircraft, a target time for the operation and the maximum allowed time instant in which the operation is allowed. A runway makes available the landing or take-off operations but can be restrictive to the aircraft class. An agenda is simply the association of a set of aircraft operations and a set of runways.

The decision problem is formulated as follows: given an agenda, assign a runway and an actual time to each of the aircraft operations. The decision problem is thus, a function which input is an Agenda and which output is an option of a Solution (in Scala and most of the languages which have some functional background, an option is a data structure which contains some value or none. It is a sound replacement for null values). The Solution aggregates a non-empty set of ScheduleOperation. The ScheduleOperation is just an AircraftOperation, which has already been scheduled for an actual time, on a specific Runway.

The resulting solution (if it exists) must meet minimum time separation requirements (defined by international aviation authorities) that are sequence-dependent, as they depend on the operation type and the respective aircraft class of both the preceding and succeeding operation. When an operation is delayed, a delay penalty cost is incurred that depends on the respective operation class and the length of the delay. If an operation must be delayed to a time outside its allowed time window, given a previous sequence of aircraft operations and the time constraints, the whole schedule is invalidated.

Property Requirements

The ASP has the following properties, for a valid schedule:

- Each aircraft operation must be scheduled within its allowed time window.
- For each solution, all the aircraft operations must be scheduled, and schedule operations must use only existing runways.
- Each solution's cost must represent the accumulated cost of each of the scheduled operations' costs.
- Each aircraft operation must comply with the sequence-dependent time separation requirements with the previous aircraft operations.

Students were required to implement these properties in the MS2 phase of the capstone project. The task consisted of identifying and developing the properties from the problem definition. The properties are not complex in themselves but required some complexity in their generators. Once the generators are created, the properties can be easily defined, since the properties merely define restrictions that the solution must comply with.

Generators

From a property-based testing perspective, the development included the automatic generation of sets of aircraft operations and sets of runways. The generation should be as realistic as possible (e.g. based on probability distributions), and such that it can be known whether a valid schedule is possible. The generation of random sets of aircraft operations and sets of runways will almost always lead to impossible scheduling problems, but the defined properties must hold only for valid schedules (that is, for scheduling problems with at least one solution). In other words, for a scheduling problem to be valid, the set of aircraft operations is dependent on the set of available runways. To consider this restriction, a random non-empty set of runways (not too many due to the NP-completeness of the problem) should be initially created. The generation of aircraft operations, even though it can have some randomness regarding the aircraft's class and operation's target time, must be dependent on the random set of runways already generated, for the problem to be feasible.

For a single runway, a criterion that can be used, to ensure there is a valid schedule is a random separation time between aircraft operations, in which the minimum possible value is the minimum aircraft separation time. This criterion could be enhanced to allow a distribution for the various available runways, by dividing the minimum aircraft separation time by the number of available runways.

The final goal is the generation of an Agenda. This will be accomplished with the definition of a generator of non-empty sets of both AircraftOperation and Runway.

Property Development

Given the implementation of the generators, it should be simple to prove the properties. The generation of testing instances with classification is the most challenging part of the problem.

The proposed algorithms, for each of the property requirements, are given in Table 3.

Table 3. Property development algorithms

Property	Development
Each aircraft operation must be scheduled within its allowed time window	From the generated Solution, examine each of the ScheduleOperation and validate that actual is included in the interval from target to limit of the associated AircraftOperation
For each solution, all the aircraft operations must be scheduled, and schedule operations must use only existing runways	Compare the Solution's ScheduleOperation set to the generated Agenda's AircraftOperation set.
	Use the Solution's ScheduleOperation set to generate all used Runway. Compare it to the generated Agenda's Runway set
Each solution's cost must represent the accumulated cost of each of the scheduled operations' costs	Use the Solution's ScheduleOperation set to accumulate the Solution's cost and compare it to the Solution's cost attribute
Each aircraft operation must comply with the sequence-dependent time separation requirements with the previous aircraft operations	Compare each of the Solution's ScheduleOperation, to all of the earlier scheduled ScheduleOperation. Verify that it has the correct time separation of actual time concerning its earlier set, given the aeronautic industry separation matrix.

The Survey

To measure the impact of the PBT technology on the students, an elective online survey was created on the learning management system in use. The students had access to it at the end of the course. This survey was answered by twenty-eight (28) students from a universe of sixty-five (65) students which effectively participated in the course.

The questionnaire was divided into the following sections: student background, PBT concepts, and PBT expected use.

The students' background questions gave a sense of previous familiarity with the PBT paradigm. The section on PBT concepts tried to capture the perceived importance of the paradigm and the depth to which it was understood. Finally, the PBT expected use tried to measure the importance attributed to the paradigm by the student.

The survey was composed of four types of questions:

- Yes/No
- Forced-choice Likert scale (Strongly agree; Agree; Disagree; Strongly disagree)
- Reduced, forced-choice Likert scale (Strongly agree; Agree; Disagree)
- Multiple-choice questions

The survey and respective results are shown in Table 4. The number of students who chose the option is shown in parentheses.

SURVEY RESULTS AND DISCUSSION

The students' background section shows that even though the majority of students work in software development, the vast majority have never heard of PBT before the course (79%). Only one student applied PBT in any way before the course. Even though not completely unknown, the technique seems to be underused in the industry.

Table 4. PBT survey

	Question	Answers
	Students' background	
1	Are you currently working in software development?	Yes (25) No (3)
2	The course belongs to your:	Favorite subjects (7) Rather favorite subjects (11) Rather not favorite subjects (5) Not favorite subjects (5)
3	Does your company use Property-Based Testing in any way?	Yes (1) No (27)
4	What were your experiences with Property-Based Testing (PBT), in any programming language, before this course?	I have never heard of it before. (22) I have heard of it before but have never used it. (5) I have already used this paradigm before this course. (1)

We can conclude that the majority (86%) of students think they understood the PBT concepts and that the technique can help them to produce more robust software. The majority (89%) of students was able to see the confidence increase from using case-based to property-based testing.

Nevertheless, some work needs to be done as there is a significant number of students (32%) which considers the PBT paradigm hard to understand. The fact that most of the PBT libraries and concepts come from functional programming, which is not part of the students' previous curriculum and is introduced in this course, could be a part of the problem. Additionally, generator design for complex algorithms is not trivial and classroom exercises are being prepared to cope with this problem.

As for future use of the technique, 64% of the inquired think that they would use it in practice, given the opportunity, which could lead to the spread of the technique throughout the students' software companies.

Finally, the Pearson correlation test was performed on the answers' data of different questions. We were expecting a positive correlation between questions:

- 2 (The course belongs to your: Favorite subjects, … Not favorite subjects) and 5 (Do you think you understood the PBT concepts?).
- 6 (PBT helps with your ability to produce more robust and less error-prone software) and 11 (Would you use the PBT techniques learned in this course in practice?).
- 10 (The concepts used in PBT are easy to use and the libraries are easy to understand) and 11 (Would you use the PBT techniques learned in this course in practice?).

Their values were, respectively, 0.02; 0.52; 0.30. The first correlation may imply that the feelings on the course do not impair the ability to learn. The second and third correlations imply that students who see a benefit in PBT and find it easy, are also prone to want to use it in their daily lives.

Other meaningful correlations between answers for some questions are shown in Table 5. The correlation between answers provided for questions 6 and 9 shows that, when students finished the course, they had understood the potential of the PBT technique and its relation to traditional case-based testing.

Table 5. PBT survey and some correlations

Question number	Other question number	Correlation value
6	9	0.71
6	7	0.50
7	8	0.48
5	10	0.45
6	19	0.42

CONCLUSION

The time and knowledge needed to create accurate tests are challenges when trying to improve software reliability and reduce coding defects. The method used for their identification depends on many factors, including the person in charge of the detection (Runeson, Andersson, Thelin, Andrews, & Berling, 2006). Recent studies have shown that many testing methods are unknown, and tools regarded as complex to use by professionals who develop tests (Hynninen, Kasurinen, Knutas, & Taipale, 2018; Strazdiņa et al., 2018). Therefore, many testing approaches must be taught to let people have a wider choice from the many possibilities that exist to ensure some quality of their applications and at an early stage. In this sense, the sharing of teaching experiences is of great importance for their replication, with or without major changes, according to their audience, in higher education or even as autonomous training.

The ability to verify the application's properties against expected properties without specifying concrete values, but generating them, is an asset in software testing. Moreover, it does not compromise its evolution, as these values, if directly indicated, may no longer be valid in the future. Testing is considered "a critical component to the incremental change aspect of evolutionary architecture" and property-based testing is seen as a promising area (Ford, Parsons, & Kua, 2017). Constant changes to software products imply a testing process that can keep up with them, and PBT has advantages over other approaches in this respect.

PBT has matured over the years and many supporting platforms have been made available, which can be seen as an indicator that the approach can be widely adopted. However, an effort in its dissemination is needed, without forgetting it is more demanding and requires more practice time than others.

The course of Advanced Programming Techniques, here described, will continue to include PBT and even dedicate to the subject additional hours. Students' comments were generally positive and the use of expressions such as "open our minds" and "think differently" was common.

In the coming months, industry research is planned. We aim to understand the importance attached to testing in the software development process and the way lesser-known approaches are used. The possibility of providing short courses especially dedicated to people other than our master's students is not ruled out.

ACKNOWLEDGMENT

We are grateful to Nuno Ferreira, an experienced software engineer, for sharing his experience in developing and testing applications for an industry with many regulations that must be adhered to. His valuable suggestions and comments on PBT have enabled us to improve this chapter.

REFERENCES

Agile Testing Days. (2018). Property-based Testing with Java. *Agile Testing Days*. Retrieved from https://agiletestingdays.com/2018/session/property-based-testing-with-java/

Amaral, C., Florido, M., & Costa, V. S. (2014, June). PrologCheck–property-based testing in prolog. In *International Symposium on Functional and Logic Programming* (pp. 1-17). Springer.

Arts, T., Hughes, J., Johansson, J., & Wiger, U. (2006, September). Testing telecoms software with quviq QuickCheck. In *Proceedings of the 2006 ACM SIGPLAN workshop on Erlang* (pp. 2-10). ACM. 10.1145/1159789.1159792

Arts, T., Hughes, J., Norell, U., & Svensson, H. (2015, April). Testing AUTOSAR software with QuickCheck. In *2015 IEEE Eighth International Conference on Software Testing, Verification and Validation Workshops (ICSTW)* (pp. 1-4). IEEE.

Basili, V., Briand, L., Bianculli, D., Nejati, S., Pastore, F., & Sabetzadeh, M. (2018). Software engineering research and industry: A symbiotic relationship to Foster impact. *IEEE Software*, *35*(5), 44–49. doi:10.1109/MS.2018.290110216

Beszédes, Á., & Vidács, L. (2016, April). Academic and Industrial Software Testing Conferences: Survey and Synergies. In *2016 IEEE Ninth International Conference on Software Testing, Verification and Validation Workshops (ICSTW)* (pp. 240-249). IEEE. 10.1109/ICSTW.2016.30

Brünjes, L. (2018). *IOHK | Director of Education - Lars Brünjes - Property Based Testing* [Video file]. Retrieved from https://www.youtube.com/watch?v=8p5YZpre0lY

Castro, L. M. (2015). Advanced management of data integrity: Property-based testing for business rules. *Journal of Intelligent Information Systems*, *44*(3), 355–380. doi:10.100710844-014-0335-2

Chen, T. Y., Kuo, F. C., Liu, H., Poon, P. L., Towey, D., Tse, T. H., & Zhou, Z. Q. (2018). Metamorphic testing: A review of challenges and opportunities. *ACM Computing Surveys*, *51*(1), 4. doi:10.1145/3143561

Chen, T. Y., Kuo, F. C., Tse, T. H., & Zhou, Z. Q. (2003, September). Metamorphic testing and beyond. In *Eleventh Annual International Workshop on Software Technology and Engineering Practice* (pp. 94-100). IEEE. 10.1109/STEP.2003.18

Chepurnoy, A., & Rathee, M. (2018, March). Checking laws of the blockchain with property-based testing. In *2018 International Workshop on Blockchain Oriented Software Engineering (IWBOSE)* (pp. 40-47). IEEE. 10.1109/IWBOSE.2018.8327570

Claessen, K., & Hughes, J. (2000). *QuickCheck: a lightweight tool for random testing of Haskell programs.* Paper presented at the fifth ACM SIGPLAN international conference on Functional programming. 10.1145/351240.351266

Claessen, K., Hughes, J., Pałka, M., Smallbone, N., & Svensson, H. (2010, May). Ranking programs using black box testing. In *Proceedings of the 5th Workshop on Automation of Software Test* (pp. 103-110). ACM. 10.1145/1808266.1808282

Dalal, S. R., Jain, A., Karunanithi, N., Leaton, J. M., Lott, C. M., Patton, G. C., & Horowitz, B. M. (1999, May). Model-based testing in practice. In *Proceedings of the 1999 International Conference on Software Engineering (IEEE Cat. No. 99CB37002)* (pp. 285-294). IEEE. 10.1145/302405.302640

Derrick, J., Walkinshaw, N., Arts, T., Earle, C. B., Cesarini, F., Fredlund, L. A., ... Thompson, S. (2009, November). Property-based testing-the protest project. In *International Symposium on Formal Methods for Components and Objects* (pp. 250-271). Springer.

Fast-check. (2019). *Property based testing framework for JavaScript (like QuickCheck) written in TypeScript.* Retrieved from https://github.com/dubzzz/fast-check

Fielding, R. T. (2000). *Architectural styles and the design of network-based software architectures.* Irvine, CA: University of California.

Fink, G., & Bishop, M. (1997). Property-based testing: A new approach to testing for assurance. *Software Engineering Notes*, *22*(4), 74–80. doi:10.1145/263244.263267

Fink, G., Ko, C., Archer, M., & Levitt, K. (1994). *Towards a property-based testing environment with applications to security-critical software.* California Univ Davis Dept of Computer Science.

Fink, G., & Levitt, K. (1994, December). Property-based testing of privileged programs. In *Tenth Annual Computer Security Applications Conference* (pp. 154-163). IEEE. 10.1109/CSAC.1994.367311

Ford, N., Parsons, R., & Kua, P. (2017). *Building evolutionary architectures: Support constant change.* O'Reilly Media, Inc.

FsCheck Web site. (2019). *Random Testing for .NET.* Retrieved from https://fscheck.github.io/FsCheck/index.html

Garousi, V., & Felderer, M. (2017). Worlds apart: Industrial and academic focus areas in software testing. *IEEE Software*, *34*(5), 38–45. doi:10.1109/MS.2017.3641116

Gulías, V. M., Abalde, C., Castro, L. M., & Varela, C. (2006). Formalisation of a Functional Risk Management System. ICEIS, (3), 516-519.

Hanus, M. (2016, September). CurryCheck: Checking properties of Curry programs. In *International Symposium on Logic-Based Program Synthesis and Transformation* (pp. 222-239). Springer.

Hebert, F. (2019, January). Property-Based Testing with PropEr, Erlang, and Elixir: Find Bugs Before Your Users Do. *Pragmatic Bookshelf.*

Hughes, J. (2016). Experiences with QuickCheck: testing the hard stuff and staying sane. In *A List of Successes That Can Change the World* (pp. 169–186). Cham: Springer. doi:10.1007/978-3-319-30936-1_9

Hynninen, T., Kasurinen, J., Knutas, A., & Taipale, O. (2018, May). Software testing: Survey of the industry practices. In *2018 41st International Convention on Information and Communication Technology, Electronics and Microelectronics (MIPRO)* (pp. 1449-1454). IEEE.

JCheck. (2013). Retrieved from http://www.jcheck.org/

jqwik. (2019). *Property-Based Testing in Java*. Retrieved from https://jqwik.net/

JungT. (2012). *Quickcheck for Java*. Retrieved from https://bitbucket.org/blob79/quickcheck/src/default/

Kuo, F. C., Chen, T. Y., & Tam, W. K. (2011, October). Testing embedded software by metamorphic testing: A wireless metering system case study. In *2011 IEEE 36th Conference on Local Computer Networks* (pp. 291-294). IEEE. 10.1109/LCN.2011.6115306

Labuschagne, A., Inozemtseva, L., & Holmes, R. (2017, August). Measuring the cost of regression testing in practice: a study of Java projects using continuous integration. In *Proceedings of the 2017 11th Joint Meeting on Foundations of Software Engineering* (pp. 821-830). ACM. 10.1145/3106237.3106288

Laucher, A. (2015). *Property Based Testing: Shrinking Risk in Your Code*. Paper presented at YOW! 2015 Conference, Brisbane, Australia.

Le, V., Afshari, M., & Su, Z. (2014, June). Compiler validation via equivalence modulo inputs. *ACM SIGPLAN Notices*, *49*(6), 216–226. doi:10.1145/2666356.2594334

Lieder, A., & Stolletz, R. (2016, April). Scheduling aircraft take-offs and landings on inter-dependent and heterogeneous runways. *Transportation Research Part E, Logistics and Transportation Review*, *88*, 167–188. doi:10.1016/j.tre.2016.01.015

MacIver, D. (2016). *What is Property Based Testing?* Retrieved from https://hypothesis.works/articles/what-is-property-based-testing/.

MacIver, D. (2019a). *Welcome to Hypothesis!* Retrieved from https://hypothesis.readthedocs.io/en/latest/

MacIver, D. (2019b). *Stateful testing*. Retrieved from https://hypothesis.readthedocs.io/en/latest/stateful.html

Moura, R. (2019). *European Testing Conference*. Retrieved from https://europeantestingconference.eu/2019/

Nilsson, R. (2014a). *ScalaCheck: The Definitive Guide*. Artima Press.

Nilsson, R. (2014b). *Testing Stateful Systems with ScalaCheck*. Berlin: ScalaDays.

Nilsson, R. (2018). *ScalaCheck: Property-based testing for Scala*. Retrieved from http://www.scala-check.org

O'Farrell, C. (2015). *Practical Property-Based Testing*. Paper presented at YOW! Lambda Jam 2015 Conference.

Page, R. (2011, October). Property-based testing and verification: a catalog of classroom examples. In *International Symposium on Implementation and Application of Functional Languages* (pp. 134-147). Springer.

PropEr. (2018). *PropEr: a QuickCheck-inspired property-based testing tool for Erlang.* Retrieved from https://github.com/proper-testing/proper

QuickCheck. (2019). *QuickCheck: Automatic testing of Haskell programs.* Retrieved from http://hackage.haskell.org/package/QuickCheck-2.13.2

QuviQ. (2019a). *QuviQ.* Retrieved from http://www.quviq.com/contact-2/about/

QuviQ. (2019b). *QuviQ testing tools.* Retrieved from http://www.quviq.com/products/

Runciman, C., Naylor, M., & Lindblad, F. (2008). SmallCheck and Lazy SmallCheck. In *Proceedings of the first ACM SIGPLAN symposium on Haskell (Haskell '08).* ACM. 10.1145/1411286.1411292

Runeson, P., Andersson, C., Thelin, T., Andrews, A., & Berling, T. (2006). What do we know about defect detection methods? *IEEE Software, 23*(3), 82–90. doi:10.1109/MS.2006.89

ScalaCheck. (2019). *ScalaCheck User Guide.* Retrieved from https://github.com/typelevel/scalacheck/blob/master/doc/UserGuide.md#stateful-testing

Stahlbauer, A., Kreis, M., & Fraser, G. (2019, August). Testing scratch programs automatically. In *Proceedings of the 2019 27th ACM Joint Meeting on European Software Engineering Conference and Symposium on the Foundations of Software Engineering* (pp. 165-175). ACM.

Strazdiņa, L., Arnicane, V., Arnicans, G., Bičevskis, J., Borzovs, J., & Kuļešovs, I. (2018). What Software Test Approaches, Methods, and Techniques are Actually Used in Software Industry? *Joint Proceedings of Baltic DB&IS 2018 Conference Forum and Doctoral Consortium.*

Tao, Q., Wu, W., Zhao, C., & Shen, W. (2010, November). An automatic testing approach for compiler based on metamorphic testing technique. In *2010 Asia Pacific Software Engineering Conference* (pp. 270-279). IEEE. doi:10.1109/APSEC.2010.39

Waldmann, J. (2017). How I Teach Functional Programming. *Workshop on Functional Logic Programming (WFLP 2017).*

Wikipedia. (2019). *QuickCheck.* Retrieved from https://en.wikipedia.org/wiki/QuickCheck

Wlaschin, S. (2015). *An introduction to property based testing.* Paper presented at Functional Programming eXchange Conference, London, UK.

Chapter 11
Investigating Software Testing Practices in Software Development Organizations:
Sri Lankan Experience

Shanmuganathan Vasanthapriyan
https://orcid.org/0000-0002-0597-0263
Sabaragamuwa University of Sri Lanka, Sri Lanka

ABSTRACT

Software testing, which is a knowledge-intensive and collaborative activity, is a sub-area of software engineering. Software testing knowledge can be applied to different testing tasks and purposes. Since software development is an error-prone task, in order to achieve quality software products, validation and verification should be carried throughout the development. This study, using qualitative methods, investigates the current practice of software testing practices in two software companies on the basis that they both claimed to apply software testing practices in their software development work. Interview results revealed some interesting latest trends in software testing from both companies.

INTRODUCTION

Software testing which is also a knowledge-intensive and collaborative activity is a sub-area of software engineering. Software testing knowledge can be applied to different testing tasks and purposes. Since software development is an error-prone task, in order to achieve quality software products, Validation and Verification should be carried out throughout the development. Software testers must, therefore, work with all the other software professionals involved in the development operations. Importantly, software testers are not only acquainted with countless test techniques for software but are also conscious of approaches to software development. Software testers, for example, may either need help with a test case design data appropriate to the comparable project that was earlier treated for testing reasons or design a

DOI: 10.4018/978-1-7998-2531-9.ch011

test case. This motivates software firms to handle their reuse understanding in creative ways of solving issues.

In several kinds of research in several nations, software testing in software businesses has been widely investigated and analyzed. A number of researches were recognized in our literature search (Causevic, Sundmark, & Punnekkat, 2010; Garousi & Varma, 2010; Garousi & Zhi, 2013; Geras, Smith, & Miller, 2004).

A code deployment transferred from one setting to another must endure a rigorous testing process to decide what problems arose. However, this form of transition was not included at the initial Software Development Lifecycle (SDLC) and thus it is not obvious whether all the historically standard application review steps were suitable for this reason (Mullen, 2018). Application verification is an essential aspect of the lifecycle of software development. Application testing has traditionally centered on software programs built on "personal" devices, i.e., on-premises. Since the industry trend changed dramatically in favor of technology hosted by the internet, software testing methods, approaches and implementation strategies had to evolve and upgrade according to these changes (Mullen, 2018).

Learning, cultural attitudes, employee behaviors, and reward systems are some of the key issues organizations should consider to present themselves as highly creative in the current marketplace. Importantly, it has been revealed from SLAASCOM (Sri Lanka Association for Software and Services Companies) that the Sri Lankan software engineering sector or other Sri Lankan organizations have not undertaken any inquiry to evaluate elements of Knowledge Management (KM) practices in Sri Lankan software sectors. The writers think that this experience can be commonly used in software sectors to reference and update promising methods in science KM and promote creativity.

In the context of software testing, knowledge and experience can be captured by the KM practices. This knowledge is usually stored on papers or in peoples' minds. When a problem arises, the team members look for experts in their own work environment, relying on people they know or look for documents. Desai and Shah (2011) identified various problems faced by organizations in KM including low rate of use and reuse of software testing knowledge, barriers in software testing knowledge transfer and poor sharing environment for software testing knowledge. Liu et al. (Liu, Wu, Liu, & Gu, 2009) also presented the current state of KM in software testing and the major existing problems. Abdullah et al. (Abdullah, Eri, & Talib, 2011) proposed and formulated a model in order to facilitate a knowledge managing of the best quality of software testing environment. Further, they stated that community of practice (CoP) can utilize the knowledge in KMS and it will reduce the mistakes or errors, so that a good product can be delivered. A series of systematic mapping research was carried out by Souza et al. (De Souza, de Almeida Falbo, & Vijaykumar, 2015; Souza, Falbo, & Vijaykumar, 2013) on the KM to software testing. They investigated some aspects associated with applying KM to software testing through this systematic mapping of the literature.

The Sri Lankan software companies have to succeed in the quality standards of leading software organizations in order to achieve global success on the international market. In order to extend our study towards the current status of software testing practices in Sri Lankan software companies, the authors of this research intended to carry out qualitative research work. Unfortunately, authors found that presently there is a gap in literature concerning the deep knowledge of current status of software testing practices in software companies in the context of Sri Lanka. Therefore, software testing practices cannot be analyzed or reviewed in software businesses in Sri Lanka. So this research seeks to decrease this gap by using an empirical inquiry to evaluate the current status of software testing practices in Sri Lankan software businesses. Also providing quantitative and qualitative approaches as complementary epistemological orientations is helpful in triangulation, and offers better understanding of the findings. Such that, this study aims to study the current status of software testing practices in Sri Lankan software companies using a qualitative method.

The related study is presented in the second section and the research design is discussed in the third section. Section four is comprised of the complete analysis of the results of the online survey and the interviews held with management and senior software engineers. Our discussion and conclusions are presented in section five.

RELATED STUDY

Numerous surveys have been conducted on the subject of software testing practices in different countries and scales. A qualitative survey was conducted for verification and validation processes almost fifteen years before in 11 Swedish companies (Runeson, Andersson, & Höst, 2003). They had invited many experts from academia and industry to study the current status of software testing practices. Most of the research has a study on (1) test process improvement, (2) testing automation and testing tools, and (3) standardization, (4) Test-Driven Development (5) test metrics (6) test management and training, (7) academic involvement.

KM has now become a trendy buzzword as a result of the transformation of industrial economics from the platform of natural resources into intellectual assets (Desouza & Pacquette, 2011). Even though its popularity is reflected in the growing number of books and articles; there is still no agreed definition for KM, even among practitioners.

However, there are many explanations that cover more alike about the topic with similar terms. One of them defines: KM is about developing, sharing and applying knowledge within the firm to gain and sustain a competitive advantage (Edvardsson, 2008). Furthermore, 'KM is the acquisition and use of resources to create an environment in which information is accessible to individuals and in which individuals acquire, share and use that information to develop their own knowledge and are encouraged and enabled to apply their knowledge for the benefit of the organization' (Harman & Brelade, 2007). It is also defined as a conscious strategy of getting the right knowledge to the right people at the right time and helping people share and put information into action in ways that strive to improve organizational performance (Girard & Girard, 2015).

Knowledge could be found in two forms such as tacit knowledge and explicit knowledge (Edvardsson, 2008; Murali & Kumar, 2014; Vasanthapriyan, Xiang, Tian, & Xiong, 2017). Tacit knowledge is what people carry in their minds and we find it difficult to access as it is developed by self-learning and experiences built over time, or maybe as a result of inborn skills. Explicit knowledge, on the other hand, is documented or codified and can be transferred easily to others due to its tangibility. The processes, procedures, journals, manuals, drawings or any such artifacts come under this category (Edvardsson, 2008; Murali & Kumar, 2014).

Omotayo (2015) states the important factors that drive KM requirement for an organization, are: organizational survival, competitive differentiation, globalization effects and aging of the workforce. Like his explanation, it is an undisputed fact that organizations have to compete on the basis of knowledge since products and services are becoming increasingly complex and competitive (Omotayo, 2015).

Focusing on the question 'Is KM important for an organization?' Omotayo (2015) suggested: 'when you know better, you do better'. Therefore, in order to succeed in the corporate world and put your business on top, the company needs to possess the best management of knowledge (Omotayo, 2015).

A survey was conducted in Alberta (Geras et al., 2004). The Alberta market performs less than the US IT sector. One of the main reasons why extreme programming is less accepted. This survey revealed that most companies produce test cases that are prone to error and lack of requirements for stopping the experiment. As a result, these organizations are releasing faulty software products. The most common technique in the development community is that unit testing and automated unit testing are increased. Only 30 percent of businesses use JUnit, NUnit, and CPPUnit automated software.

Kasurinen, Taipale, and Smolander (2010) have carried out a detailed industrial review of 31 organizations. For application test automation, 55 industry experts were interviewed. The testing process is equipped with only three fourth tools, and access to these resources is limited. The use of automated testing software in the industry is challenging. Only 26% of participants are using automated test cases. There is uncertainty that relies on what company uses technology and how it is applied.

Deak and Stålhane (2013) undertook a study that mixed interviews and surveys with a mixture of performance and qualitative queries. Its research shows current trends in the organization of software testing in the IT sector. A new trend is that the tester is a development team leader or a secondary developer's job. There is no research team for small or medium-sized businesses. Automated experiments need more investment and are complicated, which is why limited automation is accomplished.

Mailewa, Herath, and Herath (2015) purposed a new testing technique for large-scale test cases, a mix check. Test optimization is the remedy to software testing time problems. Testing in pairs combines testing and selenium tools for web projects testing automation. The advantages of software training in conjunction with manual analysis is also stressed.

In 2019, Jahan, Riaz, and Abbas study, some successful developments have been found in Pakistan. Many testers start their career as a programmer and switch to software testing when they have expertise. Most of the participants are well-trained or freshly IT experts. Industry takes control of check assessment. Research spending is lower than certain developed countries. The complexity of the IT industry was key to success. Most IT companies in Canada are using TLD, but TLD, TDD, and BDLL are used in Pakistani sector. Companies are using quantitative methods in testing (Jahan, Riaz, & Abbas, 2019).

RESEARCH DESIGN

The main objective of this research project is to understand the current status of Software Testing Practices in Sri Lankan Software companies by adopting a qualitative research method. In order to attain this objective, we target six research questions.

- (RQ1): What are the Test Types used?
- (RQ2): What are the Test Techniques used?
- (RQ3): What is the Test Automation and Test Tools used?
- (RQ4): What are the Test Metrics used?

- (RQ5): What are the Test Management practices used?
- (RQ6): What are the Test Training Techniques used?
- (RQ7): What is the current status of the Interaction with Academia and Software Testing professionals?

Semi-Structured Interviews

Semi-structured interviews were conducted in order to get a clear idea about how software testing is conducted during software development and the interviewees' perception of how to manage software testing during the software development process. The interview questions primarily focused on the current practice of software testing based on six areas as mentioned earlier.

The main purpose of these interviews was to collect qualitative data. From each project in both companies, one software quality assurance (QA) engineer and one test engineer (or equivalent to tester) were selected for the interview. All of them are qualified for the ISTQB certification. The interviews were held at suitable times for participants, with the duration ranging 30–45 min. They were conducted in board rooms at the premises of the corresponding organizations involved. Each participant was given a brief idea of the research, and detailing the participant's rights and responsibilities. Each participant then was asked a series of questions, with both the researcher and participant seeking clariôcation or more information wherever required. Semi-structured interviews started with background information of the candidates, their working experiences, their educational qualifications, and general information about the project (not the sensitive information). This helped the interviewer to develop his skills in conducting semi-structured interviews including dealing with participants, conducting the in-depth interview and managing the personal traits and language barriers.

Description of the Questions

The criteria we used to design the question set for our survey were to ensure that the issues were applicable to the sector as well as capturing the most helpful data. Most of our issues had quantitatively pre-designed multiple-choice responses (e.g., the first question about the present situation of the participant), while some had qualitative (free text) responses, e.g., "What difficulties would you like to pose to the research community?".

The first question class (#1–8) gathered the profiles of the participants. Type/level related information was gathered by the second group of issues (#9–#11). Test types/levels refer to the training phases (unit, inclusion, and system testing) and the capacity of the experiment to evaluate certain characteristics of the system being tested. Our study was targeted at determining the extent to which the sample rates are used by businesses and identifying the item features they are presently looking for.

The 3rd question section (#12 and #13) gathered the experiment technique data. Test techniques are mechanisms to identify test instances and include a broad range of methods ranging from ad hoc to formalized call graphs. The study query #12 attempted to define (and not using) the sample methods used by computer organizations. We also had a specific query (#13) about mutation screening (fault injection), as our knowledge shows that a few test professionals understand or use it (even if they understand it).

The two issues in the category test automation and testing instruments strive to collect the amount of test automation (#14) as well as specific testing instruments used in businesses (#15). Test metrics used by organizations (issues #16 and #17) were also explored. Our objective was to obtain sample coverage metrics (e.g. line and choice coverage) as well as the project or company-wide performance software metrics (e.g., code line failures, identified faults per day). As agile methods such as Scrum and Extreme Programming (XP) depend on statistics to guide the strategy to subsequent iterations, the level to which these metrics were used is crucial. Scrum, for example, is positioned as an "empirical" method for "controlling chaos" (Schwaber & Beedle, 2001).

We also tried to comprehend how organizations are managing their inspection procedures (issues #18–#21). Recent changes in manufacturing best practices render experimentation in the design phase even more pervasive. It makes sense that it is also increasingly essential to manage the test effort. The study evaluated this aspect with a number of issues linked to the sample process management.

Test preparation (questions #22–#25) was the next class of issues. The rationale for these three issues was: (1) to know the amount of official testing received by professionals on the topic of testing, (2) if organizations have a specific testing coaching program, and (3) obstacles stopping businesses from providing software testing instruction.

We also wished to assess the magnitude of studies within businesses on software testing (e.g. having corporate R&D centers), their relationship with college scientists (academia) and studying technical papers on testing and participation at software testing meetings. To this end, Questions #26–#32 served.

Selection of Case Studies and Data Collection

The two software firms (Company X and Company Y) were chosen mainly in this research on the grounds that both asserted to apply KM methods in their software development job. One of the writers who had previously operated in Company X also worked in Company Y during the inquiry. For reasons of confidentiality, the two companies are identified by the letters X and Y.

Company X is a multinational organization with a special interest group for KM, with a region assigned to its intranet from which papers and posts related to KM can be accessed. Company Y is also an organization where meetings were held where another employee was introduced to his job by an employee who is considered an "expert". The knowledge that each of their staff possessed was recognized by both organizations. Both allocated time and resources with blended outcomes to attempt and tap this understanding. Both of these firms have already invested considerable time and money in enhancing the quality of their software development procedures and would, therefore, be perfect candidates for assessing the effectiveness of a KM method as implemented in SE.

The questionnaire and interviews gathered data. This research was attended by a total of 12 individuals (six individuals from each organization). Data was gathered at each business from two projects. The questionnaires were also filled out by the same respondents who participated in interviews. In the projects examined, all respondents were in software development positions, including one project team leader, six software developers, two programmers, one system analyst, and two advisors. Because of their exposure to many elements of the software development lifecycle and their wide technical viewpoint, software developers were targeted. Their experience in software development ranged from 2 to 24 years.

Description of the Projects

The project for company X is denoted by X1 while the project for company Y is denoted by Y1. Generic details about the project are shown in Table 1.

Table 1. Generic details about the project X1 and Y1

	X1	**Y1**
Product	Online Reservation for Airline System	University Administrative Management System
Customer	External	Internal
Location	Different Sites	Same site
No. of team members	40 – 100	15 – 20
Team of QA	• Test Engineer • Automation Specialist • Trainee Automation • Software QA Engineer • QA Lead • Requirement Engineer	• Tester • Software QA Engineer • QA Lead • Business Analysist

Project X1: Project X1's main objective is to create a portal for online reservations for airline system. They were required to produce a mini-version which releases scheduled every two months. The number of team members utilized is around 40 to 100.

Project Y1: Developing a University Administrative Management System is the main goal of Project Y1. It is an internal project with the team members around 15 to 20. They have a software testing team with Tester, Software QA Engineer, QA Lead and Business Analysist.

DATA ANALYSIS, RESULTS, AND DISCUSSIONS

Semi-Structured Interviews were carried out based on grounded theory methodology (Strauss & Corbin, 1997). Not only Software testing is a knowledge-intensive and collaborative activity where software testers are involved, and grounded theory is best fitted for studying people-related issues but also grounded theory is an advisable method for studying a phenomenon that is not studied in deep. Semi-Structured Interview data were analyzed manually and the following steps were followed: a) Semi-structured interviews were recorded. b) Recorded interviews were transcribed to verbatim and developed transcriptions. c) Re-reading the transcript in order to grasp deeper meanings. d) Coding was done by using transcriptions according to prominent topics e) Categories were developed by using codes. f) Identifying central issues and developing themes that were common to all participants.

Test Types

In analyzing RQ1, this section examines the test types used in two companies. The objective was to assess the software testers' understanding and perception of test types and the frequency of usage of different test types. In terms of frequency of usage of different test types, Company X uses mostly unit and functional/system testing. This is because unit testing focuses on testing each program unit or component, isolated from the other components in the system. Further, they also stated that so far no any integration testing has been conducted. In contrast, the respondent from Company Y stated that his team used to spend 60% of the testing efforts on unit testing, 30% on system testing and 10% on performance testing.

In addition, the participants were asked: "In terms of the type and phasing of software development life-cycle, when does your testing life cycle start?". Both respondents from Company X replied they are mostly following the traditional Test-last Development (TLD) approach where the code is generated first and then testing. It means testing is done only after the implementation code has been written. TLD is a traditional and most common approach to testing. On the other hand, testers from Company Y mostly practice Test-driven (first) Development (TDD) approach. This approach allows the developers think of test cases before implementation, which they are unfamiliar to Hilton (2017).

Both of them have their own strengths and weakness. TDD is generally advised over TLD if the product is big, has several updates, has a longer life cycle, or requires a large number of customizations and maintenance. TDD massively increases overall efficiency by reducing the cost and period of repairs. Maintenance and configuration involve modification of software. Changing code may result in unwanted behavior in the output of the program. But because of test cases, this can be avoided by TDD. Since most agile projects have multiple releases, a long life cycle, and a large number of customizations and maintenance, TDD is promoted. Further, TDD is a methodology used by agile software development groups to design and develop code (Choma, Guerra, & da Silva, 2018). In agile development, TDD truly benefits compared to the TLD approach. But in our case both the projects are agile based. Since one project utilizes TLD while the other uses TDD, we dig further.

When implementing this method for the first time, Choma et al. (2018) stated novices and programmers who considered novices to the TDD can encounter difficulties. Programmers can become unmotivated as a result of these initial difficulties because they do not feel successful using TDD. When we consider the novices in project X1 and project Y1 as a ratio between expert and novices, project Y1 have more ratio for experts. Therefore, we concluded that even though both are agile projects, Project Y1 uses TDD because they have more experts in their team.

Test Techniques

Test Engineer from Company X stated that the choice of which test techniques to use depends on a number of factors, including the type of system, regulatory standards and knowledge of the testers, etc. They stated that four specification-based techniques such as equivalence partitioning, boundary value analysis, decision tables, and state transition testing are used most popularly in their projects. Equivalence partitioning is a black box technique that can be applied to all levels of testing like unit, integration, system, etc. One respondent mentioned that equivalence partitioning helped them to reduce the maximum number of test cases to a fixed array of test cases while meeting the maximum demands. Boundary value analysis is the method of checking between extreme ends or limits of input value partitions. One of the respondents stated that he noticed that input values at the output domain's extreme ends triggered further device errors. However, the respondent stated that the boundary value analysis helped them define errors at boundaries rather than locating those in the middle of the output domain.

Decision table testing is a software testing methodology for evaluating system actions with various combinations of inputs. One respondent stated that it is a systematic approach in which the different combinations of inputs and their corresponding process actions (output) are collected in a tabular type. State Transition Testing is characterized as the strategy of software testing where changes in input conditions cause changes in the Application under Test (AUT) status. All the participants in company X mentioned that State Transition Testing is effective for testing various system transitions. They have not used much on white box testing.

At the same time, a respondent from Company Y stated that they are mostly using black-box testing for their projects. On the positive side, Software QA Engineer from Company Y stated that they are familiar with using the vocabularies code coverage, decision coverage, and structural testing instead of black-box techniques.

Code coverage is a metric that measures the degree to which the software source code is checked. It is one way of white box testing in which detects places that are not checked in a number of test scenarios. Respondents mentioned, it also provides several test cases to increase the scope and calculate software performance quantitatively. Structural tests are the types of tests performed to check the software design. The code needs an understanding of this type of testing so that the programmers primarily do so. It is more about how the system behaves than about the system's functionality

Test Automation and Test Tools

The demand for delivering quality software faster is very important in software engineering. In this case, Test automation cannot be realized without good tools; as they determine how automation is performed and whether the benefits of automation can be delivered. Test automation of software testing is the use of independent code from the program being evaluated to monitor test execution and to compare actual tests with expected outcomes. In a formalized testing process already in place, test automation may automate certain routine yet necessary tasks and execute additional tests that would be difficult to perform manually. To understand this goal, Research question 3 was formulated. The use of testing tools was calculated in comparison to the previous findings by the query, implementation level of software testing tools and improvements. In this study, "an application, platform, web service, external database, design environment function, etc. were described as resources to complete the above mission" (Hynninen, Kasurinen, Knutas, & Taipale, 2018).

Both companies stated that they use manual testing in the dominant position. They use a kind of automated software testing tools for day to days testing activities. Such Test Management tools are used to facilitate regular Software Development activities, automate & manage the testing activities. Company X uses Selenium and Javascript as their automation tools. Company Y uses Selenium and TestComplete. Selenium is a great tool to automate our functional tests on websites and web applications in our favorite language. Using the Selenium WebDriver API, we can create web tests in any programming language. With TestComplete, we can re-use our Selenium scripts to scale our browser testing efforts and build the ultimate test automation solution, which includes Selenium, unit, and functional tests for desktop and mobile applications.

Test Metrics

Code coverage is a term used in software testing to describe how much program source code is covered by a testing plan (Abran, Bourque, Dupuis, & Moore, 2001). This is very much needed to the higher the value, the better, as a more thoroughly tested software product for the company. There are a couple of ways to determine how well your code is covered by the tests you run. They are Statement coverage, Function coverage, Branch coverage, Condition coverage and any other kind of coverage technique. In both companies, participants claimed both Branch coverage and Condition coverage techniques are used mostly by their testers in their projects.

Condition Coverage technique aims to cover the various conditions and its consecutive flow. A condition or predicate when evaluates to true must execute the next relevant line of code that follows. Branch Coverage technique involves checking whether every possible path or branch is covered. Branching is actually a jump from one decision point to another. In addition to that, company Y uses "Total number of defects detected per day" and "Average Defect per Line of Code (LOC)" metrics too to measure how well an application has been tested.

Test Management Practices

Many of the agile project management software that simplifies user story-based design does not adapt itself well to test management, resulting in the need for centric test-suite applications. Although test management software allows a QA person's life much simpler, it creates a different challenge–handling a product backlog system as well as a performance management system.

This research question targets the experience is with the various defect tracking and test management systems used in test management practices. Both Companies are using the Jira tool in their projects. Jira is an Atlassian-developed proprietary issue tracking tool that allows for bug tracking and agile project management. Jira Software is designed to prepare, monitor and launch great software for each part of your software team. Participants from both companies mentioned that Jira lets them (i) build customer narratives and problems, schedule sprints, and delegate activities around the technology group, (ii) organize and address the work of your team in entire context with maximum transparency, (iii) securely and comfortably ship ensuring that the data you have is still up-to-date and (iv) improve real-time team success. They also mentioned that Jira can be integrated with Confluence, Bitbucket, and hundreds of other developer tools as well. Therefore they do not need to change their existing developer tool because of the Jira.

Further, the participant from Company Y stated that they also started to use the TestLink tool. This is because of its simple interface and "technical" design with no frills. TestLink is an open-source application that can be downloaded in a matter of minutes on almost every LAMP host. We can start creating and controlling (i) Test Cases, (ii) Requirements and (iii) Test Plans when TestLink is installed and configured. The participants from Company Y mentioned that TestLink has a user-friendly interface that allows test cases to be exported or imported and it has all the key features such as generating test cases, combining maintenance with common issue trackers, etc.

Test Training

In Company X, participants preferred a 'Learn by Doing' approach to acquiring software testing knowledge, rather than attending formal training programs. This is because of the lack of support from high-level management. Also, they stated that lack of time for employees and expenditure cost for such training made them do so. Participants from Company Y raised the need for better training for testing tools. From their point of view, they face such difficulties to use new tools. Because of this, some of the team members are low expertise which delays the regular testing activities.

Interaction With Academia and Software Testing Professionals

Participants were asked whether their companies or themselves involved in any research to develop new test techniques/ tools with the university academia. Test Engineer from Company X stated that their company has already announced its partnership with the leading university to establish a testing laboratory that targets both side active involvements in the aspect of research and development. In contrast, participants from Company Y could not respond to this question since they are not aware of anything related to any collaborations.

CONCLUSION

In this paper, we presented a qualitative study of the current status of software testing in Software testing companies. Seven research questions were defined and addressed to investigate the facets. Almost all two companies are using Agile software development and that represents a major departure from traditional, plan-based approaches to software engineering. These Agile teams tend to be small comprising of heterogeneous and capable of engaging in several distinct types of work such as analysis, development, and testing together. Further, these companies are engaged with new automated tools introduced in the market to handle the manual testing and Selenium is highly recommended at these companies. Importantly, both Black-box testing and White-box testing are popular among these communities. Most importantly, money, cost and lack of resources are the barriers for these companies to purchase or spend more time on systematic testing methodologies and testing tools. Further, these companies should involve in providing training to their employees. This is witnessed when respondents answered as No. They should focus on training programs targeting most of the test types, such as unit testing, functional or system testing, performance testing, and user acceptance testing.

ACKNOWLEDGMENT

We thank the software companies participated and its testing team members who were actively facilitating this research since beginning. We also thank both Academic Staffs who provided their immense support through expert evaluation. This work is partially supported by Sabaragamuwa University of Sri Lanka Research Grant SUSL/RG/2018/04.

REFERENCES

Abdullah, R., Eri, Z. D., & Talib, A. M. (2011). *A model of knowledge management system in managing knowledge of software testing environment.* Paper presented at the Software Engineering (MySEC), 5th Malaysian Conference in. 10.1109/MySEC.2011.6140675

Abran, A., Bourque, P., Dupuis, R., & Moore, J. W. (2001). *Guide to the software engineering body of knowledge-SWEBOK.* IEEE Press.

Causevic, A., Sundmark, D., & Punnekkat, S. (2010). *An industrial survey on contemporary aspects of software testing.* Paper presented at the 2010 Third International Conference on Software Testing, Verification and Validation. 10.1109/ICST.2010.52

Choma, J., Guerra, E. M., & da Silva, T. S. (2018). *Developers' Initial Perceptions on TDD Practice: A Thematic Analysis with Distinct Domains and Languages.* Paper presented at the International Conference on Agile Software Development. 10.1007/978-3-319-91602-6_5

De Souza, E. F., de Almeida Falbo, R., & Vijaykumar, N. L. (2015). Knowledge management initiatives in software testing: A mapping study. *Information and Software Technology, 57*(1), 378–391. doi:10.1016/j.infsof.2014.05.016

Deak, A., & Stålhane, T. (2013). *Organization of testing activities in Norwegian Software Companies.* Paper presented at the 2013 IEEE Sixth International Conference on Software Testing, Verification and Validation Workshops. 10.1109/ICSTW.2013.18

Desai, A., & Shah, S. (2011). *Knowledge management and software testing.* Paper presented at the Proceedings of the International Conference & Workshop on Emerging Trends in Technology, Mumbai, Maharashtra, India.

Desouza, K. C., & Pacquette, S. (2011). *Knowledge management: An introduction.* Neal-Schuman Publishers.

Edvardsson, I. R. (2008). HRM and knowledge management. *Employee Relations, 30*(5), 553–561. doi:10.1108/01425450810888303

Garousi, V., & Varma, T. (2010). A replicated survey of software testing practices in the Canadian province of Alberta: What has changed from 2004 to 2009? *Journal of Systems and Software, 83*(11), 2251–2262. doi:10.1016/j.jss.2010.07.012

Garousi, V., & Zhi, J. (2013). A survey of software testing practices in Canada. *Journal of Systems and Software, 86*(5), 1354–1376. doi:10.1016/j.jss.2012.12.051

Geras, A. M., Smith, M. R., & Miller, J. (2004). A survey of software testing practices in Alberta. *Canadian Journal of Electrical and Computer Engineering, 29*(3), 183–191. doi:10.1109/CJECE.2004.1532522

Girard, J., & Girard, J. (2015). Defining knowledge management: Toward an applied compendium. *Online Journal of Applied Knowledge Management, 3*(1), 1–20.

Harman, C., & Brelade, S. (2007). *Managing human resources in the knowledge economy.* Paper presented at the United Nations 7th Global Forum on Reinventing Government Building Trust in government. Vienna, Austria.

Hilton, M. M. E. (2017). *Understanding Software Development and Testing Practices.* Academic Press.

Hynninen, T., Kasurinen, J., Knutas, A., & Taipale, O. (2018). *Software testing: Survey of the industry practices.* Paper presented at the 2018 41st International Convention on Information and Communication Technology, Electronics and Microelectronics (MIPRO). 10.23919/MIPRO.2018.8400261

Jahan, M. S., Riaz, M. T., & Abbas, M. (2019). Software Testing Practices in IT Industry of Pakistan. *Proceedings of the 6th Conference on the Engineering of Computer Based Systems*. 10.1145/3352700.3352724

Kasurinen, J., Taipale, O., & Smolander, K. (2010). Software test automation in practice: Empirical observations. *Advances in Software Engineering*.

Liu, Y., Wu, J., Liu, X., & Gu, G. (2009). *Investigation of knowledge management methods in software testing process*. Paper presented at the Information Technology and Computer Science (ITCS). International Conference on, Kiev, Ukraine. 10.1109/ITCS.2009.157

Mailewa, A., Herath, J., & Herath, S. (2015). *A Survey of Effective and Efficient Software Testing*. Paper presented at the Midwest Instruction and Computing Symposium. Retrieved August 01, 2019, from http://www. micsymposium. org/mics2015/ProceedingsMICS_2015/Mailewa_ 2D1_41. pdf

Mullen, R. (2018). *An Analysis of Software Testing Practices on Migrations From on Premise to Cloud Hosted Environments*. Academic Press.

Murali, A., & Kumar, S. K. (2014). Knowledge Management and Human Resource Management (HRM): Importance of Integration. *FIIB Business Review*, *3*(1), 3–10. doi:10.1177/2455265820140101

Omotayo, F. O. (2015). Knowledge Management as an important tool in Organisational Management: A Review of Literature. *Library Philosophy and Practice*, *1*, 1–23.

Runeson, P., Andersson, C., & Höst, M. (2003). Test processes in software product evolution—a qualitative survey on the state of practice. *Journal of Software Maintenance and Evolution: Research and Practice, 15*(1), 41-59.

Schwaber, K., & Beedle, M. (2001). *Agile software development with Scrum*. Upper Saddle River, NJ: Prentice Hall PTR.

Souza, E. F., Falbo, R., & Vijaykumar, N. L. (2013). *Using ontology patterns for building a reference software testing ontology*. Paper presented at the Enterprise Distributed Object Computing Conference Workshops (EDOCW), 2013 17th IEEE International. 10.1109/EDOCW.2013.10

Strauss, A., & Corbin, J. M. (1997). Grounded theory in practice. *Sage (Atlanta, Ga.)*.

Vasanthapriyan, S., Xiang, J., Tian, J., & Xiong, S. (2017). Knowledge synthesis in software industries: A survey in Sri Lanka. *Knowledge Management Research and Practice, 15*(3), 413–430. doi:10.105741275-017-0057-7

KEY TERMS AND DEFINITIONS

Agile Software Development: Agile software development comprises various approaches to software development under which requirements and solutions evolve through the collaborative effort of self-organizing and cross-functional teams and their end-user(s). It advocates adaptive planning, evolutionary development, early delivery, and continual improvement, and it encourages rapid and flexible response to change.

Extreme Programming: Extreme programming (XP) is an agile software development framework that aims to produce higher quality software and a higher quality of life for the development team. XP is the most specific of the agile frameworks regarding appropriate engineering practices for software development.

ISTQB Certification: The International Software Testing Qualifications Board is a software testing certification board that operates internationally. Founded in Edinburgh in November 2002, the ISTQB is a non-profit association legally registered in Belgium.

Knowledge Management: Knowledge management (KM) is the process of creating, sharing, using and managing the knowledge and information of an organization. It refers to a multidisciplinary approach to achieving organizational objectives by making the best use of knowledge. Knowledge management is recognized as the fundamental activity for obtaining, growing and sustaining intellectual capital in organizations.

Scrum: Scrum is an agile process framework for managing complex knowledge work, with an initial emphasis on software development, although it has been used in other fields and is slowly starting to be explored for other complex work, research and advanced technologies. It is designed for teams of ten or fewer members, who break their work into goals that can be completed within timeboxed iterations, called sprints, no longer than one month and most commonly two weeks, then track progress and re-plan in 15-minute time-boxed stand-up meetings, called daily scrums.

Software Development Lifecycle: The software development lifecycle is a systematic process for building software that ensures the quality and correctness of the software built. SDLC process aims to produce high-quality software which meets customer expectations. The software development should be complete in the pre-defined time frame and cost.

Software Engineering: Software engineering is concerned with the study of systematic approaches towards software development and maintenance.

Software Testing: Software testing provides the mechanism for verifying that the requirements identified during the initial phases of the project were properly implemented and that the system performs as expected. The test scenarios developed through these competitions ensure that the requirements are met end-to-end.

Software Testing Metric: Software testing metric is to be defined as a quantitative measure that helps to estimate the progress, quality, and health of a software testing effort. A metric defines in quantitative terms the degree to which a system, system component, or process possesses a given attribute.

Software Testing Techniques: Software testing techniques help you design better test cases. Since exhaustive testing is not possible; manual testing techniques help reduce the number of test cases to be executed while increasing test coverage. They help identify test conditions that are otherwise difficult to recognize.

Test Automation: Test automation is the use of software separate from the software being tested to control the execution of tests and the comparison of actual outcomes with predicted outcomes. Test automation can automate some repetitive but necessary tasks in a formalized testing process already in place, or perform additional testing that would be difficult to do manually. Test automation is critical for continuous delivery and continuous testing.

Test Management: Test management most commonly refers to the activity of managing the computer software testing process. A test management tool is a software used to manage tests (automated or manual) that have been previously specified by a test procedure. It is often associated with automation software. Test management tools often include requirement and/or specification management modules that allow automatic generation of the required test matrix (RTM), which is one of the main metrics to indicate functional coverage of a system under test (SUT).

Test Tools: A product that supports one or more test activities right from planning, requirements, creating a build, test execution, defect logging, and test analysis.

Validation: At the end of the development process, validation is the method of reviewing code to decide whether it satisfies customer expectations or specifications. The aim of validation is to guarantee that the product actually meets the requirements of the consumer and to verify that the specifications are correct in the first place. "Testing like black-box testing, white box testing, gray box testing, etc." are involved in validation.

Verification: Verification is the process of evaluating a development stage of products to determine whether they comply with the requirements specified. Verification helps to ensure that the product being developed is in compliance with the standards and specifications of the model. Verification includes "reviews, meetings, and inspections."

Chapter 12
Knowledge Transfer Between Senior and Novice Software Testers:
A Qualitative Analysis in Sri Lankan Software Companies

Shanmuganathan Vasanthapriyan
https://orcid.org/0000-0002-0597-0263
Sabaragamuwa University of Sri Lanka, Sri Lanka

Kuhaneswaran Banujan
https://orcid.org/0000-0002-0265-2198
Sabaragamuwa University of Sri Lanka, Sri Lanka

ABSTRACT

Software testing is a sub-activity of software engineering, and it is also a knowledge-intensive activity. Software testing experts need to gather domain knowledge to be able to successfully test and deliver a software system. In particular, novice software testers, who have joined the company, need to acquire enough knowledge to perform their tasks. Since software development is an error-prone task, in order to achieve quality software products, validation and verification should be carried throughout the development. This means that knowledge transfer to novice software testers must be quickly and effectively performed to facilitate the onboarding process. One way to understand the knowledge transfer process is by analyzing the software development context and the involved team members. This study, using qualitative methods, investigates the current practice of knowledge transfer in software testing practices in one software company.

DOI: 10.4018/978-1-7998-2531-9.ch012

INTRODUCTION

Knowledge is a critical organizational resource and the primary source of the sustainable competitive advantage in a competitive economy. Management of this knowledge is the key to long-term sustainability and success of the organization. Effective and efficient management of knowledge is not possible without a proper process of knowledge transfer, where knowledge transfer is a cornerstone for managing knowledge. Knowledge creation and transfer in an organization are inseparable from learning; all knowledge processes are in fact the consequence of learning (Mehra & Dhawan, 2003). Knowledge Transfer in organizations can be defined as "the process through which one unit (e.g., group, department, or division) is affected by the experience of another". Knowledge Transfer, in essence, is the sharing of one's ideas, insights, solutions, experiences with another individual (Nidhra, Yanamadala, Afzal, & Torkar, 2013).

The software development process is a team effort that requires a combination of knowledge and skills of team members who involve in the software development activities (Ranasinghe & Jayawardana, 2011; Vasanthapriyan, Xiang, Tian, & Xiong, 2017a; Wickramasinghe & Widyaratne, 2012). The collaborative and knowledge-intensive characteristic of software development activities signifies the importance of effective knowledge transfer in order to disseminate required software knowledge across development teams (Kukko & Helander, 2012). Knowledge transfer is the fundamental mean in which employees can contribute their knowledge towards the competitive advantage of the organization through innovations. Knowledge transfer between employees within and across development teams allows organizations to exploit and capitalize on knowledge-based resources.

Transfer of information may take place through social systems, like organizations, groups, and individuals. Transfer of information among entities is a dyadic mechanism through which seekers/recipients learn and appreciate senders' knowledge and adapt it to a different situation. Four consecutive phases of the knowledge transfer cycle are quest, reading, training, and understand. Transfer of expertise increases team performance through cooperative training, such as software project progress and judgment reliability. Knowledge transfer varies markedly from knowledge sharing, which is often calculated by the communication of individuals' purpose and actions, as the latter stresses on the use of data and the development of knowledge values. Stresses on the use of data and the development of knowledge values relate to the "provision of job information and know-how to support others". Sharing knowledge is unable to close the "knowledge gap", which has an inconsistent effect on team performance in existing studies. They see the transfer of knowledge as a tool for advancing current understanding (Wang, Huang, Davison, & Yang, 2018).

Another distinction in knowledge transfer and knowledge sharing is that sender and recipient are similarly important in the transmission of social knowledge while exchanging knowledge focuses solely on the purpose and actions of senders to add knowledge. Several literature reviews show that in data-intensive contexts analysis of knowledge transfer enablers, obstacles, and mitigation strategies cannot neglect considerations regarding participants ' resources, their interactions, and their contexts. Work on knowledge sharing has unraveled that sharing purpose and behavior can be fostered by sharers ' personality of enjoying support, understanding of rewards, recipient confidence, and social norms such as reciprocity and participation (Wang et al., 2018).

Although software companies are still developing and growing in Sri Lanka, it is important that these companies have an indispensable aspiration to sustainable growth. In recent decades, sales of IT companies in Sri Lanka have grown rapidly (Ranasinghe & Jayawardana, 2011; Wickramasinghe & Widyaratne, 2012). In parallel, software projects have continued to be over budgeted, costing more than the expected budget and sometimes making mistakes by failing to deliver the required quality and functionality to the users (Ranasinghe & Jayawardana, 2011). Most problems that occur in software companies are due to inefficient knowledge transfer. Among the software companies in Sri Lanka, companies that are not yet developed and still growing face major barriers to knowledge transfer. It can be seen that there are more problems in growing companies in the area of knowledge transfer than in other areas, and that the growth of these companies may be faced with limitations and dilemmas due to barriers to knowledge transfer (Kukko, 2013, Kukko & Helander, 2012). As a rule, business growth creates new jobs, more career opportunities, prosperity and economic growth. However, the negative attitude of staff to sharing knowledge is hindering these benefits by reducing growth in all three growing dimensions. organic growth, acquisition growth, network growth; in software companies where knowledge transfer is a cornerstone of growth. Existing knowledge in the organization becomes valuable only when the organization's employees gain access to that knowledge. The size and diversification of organizations makes it difficult to locate and transport existing knowledge to where it is actually needed as these dimensions increase. Even the knowledge available to you could be of good quality, sometimes good quality is not good enough in the market today (Zammit, Gao & Evans, 2015). In order to improve organizational performance, the knowledge should be exchanged in a structured way so that the right knowledge is passed on to the right person at the right time.

The software industry is a much younger and knowledge-intensive industry which mostly depends on the knowledge resource (Kukko & Helander, 2012). Most of the software companies are profit-oriented organizations. Even, these companies are still under development, they have a great aspiration to grow and achieve sustainability in the market. Generally, these companies are project-based companies and therefore, the ultimate success of the business depends on the success of projects they undertake, and the success of these projects could be achieved only through satisfying the customers by completing these projects successfully within the budgeted time and cost. Therefore, these companies consider successful project completion and customer satisfaction as their short term goals. By means of customer satisfaction, they achieve sustainability in the market which is considered to be the long term goal of a software company.

Software development is a quickly changing, knowledge-intensive business, involving many people working in different phases and activities(Vasanthapriyan, Tian, & Xiang, 2015). The available resources are not increasing along with the increasing needs; therefore, software organizations expect a climb in productivity (Rus, Lindvall, & Sinha, 2002; Vasanthapriyan, Xiang, Tian, & Xiong, 2017b). Software Organizations are becoming more knowledge-intensive, they are hiring "minds" more than "hands", and the need for leveraging the value of knowledge is increasing. There is growing recognition in the business community about the importance of knowledge as a critical resource for organizations. Knowledge in software engineering is diverse and its proportions immense and steadily growing. Organizations have problems identifying the content, location, and use of knowledge. Improved use of this knowledge is the basic motivation and driver for Knowledge management (KM) in software engineering and deserves a deeper analysis. KM is recognized as the fundamental activity for obtaining, growing and sustaining intellectual capital in organizations (Quast, 2012).

Software testing is a knowledge-intensive and collaborative activity, which mainly depends on the knowledge and experience of the software testers(Vasanthapriyan, 2018). Software testing knowledge can be applied to different testing tasks and purposes. Since software development is an error-prone task, in order to achieve quality software products, Validation and Verification should be carried throughout the development. Verification is the process of evaluating a development stage of products to determine whether they comply with the requirements specified. Verification helps to ensure that the product being developed is in compliance with the standards and specifications of the model. Verification includes "Reviews, Meetings, and Inspections." (Lewis, 2017; Smith & Kandel, 2018).

At the conclusion of the development process, validation is the method of reviewing code to decide whether it satisfies customer expectations or specifications. The aim of Validation is to guarantee that the product actually meets the requirements of the consumer and to verify that the specifications are correct in the first place. "Testing like black-box testing, white box testing, gray box testing, etc." are involved in validation (Lewis, 2017; Smith & Kandel, 2018).

In particular, novice software testers need to acquire enough knowledge to perform their tasks. This means that knowledge transfer to novice software testers must be quickly and effectively performed to facilitate the onboarding process. One way to understand the knowledge transfer process is by analyzing the software testing context and the involved team members.

Further, the knowledge of the members of a team and the outside team within the organization should be properly managed by capturing, storing and reusing when needed. Traditional software methods use detailed specifications and design upfront and rigorous documentation to manage knowledge (Abrahamsson, Salo, Ronkainen, & Warsta, 2017). Agile methods and principals emerge to software development which brings collaboration and interaction within the team and the outside of the team (Petersen, Feldt, Mujtaba, & Mattsson, 2008). It helps to manage the knowledge more efficiently and effectively by presenting the right knowledge in the right form to the right person at the right time (Vasanthapriyan, 2019).

The lack of proven computer systems makes it more difficult for the examined organization to move knowledge and transmit it. It is therefore essential to examine knowledge transfer processes in this company because we can use our results to confirm the essence of such activities in a real context (Mehra & Dhawan, 2003).

Apart from that, the majority of the studies conducted previously regarding knowledge transfer have followed a qualitative research method which provides only a general description of the related subject. Therefore, most of the studies do not provide a comprehensive and in-depth explanation regarding the topic except only a few papers that have conducted a quantitative research method. When considering the literature, there is a lack of quantitative research analysis regarding this domain especially, in the context of Sri Lanka. In order to provide a better and in-depth description of the related topic, this study focuses on the quantitative method regardless of the qualitative perspective of data. Therefore, this study would be able to reduce the existing gap of quantitatively analyzed and statistically proved facts and recommendations in the past literature.

In order to extend our study towards the current status of software testing practices in Sri Lankan software companies (Vasanthapriyan, 2018), the authors of this research intended to carry out qualitative research work. Unfortunately, authors found that presently there is a gap in the literature concerning the deep knowledge of the current status of knowledge transfer in software testing practices between senior and junior software testers within the software companies in the context of Sri Lanka. Therefore, the goal of this paper is to analyze, through a qualitative empirical study, how novice software testers gain knowledge during the initial software testing activities they perform in a particular software company. This software company was selected on the basis that they claimed to apply software testing practices in their software development work. We also analyze which factors influence such knowledge transfer. Such analysis enables the development team to determine key aspects that can influence knowledge acquisition by novice software testers. We believe our results can support other software organizations to improve the sharing of knowledge and learning practices.

The rest of this paper is structured as follows: Section 2 discusses related work regarding knowledge transfer in software engineering. Section 3 presents the research design, the study settings, and the study context. Then, in Section 4 we show our results and discuss our findings. Finally, Section 5 presents our conclusions and future works.

RELATED STUDY

Insecure software development activities are widespread due to a variety of reasons, including inefficiencies within current knowledge transfer systems focused on vulnerability repositories and pattern-based strategies, protection viewed by software developers as an afterthought, and lack of security concern as part of the Software Development Lifecycle (SDLC) (Nafees, 2019).

In order to make these projects a success, the company should have good knowledge resources and better team performance. Not only the success of projects but also the sustainability of the organizations in today's competitive market is unachievable unless these companies consist of an effective knowledge resource. Also, software companies generally work on small to large scale projects which require a considerable amount of resources (time, cost, human resource, technology, etc.). These projects are accomplished by development teams consist of team members with different skills and experience levels under different roles from assistant software engineer to project manager, and from less-experienced individuals to experts in the domain. In order to make these projects a success, the knowledge of each team member should be shared within the team. Not only within the teams, but also knowledge transfer across different development teams and across different departments of the companies are mostly very crucial to the success of projects. Therefore, knowledge transfer is considered as a cornerstone for software companies to achieve their short term and long term goals and objectives.

On the other hand, the software industry does not have structured and proper processes and systems to share knowledge (Kukko & Helander, 2012). As a result, knowledge transfer is not properly taken place in these companies most of the time. Moreover, these companies face different obstacles when sharing knowledge among employees due to the influence of different factors such as individual factors, organizational factors and technical factors (Kukko, 2013; Riege, 2005). As a result of this, software companies have resulted in unbearable failures in projects causing huge damage to the sustainability of the companies in the market (Ranasinghe & Jayawardana, 2011). These failures also cause the wastage of the allocated resources to large scale projects. The failures occurred due to inappropriate knowledge transfer in the companies is a well-proved fact according to the previous literature (Kukko, 2013; Ranasinghe & Jayawardana, 2011). Therefore, identifying the root cause of these barriers is the best remedy to overcome these barriers existing in the knowledge transfer domain. By eliminating these barriers, software companies would be able to acquire the greater opportunity of achieving sustainability in the path of success and goals without any failure.

KNOWLEDGE

Knowledge has several taxonomies. These taxonomies describe various types of knowledge. The most fundamental distinction is between tacit knowledge and explicit knowledge (King, 2009). Tacit knowledge inhibits the minds of people and explicit knowledge is the articulated knowledge (King, 2009).

To maximize the use of internal knowledge, it must be shared among individuals and teams. Ezeh and Anthony (2013) argues knowledge sharing as a process of knowledge exchange and motivation for these exchanges is related to the expectation of receiving something in return. Park and Lee (2014) define knowledge sharing as the most valuable activity for successful IS implementation because it encourages project participants to become more innovative, creative and sustain high performance in IS projects, accelerate relationships among business clients, and reduce time spent on problem-solving.

Knowledge Management

According to Polanyi's definition, there are two kinds of knowledge (Nonaka, Toyama, & Konno, 2000), namely explicit and tacit knowledge. KM (Vasanthapriyan et al., 2017b) is a method that simplifies the process of sharing, distributing, creating, capturing and understanding of an organization's knowledge that should be employed. KM's mission is to move tacit information to explicit knowledge and to shift explicit knowledge within the organization from persons to classes. KM is therefore associated with the development, conservation and implementation of the information available within organizations. The recent interest in corporate awareness has contributed to the problem of using an organization's information to its benefit. This enthusiasm has created a new outlook for the KM which sees KM as a methodology to recognize and exploit collective knowledge in an organization to help the company succeed (Von Krogh, 1998; Von Krogh, Back, Enkel, & Seufert, 2004).

KM in software engineering is designed to help software developers define processes for software, to follow a process-oriented approach and to improve and adapt existing software processes for future use. Although it is recognized that computer process models can be created for use by an enterprise, they must be recognized by software developers before they can succeed in information management. However, there are no study-related software testers and KM.

Knowledge Transfer

Knowledge transfer could be identified as a process between units, teams, and organizations where people exchange their knowledge with others (Vasanthapriyan, 2019). Software companies create a lack of well-structured knowledge transfer processes within the software industry. In software companies, independent, competent and creative individuals with a high level of expertise shape the business, and knowledge and innovation are crucial to staying competitive and growing (Kukko, 2013). Hence, knowledge transfer is a cornerstone for software companies for their growth and sustainability. It can be seen that many issues are arisen in the knowledge transfer domain in software companies due to inefficient knowledge transfer (Ranasinghe & Jayawardana, 2011). If a proper knowledge transfer process is not available, employees would proceed with the knowledge that they already have or with the knowledge that is most easily available(Weerakoon & Wijayanayake, 2016). Even that knowledge is accurate and of good quality, sometimes it may not be good enough to achieve the success of the projects or the sustainability of today's market (Weerakoon & Wijayanayake, 2016; Zammit, Gao, & Evans, 2016).

The cycle of knowledge transfer is one of the key factors in the effective completion of the project. (Bao, Zhang, & Yang, 2019). Since organizational work arrangements are often shared between individuals, information transfer is needed by achieving common goals. Interpersonal transmission of information refers to the process by which knowledge seekers/receivers are influenced by knowledge senders

' experience. In general, it involves "sharing one's thoughts, observations, strategies, perceptions with another individual" as well as acquiring and implementing information transferred (Wang et al., 2018).

Knowledge Sharing in the Software Industry

Seba, Rowley, and Lambert (2012) stated that Motivation and willingness is one the enablers for knowledge transfer where knowledge transfer is not meaningful without both motivation to share knowledge and willingness to receive knowledge. Vasanthapriyan (2019) has summarized through a mapping study for initiatives taken in the recent works of literature about Knowledge Transfer in Software Companies.

According to Kukko and Helander (2012), every company has a great desire to grow and growth is described as a way to pursue success, profitability, and competitiveness from the organizational perspective. They further explain that the growth of a company can be either organically, non-organically or through networking where knowledge is a cornerstone for each of these dimensions. Organically growth is the growth that can be attained without acquiring businesses existing external to the company, and taking the usage of internal productive resources, services, and special knowledge. They further argue organically growth as a natural way of growing, especially in high technology companies such as software companies, as they are typically small and medium-sized. Acquisition growth is attained through obtaining outside resources that are external to the organization by the companies that focused on outsourcing. Network growth is a combination of organically and acquisition growth that takes place in the business environment which requires the rapid adjustment of new knowledge (Kukko, 2013; Kukko & Helander, 2012). As described by Kukko (2013), factors that influence the success of knowledge sharing activities in an organization to differ from these three growing dimensions; organically growth, acquisition growth, and network growth.

Barriers to Knowledge Transfer

Sharing knowledge among individuals, teams, and units have several knowledge barriers. Szulanski (2002) describes knowledge barriers as a set of factors which impact negatively on knowledge sharing. These knowledge barriers have different categories such as organizational, technical, individual and cultural categories (McLaughlin, Paton, & Macbeth, 2008). In this research, the objective is to investigate dominant barriers for knowledge transfer between senior and novice software testers, which influence on a software company's work. Determinants of the dominant barriers which influence the knowledge sharing classify into three categories; Individual barriers (level where knowledge resides), Organizational barriers (level that knowledge gets its economic and competitive value), and Technical barriers (level which provides integral tools for knowledge sharing) (Kukko & Helander, 2012; Riege, 2005).

Individual factors are central to the outcome of the knowledge sharing process. Without positive individual factors, knowledge will not be properly shared. Literature defines different individual factors as enablers for knowledge sharing. Motivation and willingness are described as one of the enablers for knowledge sharing where knowledge sharing is not meaningful without both motivation (intrinsic motivation and extrinsic motivation) to share knowledge and willingness to receive knowledge (Heeager & Nielsen, 2013; Seba et al., 2012). The employees who are highly educated and very familiar with their own specialist areas do not feel the benefit from the others' knowledge beyond their close circle (Kukko & Helander, 2012). Knowledge sharing activities cannot be supervised or enforced by people, instead individuals must see a value of knowledge in order to voluntarily share their knowledge and accept new knowledge from others (Heeager & Nielsen, 2013).

Time allocation is described as the main enabler for knowledge sharing by many researchers (Kukko & Helander, 2012; Mas-Machuca & Martínez Costa, 2012; Seba et al., 2012). According to Kukko (2013), growth of the firm leads to the growth of employees' workload and they have to spend much time on routine tasks with only the knowledge residing in individual employees or containing inside a particular team and they may not have enough time to seek or share knowledge. Because knowledge sharing is a time-consuming task.

Trust is a very effective fact in knowledge sharing and it is known as a key antecedent of knowledge sharing (Kukko, 2013; Park & Lee, 2014; Seba et al., 2012). Trust as well as dependence plays a central role in building and maintaining the relationship between individuals and promoting knowledge sharing activities (Park & Lee, 2014). There is considerable trust only within one's own team or, in particular, between old team members and insufficient trust between different teams and between new and old employees (Kukko, 2013). Knowledge sharing between employees needs a strong culture, as well as trust and transparency all through the organization. Park and Lee (2014) argue frequent communication between partners, the similarity between parties, the similarity between target goals and strategy, common work experience, and project complexity as the factors which improve trust among individuals and enhance organizational learning.

Endres and Chowdhury (2013) explain the expected reciprocity as one of the significant barriers in knowledge sharing. Many researchers (Endres & Chowdhury, 2013; Shoemaker, 2014; Titi Amayah, 2013) further describe rewarding as an effective motivate to improve knowledge sharing among individuals and they called this "self-determined motivation". Though most researchers (Shoemaker, 2014; Titi Amayah, 2013) argue that knowledge sharing has been dominated by motivation theory, which describes rewards are associated with knowledge sharing, Seba et al. (2012) suggest that employees are not especially interested in rewards.

Power relationships arise when individuals try to position themselves in the organizational hierarchy. Individuals who have expert and critical knowledge tend to become bottlenecks in their attempt of achieving more power, by avoiding the sharing of knowledge with others. This mainly occurs in companies that have a large hierarchy than in the small companies which have organically growth (Kukko, 2013).

Seba et al. (2012) suggest a strong relationship between attitude towards knowledge sharing and the intention to share knowledge. This relationship is a well-proven fact according to the Theory of Planned Behavior (TPB). TPB is an extended concept of predicting behavior in any social situation. It proposes intention to behavior as the most recent antecedent of a specific behavior. Then extends this theory based on attitude, and proposes attitude as an influencer on the intention of behavior (Kiriakidis, 2015). Later on, this theory seems to be used in much research as the basis of this research. The study of Seba et al. (2012) has further proved this theory regarding the knowledge sharing behavior, where they define the same relationship between attitude towards knowledge sharing, intention to share knowledge and knowledge sharing behavior.

Table 1. Description of the Project X1

	X1
Product	Online Reservation for Airline System
Customer	External
Location	Different Sites
No. of team members	40 – 100
Team of QA	Test Engineer Automation Specialist Trainee Automation Software QA Engineer QA Lead Requirement Engineer

RESEARCH DESIGN

The main objective of this study is to provide a deep and broad description of the knowledge transfer among novice and senior software testers within the software company by adopting an empirical research method. We, therefore, set out to answer the following research questions in this paper in order to provide comprehensive coverage of knowledge transfer problems and approaches between senior and novice software testers, from both literature and business insights:

- RQ 1: What are the challenges faced and the mitigation strategies for effective knowledge transfer between senior and novice software testers as reported in the literature?
- RQ 2: What are the challenges faced and the mitigation strategies for effective knowledge transfer between senior and novice software testers from an industrial perspective?
- RQ 3: What can we learn in terms of comparing the literature and the industrial perspectives regarding challenges and mitigation strategies for effective knowledge transfer between senior and novice software testers?

In such a situation, the information should be gathered from different members of the Quality Assurance (QA) team who claimed that they are engaging in such knowledge transfer practices. Even though qualitative research usually involves relatively small numbers of participants, it has been chosen for the following reasons. Qualitative methods allow face-to-face semi-structured interviews would allow to obtain the true feelings, gain insight and understanding of the interviewee (Hove & Anda, 2005). Especially, the interviewer builds up a good rapport with the interviewee. As a result, more suffice enough experience and sensitive information can be obtained (Vasanthapriyan et al., 2017b).

STUDY CONTEXT

For this study, the interviews took place in a software organization from Sri Lanka. The company is named X. The project for company X is denoted by X1.

Table 2. Questions asked for novice testers

Questions asked for novices
How do you identify important knowledge to transfer to your project?
How do team members transfer knowledge in your organization?
When you identify important project knowledge, which information do you try to get?
How can this knowledge help you during the software project?

Project X1: Project X1's main objective is to create a portal for online reservations for the airline system. They were required to produce a mini-version which releases scheduled every two months. The number of team members utilized is around 40 to 100. Description of the project X1 is shown in table 1.

Data Collection

As a preliminary step, participated QAs were requested to complete a detailed questionnaire in order to gain an understanding of the current Knowledge transfer practices they do within their company. Two questionnaires were prepared based on the Five-point Likert-type scale, where respondents had to make their level of the agreement such as; Strongly Agree, Agree, No Idea, Disagree and Strongly Disagree. Scores 5, 4, 3, 2, and 1 were assigned respectively for the above-mentioned categories (Jamieson, 2004). One for the novice employees and the other for the senior QAs. Table 2 shows some of the questions asked for novices.

The interviews were held at the company itself for suitable times for participants. So that the interviewee could express his/her opinion effectively. The duration of the interview was ranging from 25-30 minutes by the same interviewer ensuring consistency in administering the research instrument. Each participant was given the opportunity to complete the questionnaire at the beginning and then allowed them to intensify their opinion verbally at later stages.

Data Analysis

Once the interview sessions have been completed, data was analyzed manually. The following steps were followed as explained by Vasanthapriyan et al. (2017b): a) Semi-structured interviews were recorded b) Recorded interviews were transcribed to verbatim and developed transcriptions. c) Re-reading the transcript in order to grasp deeper meanings. d) Coding was done by using transcriptions according to prominent topics. e) Categories were developed by using codes. f) Identifying central issues and developing themes that were common to all participants.

STUDY RESULTS AND DISCUSSIONS

As mentioned before, project X1 develops software to create a portal for online reservation for an airline system. In addition to the lack of a specified software process, there is no structured way to transfer knowledge within the organization. Thus, by verifying this process among senior and novice testers, the primary way to examine how the transfer of knowledge takes place in practice. In fact, practitioners are committed to transferring organizational knowledge to novice practitioners whereas they actually think that the fellow members of the specialist would be such individuals.

Organization X testers have access to multiple sources of knowledge: the web, intranet, source code, training material, expertise, and documentation for testing. Though, novice testers largely ignore the documentation of the testing as a source of knowledge and prefer informal discussions that are permitted in the environment of the organization. Novice testers gain knowledge while they follow organizational procedures and when they have comprehensive guidelines for the tasks they are expected to perform. Members of the team of experts create such comprehensive guidelines because of the lack of expertise of novices. Thus, organization X emphasizes both types of knowledge (tacit and explicit).

Before beginning their testing, novice testers had to participate in diverse training focusing on manual testing, testing tools, test cases, and test automation. Such training is essential for the organization's onboarding process of novice testers by providing proper skills necessary for the tasks of novices. They receive new tasks each day after the training when novices start working. These tasks comprise guidelines to be followed in order to carry them out satisfactorily. These tasks and guidelines are sent by Slack (Slack is a cloud-based set of proprietary team collaboration software tools and online services, developed by Slack Technologies) or e-mail by either a senior team member.

During our study, we have noticed that there are many slack conversations and e-mails about organizational tasks, such as the testing procedure supporting the workouts of the customs agencies. We also saw that the most intimate knowledge is shared person by person, based on the needs of the organization. Observations are another way of acquiring knowledge. Novice testers observe how their tasks are carried out by the other members of the team. They realize how well the business process takes place. They gain tacit knowledge in the above manner.

Pair programming is an agile method for software development in which two developers at one workstation operate together. One, the writer, is writing code while the other, the analyst or navigator, is reading every line of code as it is typed in. The two programmers often switch roles (Singh & Pandey, 2017). During our study, none of them mentioned the pair programing because the selected candidates are pure software testers. So, they can't write codes for software development.

We discovered that the senior tester offered a comprehensive task guideline because he did not have a high degree of confidence in the performance and expertise of the novice tester. We also spotted that novice testers gained more understanding (about testing techniques and the business domain) when performing the tasks on their own. Even though preliminary information was available, it was necessary for most instances to search for extra sources of knowledge that helped the success of the tasks. Novice testers referred to the following sources of knowledge: (a) the web; (b) the intranet; (c) books; (d) training material; (e) members of the expert team.

Our informants informed us of some other source of knowledge, software documentation (e.g. specification requirements, UML diagrams, and plans for software). The senior member said this documentation is known to novice testers. It is outdated, however, and novice testers have not mentioned its use. Novice testers ask for assistance from expert members of the team during most of the execution of the tasks. We checked that almost all members of the testing team are in the same office. We, therefore, deduced that the configuration of the workplace promotes face-to-face communication. However, there are no records of knowledge transfer. Senior managers are then unable to know what knowledge has been transferred.

As regards the assessment of the knowledge gained by the novice software testers, the senior member shall assess the above informally by observing the quality of the releases. This assessment helps the senior team member increase the complexity of the novice testers' allocated tasks. This increase will ensure that novice practitioners acquire new knowledge and generate additional software and business model experience. While reviewing these findings, we noted certain aspects that may affect knowledge transfers.

CONCLUSION AND FUTURE WORKS

We discussed the transfer of knowledge between senior and novice software testers in a small software organization in this chapter. The lack of use of a defined software process enabled us to analyze the transfer of knowledge in the field, i.e. in the X organization context. A qualitative study aimed at understanding the transfer of knowledge between senior and novice software testers was conducted. Furthermore, tacit and explicit dissemination of knowledge could be observed. The resultant communication distance often inhibits both senior and novice software testers from effectively exchanging essential knowledge. This paper addresses the major issues in knowledge transfer utilizing current pattern-based methods that stop programmers from identifying and minimizing the triggers of errors.

We noticed that, through training provided by senior testers, novice practitioners had initial contact with the necessary knowledge to perform their assignments. However, our results suggest that during the actual software testing activities they gained more knowledge. Also, as mentioned above, it was important for the organization to successfully transfer knowledge because some of its senior testers left. The informal process of development has contributed to an informal way of transfer of knowledge.

Other software organizations can use our results as recommendations to enhance their knowledge transfer activities. Furthermore, to create benefits for organizations, it is necessary to encourage the full use of tacit and explicit knowledge.

In terms of its organizational context, this study has some limitations. We conducted interviews with testers of novice and senior software. We covered the transfer of knowledge between novices as a whole. We know, however, that we cannot generalize our results to other companies as a qualitative study. Nevertheless, we believe our study is important because each qualitative study helps to advance the state of the art in a research area, providing evidence and hypothesis that can be tested later using quantitative methods. In short, each study helps build a knowledge base about transferring knowledge. Much research was conducted in academia, while small studies on corporate environments were conducted with novices. To contribute to improving organizational practices, it is important to observe what happens in a real context of software development.

In order to understand more organizations and other contexts, we plan to carry out additional qualitative data collections. This will enable us to gain a better understanding of the transfer of knowledge and identify support strategies in software companies for organizational learning.

ACKNOWLEDGMENT

We thank the software companies participated and its testing team members who were actively facilitating this research since beginning. We also thank both Academic Staffs who provided their immense support through expert evaluation. This work is partially supported by Sabaragamuwa University of Sri Lanka Research Grant SUSL/RG/2018/04.

REFERENCES

Abrahamsson, P., Salo, O., Ronkainen, J., & Warsta, J. (2017). *Agile software development methods: Review and analysis.* Cornell University.

Bao, X., Zhang, L., & Yang, W. (2019). Empirical research for the interactive memory system research of object. In *4th International Conference on Humanities Science and Society Development (ICHSSD 2019)* (vol. 328, pp. 348-354). Atlantis Press.

Endres, M. L., & Chowdhury, S. (2013). The role of expected reciprocity in knowledge sharing. *International Journal of Knowledge Management, 9*(2), 1–19. doi:10.4018/jkm.2013040101

Ezeh, A., & Anthony, P. (2013). *Factors Influencing Knowledge Sharing in Software Development: A Case Study at Volvo Cars IT Torslanda.* Göteborgs universitet.

Heeager, L., & Nielsen, P. A. (2013). *Agile software development and the barriers to transfer of knowledge: an interpretive case study.* Paper presented at the Scandinavian Conference on Information Systems. 10.1007/978-3-642-39832-2_2

Hove, S. E., & Anda, B. (2005). *Experiences from conducting semi-structured interviews in empirical software engineering research.* Paper presented at the 11th IEEE International Software Metrics Symposium (METRICS'05). 10.1109/METRICS.2005.24

Jamieson, S. (2004). Likert scales: How to (ab) use them. *Medical Education, 38*(12), 1217–1218. doi:10.1111/j.1365-2929.2004.02012.x PMID:15566531

King, W. R. (2009). *Knowledge management and organizational learning.* Springer. doi:10.1007/978-1-4419-0011-1

Kiriakidis, S. (2015). Theory of planned behaviour: The intention-behaviour relationship and the perceived behavioural control (PBC) relationship with intention and behaviour. *International Journal of Strategic Innovative Marketing, 3*(2), 40–51.

Kukko, M. (2013). Knowledge sharing barriers in organic growth: A case study from a software company. *The Journal of High Technology Management Research, 24*(1), 18–29. doi:10.1016/j.hitech.2013.02.006

Kukko, M., & Helander, N. (2012). *Knowledge sharing barriers in growing software companies.* Paper presented at the 2012 45th Hawaii International Conference on System Sciences. 10.1109/HICSS.2012.407

Lewis, W. E. (2017). *Software testing and continuous quality improvement.* Auerbach publications. doi:10.1201/9781439834367

Mas-Machuca, M., & Martínez Costa, C. (2012). Exploring critical success factors of knowledge management projects in the consulting sector. *Total Quality Management & Business Excellence, 23*(11-12), 1297–1313. doi:10.1080/14783363.2011.637778

McLaughlin, S., Paton, R. A., & Macbeth, D. K. (2008). Barrier impact on organizational learning within complex organizations. *Journal of Knowledge Management, 12*(2), 107–123. doi:10.1108/13673270810859550

Mehra, K., & Dhawan, S. (2003). Study of the process of organisational learning in software firms in India. *Technovation, 23*(2), 121–129. doi:10.1016/S0166-4972(01)00089-X

Nafees, T. (2019). *Addressing the knowledge transfer problem in secure software development through anti-patterns*. Abertay University.

Nidhra, S., Yanamadala, M., Afzal, W., & Torkar, R. (2013). Knowledge transfer challenges and mitigation strategies in global software development—A systematic literature review and industrial validation. *International Journal of Information Management, 33*(2), 333–355. doi:10.1016/j.ijinfomgt.2012.11.004

Nonaka, I., Toyama, R., & Konno, N. (2000). SECI, Ba and leadership: A unified model of dynamic knowledge creation. *Long Range Planning, 33*(1), 5–34. doi:10.1016/S0024-6301(99)00115-6

Park, J.-G., & Lee, J. (2014). Knowledge sharing in information systems development projects: Explicating the role of dependence and trust. *International Journal of Project Management, 32*(1), 153–165. doi:10.1016/j.ijproman.2013.02.004

Petersen, K., Feldt, R., Mujtaba, S., & Mattsson, M. (2008). *Systematic mapping studies in software engineering*. Paper presented at the Ease. 10.14236/ewic/EASE2008.8

Quast, L. (2012). *Why knowledge management is important to the success of your company*. Retrieved September from https://www.forbes.com/sites/lisaquast/2012/08/20/why-knowledge-management-is-important-to-the-success-of-your-company/#673aceac3681

Ranasinghe, G., & Jayawardana, A. (2011). Impact of knowledge sharing on project success in the Sri Lankan software industry. *Sri Lankan Journal of Management, 16*(1).

Riege, A. (2005). Three-dozen knowledge-sharing barriers managers must consider. *Journal of Knowledge Management, 9*(3), 18–35. doi:10.1108/13673270510602746

Rus, I., Lindvall, M., & Sinha, S. (2002). Knowledge management in software engineering. *IEEE Software, 19*(3), 26–38. doi:10.1109/MS.2002.1003450

Seba, I., Rowley, J., & Lambert, S. (2012). Factors affecting attitudes and intentions towards knowledge sharing in the Dubai Police Force. *International Journal of Information Management, 32*(4), 372–380. doi:10.1016/j.ijinfomgt.2011.12.003

Shoemaker, N. (2014). Can Universities Encourage Students Continued Motivation For Knowledge Sharing And How Can This Help Organizations? *Journal of College Teaching and Learning, 11*(3), 99–114. doi:10.19030/tlc.v11i3.8757

Singh, A., & Pandey, D. (2017). Implementation of Requirement Engineering in Extreme Programing and SCRUM. *International Journal of Advanced Research in Computer Science, 8*(5).

Smith, S., & Kandel, A. (2018). *Verification and validation of rule-based expert systems*. CRC Press.

Szulanski, G. (2002). Sticky knowledge: Barriers to knowing in the firm. *Sage (Atlanta, Ga.)*.

Titi Amayah, A. (2013). Determinants of knowledge sharing in a public sector organization. *Journal of Knowledge Management, 17*(3), 454–471. doi:10.1108/JKM-11-2012-0369

Vasanthapriyan, S. (2018). *A Study of Software Testing Practices in Sri Lankan Software Companies.* Paper presented at the 2018 IEEE International Conference on Software Quality, Reliability and Security Companion (QRS-C). 10.1109/QRS-C.2018.00066

Vasanthapriyan, S. (2019). *Knowledge Sharing Initiatives in Software Companies: A Mapping Study. In Human Factors in Global Software Engineering* (pp. 84–108). IGI Global. doi:10.4018/978-1-5225-9448-2.ch004

Vasanthapriyan, S., Tian, J., & Xiang, J. (2015). *A survey on knowledge management in software engineering.* Paper presented at the Software Quality, Reliability and Security-Companion (QRS-C), 2015 IEEE International Conference on, Vancouver, Canada. 10.1109/QRS-C.2015.48

Vasanthapriyan, S., Xiang, J., Tian, J., & Xiong, S. (2017a). Knowledge synthesis in software industries: A survey in Sri Lanka. *Knowledge Management Research and Practice, 15*(3), 413–430. doi:10.105741275-017-0057-7

Vasanthapriyan, S., Xiang, J., Tian, J., & Xiong, S. (2017b). Knowledge synthesis in software industries: A survey in Sri Lanka. *Knowledge Management Research and Practice,* 1–18. doi:10.105741275-017-0057-7

Von Krogh, G. (1998). Care in knowledge creation. *California Management Review, 40*(3), 133–153. doi:10.2307/41165947

Von Krogh, G., Back, A., Enkel, E., & Seufert, A. (2004). *Putting knowledge networks into action.* Springer-Verlag.

Wang, Y., Huang, Q., Davison, R. M., & Yang, F. (2018). Effect of transactive memory systems on team performance mediated by knowledge transfer. *International Journal of Information Management, 41,* 65–79. doi:10.1016/j.ijinfomgt.2018.04.001

Weerakoon, S., & Wijayanayake, J. (2016). *Propensity of Knowledge Sharing in Software Development Case in Sri Lanka.* Paper presented at the International Conference on Multidisciplinary Approaches.

Wickramasinghe, V., & Widyaratne, R. (2012). Effects of interpersonal trust, team leader support, rewards, and knowledge sharing mechanisms on knowledge sharing in project teams. *Vine, 42*(2), 214–236. doi:10.1108/03055721211227255

Zammit, J., Gao, J., & Evans, R. (2016). Capturing and sharing product development knowledge using storytelling and video sharing. *Procedia CIRP, 56,* 440–445. doi:10.1016/j.procir.2016.10.081

Zammit, J. P., Gao, J., & Evans, R. (2015). *A framework to capture and share knowledge using storytelling and video sharing in global product development.* Paper presented at the IFIP International Conference on Product Lifecycle Management.

KEY TERMS AND DEFINITIONS

Agile Software Method: Agile software method comprises various approaches to software development under which requirements and solutions evolve through the collaborative effort of self-organizing and cross-functional teams and their end-user(s). It advocates adaptive planning, evolutionary development, early delivery, and continual improvement, and it encourages rapid and flexible response to change.

Knowledge Management: Knowledge management (KM) is the process of creating, sharing, using and managing the knowledge and information of an organization. It refers to a multidisciplinary approach to achieving organizational objectives by making the best use of knowledge. Knowledge management is recognized as the fundamental activity for obtaining, growing and sustaining intellectual capital in organizations.

Knowledge Transfer: Sharing of one's ideas, insights, solutions, experiences with another individual.

Novice Software Tester: A software professional who has just stepped into the software testing industry.

Quality Assurance Team: A team conducts activities that validate quality requirements.

Senior Software Tester: A software professional who has a lot of working experience in the software testing industry.

Software Development Lifecycle: The software development lifecycle is a systematic process for building software that ensures the quality and correctness of the software built. SDLC process aims to produce high-quality software which meets customer expectations. The software development should be complete in the pre-defined time frame and cost.

Software Engineering: Software engineering is concerned with the study of systematic approaches towards software development and maintenance.

Software Testing: Software testing provides the mechanism for verifying that the requirements identified during the initial phases of the project were properly implemented and that the system performs as expected. The test scenarios developed through these competitions ensure that the requirements are met end-to-end.

Test Automation: Test automation is the use of software separate from the software being tested to control the execution of tests and the comparison of actual outcomes with predicted outcomes. Test automation can automate some repetitive but necessary tasks in a formalized testing process already in place, or perform additional testing that would be difficult to do manually. Test automation is critical for continuous delivery and continuous testing.

Test Tools: A product that supports one or more test activities right from planning, requirements, creating a build, test execution, defect logging, and test analysis.

Theory of Planned Behavior: An extended concept of predicting behavior in any social situation. It proposes intention to behavior as the most recent antecedent of a specific behavior.

Validation: At the end of the development process, validation is the method of reviewing code to decide whether it satisfies customer expectations or specifications. The aim of Validation is to guarantee that the product actually meets the requirements of the consumer and to verify that the specifications are correct in the first place. "Testing like black-box testing, white box testing, gray box testing, etc." are involved in validation

Verification: Verification is the process of evaluating a development stage of products to determine whether they comply with the requirements specified. Verification helps to ensure that the product being developed is in compliance with the standards and specifications of the model. Verification includes "reviews, meetings, and inspections."

Chapter 13
Effectiveness of Scrum and Kanban on Agile-Based Software Maintenance Projects

Shanmuganathan Vasanthapriyan

iD https://orcid.org/0000-0002-0597-0263

Sabaragamuwa University of Sri Lanka, Sri Lanka

Kalpani Madushika Udawela Arachchi

Sabaragamuwa University of Sri Lanka, Sri Lanka

ABSTRACT

Software maintenance is an important phase in the lifespan of a software system. This chapter examines the effectiveness of Scrum and Kanban methods in terms of their impacts on project management factors for a software maintenance project. The six-point star model defines project management factors like schedule, scope, budget, risk, resources, quality, and study, and uses two other non-quantitative techniques such as team commitment and work organization. A quantitative survey was carried out together with the questionnaire distributed to IT industry professionals in Sri Lanka. Each question in the questionnaire was related to one of the above factors. The Pearson correlation coefficient was used to find the correlation between the coefficients. A strong correlation was identified. Based on the results of multiple linear regression modeling, a model has been proposed. Scrum-based software maintenance projects can improve project quality by managing work organization and resources whereas Kanban-based can improve project quality by controlling the risk and scope of the project.

INTRODUCTION

Software Maintenance

Software maintenance is a very important phase in the lifespan of a software system. As a result of maintenance, the software system fully or partially deviates from its original state and evolved into a new

DOI: 10.4018/978-1-7998-2531-9.ch013

system (Lei, Ganjeizadeh, Jayachandran, & Ozcan, 2017). According to IEEE, software maintenance can be defined as the modification of a software system or its components, after its delivery to correct its faults, adapting to a changing environment or improving its performance (Larman & Basili, 2003). The software maintenance process plays a vital role in an organization because it consumes a considerable amount of overall lifecycle costs. Failure to change the software quickly and reliably according to the organization's requirements leads to loss of business opportunities (Ågerfalk, Fitzgerald, & In, 2006).

Mostly software maintenance is carried out by a heavyweight method or even without any particular method. Several maintenance models, such as Boehm, quick-fix, Osborne, full reuse, iterative-enhancement and the ISO/IEC 14764 and IEEE-1219 IEEE standards for maintenance have been proposed. Those existing models generate challenges because they are largely based on the Waterfall model. It is difficult to handle problems properly due to their limitations such as team morale, lack of communication among stakeholders, unstructured code, and frequent prioritization of customer requests and poor visibility of the project flow. Agile methodologies were able to handle limitations by providing continuous testing, customer collaboration, incremental development and refactoring (Dyba, 2000).

Agile Methods

Anterior software development methods have been used to capture approaches to define and gather project requirements, investigate problems, and systematically implement problem solutions (Lei et al., 2017). Although most companies consider iterative and incremental methods as modern developmental practices, their application dates back to the mid-1950s (Larman & Basili, 2003), when other methods were sequential and linear and called "waterfall models" (Lei et al, 2017). In 2001, problems in the waterfall model were identified and the agile methodology introduced (Lei et al., 2017). Agile development methods are a set of software development practices defined by experienced practitioners (Ågerfalk et al., 2006). These agile development practices responded to traditional or plan-driven approaches that focus on "an engineering-based, rationalized approach" (Dyba, 2000; Nerur, Mahapatra & Mangalaraj, 2005).

Agile methods have some common features: iterative development process, adaptation to change, less documentation, customer interaction, focus on delivery, frequent testing, communication and collaboration among team members, motivation enhancement, high quality codes, knowledge transfer through openness and high quality products with customer (Ahmad, Kuvaja, Oivo, & Markkula, 2016; Devulapally, 2015; Rehman, Maqbool, Riaz, Qamar, & Abbas, 2018). Agile software engineering practices include simple design, small releases, pair programming, test-driven development, daily stand-up meetings, task boards, product backlog, user stories, and on-site customers. Agile practitioners have recognized benefits that include cost reduction, quality improvement, flexibility of development teams, increased productivity, and customer satisfaction and reduced time to market. These benefits are achieved in the software development phase and it needs to be examined whether these benefits are taken into account in the software maintenance phase (Devulapally, 2015; Heeager & Rose, 2015).

Scrum Theory

Scrum is an iterative and incremental project management methodology based on empirical process control theory. It is about optimizing predictability and controlling the risk of a project. The Scrum process consists of three key factors such as transparency, inspection, and adaptation. Transparency is the visibility of the project for each project participant. Inspection is the frequent review of Scrum artifacts to capture issues in previous phases. If an inspector detects a defect, the process can be adjusted to avoid further problems and it is an adaptation.

The Scrum process contains Scrum artifacts, rules, teams, and events, while the rules affect how to bind Scrum artifacts, rules, and teams together. The Scrum team has a product owner, a Scrum master and developers. The role of the product owner is to maximize the value of the project by managing the product backlog and explaining the product backlog and project goals to the developers. The product backlog is the list of project requirements. Scrum master is responsible for managing the product backlog, and directing developers to create product backlog elements perfectly. Developers are an essential part of supporting implementation and on-time delivery at the end of a sprint. Sprint is a time needed for an increment. They are self-organized and do not form subgroups (Rehman et al., 2018).

Kanban Theory

Kanban grants a Japanese meaning, which means a signboard that is used in manufacturing companies as a scheduling system. It is considered as a flow control mechanism used for just-in-time pull driven production where the upstream processing activities are started by the downstream process request signals (Ahmad et al., 2016). It has been successfully used by Toyota in practice (Ahmad et al., 2016). Anderson has proposed five principles for Kanban theory (Rehman et al., 2018).

The first principle is the visualization of the workflow. In an organization, the work goes through various states such as planned, in progress, and done. The Kanban promotes the visualization of the workflow by applying virtual or physical boards and maps. The cards allow team members to see the ongoing work-in-progress and being self-organized by placing their tasks and finishing the work without the admonition of a manager.

Limit Work in Progress (WIP) is the next principle and means managing the amount of work-in-progress at a particular stage of the workflow. To be considered a Kanban system, there must be explicit WIP limits and signaling to attract new workers through the system.

Motivation of the Research

The motivation of the research is based on the inclusion of research papers and, in essence, on the expertise experience at industry-level. Agile is an incremental and iterative methodology that makes an effective contribution to project management. It was traditionally based on the models "waterfall" and "V". In comparison, the application of a project management method effectively and efficiently contributes to setting of timelines, planning, budget control, and project quality improvement (Rehman et al., 2018). According to the literature, the applicability of agile methodology was only for software development, and the handling of software maintenance was not well considered. So look at the effect of agile project management methodology for software maintenance, which is considered a necessary requirement.

In the Sri Lankan software industry, software maintenance is mainly based on Scrum practices, and some small companies do not follow a project management methodology. There are leading software companies that use Kanban for software maintenance projects, and they have explored their idea for the effectiveness and efficient use of Kanban to improve software maintenance. There have been fewer studies on Scrum for software maintenance although the Scrum is frequently used in industry in projects. This study has therefore set itself the goal of analyzing the effectiveness of Scrum and Kanban in the area of software maintenance.

According to the software industry employees, they faced many problems, such as non-adherence to schedule and budget, failure to meet customer expectations, etc. Business people need to adapt to change in the face of rapid technological improvements and changing business environment. Applications are expected to change. In such a situation, software maintainers have a great responsibility to meet customer expectations. So they have to choose the right path. There should be a standard way to deliver the expected results in time with the expected quality, by properly deploying resources and properly reducing the risk, planning scope and schedule. For these reasons, the authors have looked at the impact of Scrum and Kanban on software maintenance.

Research Objectives and Goals

Scrum and Kanban are the two outstanding agile methods in the software industry. In Sri Lanka, both methods are often used in software development and rarely in software maintenance. Industry experts from Sri Lanka have found that Kanban is often suitable for software maintenance and Scrum are more frequently used. There is also a lack of literature on Scrum- or Kanban-based software maintenance. Therefore, this study was conducted to close the gap in the literature on Scrum or Kanban based software maintenance.

This research will give an overview of how Scrum and Kanban affect software maintenance projects. The effectiveness are measured taking into account schedule management, scope management, budget handling, risk management, resource management, team commitment and work organization of the project. Scope, timeline, budget, risk, resources, and quality are project management factors defined in the six-point star model (Guide, 2001). In addition, team commitment and work organization are considered as two non-quantitative techniques. Quality is the dependent variable of the study used to determine the success of the software maintenance project. To achieve the goals of the study, the following research objectives were addressed.

Main objective: To investigate the effectiveness of Scrum and Kanban methods in terms of their impact on project management factors for a software maintenance project.

Sub-objective 1: To examine the effect of team commitment on Scrum or Kanban based software maintenance projects.

Sub-objective 2: To identify the effect of scope management on Scrum or Kanban based software maintenance projects.

Sub-objective 3: To determine the effect of budget handling on Scrum or Kanban based software maintenance projects.

LITERATURE REVIEW

The characterization of software maintenance is an important issue as it differs from software development (Rehman et al., 2018). Castro Sousa et al. pointed out three major software maintenance issues, namely the lack of a software maintenance process model, the lack of clear documentation on application development, and the difficulty of balancing time within maintenance. The study found that most projects in Portugal use the quick-fix model for software maintenance (Sousa & Moreira, 1998). Stephen W.L. Yip et al. surveyed in Hong Kong in 1994, and they concluded that software maintenance costs are still high and the significance of software maintenance has not been properly established (Yip & Lam, 1994). In 2011, Meananeatra et al. investigated software maintenance in the Thai software industry. The study is based on four topics: techniques, awareness, refactoring practices, and software maintenance issues. The study indicated that the Thai software industry was aware of the importance of software maintenance, and the results suggested that the design pattern technique is preferable to the refactoring technique (Meananeatra, Rongviriyapanish & Apiwattanapong, 2011).

In 2016, Sokappadu et al. reviewed software maintenance problems and suggested solutions for them (Sokappadu, Mattapullut, Paavan & Ramdoo, 2016). According to the study, common causes for the problems were defined in two categories as technical and non-technical problems. Technical problems include program understanding, change impact analysis, implementation and propagation of changes, regression testing, database size, system quality, system age and obsolescence, operating environment, system size and complexity, legacy software, types of frameworks and building blocks used, and re-structuring change. Non-technical problems include the availability of the programmer, the needs and expectations of the users, the size of the staff, the turnover of staff, the maintenance budget, the quality of the documentation, the development experience of the maintenance staff, project management issues and errors, and the lack of skilled labor. Problems are caused by product quality, re-documentation of the proposed solutions, the removal of dead code, and cloned code. If the code is flawed and ugly, eliminate errors and a restructuring has been proposed. If restructuring is not enough, reengineering is the answer. Staff-related issues are resolved through technical training, outsourcing, recruiting, and employee training (Doomun, Khedo & Khedo, 2016).

Kajko-Mattsson and Nyfjord presented a process model for maintenance that is a subset of other agile process models. According to their results, they concluded the degree of agility change according to the phase and it is higher in the implementation phase, while it is lower in the pre-implementation phase. According to these observations, some agile practices during the maintenance and evaluation phase were approved (Kajko-Mattsson & Nyfjord, 2009). Accordingly, several research studies have demonstrated the applicability of Agile in software maintenance projects.

The terms project and project management are two different terms that are confused with each other. The aim of both terms, however, is to achieve project success. The distinction between the two terms is due to the scope of the project life cycle. The project focuses on long-term goals such as increased productivity and return on investment, while project management focuses on short-term goals such as on-time completion, meeting expected requirements, and developing the project within the budget (Demir, 2008). Traditionally, the project's success has depended on cost, time and scope (Lei et al., 2017). Later, an expanded triple constraint model was defined based on six factors such as schedule, scope, budget, risk, resources, and quality. It was defined by Project Management Body of Knowledge in 2001 (Guide, 2001).

According to many studies, a large part of the software costs are spent on maintenance. Therefore, researchers have begun to look for techniques that can improve software maintenance. F. Ruiz et al. have investigated the development of a management environment for software maintenance. It is MANTIS, which is called the extended software development environment. As an extended approach, a new module has been added, called the KM module, which provides the ability to reuse information and expertise generated during software maintenance. They mentioned that the software maintenance process is a collection of information that comes from different sources such as projects, methodologies, teams, and so on. Due to the enormous complexity, they also proposed an ontology. Their ontology is a collection of ontologies such as maintenance, workflow and measurement. This ontology deals with the main aspects of software maintenance as products, processes, activities, agents, workflows and measures (Ruiz, Vizcaíno, Piattini & García, 2004).

The scope factor of a project is to consider project goals, missions, and requirements. G.E. Stark et al. have investigated the implications of changing the requirement for a software maintenance release (Stark, Oman, Skillicorn & Ameele, 1999). Requirements form the basis for estimating the cost and schedule of the project. The scope factor has a direct or indirect impact on the schedule, the budget and the quality factor. Here two quantitative techniques have been used to handle requirement changes in a software maintenance environment. The first is exploratory data analysis, which determines the source, frequency and type of the change. The second is the regression model, which allows the management level to estimate the impact of cost and timing due to requirement changes. Based on their findings, they conclude that collaborative application development and prototyping are useful for dealing with customers, while dealing with software maintainers requires more detailed documentation and discipline. They suggest an economic impact model to conduct a discussion between the client and the supplier when a change of requirement occurs (Stark et al., 1999). According to Guide (2001), the schedule factor focuses on the on-time completion of the project. Aversano et al. have discussed the introduction of workflow management in software maintenance (Aversano, de Lucia, Stefanucci & Betti, 2001). They conducted a case study and proposed a workflow-based prototype implementation.

RESEARCH METHOD

Sample Selection

The study deals with agile software maintenance projects and is conducted in the context of Sri Lanka. Therefore, the Sri Lankan software company is the targeted sample for the study. Agile methodology is a recent iterative approach to project management and is widely used only in software development projects. Software maintenance and development also have a significant difference. Thus the selection of samples involves considerable effort. Because selecting a sample by those who do not use agile methodologies in their maintenance projects can lead to project failures and wasted time. Therefore, a targeted sampling was performed for the sample selection procedure.

Data Collection

The study has selected quantitative data collection techniques to collect data from the selected sample. The data collection approach selected was the most common quantitative data collection technique, which is a questionnaire. Literature research and the ideas of industry experts with experience in agile software maintenance contributed to the creation of the questionnaire content. To confirm the quality of the questionnaire, a pilot study was carried out and the answers carefully managed. The questionnaire was electronically formatted using Google Forms and reached the desired sample using social media (LinkedIn). The timeframe of the study was from 5/13/2019 to 6/22/2013. The privacy of the respondents was protected.

Pilot Survey Study

This study focuses on the pilot study for a variety of reasons, mainly due to the agile approach, which is new in software maintenance projects. It also provides a guide to research design, testing instrument and research design, testing techniques for the survey (e.g. email and social media), testing the viability of the selected sample, understanding survey limitations, and testing sentence comprehension in the questionnaires as well often beneficial for conducting a pilot survey. So this is an extremely valuable approach to the success of the study. Finally, it leads to improvements and modifications of the full-scale study.

The instrument of the pilot study was a self-administered questionnaire. It consists of an administrative introductory section and two research-related sections. The first section contains general information and the second section looks at the impact of agile methodologies on the software maintenance process. Each question in section 2 was based on one of the aforementioned factors.

Survey Instrument (Questionnaire)

Taking into account the results of the pilot survey, a well-organized questionnaire was prepared. The first section contains general information, such as the experienced agile method (among the responses given), age, specialty, level of experience, size of the company, and the size of the maintenance project team. Each of these questions had five answers. The second section dealt with the experience of agile software maintenance. Each question in the second section was included in one of the above factors. The answers to these questions were given according to the five-point Likert scale.

Hypothesis Development

The study-related hypothesis was constructed as follows and the conceptual model of the research (Figure 1) was constructed using the hypothesis.

H1 – Schedule management influences on the success of a software maintenance project
    On-time completion of a project was considered as the schedule management. This study was used past literature to address the schedule dimension. The schedule is considered as a time table for a project. Project progress is defined over a certain time by considering the on-time completion and available resources.
H2 – Scope management influences on the success of a software maintenance project
    The scope factor determines the goals, missions, and requirements of a project (Lei et al., 2017). A clear understanding of the project can be gained by the scope definition. Resource allocations and all planning of the project are discussed within the scope management scenario. Better scope management ensures that all the work required is included to gain a successful project outcome.
H3 – Budget management influences on the success of a software maintenance project
    According to (Abdullah, 2018; Ahmad et al., 2016), a significant portion of a software cost is taken by software maintenance. Literature has shown that 5% of the total software cost is spent on preventive maintenance. Sousa and Moreira have mentioned that the costly maintenance type is adaptive maintenance (Reyes, Smith, & Fraunholz, 2007).
H4 – Risk management influences on the success of a software maintenance project

Risk management focuses on risk mitigation of the relevant project. Identification, analyze and mitigation needs to be done in risk management. The focus of risk management is to minimize unfortunate issues for the project. The project may have redundant and incorrect things. To protect the quality of the project incorrect things need to be eliminated.

H5 – Resource management influences on the success of a software maintenance project

A software maintenance project includes human and material resources. They ensure that the project has enough staff. The team members with knowledge of the application are an important resource for a maintenance project. The most significant material resource of a maintenance project is up to date documentation (Choudhari & Suman, 2010; Sousa & Moreira, 1998).

H6 – Team commitment influences on the success of a software maintenance project

The team has the major place in a project. Commitment to a specific goal as a team is a cornerstone of a project. The team commitment is fulfilled when the goal of all team members has focused on the project goal. The commitment of all team members to reach a specific goal as a team is a deciding factor for both team success and project quality. Changes to team members are common in projects. To sustain the success of the overall project, effective management of the change of team members is required (Bennett & Rajlich, 2000; Sousa & Moreira, 1998).

H7 – Work organization influences on the success of a software maintenance project

The organization of work is an important thing in the daily work. In a software maintenance project, a work organization facilitates the coordination and execution of project activities. Proper work organizations minimize disruptions and conflicts. Better task assignment and workload management, as well as the management of unpredictable tasks require work organization (Bennett & Rajlich, 2000). The goal is to improve the quality of the project.

RESULTS AND DISCUSSIONS

Descriptive Statistics for Demographic Data

Demographic analyze was done using frequencies of demographic data (Table 1). A data set consisted of 225 valid responses was used to carry out the analysis. Among them, 141 (62.7%) respondents had experience with Scrum, while 4 (1.8%) respondents had experience with Kanban. The rest of the respondents, 80 (35.6%), had experience with both Scrum and Kanban. Of all respondents, 153 (67.6%) were answered with Scrum skills, while 72 (32.4%) were answered with Kanban skills. Therefore, the majority had experience with Scrum.

Assessment of the Measurement Model

The measurement model was evaluated prior to descriptive, correlation and regression analysis. It was performed to verify the reliability and validity of the key figures used in latent variables. Later, the analysis was performed on the basis of reliability and validity. The validity takes into account evidence for the correctness of the assumptions about the questions that need to be answered in the study, while the reliability measures the stability and consistency of the results (Vasanthapriyan, Xiang, Tian & Xiong, 2017).

Figure 1. Conceptual research model

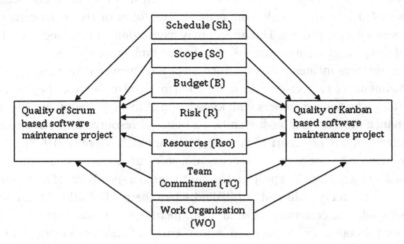

Validity Test

The validity analysis was performed using the Kaiser-Meyer-Olkin coefficient (KMO) and the Bartlett Test of Sphericity (BTS). The adequacy of the samples was measured by the value of KMO, while the overall significance of all correlations within the correlation matrix factors was measured by BTS. KMO scores are rated as marvelous at 0.9 s, meritorious at 0.8 s, middling at 0.7 s, miserable at 0.5 s and unacceptable at less than 0.5 s (Vasanthapriyan et al., 2017). The cutoff value was 0.8 to conclude the significance of the analysis. Table 2 shows KMO values obtained for Scrum and Kanban datasets of 0.90 and 0.78, respectively, while BTS has been found to be significant even in strong relationships. In this way it was shown that both tests provide strong evidence for the appropriateness of a sample size to perform the analysis.

Reliability Test

Cronbach's Alpha (Cronbach, 1951) was used to measure the internal consistency of the questionnaire and noted that the questionnaire was very consistent. Vasanthapriyan et al. (2017) recommended setting the threshold for Cronbach's Alpha at 0.5. According to the results in Table 3, the Cronbach's Alpha is greater than 0.5 for all coefficients. The reliability level can therefore be considered as high and the internal consistency of the questionnaire as good.

Table 1. Demographic analysis

	Demographic variable	Percent (%)
Experienced agile method	Scrum	62.7
	Kanban	1.8
	Both(Scrum and Kanban)	35.6
Age	Below 25	16.0
	25 – 30	68.0
	30 – 35	14.7
	35 – 40	0.9
	Above 40	0.4
Specialty	Software Engineering	75.6
	Project Management	4.9
	Business Analysts	4.0
	QA Engineering	11.6
	UI/UX Engineer	0.4
	Software Architect	0.9
	Database Administrator	0.4
	DevOps Engineer	2.2
Experience level in industry	Below 1 year	16.0
	1 – 3 years	37.3
	3 – 5 years	27.6
	5 – 10 years	16.9
	Above 10 years	2.2
Company size	Below 50	16.0
	51 – 100	11.6
	101 – 250	19.6
	251 – 500	28.0
	Above 501	24.9
Team size	Below 3	6.7
	4 – 9	45.3
	10 – 14	20.9
	15 – 25	10.7
	Above 26	16.4

Table 2. KMO and Bartlett's test

		Scrum	Kanban
Kaiser-Meyer-Olkin Measure of Sampling Adequacy.		0.90	0.78
Bartlett's Test of Sphericity	Approx. Chi-Square	2185.43	1146.92
	Df	435	435
	Sig.	.000	.000

Table 3. Reliability analysis

Factor	No. of item	Mean		Std. Deviation		Cronbach's Alpha	
		Scrum	Kanban	Scrum	Kanban	Scrum	Kanban
Sh	3	4.08	4.03	0.54	0.48	0.62	0.54
Sc	5	3.84	3.84	0.55	0.55	0.73	0.71
B	3	3.64	3.60	0.68	0.64	0.78	0.65
R	3	3.81	3.79	0.59	0.65	0.56	0.58
Rso	4	3.91	3.96	0.56	0.56	0.64	0.64
Q	6	3.98	3.96	0.59	0.59	0.87	0.87
TC	4	4.01	4.06	0.56	0.47	0.73	0.61
WO	2	3.85	3.87	0.66	0.58	0.61	0.51

Assessment of the Structural Model

Check Linearity of Variables

The linearity of the variables was checked by the Pearson correlation coefficient (r), which is used to measure the linear correlation between two variables. The value of r ranges from -1 to +1 for continuous data (Benesty, Chen, Huang & Cohen, 2009). Positive correlation means either variable increase or decrease together. A negative correlation means that one variable increases and the other decreases and vice versa. A zero-value correlation means that there is no correlation between variables, while one means a perfect correlation. According to Benesty et al. (2009) the magnitude of the correlation coefficient is ranked, very high correlation at 0.9 s, high correlation at 0.7 to 0.9 s, moderate correlation at 0.5 to 0.7 s, low correlation at 0.3-0.5s and little linear correlation at less than 0.3s. Table 4 shows Pearson's correlation coefficients of constructs after grouping in Scrum and Kanban. All correlations are significant at 0.01 level.

According to the results of Table 4, all variables appear to have a positive correlation between the dependent variable and the independent variable in both Scrum and Kanban data sets. Each correlation value is greater than 0.5, indicating that there is a moderate correlation between variables. With a sig. value of less than 0.05 and a Pearson correlation coefficient close to 1, a higher correlation can be assumed. Therefore, the effect of Scrum and Kanban on each construct can affect the overall success of the project.

Table 4. Pearson correlation of variables

			Sh	Sc	B	R	Rso	TC	WO
Q	Scrum	Sh	1						
		Sc	.59**	1					
		B	.48**	.54**	1				
		R	.49**	.51**	.38**	1			
		Rso	.50**	.48**	.46**	.50**	1		
		TC	.63**	.50**	.46**	.59**	.66**	1	
		WO	.64**	.60**	.42**	.53**	.51**	.58**	1
		Q	.60**	.52**	.51**	.57**	.67**	.70**	.64**
1	Kanban	Sh	1						
		Sc	.41**	1					
		B	.45**	.36**	1				
		R	.31**	.44**	.46**	1			
		Rso	.31**	.48**	.51**	.48**	1		
		TC	.56**	.55**	.51**	.58**	.56**	1	
		WO	.44**	.65**	.26*	.44**	.31**	.51**	1
		Q	.53**	.56***	.57**	.60**	.56**	.69**	.51**

** Correlation is significant at the 0.01 level (2-tailed).
*Correlation is significant at the 0.05 level (2-tailed).

Model Adequacy (Model Fit)

The model adequacy was measured using the model summary table, which indicates the strength of the relationships between the dependent variable and the model. Table 5 shows the model summary. R denotes the multiple correlation coefficient. The linear correlation between the model-predicted and observed dependent variable values is defined by R. R Square denotes coefficient of determination and it is the squared value of multiple correlation coefficient. The adjusted R square checks how good the model is. According to Table 5, the model adequacy of the Scrum-related model is 63.5% and the model adequacy of the Kanban-related model is 60.9%. If the model adequacy is greater than 70%, it means that the model is very good, while the model adequacy is less than 50%, it means that the model is not good. So these two models are relatively good. Among them, the Scrum-related model is better than the Kanban-related model. However, each of the models has several other factors that affect the quality of a software maintenance project, except for the factors considered.

Table 5. Model summary

Method	Model	R	R Square	Adjusted R Square	Std. Error of the Estimate
Scrum	1	.695[a]	.483	.479	.42733
	2	.754[b]	.568	.562	.39182
	3	.788[c]	.622	.614	.36792
	4	.797[d]	.635	.625	.36277
Kanban	5	.694[a]	.481	.474	.42968
	6	.739[f]	.546	.533	.40481
	7	.763[g]	.583	.565	.39090
	8	.780[h]	.609	.586	.38130

a. Predictors: (Constant), TC

b. Predictors: (Constant), TC, WO

c. Predictors: (Constant), TC, WO, Rso

d. Predictors: (Constant), TC, WO, Rso, B

e. Dependent Variable: Q

f. Predictors: (Constant), TC, B

g. Predictors: (Constant), TC, B, R

h. Predictors: (Constant), TC, B, R, Sc

Discussion of Hypothesis

In this study, two models for Scrum and Kanban were identified. Both models were identified using schedule, scope, budget, risk, resources, team commitment, and work organization as independent variables, using the quality of the project as a dependent variable. After checking whether the dependent variable depends on the independent variable, some of the hypotheses were accepted while others were rejected.

Scrum

H1 – Schedule management influences on the success of a software maintenance project

Looking at the Scrum model, the schedule, scope, and risk-related hypothesis have shown negative results. So they rejected the model. The correlation between schedule and quality is 0.6, with a correlation that is significant at 0.01 level (Table 4). Therefore, the H1 hypothesis is accepted. Since the results have a negative correlation, there is no relationship between the schedule and quality factors associated with Scrum-based software maintenance.

H2 – Scope management influences on the success of a software maintenance project

When considering the scope dimension, the correlation between scope and quality is 0.52, with the correlation being significant at 0.01 level (Table 4). Therefore, the H2 hypothesis is accepted. Although the correlation is greater than 0.5, the significant value of the scope is greater than 0.05. Therefore, there is no relationship between scope and quality factors associated with Scrum-based software maintenance.

H3 – Budget management influences on the success of a software maintenance project

The correlation between budget and quality is 0.51 where correlation is significant at the 0.01 level (Table 4). Therefore H3 hypothesis is rejected. As results show a positive relationship, the budget positively influences the quality of Scrum-based software maintenance.

H4 – Risk management influences on the success of a software maintenance project

Taking into account the risk dimension, the correlation between risk and quality is 0.57, with a correlation being significant at 0.01 level (Table 4). Therefore, the H4 hypothesis is accepted. Although the correlation is greater than 0.5, the significant risk value is greater than 0.05. Therefore, there is no correlation between risk and quality factors associated with Scrum-based software maintenance.

H5 – Resource management influences on the success of a software maintenance project

The correlation between resources and quality is 0.67 with a correlation being significant at 0.01 level (Table 4). Therefore H5 hypothesis is rejected. As results show a positive relationship, resources positively influence the quality of Scrum-based software maintenance.

H6 – Team commitment influences the success of a software maintenance project

When considering team commitment dimension, the correlation between team commitment and quality is 0.70 with a correlation being significant at 0.01 level (Table 4). Therefore H6 hypothesis is rejected. Since the correlation is greater than 0.5 and the significant value of team commitment is greater than 0.05, there is a positive relationship between team commitment and the quality of Scrum-based software maintenance.

H7 – Work organization influences on the success of a software maintenance project

The correlation between work organization and quality is 0.64 with a correlation being significant at 0.01 level (Table 4). Therefore H7 hypothesis is rejected. As results show a positive relationship, work for organization positively influences the quality of Scrum-based software maintenance.

Kanban

H1 – Schedule management influences the success of a software maintenance project

When considering the Kanban model, schedule, resource, and work organization hypotheses have shown negative results. So they rejected the model. The correlation between schedule and quality is 0.53, with a correlation being significant at 0.01 level (Table 4). Therefore, the H1 hypothesis is accepted. Since the results show a negative relationship, there is no relationship between schedule and quality factors related to Kanban-based software maintenance.

H2 – Scope management influences on the success of a software maintenance project

When considering the scope dimension, the correlation between scope and quality is 0.56, with the correlation being significant at 0.01 level (Table 4). Therefore, the H2 hypothesis is rejected. Since the correlation is greater than 0.5 and the significant value of the scope is less than 0.05, there is a relationship between the scope and quality factors associated with Kanban-based software maintenance. Scope therefore has a positive effect on the quality of Kanban-based software maintenance.

H3 – Budget management influences the success of a software maintenance project

The correlation between budget and quality is 0.50 with the correlation being significant at 0.01 level (Table 4). Therefore H3 hypothesis is rejected. Since the results show a positive relationship, the budget has a positive effect on the quality of Kanban-based software maintenance.

H4 – Risk management influences the success of a software maintenance project

When considering risk dimension, the correlation between risk and quality is 0.60 with the correlation being significant at 0.01 level (Table 4). Therefore H4 hypothesis is rejected. Since the correlation is greater than 0.5 and the significant risk value is less than 0.05, the risk factor positively influences the quality of Kanban-based software maintenance.

H5 – Resource management influences the success of a software maintenance project

The correlation between resources and quality is 0.56, with the correlation being significant at 0.01 level (Table 4). Therefore, the H5 hypothesis is accepted. According to the results, there is no correlation between resources and the quality of Kanban-based software maintenance.

H6 – Team commitment influences the success of a software maintenance project

Considering the team commitment dimension, the correlation between team commitment and quality is 0.69, with the correlation being significant at 0.01 level (Table 4). Therefore, the H6 hypothesis is rejected. Because the correlation is greater than 0.5 and the significant value of the team commitment is greater than 0.05, there is a positive relationship between team commitment and the quality of Kanban-based software maintenance.

H7 – Work organization influences the success of a software maintenance project

The correlation between work organization and quality is 0.51, with a correlation that is significant at 0.01 level (Table 4). Therefore, the H7 hypothesis is accepted. The results indicate that there is no relationship between work organization and quality of Kanban-based software maintenance.

Taking into account the results of the hypothesis, the conceptual research model was reconstructed as shown in Figure 2.

CONCLUSION

A review of the literature revealed that there is a lack of advanced evidence for the effectiveness of Scrum and Kanban in software maintenance projects. The study was conducted to find out if there is a difference between two approaches that affect the project management factors specified in the six-star model, and two other quantitative techniques such as work organization and team commitment (Guide, 2001). Schedule management, scope definition, budget handling, risk control, resource management and project quality are the six project management factors that have been considered in the study. To compare the effectiveness of Scrum versus Kanban in software maintenance projects, a survey-based questionnaire

Figure 2. Reconstructed research model

was designed that included various questions about responders, company, software maintenance project, and project management methodology.

An advanced analysis technique called structured regression modeling was used to compare the effectiveness of Scrum and Kanban on selected factors. For each factor, the highest correlation was found with the quality of the software maintenance project. The results showed that there is no significant difference in the 95% confidence level between Scrum and Kanban for the selected dimensions. The results also showed that both Scrum and Kanban are influencing the team's commitment and budget management to improve the quality of software maintenance projects. In addition, work organization and resources were impacted by the quality of Scrum-based software maintenance projects, while risk and scope were affected by the quality of Kanban-based software maintenance projects. The research model was reconstructed on the basis of these results (Figure 2) and was the model suit for the context of Sri Lanka. Eliminated factors in any agile methodology were not suitable for the context of Sri Lanka.

According to the results of additional analysis, it is efficient to allow tasks with the highest priority when Kanban is used for software maintenance. The team size of a software maintenance project is not the size of software development projects. The results show that members of less than or equal to three are most suitable for software maintenance projects. In the Sri Lankan context, Kanban can do better correction, perfection, and adaptation in software maintenance processes to improve the quality of the project. Budget management was also effective when using Kanban. For maintenance projects using Kanban, greater consistency in team commitment has been identified. Kanban showed better results in most situations. However, the overall result has shown that both Kanban and Scrum lead to a successful software maintenance project. Variables for result analysis were selected from previous literature and this study was conducted in the context of Sri Lanka. Different results have emerged due to cultural differences between Sri Lanka and other countries.

There were several limitations in the circumstances research was conducted. Thus, threats and errors can be linked to the validity of research results. This study was conducted by a single author under supervision. Therefore, decisions regarding study, dimension selection, and hypothesis construction may not be significant for each dimension. The questionnaire was sent to respondents via LinkedIn. The selected sample may therefore show deviations because the respondents have different backgrounds. They come from different company sizes, different experience levels and corporate cultures. This may cause deviations in the selected sample. The survey duration was one and a half months. This time cannot be considered sufficient for data collection. Due to the limited timeframe for the research study, this study was unable to separate more time for data collection. The study was used as the only quantitative approach for data collection. It was a questionnaire. There are limitations in conducting only quantitative research because respondents have no way of expressing their own ideas. In some cases, respondents mentioned ideas in private messages. For a successful research result, therefore, a qualitative technique is required due to the sensitive and detailed information. Both quantitative and qualitative techniques are able to achieve the most successful research results. Because this research is conducted in a geographically diverse context, results related to the context of Sri Lanka may not be generalized to the results of other countries. To be valid, more research on this topic needs to be carried out both in the Sri Lankan context and in other countries.

In the future, the plan will be expanded to consider a qualitative technique using the quantitative method to improve probative value. The proposed model is reviewed at the organizational level to verify its validity in the Sri Lankan context. Other dimensions are considered visibility and communication to explore research in a wide range.

ACKNOWLEDGMENT

We thank the software companies participated and its testing team members who were actively facilitating this research since beginning. We also thank both Academic Staffs who provided their immense support through expert evaluation. This work is partially supported by Sabaragamuwa University of Sri Lanka Research Grant SUSL/RG/2018/04.

REFERENCES

Abdullah, S. (2018). Improving the Governance of Software Maintenance Process for Agile Software Development Team. *International Journal of Engineering and Technology, 7*(4.31). doi:10.14419/ijet.v7i4.31.23352

Ågerfalk, J., Fitzgerald, B., & In, O. P. (2006). *Flexible and distributed software processes: old petunias in new bowls.* Paper presented at the Communications of the ACM.

Ahmad, M. O., Kuvaja, P., Oivo, M., & Markkula, J. (2016). *Transition of software maintenance teams from Scrum to Kanban.* Paper presented at the 2016 49th Hawaii International Conference on System Sciences (HICSS). 10.1109/HICSS.2016.670

Aversano, L., de Lucia, A., Stefanucci, S., & Betti, S. (2001). Introducing workflow management in software maintenance processes. *Proceedings of the IEEE International Conference on Software Maintenance (ICSM'01).* 10.1109/ICSM.2001.972757

Benesty, J., Chen, J., Huang, Y., & Cohen, I. (2009). *Pearson correlation coefficient. In Noise reduction in speech processing* (pp. 1–4). Springer.

Bennett, K. H., & Rajlich, V. T. (2000). Software maintenance and evolution: a roadmap. *Proceedings of the Conference on the Future of Software Engineering.*

Choudhari, J., & Suman, U. (2010). *Iterative maintenance life cycle using extreme programming.* Paper presented at the 2010 International Conference on Advances in Recent Technologies in Communication and Computing. 10.1109/ARTCom.2010.52

Cronbach, L. J. (1951). Coefficient alpha and the internal structure of tests. *Psychometrika, 16*(3), 297-334.

Demir, K. A. (2008). *Measurement of software project management effectiveness.* Retrieved from https://core.ac.uk/download/pdf/36739565.pdf

Devulapally, G. K. (2015). *Agile in the context of Software Maintenance: A Case Study.* Academic Press.

Doomun, R., Khedo, K. K., & Khedo, K. (2016). Review of Software Maintenance Problems and Proposed Solutions in IT consulting firms in Mauritius. *International Journal of Computers and Applications, 156*(4), 975–8887.

Dyba, T. (2000). Improvisation in small software organizations. *IEEE Software, 17*(5), 82–87. doi:10.1109/52.877872

Guide, A. (2001). *Project management body of knowledge (pmbok® guide).* Paper presented at the Project Management Institute.

Heeager, L. T., & Rose, J. (2015). Optimising agile development practices for the maintenance operation: Nine heuristics. *Empirical Software Engineering, 20*(6), 1762–1784. doi:10.100710664-014-9335-7

Kajko-Mattsson, M., & Nyfjord, J. (2009). *A model of agile evolution and maintenance process.* Paper presented at the 2009 42nd Hawaii International Conference on System Sciences.

Larman, C., & Basili, V. R. (2003). Iterative and incremental developments. a brief history. *Computer, 36*(6), 47–56. doi:10.1109/MC.2003.1204375

Lei, H., Ganjeizadeh, F., Jayachandran, P. K., & Ozcan, P. (2017). A statistical analysis of the effects of Scrum and Kanban on software development projects. *Robotics and Computer-integrated Manufacturing, 43*, 59–67. doi:10.1016/j.rcim.2015.12.001

Meananeatra, P., Rongviriyapanish, S., & Apiwattanapong, T. (2011). *A Survey on the Maintenance of Software Structure in Thai Software Industries.* Paper presented at the 2011 International Conference on Modeling, Simulation and Control, Singapore.

Nerur, S., Mahapatra, R., & Mangalaraj, G. (2005). Challenges of migrating to agile methodologies. *Communications of the ACM, 48*(5), 72–78. doi:10.1145/1060710.1060712

Rehman, F., Maqbool, B., Riaz, M. Q., Qamar, U., & Abbas, M. (2018). *Scrum Software Maintenance Model: Efficient Software Maintenance in Agile Methodology.* Paper presented at the 2018 21st Saudi Computer Society National Computer Conference (NCC). 10.1109/NCG.2018.8593152

Reyes, W., Smith, R., & Fraunholz, B. (2007). *Agile approaches to software maintenance: an exploratory study of practitioner views.* Paper presented at the Managing worldwide operations and communications with information technology: 2007 Information Resources Management Association International Conference, Vancouver, British Columbia, Canada.

Ruiz, F., Vizcaíno, A., Piattini, M., & García, F. (2004). An ontology for the management of software maintenance projects. *International Journal of Software Engineering and Knowledge Engineering, 14*(03), 323–349. doi:10.1142/S0218194004001646

Sokappadu, B., Mattapullut, S., Paavan, R., & Ramdoo, V. D. (2016). Review of Software Maintenance Problems and Proposed Solutions in IT consulting firms in Mauritius. *International Journal of Computers and Applications, 156*(4), 975–8887.

Sousa, M. J. C., & Moreira, H. M. (1998). A survey on the software maintenance process. *Proceedings of the International Conference on Software Maintenance* (Cat. No. 98CB36272). 10.1109/ICSM.1998.738518

Stark, G. E., Oman, P., Skillicorn, A., & Ameele, A. (1999). An examination of the effects of requirements changes on software maintenance releases. *Journal of Software Maintenance: Research and Practice, 11*(5), 293–309. doi:10.1002/(SICI)1096-908X(199909/10)11:5<293::AID-SMR198>3.0.CO;2-R

Vasanthapriyan, S., Xiang, J., Tian, J., & Xiong, S. (2017). Knowledge synthesis in software industries: A survey in Sri Lanka. *Knowledge Management Research and Practice, 15*(3), 413–430. doi:10.105741275-017-0057-7

Yip, S. W., & Lam, T. (1994). A software maintenance survey. *Proceedings of 1st Asia-Pacific Software Engineering Conference.* 10.1109/APSEC.1994.465272

KEY TERMS AND DEFINITIONS

Agile Software Methodology: An evolutionary and iterative approach to software development with focuses on adaptation to changes.

Kanban: An agile process framework with a flow control mechanism used for just-in-time pull driven production where the upstream processing activities are started by the downstream process request signals.

Product Backlog: An ordered list of everything that is known to be needed in the product.

Scrum: An agile process framework for managing knowledge work, with an emphasis on software development.

Software Engineering: The application of engineering to the development of software in a systematic method.

Software Maintenance: Software activities for the modification of a software system or its components, after its delivery to correct its faults, adapting to a changing environment or improving its performance.

Waterfall Model: A sequential design, used in software development processes, in which progress is seen as flowing steadily downwards (like a waterfall) through the phases of Conception, Initiation, Analysis, Design, Construction, Testing, Deployment, and Maintenance.

Compilation of References

Abdou, T., Kamthan, P., & Shahmir, N. (2014). User Stories for Agile Business: INVEST, Carefully! *ResearchGate*. Retrieved May 25, 2019, from https://www.researchgate.net/publication/267515016_User_Stories_for_Agile_Business_INVEST_Carefully

Abdullah, R., Eri, Z. D., & Talib, A. M. (2011). *A model of knowledge management system in managing knowledge of software testing environment.* Paper presented at the Software Engineering (MySEC), 5th Malaysian Conference in. 10.1109/MySEC.2011.6140675

Abdullah, S. (2018). Improving the Governance of Software Maintenance Process for Agile Software Development Team. *International Journal of Engineering and Technology, 7*(4.31). doi:10.14419/ijet.v7i4.31.23352

Abrahamsson, P., Salo, O., Ronkainen, J., & Warsta, J. (2017). *Agile software development methods: Review and analysis.* Cornell University.

Abran, A., Bourque, P., Dupuis, R., & Moore, J. W. (2001). *Guide to the software engineering body of knowledge-SWEBOK.* IEEE Press.

Ågerfalk, J., Fitzgerald, B., & In, O. P. (2006). *Flexible and distributed software processes: old petunias in new bowls.* Paper presented at the Communications of the ACM.

Aggarwal, A., Kapoor, N., & Gupta, A. (2013). Health Insurance: Innovation and challenges ahead. *Global Journal of Management and Business Studies, 3*(5), 475-780.

Agile Alliance. (2019). *Agile Alliance.* Retrieved July 26, 2019 from https://www.agilealliance.org/

Agile Business Consortium. (2019). Chapter 15: Requirements and User Stories. *Agile Business Consortium*. Retrieved July 26, 2019 from https://www.agilebusiness.org/page/ProjectFramework_15_RequirementsandUserStories

Agile Manifesto Group. (2001). Manifesto for Agile Software Development. *Agile Manifesto*. Retrieved July 26, 2010, from http://agilemanifesto.org

Agile Testing Days. (2018). Property-based Testing with Java. *Agile Testing Days*. Retrieved from https://agiletestingdays.com/2018/session/property-based-testing-with-java/

Agile Testing. (2016). Agile Testing Tutorial. *Tutorials Point*. Retrieved September 09, 2019, from https://www.tutorialspoint.com/agile_testing/index.htm

Agostinho, C., Ducq, Y., Zacharewicz, G., Sarraipa, J., Lampathaki, F., Poler, R., & Jardim-Goncalves, R. (2016). Towards a sustainable interoperability in networked enterprise information systems: Trends of knowledge and model-driven technology. *Computers in Industry, 79*, 64–76. doi:10.1016/j.compind.2015.07.001

AguiarP. (2019, March 22). *Gamify.* Retrieved from: https://bitbucket.org/1140459/gamify/src/master/

Ahmad, M. O., Kuvaja, P., Oivo, M., & Markkula, J. (2016). *Transition of software maintenance teams from Scrum to Kanban.* Paper presented at the 2016 49th Hawaii International Conference on System Sciences (HICSS). 10.1109/HICSS.2016.670

Aitken, A. (2014). Dual Application Model for Agile Software Engineering. *47th Hawaii International Conference on System Sciences*, 4789-4798. 10.1109/HICSS.2014.588

Al-Baity, A. A., Faisal, K., & Ahmed, M. (2013). Software reuse: the state of art. *Proceedings of the International Conference on Software Engineering Research and Practice (SERP)*, 1–7.

Alenezi, M., & Magel, K. (2014). Empirical evaluation of a new coupling metric: Combining structural and semantic coupling. *International Journal of Computers and Applications*, *36*(1). doi:10.2316/Journal.202.2014.1.202-3902

Al-Sakran, H. O. (2015, February). Framework Architecture For Improving Healthcare Information Systems using Agent Technology. *International Journal of Managing Information Technology*, *7*(1), 17–31. doi:10.5121/ijmit.2015.7102

Amaral, C., Florido, M., & Costa, V. S. (2014, June). PrologCheck–property-based testing in prolog. In *International Symposium on Functional and Logic Programming* (pp. 1-17). Springer.

Ambler, S. W. (2010). Agile Modeling. *Ambysoft*. Retrieved July 26, 2010, from http://www.agilemodeling.com/

Ambler, S. W., & Astels, D. (2003). *Test Driven development: A Practical Guide*. Upper Saddle River, NJ: Prentice Hall PTR.

Ammenwerth, E., Ehlers, F., Eichstädter, R., Haux, R., Pohl, U., & Resch, F. (2002). Systems Analysis in Health Care: Framework and Example. *Methods of Information in Medicine*, *2/2002*, 134–140. PMID:12061120

Anam, S., Kim, Y., Kang, B., & Liu, Q. (2016). Adapting a knowledge-based schema matching system for ontology mapping. In *Proceedings of the Australasian Computer Science Week Multiconference* (p. 27). New York, NY: ACM Press. 10.1145/2843043.2843048

Anand, S., Burke, E. K., Chen, T. Y., Clark, J. A., Cohen, M. B., Grieskamp, W., ... McMinn, P. (2013). An orchestrated survey of methodologies for automated software test case generation. *Journal of Systems and Software*, *86*(8), 1978–2001. doi:10.1016/j.jss.2013.02.061

Andrade, H., & Crnkovic, I. (2019, May). A Review on Software Architectures for Heterogeneous Platforms. *IEEE 25th Asia-Pacific Software Engineering Conference (APSEC)*.

Anita, J. (2008). Emerging Health Insurance in India–An overview. *10th Global Conference of Actuaries*, 81-97.

Arts, T., Hughes, J., Johansson, J., & Wiger, U. (2006, September). Testing telecoms software with quviq QuickCheck. In *Proceedings of the 2006 ACM SIGPLAN workshop on Erlang* (pp. 2-10). ACM. 10.1145/1159789.1159792

Arts, T., Hughes, J., Norell, U., & Svensson, H. (2015, April). Testing AUTOSAR software with QuickCheck. In *2015 IEEE Eighth International Conference on Software Testing, Verification and Validation Workshops (ICSTW)* (pp. 1-4). IEEE.

Aversano, L., de Lucia, A., Stefanucci, S., & Betti, S. (2001). Introducing workflow management in software maintenance processes. *Proceedings of the IEEE International Conference on Software Maintenance (ICSM'01)*. 10.1109/ICSM.2001.972757

Babar, M. A., Brown, A. W., & Mistrik, I. (2014). *Agile Software Architecture*. Waltham, MA: Morgan Kaufmann.

Babu, D., & Darsi, M. (2013). A Survey on Service Oriented Architecture and Metrics to Measure Coupling. *International Journal on Computer Science and Engineering*, *5*(8), 726–733.

Badri, A. (2016). User Stories and Technical Stories in Agile Development. *Seilevel*. Retrieved May 26, 2017, from https://seilevel.com/requirements/user-stories-technical-stories-agile-development

Balamurugan, M. (2019). 17 Best Tips to Write Effective Test Cases. *Java Code Greeks*. Retrieved September 09, 2019, from https://www.javacodegeeks.com/2019/09/17-best-tips-to-write-effective-test-cases.html

Baldwin, C. Y., & Clark, K. B. (2000). *Design Rules: The power of modularity*. Cambridge, MA: MIT Press. doi:10.7551/mitpress/2366.001.0001

Bao, X., Zhang, L., & Yang, W. (2019). Empirical research for the interactive memory system research of object. In *4th International Conference on Humanities Science and Society Development (ICHSSD 2019)* (vol. 328, pp. 348-354). Atlantis Press.

Bartle, R. (1996). Hearts, clubs, diamonds, spades: Players who suit MUDs. *Journal of MUD Research, 1*(1), 19. Retrieved from https://www.researchgate.net/directory/publications

Basili, V., Briand, L., Bianculli, D., Nejati, S., Pastore, F., & Sabetzadeh, M. (2018). Software engineering research and industry: A symbiotic relationship to Foster impact. *IEEE Software, 35*(5), 44–49. doi:10.1109/MS.2018.290110216

Bassett, L. (2015). *Introduction to JavaScript Object Notation: A to-the-point Guide to JSON*. Sebastopol, CA: O'Reilly Media, Inc.

Beck, B. (2002). *Test Driven Development: By Example*. Reading, MA: Addison-Wesley.

Beck, K. (1999). Embracing change with extreme programming. *Computer, 32*(10), 70–77. doi:10.1109/2.796139

Beck, K., Beedle, M., Bennekum, A. V., Cockburn, A., & Cunningham, W. (2001). *The Agile Manifesto*. Software Development.

Bell, T. E., & Thayer, T. A. (1976). Software Requirements: Are They Really a Problem? In *Proceedings of the 2nd International Conference on Software Engineering*, (pp. 61-68). IEEE Computer Society Press.

Benesty, J., Chen, J., Huang, Y., & Cohen, I. (2009). *Pearson correlation coefficient. In Noise reduction in speech processing* (pp. 1–4). Springer.

Bennett, K. H., & Rajlich, V. T. (2000). Software maintenance and evolution: a roadmap. *Proceedings of the Conference on the Future of Software Engineering*.

Bertolino, A. (2007). *Software Testing Research: Achievements, Challenges, Dreams*. Software Verification and Validation Lab, University of Kentucky. Retrieved May 26, 2019, from http://selab.netlab.uky.edu/homepage/sw-test-roadmap-bertolino.pdf

Beszédes, Á., & Vidács, L. (2016, April). Academic and Industrial Software Testing Conferences: Survey and Synergies. In *2016 IEEE Ninth International Conference on Software Testing, Verification and Validation Workshops (ICSTW)* (pp. 240-249). IEEE. 10.1109/ICSTW.2016.30

Bhaggan, K. (2009). *Test Automation in Practice*. Delft University of Technology.

Bidve, V. S., & Sarasu, P. (2016). Tool for measuring coupling in object-oriented java software. *IACSIT International Journal of Engineering and Technology, 8*(2), 812–820.

Bielecki, A., & Nieszporska, S. (2019, April). Analysis of Healthcare Systems by Using Systemic Approach. Hindwani Complexity, Volume 2019, Article ID 6807140, 12 pages.

Biggerstaff, T. J., & Perlis, A. J. (1989). *Frontier Series: Software Reusability* (Vols. 1-2). New York, N.Y.: ACM Press.

Biggerstaff, T. J., & Richter, C. (1989). Reusability Framework, Assessment, and Directions. Frontier Series: Software Reusability: Vol. I. *Concepts and Models*. ACM Press.

Binder, R. V., Legeard, B., & Kramer, A. (2015). Model-based testing: Where does it stand? *Communications of the ACM, 58*(2), 52–56. doi:10.1145/2697399

Boehm, B. W. (1988). A spiral model of software development and enhancement. *Computer, 21*(5), 61–72. doi:10.1109/2.59

Bohnsack, R., Hanelt, A., Marz, D., & Marante, C. (2018). Same, same, but different!? A systematic review of the literature on digital transformation. Academy of Management Proceedings, 2018(1), 16262.

Booch, G., Maksimchuk, R. A., Engle, M. W., Young, B. J., Conallen, J., & Houston, K. A. (2007). *Object-Oriented Analysis and Design with Applications* (3rd ed.). Upper Saddle River, NJ: Addison-Wesley.

Brambilla, M., Cabot, J., & Wimmer, M. (2017). *Model-Driven Software Engineering in Practice* (2nd ed.). San Rafael, CA: Morgan & Claypool Publishers.

Brathwaite, B., & Schreiber, I. (2008). *Challenges for Game Designers* (1st ed.). Rockland, MA: Charles River Media, Inc.

Brito, G., Mombach, T., & Valente, M. T. (2019). Migrating to GraphQL: A Practical Assessment. *2019 IEEE 26th International Conference on Software Analysis, Evolution and Reengineering (SANER)*, 140–150. 10.1109/SANER.2019.8667986

Brooks, F. P. (1987). No Silver Bullet: Essence and Accidents of Software Engineering. *Computer, 20*(4), 10–19. doi:10.1109/MC.1987.1663532

Brünjes, L. (2018). *IOHK | Director of Education - Lars Brünjes - Property Based Testing* [Video file]. Retrieved from https://www.youtube.com/watch?v=8p5YZpre0lY

Budanitsky, A., & Hirst, G. (2001). Semantic Distance in WordNet: An Experimental Application-Oriented Evaluation of Five Measure. *Proceeding Workshop WordNet and Other Lexical Resources, Second Meeting of the North American Chapter of the Association for Computational Linguistics*.

Burke, B. (2014). *Gamify: How Gamification Motivates People to Do Extraordinary Things*. Abingdon, UK: Routledge.

Cai, L., Rensing, C., Li, X., & Wang, G. (2009). Novel gene clusters involved in arsenite oxidation and resistance in two arsenite oxidizers: Achromobacter sp. SY8 and Pseudomonas sp. TS44. *Applied Microbiology and Biotechnology, 83*(4), 715–725. doi:10.100700253-009-1929-4 PMID:19283378

Calderón, A., Boubeta-Puig, J., & Ruiz, M. (2018). MEdit4CEP-Gam: A model-driven approach for user-friendly gamification design, monitoring and code generation in CEP-based systems. *Information and Software Technology, 95*, 238–264. doi:10.1016/j.infsof.2017.11.009

Carmona, J., van Dongen, B., Solti, A., & Weidlich, M. (Eds.). (2018). *Conformance Checking: Relating Processes and Models*. Cham, Switzerland: Springer. doi:10.1007/978-3-319-99414-7

Castro, L. M. (2015). Advanced management of data integrity: Property-based testing for business rules. *Journal of Intelligent Information Systems, 44*(3), 355–380. doi:10.100710844-014-0335-2

Causevic, A., Sundmark, D., & Punnekkat, S. (2010). *An industrial survey on contemporary aspects of software testing*. Paper presented at the 2010 Third International Conference on Software Testing, Verification and Validation. 10.1109/ICST.2010.52

Chan, M. (2019). SQL vs. NoSQL – what's the best option for your database needs? *Thorn Technologies*. Retrieved July 19, 2019, from https://www.thorntech.com/2019/03/sql-vs-nosql

Chappell, D. A. (2004). *Enterprise Service Bus*. Sebastopol, CA: O'Reilly.

Charette, R. N. (2005). Why Software Fails. *IEEE Spectrum, 2*.

Charette, R. N. (2009). This Car Runs on Code. *IEEE Spectrum, 1*.

Chaudhary, S. (2017). Latest Software Testing Tools and Techniques: A Review. *International Journal of Advanced Research in Computer Science and Software Engineering*. Retrieved May 26, 2019, from https://pdfs.semanticscholar.org/87eb/9a3d22bca4397e8b5e53a5e852457f18ccfd.pdf

Chauhan, R., & Singh, I. (2014). Latest Research and Development on Software Testing Techniques and Tools. *International Journal of Current Engineering and Technology, 4*(4), 2368–2372.

Chen, T. Y., Kuo, F. C., Liu, H., Poon, P. L., Towey, D., Tse, T. H., & Zhou, Z. Q. (2018). Metamorphic testing: A review of challenges and opportunities. *ACM Computing Surveys, 51*(1), 4. doi:10.1145/3143561

Chen, T. Y., Kuo, F. C., Tse, T. H., & Zhou, Z. Q. (2003, September). Metamorphic testing and beyond. In *Eleventh Annual International Workshop on Software Technology and Engineering Practice* (pp. 94-100). IEEE. 10.1109/STEP.2003.18

Chepurnoy, A., & Rathee, M. (2018, March). Checking laws of the blockchain with property-based testing. In *2018 International Workshop on Blockchain Oriented Software Engineering (IWBOSE)* (pp. 40-47). IEEE. 10.1109/IWBOSE.2018.8327570

Chinosi, M., & Trombetta, A. (2012). BPMN: An introduction to the standard. *Computer Standards & Interfaces, 34*(1), 124–134. doi:10.1016/j.csi.2011.06.002

Choma, J., Guerra, E. M., & da Silva, T. S. (2018). *Developers' Initial Perceptions on TDD Practice: A Thematic Analysis with Distinct Domains and Languages*. Paper presented at the International Conference on Agile Software Development. 10.1007/978-3-319-91602-6_5

Choudhari, J., & Suman, U. (2010). *Iterative maintenance life cycle using extreme programming*. Paper presented at the 2010 International Conference on Advances in Recent Technologies in Communication and Computing. 10.1109/ARTCom.2010.52

Chou, Y. (2015). *Actionable gamification: Beyond points, badges, and leaderboards*. Fremont, CA: Octalysis Media.

Claessen, K., & Hughes, J. (2000). *QuickCheck: a lightweight tool for random testing of Haskell programs*. Paper presented at the fifth ACM SIGPLAN international conference on Functional programming. 10.1145/351240.351266

Claessen, K., Hughes, J., Pałka, M., Smallbone, N., & Svensson, H. (2010, May). Ranking programs using black box testing. In *Proceedings of the 5th Workshop on Automation of Software Test* (pp. 103-110). ACM. 10.1145/1808266.1808282

Clark, L. (2019). No developers required: Why this company chose no-code over software devs. *ZDNet*. Retrieved June 26, 2019, from https://www.zdnet.com/google-amp/article/no-developers-required-why-this-company-chose-no-code-over-software-devs/

Clements, P., Bachmann, F., Bass, L., Garlan, D., Ivers, J., Little, R., Merson, P., Nord, R., & Stafford, J. (2010, October). *Documenting Software Architectures: Views and Beyond*. Pearson Education.

Clements, D., Dault, M., & Priest, A. (2007). Effective Teamwork in Healthcare: Research and Reality. *Healthcare Papers, 7*(sp), 26–34. doi:10.12927/hcpap.2013.18669 PMID:17478997

Cockburn, A. (1998). Origin of story card is a promise for a conversation. *Alistair.Cockburn*. Retrieved May 26, 2017, from http://alistair.cockburn.us/Origin+of+user+story+is+a+promise+for+a+conversation

Cohn, M. (2015). Not Everything Needs to Be a User Story: Using FDD Features. *Mountain Goat Software*. Retrieved May 26, 2017, from https://www.mountaingoatsoftware.com/blog/not-everything-needs-to-be-a-user-story-using-fdd-features

Colburn, T., & Shute, G. (2007). Abstraction in Computer Science. *Minds and Machines, 17*(2), 169–184. doi:10.100711023-007-9061-7

Collins, E., Dias-Neto, A., & de Lucena, V. F., Jr. (2012). Strategies for Agile Software Testing Automation: An Industrial Experience. In *IEEE 36th Annual Computer Software and Applications Conference Workshops* (440-445). IEEE.

Conway, P. H., & Clancy, C. (2009). Transformation of health care at the front line. *Journal of the American Medical Association, 301*(7), 763–765. doi:10.1001/jama.2009.103 PMID:19224753

Crispin, L., & Gregory, J. (2009). *Agile Testing: A Practical Guide for Testers and Agile Teams*. Reading, MA: Addison-Wesley.

Cronbach, L. J. (1951). Coefficient alpha and the internal structure of tests. *Psychometrika, 16*(3), 297-334.

Czepa, C., Tran, H., Zdun, U., Kim, T., Weiss, E., & Ruhsam, C. (2017). On the understandability of semantic constraints for behavioral software architecture compliance: A controlled experiment. In *Proceedings of the International Conference on Software Architecture* (pp. 155-164). Piscataway, NJ: IEEE Computer Society Press. 10.1109/ICSA.2017.10

Dalal, S. R., Jain, A., Karunanithi, N., Leaton, J. M., Lott, C. M., Patton, G. C., & Horowitz, B. M. (1999, May). Model-based testing in practice. In *Proceedings of the 1999 International Conference on Software Engineering (IEEE Cat. No. 99CB37002)* (pp. 285-294). IEEE. 10.1145/302405.302640

De Lucia, A., & Qusef, A. (2017). Requirements Engineering in Agile Software Development. *Journal of Emerging Technologies in Web Intelligence, 2*(3), 212–220.

De Souza, E. F., de Almeida Falbo, R., & Vijaykumar, N. L. (2015). Knowledge management initiatives in software testing: A mapping study. *Information and Software Technology, 57*(1), 378–391. doi:10.1016/j.infsof.2014.05.016

Deak, A., & Stålhane, T. (2013). *Organization of testing activities in Norwegian Software Companies*. Paper presented at the 2013 IEEE Sixth International Conference on Software Testing, Verification and Validation Workshops. 10.1109/ICSTW.2013.18

Deci, E. L., & Ryan, R. M. (2012). Motivation, personality, and development within embedded social contexts: An overview of self-determination theory. The Oxford Handbook of Human Motivation, 85–107. doi:10.1093/oxfordhb/9780195399820.013.0006

Delgado, J. (2019). Cloud-Based Application Integration in Virtual Enterprises. In N. Raghavendra Rao (Ed.), *Global Virtual Enterprises in Cloud Computing Environments* (pp. 46–85). Hershey, PA: IGI Global. doi:10.4018/978-1-5225-3182-1.ch003

Demir, K. A. (2008). *Measurement of software project management effectiveness*. Retrieved from https://core.ac.uk/download/pdf/36739565.pdf

Derrick, J., Walkinshaw, N., Arts, T., Earle, C. B., Cesarini, F., Fredlund, L. A., ... Thompson, S. (2009, November). Property-based testing-the protest project. In *International Symposium on Formal Methods for Components and Objects* (pp. 250-271). Springer.

Desai, A., & Shah, S. (2011). *Knowledge management and software testing*. Paper presented at the Proceedings of the International Conference & Workshop on Emerging Trends in Technology, Mumbai, Maharashtra, India.

Desouza, K. C., & Pacquette, S. (2011). *Knowledge management: An introduction*. Neal-Schuman Publishers.

Deterding, S., Dixon, D., Khaled, R., & Nacke, L. (2011, September 28). From Game Design Elements to Gamefulness. *Defining Gamification, 11*, 9–15.

Deterding, S. (2015). The Lens of Intrinsic Skill Atoms: A Method for Gameful Design. *Human-Computer Interaction, 30*(3-4), 294–335. doi:10.1080/07370024.2014.993471

Devi, S., & Nehra, V.S. (2015). The problems with health insurance sector in India. *Indian Journal of Research, 4*(3), 6-8.

Devulapally, G. K. (2015). *Agile in the context of Software Maintenance: A Case Study*. Academic Press.

Djaouti, D., Alvarez, J., Jessel, J.-P., & Rampnoux, O. (2011). Origins of serious games. In *Serious games and edutainment applications* (pp. 25–43). New York, NY: Springer. doi:10.1007/978-1-4471-2161-9_3

Doomun, R., Khedo, K. K., & Khedo, K. (2016). Review of Software Maintenance Problems and Proposed Solutions in IT consulting firms in Mauritius. *International Journal of Computers and Applications, 156*(4), 975–8887.

Dornberger, R. (Ed.). (2018). *Business Information Systems and Technology 4.0: New Trends in the Age of Digital Change* (Vol. 141). Cham, Switzerland: Springer. doi:10.1007/978-3-319-74322-6

Drumond, C. (2019). What is Scrum? *Atlassian*. Retrieved July 11, 2019, from https://www.atlassian.com/agile/scrum

Drumond, C. (2019). What is Scrum? *Atlassian*. Retrieved July 11, 2019, from https://www.atlassian.com/agile/Scrum

Dubitzky, W., Wolkenhauer, O., Cho, K.-H., & Yokota, H. (Eds.). (2013). Tukey's Honestly Significant Difference Test. In Encyclopedia of Systems Biology (pp. 2303–2303). doi:10.1007/978-1-4419-9863-7_101572

Dutta, S., Wassenhove, L. N. V., & Kulandaiswamy, S. (1998). Benchmarking European Software Management Practices. *Communications of the ACM, 41*(6), 77–86. doi:10.1145/276609.276623

Dyba, T. (2000). Improvisation in small software organizations. *IEEE Software, 17*(5), 82–87. doi:10.1109/52.877872

Edvardsson, I. R. (2008). HRM and knowledge management. *Employee Relations, 30*(5), 553–561. doi:10.1108/01425450810888303

Elshwimy, F., Algergawy, A., Sarhan, A., & Sallam, E. (2014). Aggregation of similarity measures in schema matching based on generalized mean. *Proceedings of the IEEE International Conference on Data Engineering Workshops* (pp. 74-79). Piscataway, NJ: IEEE Computer Society Press. 10.1109/ICDEW.2014.6818306

Endres, M. L., & Chowdhury, S. (2013). The role of expected reciprocity in knowledge sharing. *International Journal of Knowledge Management, 9*(2), 1–19. doi:10.4018/jkm.2013040101

Erl, T., Merson, P., & Stoffers, R. (2017). *Service-oriented Architecture: Analysis and Design for Services and Microservices*. Upper Saddle River, NJ: Prentice Hall PTR.

Ezeh, A., & Anthony, P. (2013). *Factors Influencing Knowledge Sharing in Software Development: A Case Study at Volvo Cars IT Torslanda*. Göteborgs universitet.

Fairbanks, G. (2010). *Just enough software architecture: A risk-driven approach*. Boulder, CO: Marshall & Brainerd.

Farid, A. (2017). Measures of reconfigurability and its key characteristics in intelligent manufacturing systems. *Journal of Intelligent Manufacturing, 28*(2), 353–369. doi:10.100710845-014-0983-7

Fast-check. (2019). *Property based testing framework for JavaScript (like QuickCheck) written in TypeScript*. Retrieved from https://github.com/dubzzz/fast-check

Fawcett, J., Ayers, D., & Quin, L. (2012). *Beginning XML*. Indianapolis, IN: John Wiley & Sons.

Fellbaum, C. (1998). *WordNet: An Electronic Lexical Database*. Cambridge, MA: MIT Press. doi:10.7551/mitpress/7287.001.0001

Fielding, R. T. (2000). *Architectural styles and the design of network-based software architectures*. Irvine, CA: University of California.

Fielding, R. T., & Taylor, R. N. (2000). Principled design of the modern Web architecture. *Proceedings of the 2000 International Conference on Software Engineering. ICSE 2000 the New Millennium*, 407–416. 10.1145/337180.337228

Fielding, R., Taylor, R., Erenkrantz, J., Gorlick, M., Whitehead, J., Khare, R., & Oreizy, P. (2017). Reflections on the REST architectural style and principled design of the modern web architecture. In *Proceedings of the 2017 11th Joint Meeting on Foundations of Software Engineering* (pp. 4-14). New York, NY: ACM Press. 10.1145/3106237.3121282

Fink, G., & Bishop, M. (1997). Property-based testing: A new approach to testing for assurance. *Software Engineering Notes*, *22*(4), 74–80. doi:10.1145/263244.263267

Fink, G., Ko, C., Archer, M., & Levitt, K. (1994). *Towards a property-based testing environment with applications to security-critical software*. California Univ Davis Dept of Computer Science.

Fink, G., & Levitt, K. (1994, December). Property-based testing of privileged programs. In *Tenth Annual Computer Security Applications Conference* (pp. 154-163). IEEE. 10.1109/CSAC.1994.367311

Ford, N., Parsons, R., & Kua, P. (2017). *Building evolutionary architectures: Support constant change*. O'Reilly Media, Inc.

Forsberg, K., & Mooz, H. (1991). The relationship of system engineering to the project cycle. In *Proceedings of Annual Conference of the National Council on System Engineering*. National Council on Systems Engineering. 10.1002/j.2334-5837.1991.tb01484.x

Fowler, M. (1996). *Analysis Patterns: Reusable Object Models*. Boston, MA: Addison-Wesley.

Fowler, M. (2006). *Patterns of Enterprise Application Architecture*. Boston, MA: Addison-Wesley.

Frakes, W. B., & Kang, K. (2005). Software Reuse Research: Status and Future. *IEEE Transactions on Software Engineering*, *13*(7), 529–536. doi:10.1109/TSE.2005.85

Freeman, P. (1987). *Tutorial: Software Reusability*. Los Alamitos, CA: IEEE Computer Society Press.

FsCheck Web site. (2019). *Random Testing for .NET*. Retrieved from https://fscheck.github.io/FsCheck/index.html

Galen, R. (2013). Technical User Stories – What, When, and How? *RGALEN Consulting*. Retrieved July 11, 2019, from http://rgalen.com/agile-training-news/2013/11/10/technical-user-stories-what-when-and-how

Gamma, E., Helm, R., Johnson, R., & Vlissides, L. (1995). *Design Patterns: Elements of Reusable Object-Oriented Software*. Reading, MA: Addison-Wesley.

Ganton, J. (2018, June). *Engaging Individuals with Lived Experience A Framework*. Primary Health care Opioid Response Initiative.

Garlan, D. (2000, June). Software architecture: a roadmap. In *The Future of Software Engineering 2000, Proceedings 22nd International Conference on Software Engineering*. ACM Press.

Garousi, V., & Felderer, M. (2017). Worlds apart: Industrial and academic focus areas in software testing. *IEEE Software*, *34*(5), 38–45. doi:10.1109/MS.2017.3641116

Garousi, V., & Varma, T. (2010). A replicated survey of software testing practices in the Canadian province of Alberta: What has changed from 2004 to 2009? *Journal of Systems and Software*, *83*(11), 2251–2262. doi:10.1016/j.jss.2010.07.012

Garousi, V., & Zhi, J. (2013). A survey of software testing practices in Canada. *Journal of Systems and Software, 86*(5), 1354–1376. doi:10.1016/j.jss.2012.12.051

Geetha, C., Subramanian, C., & Dutt, S. (2015). *Software Engineering*. Delhi, India: Pearson Education India.

Geetika, R., & Singh, P. (2014). Dynamic coupling metrics for object oriented software systems: A survey. *Software Engineering Notes, 39*(2), 1–8. doi:10.1145/2579281.2579296

Geras, A. M., Smith, M. R., & Miller, J. (2004). A survey of software testing practices in Alberta. *Canadian Journal of Electrical and Computer Engineering, 29*(3), 183–191. doi:10.1109/CJECE.2004.1532522

Geyer-Schulz, A., & Hahsler, M. (2001). Software Engineering with Analysis Patterns. *CiteSeerX*. Retrieved May 26, 2019, from http://citeseerx.ist.psu.edu/viewdoc/summary?doi=10.1.1.70.8415

Girard, J., & Girard, J. (2015). Defining knowledge management: Toward an applied compendium. *Online Journal of Applied Knowledge Management, 3*(1), 1–20.

Goel, A. K., & Diaz-Agudo, B. (2017). *What's hot in case-based reasoning?* AAAI.

Gronback, R. C. (2009). *Eclipse modeling project: A domain-specific language (DSL) toolkit*. London, UK: Pearson Education.

Guide, A. (2001). *Project management body of knowledge (pmbok® guide)*. Paper presented at the Project Management Institute.

Guillen-Drija, C., Quintero, R., & Kleiman, A. (2018). GraphQL vs REST: una comparación desde la perspectiva de eficiencia de desempeño. Retrieved November 20, 2019, from doi:10.13140/RG.2.2.25221.19680

Gulías, V. M., Abalde, C., Castro, L. M., & Varela, C. (2006). Formalisation of a Functional Risk Management System. ICEIS, (3), 516-519.

Guo, S., Tong, W., Zhang, J., & Liu, Z. (2011). An Application of Ontology to Test Case Reuse. *International Conference on Mechatronic Science, Electrical Engineering and Computer*, Jilin, China.

Hamari, J., & Koivisto, J. (2015). Why do people use gamification services? *International Journal of Information Management, 35*(4), 419–431. doi:10.1016/j.ijinfomgt.2015.04.006

Hamari, J., Koivisto, J., & Sarsa, H. (2014). Does Gamification Work? - A Literature Review of Empirical Studies on Gamification. *Proceedings of the Annual Hawaii International Conference on System Sciences, 14*, 3025–3034. 10.1109/HICSS.2014.377

Hanus, M. (2016, September). CurryCheck: Checking properties of Curry programs. In *International Symposium on Logic-Based Program Synthesis and Transformation* (pp. 222-239). Springer.

Harlow, M. (2014). Coconut Headphones: Why Agile Has Failed. *Code Rant*. Retrieved December 11, 2014, from http://mikehadlow.blogspot.ch/2014/03/coconut-headphones-why-agile-has-failed.html

Harman, C., & Brelade, S. (2007). *Managing human resources in the knowledge economy*. Paper presented at the United Nations 7th Global Forum on Reinventing Government Building Trust in government. Vienna, Austria.

Hartmann Preuss, D. (2006). Interview: Jim Johnson of Standish Group. *InfoQ*. Retrieved July 26, 2010, from http://www.infoq.com/articles/Interview-Johnson-Standish-CHAOS

Hastie, S., & Wojewoda, S. (2015). Standish Group 2015 Chaos Report - Q&A with Jennifer Lynch. *InfoQ*. Retrieved from May 26, 2019, from https://www.infoq.com/articles/standish-chaos-2015

Hayes, L. (2004). *The Automated Testing Handbook*. Automated Testing Institute.

Hebert, F. (2019, January). Property-Based Testing with PropEr, Erlang, and Elixir: Find Bugs Before Your Users Do. *Pragmatic Bookshelf*.

Heeager, L., & Nielsen, P. A. (2013). *Agile software development and the barriers to transfer of knowledge: an interpretive case study*. Paper presented at the Scandinavian Conference on Information Systems. 10.1007/978-3-642-39832-2_2

Heeager, L. T., & Rose, J. (2015). Optimising agile development practices for the maintenance operation: Nine heuristics. *Empirical Software Engineering*, *20*(6), 1762–1784. doi:10.100710664-014-9335-7

Herzig, P., Jugel, K., Momm, C., Ameling, M., & Schill, A. (2013). GaML-A modeling language for gamification. *2013 IEEE/ACM 6th International Conference on Utility and Cloud Computing*, 494–499.

Hilton, M. M. E. (2017). *Understanding Software Development and Testing Practices*. Academic Press.

Hinings, B., Gegenhuber, T., & Greenwood, R. (2018). Digital innovation and transformation: An institutional perspective. *Information and Organization*, *28*(1), 52–61. doi:10.1016/j.infoandorg.2018.02.004

Hoda, R., Salleh, N., & Grundy, J. (2018). The rise and evolution of agile software development. *IEEE Software*, *35*(5), 58–63. doi:10.1109/MS.2018.290111318

Holcombe, M. (2008). *Running an Agile Software Development Project*. Hoboken, NJ: John Wiley & Sons; doi:10.1109/MEC.2011.6025579.

Hopkins, R., & Harcombe, S. (2014). Agile Architecting: Enabling the Delivery of Complex Agile Systems Development Projects. In M. A. Babar, A. W. Brown, & I. Mistrik (Eds.), *Agile Software Architecture*. Waltham, MA: Morgan Kaufmann. doi:10.1016/B978-0-12-407772-0.00011-3

Horowitz, E., & Munson, J. B. (1984, September). An Expansive View of Reusable Software. *IEEE Transaction on Software Engineering SE*, *10*(5), 477–487. doi:10.1109/TSE.1984.5010270

Hove, S. E., & Anda, B. (2005). *Experiences from conducting semi-structured interviews in empirical software engineering research*. Paper presented at the 11th IEEE International Software Metrics Symposium (METRICS'05). 10.1109/METRICS.2005.24

Huang, M. (2010) Software Engineering Principles. *Lecture Note from University of Arkansas*. Retrieved May 26, 2019, from http://www.csce.uark.edu/~mqhuang/courses/3513/s2010/lectures/SE_Lecture_3.pdf

Hughes, J. (2016). Experiences with QuickCheck: testing the hard stuff and staying sane. In *A List of Successes That Can Change the World* (pp. 169–186). Cham: Springer. doi:10.1007/978-3-319-30936-1_9

Hunicke, R., Leblanc, M., & Zubek, R. (2004). MDA: A Formal Approach to Game Design and Game Research. *AAAI Workshop - Technical Report, 1*.

Huotari, K., & Hamari, J. (2012). Defining gamification: A service marketing perspective. In *Proceeding of the 16th International Academic MindTrek Conference*, (pp. 17–22). New York, NY: ACM. 10.1145/2393132.2393137

Huynh, D., Zuo, L., & Iida, H. (2018). An Assessment of Game Elements in Language-Learning Platform Duolingo. In *2018 4th International Conference on Computer and Information Sciences (ICCOINS)*, (pp. 1–4). Piscataway, NJ: IEEE.

Hynninen, T., Kasurinen, J., Knutas, A., & Taipale, O. (2018). *Software testing: Survey of the industry practices*. Paper presented at the 2018 41st International Convention on Information and Communication Technology, Electronics and Microelectronics (MIPRO). 10.23919/MIPRO.2018.8400261

Hynninen, T., Kasurinen, J., Knutas, A., & Taipale, O. (2018, May). Software testing: Survey of the industry practices. In *2018 41st International Convention on Information and Communication Technology, Electronics and Microelectronics (MIPRO)* (pp. 1449-1454). IEEE.

INESC TEC. (2017). Retrieved 22 February 2019, from INESC TEC. Retrieved November 20, 2019, from https://www.inesctec.pt/en/institution

Ipate, F., & Holcombe, M. (1997). An integration testing method that is proved to find all faults. *International Journal of Computer Mathematics*, *63*(3-4), 159–178. doi:10.1080/00207169708804559

Ismail, N. (2017). UK wasting 37 billion a year on failed agile IT projects. *Information Age*. Retrieved May 26, 2019, from https://www.information-age.com/uk-wasting-37-billion-year-failed-agile-it-projects-123466089/

ISO. (2010). *Systems and software engineering – Vocabulary. ISO/IEC/IEEE 24765:2010(E) International Standard.* Geneva, Switzerland: International Organization for Standardization.

Isotta-Riches, B., & Randell, J. (2014). Architecture as a Key Driver for Agile Success. In M. A. Babar, A. W. Brown, & I. Mistrik (Eds.), *Agile Software Architecture*. Waltham, MA: Morgan Kaufmann. doi:10.1016/B978-0-12-407772-0.00014-9

Itumalla, R., Acharyulu, G. V. R. K., & Reddy, L. K. V. (2016). Health Insurance in India: Issues and challenges. *International Journal of Current Research*, *8*(2), 26815–26817.

Jackson, M. A. (1975). *Principles of Program Design*. Cambridge, MA: Academic Press.

Jacobson, I., Christerson, M., Jonsson, P., & Oevergaard. (1992). *Object-Oriented Software Engineering*. New York: ACM Press.

Jacobson, I., Griss, M., & Jonsson, P. (1997). *Software Reuse. Architecture, Process and Organization for Business Success*. Reading, MA: Addison Wesley.

Jahan, M. S., Riaz, M. T., & Abbas, M. (2019). Software Testing Practices in IT Industry of Pakistan. *Proceedings of the 6th Conference on the Engineering of Computer Based Systems*. 10.1145/3352700.3352724

Jalote, P., & Jain, G. (2006). Assigning tasks in a 24-h software development model. *Journal of Systems and Software*, *79*(7), 904–911. doi:10.1016/j.jss.2005.06.040

Jamieson, S. (2004). Likert scales: How to (ab) use them. *Medical Education*, *38*(12), 1217–1218. doi:10.1111/j.1365-2929.2004.02012.x PMID:15566531

Jazayeri, M., Loos, R. G. K., & Musser, D. R. (1998). Generic Programming. In *International Seminar on Generic Programming Dagstuhl Castle, Germany*. Berlin, Germany: Springer.

JCheck. (2013). Retrieved from http://www.jcheck.org/

Johnson, J., Boucher, K. D., Connors, K., & Robinson, J. (2001). Collaborating on Project Success. *SOFTWAREMAG*. Retrieved July 26, 2010, from http://www.softwaremag.com/archive/2001feb/collaborativemgt.html

Jones, C. (1984). Reusability in programming: A survey of the state of the art. *IEEE Transactions on Software Engineering*, *10*(5), 488–494. doi:10.1109/TSE.1984.5010271

Josika, K. (2017) Software Engineering | Coupling and Cohesion. *GeeksForGreeks*. Retrieved June 6, 2019, from https://www.geeksforgeeks.org/software-engineering-coupling-and-cohesion/

jqwik. (2019). *Property-Based Testing in Java*. Retrieved from https://jqwik.net/

JungT. (2012). *Quickcheck for Java*. Retrieved from https://bitbucket.org/blob79/quickcheck/src/default/

Kajko-Mattsson, M., & Nyfjord, J. (2009). *A model of agile evolution and maintenance process.* Paper presented at the 2009 42nd Hawaii International Conference on System Sciences.

Kapp, K. M. (2012). *The gamification of learning and instruction.* San Francisco, CA: Wiley.

Kasurinen, J., Taipale, O., & Smolander, K. (2010). Software test automation in practice: Empirical observations. *Advances in Software Engineering.*

Kaufmann, D., & Kraay, A. (2007). Governance Indicators: Where Are We, Where Should We Be Going? *The World Bank Research Observer, 23*(1), 1–30. doi:10.1093/wbro/lkm012

Khajehpour, S., & Raheleh, E. (2013). Advancements and Trends in Medical Case-Based Reasoning: An Overview of Systems and System Development. *Iran J. Medical Informatics, 2*(4), 12–16.

Khalfallah, M., Figay, N., Barhamgi, M., & Ghodous, P. (2014). Model driven conformance testing for standardized services. In *IEEE International Conference on Services Computing* (pp. 400–407). Piscataway, NJ: IEEE Computer Society Press. 10.1109/SCC.2014.60

King, W. R. (2009). *Knowledge management and organizational learning.* Springer. doi:10.1007/978-1-4419-0011-1

Kiriakidis, S. (2015). Theory of planned behaviour: The intention-behaviour relationship and the perceived behavioural control (PBC) relationship with intention and behaviour. *International Journal of Strategic Innovative Marketing, 3*(2), 40–51.

Kolodner, J. (1993). *Case Based Reasoning.* Morgan Kaufmann. doi:10.1016/B978-1-55860-237-3.50005-4

Kostoska, M., Gusev, M., & Ristov, S. (2016). An overview of cloud interoperability. In *Federated Conference on Computer Science and Information Systems* (pp. 873-876). Piscataway, NJ: IEEE Computer Society Press. 10.15439/2016F463

Kouroshfar, E., Mirakhorli, M., Bagheri, H., Xiao, L., Malek, S., & Cai, Y. (2015). A Study on the Role of Software Architecture in the Evolution and Quality of Software. *12th Working Conference on Mining Software Repositories,* 246-257. 10.1109/MSR.2015.30

Kramer, J., & Finkelstein, A. (1991). A Configurable Framework for Method and Tool Integration. *European Symposium on Software Development Environments and CASE Technology.* Retrieved May 26, 2019, from http://citeseerx.ist.psu.edu/viewdoc/download?doi=10.1.1.129.7971&rep=rep1&type=pdf

Krigsman, M. (2006). Success Factors. *ZDNet.* Retrieved July 26, 2010, from http://www.zdnet.com/blog/projectfailures/success-factors/183

Krivtsov, R. (2019a). *Swagger to GraphQL API adapter. Contribute to yarax/swagger-to-graphql development by creating an account on GitHub* [JavaScript]. Retrieved November 20, 2019, from https://github.com/yarax/swagger-to-graphql (Original work published 2016)

Krivtsov, R. (2019b). *Yarax/swagger-to-graphql* [TypeScript]. Retrieved November 20, 2019, from https://github.com/yarax/swagger-to-graphql (Original work published 2016)

Kruchten, P. (2000). *The Rational Unified Process: An Introduction* (2nd ed.). Boston, MA: Addision Wesley Longman Publishing.

Krueger, C. W. (1992). Software Reuse. *ACM Computing Surveys, 24*(2), 131–183. doi:10.1145/130844.130856

Kuehl, R., & Hawker, J. S. (2019). Requirements – Architecture – Agility. *SWEN 440-01 Software Requirements and Architecture Engineering.* Retrieved October 28, 2019, from http://www.se.rit.edu/~swen-440/slides/instructor-specific/Kuehl/Lecture%2026%20Requirements%20Architecture%20Agility.pdf

Kukko, M., & Helander, N. (2012). *Knowledge sharing barriers in growing software companies.* Paper presented at the 2012 45th Hawaii International Conference on System Sciences. 10.1109/HICSS.2012.407

Kukko, M. (2013). Knowledge sharing barriers in organic growth: A case study from a software company. *The Journal of High Technology Management Research, 24*(1), 18–29. doi:10.1016/j.hitech.2013.02.006

Kumar, J. (2013). Gamification at work: Designing engaging business software. In *International Conference of Design, User Experience, and Usability,* (pp. 528–537). New York, NY: Springer. 10.1007/978-3-642-39241-2_58

Kuo, F. C., Chen, T. Y., & Tam, W. K. (2011, October). Testing embedded software by metamorphic testing: A wireless metering system case study. In *2011 IEEE 36th Conference on Local Computer Networks* (pp. 291-294). IEEE. 10.1109/LCN.2011.6115306

Labuschagne, A., Inozemtseva, L., & Holmes, R. (2017, August). Measuring the cost of regression testing in practice: a study of Java projects using continuous integration. In *Proceedings of the 2017 11th Joint Meeting on Foundations of Software Engineering* (pp. 821-830). ACM. 10.1145/3106237.3106288

Laing, S. (2015). The Testing Manifesto. *Growing Agile Coaches.* Retrieved May 26, 2019, from http://www.growing-agile.co.nz/2015/04/the-testing-manifesto

Land, S. K., & Wilson, B. (2006). Using IEEE standards to support America's Army gaming development. *Computer, 39*(11), 105–107. doi:10.1109/MC.2006.405

Laplante, P. A. (2007). *What Every Engineer Should Know about Software Engineering* (1st ed.). CRC Press. doi:10.1201/9781420006742

Larman, C. (2003). *Agile and Iterative Development: A Manager's Guide.* Reading, MA: Addison-Wesley.

Larman, C., & Basili, V. R. (2003). Iterative and incremental developments. a brief history. *Computer, 36*(6), 47–56. doi:10.1109/MC.2003.1204375

Laucher, A. (2015). *Property Based Testing: Shrinking Risk in Your Code.* Paper presented at YOW! 2015 Conference, Brisbane, Australia.

Lawrence, R. (2009). Making Agile a Reality. *Agile for All.* Retrieved July 20, 2019 from https://agileforall.com/patterns-for-splitting-user-stories/

Leach, R. J. (2011). *Software Reuse: Methods, Models, and Costs.* Retrieved May 26, 2019, from https://pdfs.semantic-scholar.org/700b/83bc8d4a2e4c1d1f4395a4c8fb78462c9f5a.pdf

Lei, H., Ganjeizadeh, F., Jayachandran, P. K., & Ozcan, P. (2017). A statistical analysis of the effects of Scrum and Kanban on software development projects. *Robotics and Computer-integrated Manufacturing, 43*, 59–67. doi:10.1016/j.rcim.2015.12.001

Le, V., Afshari, M., & Su, Z. (2014, June). Compiler validation via equivalence modulo inputs. *ACM SIGPLAN Notices, 49*(6), 216–226. doi:10.1145/2666356.2594334

Lewis, W. E. (2017). *Software testing and continuous quality improvement.* Auerbach publications. doi:10.1201/9781439834367

Liao, Y., Deschamps, F., Loures, E., & Ramos, L. (2017). Past, present and future of Industry 4.0 - a systematic literature review and research agenda proposal. *International Journal of Production Research, 55*(12), 3609–3629. doi:10.1080/00207543.2017.1308576

Lieder, A., & Stolletz, R. (2016, April). Scheduling aircraft take-offs and landings on inter-dependent and heterogeneous runways. *Transportation Research Part E, Logistics and Transportation Review, 88*, 167–188. doi:10.1016/j.tre.2016.01.015

Lina, M. G. R., Ampatzoglou, A., Avgeriou, P., & Nakagawa, E. Y. (2015, June). A Comparative Analysis of Reference Architectures for Healthcare in the Ambient Assisted Living Domain. *28th International Symposium on Computer-Based Medical Systems*, 270-275.

Liskov, B. (1988). Keynote address - data abstraction and hierarchy. *ACM SIGPLAN Notices, 23*(5), 17–34. doi:10.1145/62139.62141

Liu, Y., Wu, J., Liu, X., & Gu, G. (2009). *Investigation of knowledge management methods in software testing process.* Paper presented at the Information Technology and Computer Science (ITCS). International Conference on, Kiev, Ukraine. 10.1109/ITCS.2009.157

Ludík, T., Barta, J., & Navrátil, J. (2013). Design Patterns for Emergency Management Processes, World Academy of Science, Engineering and Technology. *International Journal of Economics and Management Engineering, 7*(12), 3026–3033.

Macedo, A. A., Pollettini, J. T., Baranauskas, J. A., & Chaves, J. C. A. (2016, August). A health surveillance software framework to design the delivery of information on preventive healthcare strategies. *Journal of Biomedical Informatics, 62*, 159–170. doi:10.1016/j.jbi.2016.06.002 PMID:27318270

MacIver, D. (2016). *What is Property Based Testing?* Retrieved from https://hypothesis.works/articles/what-is-property-based-testing/.

MacIver, D. (2019a). *Welcome to Hypothesis!* Retrieved from https://hypothesis.readthedocs.io/en/latest/

MacIver, D. (2019b). *Stateful testing.* Retrieved from https://hypothesis.readthedocs.io/en/latest/stateful.html

Madanayake, R., Dias, G. K. A., & Kodikara, N. D. (2016). Use Stories vs UML Use Cases in Modular Transformation. *International Journal of Scientific Engineering and Applied Science, 3*(1), 1–5.

Mailewa, A., Herath, J., & Herath, S. (2015). *A Survey of Effective and Efficient Software Testing.* Paper presented at the Midwest Instruction and Computing Symposium. Retrieved August 01, 2019, from http://www. micsymposium. org/mics2015/ProceedingsMICS_2015/Mailewa_ 2D1_41. pdf

Mair, C., Martincova, M., & Shepperd, M. (2012). An Empirical Study of Software Project Managers Using a Case-Based Reasoner. In *Proceedings of 45th Hawaii International Conference on System Science*, (pp. 1030-1039). IEEE Computer Society. 10.1109/HICSS.2012.96

Malan, R., & Bredemeyer, D. (2010). Software Architecture and Related Concerns. *Resources for Software Architects.* Retrieved July 26, 2010, from http://www.bredemeyer.com/whatis.htm

Mall, R. (2006). *Fundamentals of Software Engineering* (2nd ed.). Prentice Hall.

Martin, R. (2000). *Design Principles and Design Patterns.* Retrieved July 12, 2017, from https://web.archive.org/web/20150906155800/http://www.objectmentor.com/resources/articles/Principles_and_Patterns.pdf

Martin, R. (2017). *Clean Architecture: A Craftsman's Guide to Software Structure and Design.* Upper Saddle River, NJ: Prentice Hall PTR.

Mas-Machuca, M., & Martínez Costa, C. (2012). Exploring critical success factors of knowledge management projects in the consulting sector. *Total Quality Management & Business Excellence, 23*(11-12), 1297–1313. doi:10.1080/14783363.2011.637778

Matallaoui, A., Herzig, P., & Zarnekow, R. (2015). Model-Driven Serious Game Development Integration of the Gamification Modeling Language GaML with Unity. *2015 48th Hawaii International Conference on System Sciences*, 643–651. 10.1109/HICSS.2015.84

Mayrhauser, A. v., Walls, J., & Mraz, R. (1994). Sleuth: A Domain Based Testing Toll. In *IEEE International Test Conference* (pp. 840-849). 10.1109/TEST.1994.528031

McGovern, J., Ambler, S. W., Stevens, M. E., Linn, J., Sharan, V., & Jo, E. K. (2003). *A Practical Guide To Enterprise Architecture*. Upper Saddle River, NJ: Prentice Hall PTR.

McKinsey Global Institute. (2006, October). *A Framework to Guide Healthcare System Reform*. San Francisco, CA: Author.

McLaughlin, S., Paton, R. A., & Macbeth, D. K. (2008). Barrier impact on organizational learning within complex organizations. *Journal of Knowledge Management*, *12*(2), 107–123. doi:10.1108/13673270810859550

McMeekin, K. (2017). Test Automation vs. Automated Testing. *DZone*. Retrieved May 26, 2019, from https://dzone. com/articles/test-automation-vs-automated-testing-the-differenc

MDA. (2010). MDA – The Architecture of Choice for a Changing World. *OMG*. Retrieved July 12, 2017, from https:// www.omg.org/mda/

Meananeatra, P., Rongviriyapanish, S., & Apiwattanapong, T. (2011). *A Survey on the Maintenance of Software Structure in Thai Software Industries*. Paper presented at the 2011 International Conference on Modeling, Simulation and Control, Singapore.

Mehra, K., & Dhawan, S. (2003). Study of the process of organisational learning in software firms in India. *Technovation*, *23*(2), 121–129. doi:10.1016/S0166-4972(01)00089-X

Mehta, P. (2017, January). Framework of Indian Healthcare System and its Challenges: An Insight. In *Healthcare Community Synergism between Patients, Practitioners, and Researchers* (pp. 247-271). IGI Global.

Mellor, S. J., Scott, K., Uhl, A., & Weise, D. (2004). *MDA Distilled: Principles of Model-Driven Architecture*. Reading, MA: Addison-Wesley.

Meyer, B. (1988). Genericity Versus Inheritance. *Journal of Pascal, Ada, & Modula-2*, *7*(2), 13-30.

Meyer, B. (1988). *Object-oriented Software Construction*. Upper Saddle River, NJ: Prentice Hall PTR.

Milad, H., Nahla, E., & Mostafa, S. (2014). A Review of Scripting Techniques Used in Automated Software Testing. *International Journal of Advanced Computer Science and Applications*, *5*(1), 194–202.

Miller, G. A. (1995). WordNet: A Lexical Database for English. *Communications of the ACM*, *38*(11), 39–41. doi:10.1145/219717.219748

Möller, S. (2010). Usability Engineering. In S. Möller (Ed.), Quality Engineering: Qualität kommunikationstechnischer Systeme (pp. 57–74). doi:10.1007/978-3-642-11548-6_4

Mora, A., Riera, D., González, C., & Arnedo-Moreno, J. (2017). Gamification: A systematic review of design frameworks. *Journal of Computing in Higher Education*, *29*(3), 516–548. doi:10.100712528-017-9150-4

Morschheuser, B., Hamari, J., Werder, K., & Abe, J. (2017). How to gamify? A method for designing gamification. *Proceedings of the 50th Hawaii International Conference on System Sciences 2017*. 10.24251/HICSS.2017.155

Morschheuser, B., Hassan, L., Werder, K., & Hamari, J. (2018). How to design gamification? A method for engineering gamified software. *Information and Software Technology*, *95*, 219–237. doi:10.1016/j.infsof.2017.10.015

Moura, R. (2019). *European Testing Conference*. Retrieved from https://europeantestingconference.eu/2019/

Mullen, R. (2018). *An Analysis of Software Testing Practices on Migrations From on Premise to Cloud Hosted Environments*. Academic Press.

Murali, A., & Kumar, S. K. (2014). Knowledge Management and Human Resource Management (HRM): Importance of Integration. *FIIB Business Review*, *3*(1), 3–10. doi:10.1177/2455265820140101

Myers, G. (1979). *The Art of Software Testing. IBM Systems Research Institute, Lecturer in Computer Science, Polytechnic Institute of New York*. John Wiley & Sons.

Myers, G. J. (2004). *The Art of Software Testing* (2nd ed.). Hoboken, NJ: John Wiley & Sons.

Nafees, T. (2019). *Addressing the knowledge transfer problem in secure software development through anti-patterns*. Abertay University.

Nauman, J. D., & Jenkins, A. M. (1982). Prototyping: The New Paradigm for System Development. *Management Information Systems Quarterly*, *6*(3), 29–44. doi:10.2307/248654

Naveen, K. (2015). Step by Step Process to Perform Automation Test using SoapUI. *TESTINGFREAK*. Retrieved May 26, 2019, from http://testingfreak.com/step-by-step-process-to-perform-automation-test-using-soapui

Nerur, S., Mahapatra, R., & Mangalaraj, G. (2005). Challenges of migrating to agile methodologies. *Communications of the ACM*, *48*(5), 72–78. doi:10.1145/1060710.1060712

Nicolini, D., Powell, J., Convile, P., & Martinez-Solano, L. (2008, August). Managing knowledge in the healthcare sector, A review. *International Journal of Management Reviews*, *10*(3), 245–263. doi:10.1111/j.1468-2370.2007.00219.x

Nidhra, S., Yanamadala, M., Afzal, W., & Torkar, R. (2013). Knowledge transfer challenges and mitigation strategies in global software development—A systematic literature review and industrial validation. *International Journal of Information Management*, *33*(2), 333–355. doi:10.1016/j.ijinfomgt.2012.11.004

Nikolik, B. (2012). Software quality assurance economics. *Information and Software Technology*, *54*(11), 1229–1238. doi:10.1016/j.infsof.2012.06.003

Nilsson, R. (2018). *ScalaCheck: Property-based testing for Scala*. Retrieved from http://www.scalacheck.org

Nilsson, R. (2014a). *ScalaCheck: The Definitive Guide*. Artima Press.

Nilsson, R. (2014b). *Testing Stateful Systems with ScalaCheck*. Berlin: ScalaDays.

Nonaka, I., Toyama, R., & Konno, N. (2000). SECI, Ba and leadership: A unified model of dynamic knowledge creation. *Long Range Planning*, *33*(1), 5–34. doi:10.1016/S0024-6301(99)00115-6

O'Farrell, C. (2015). *Practical Property-Based Testing*. Paper presented at YOW! Lambda Jam 2015 Conference.

Oh, S., Cha, J., Ji, M., Kang, H., Kim, S., Heo, E., ... Yoo, S. (2015, April). Architecture Design of Healthcare Software-as-a-Service Platform for Cloud-Based Clinical Decision Support Service. *Healthcare Informatics Research*, *21*(2), 102–110. doi:10.4258/hir.2015.21.2.102 PMID:25995962

Omar, W., & Bendiab, A. T. (2006). *E-Health Support Services Based on Service-Oriented Architecture*. IEEE Computer Society.

Omotayo, F. O. (2015). Knowledge Management as an important tool in Organisational Management: A Review of Literature. *Library Philosophy and Practice*, *1*, 1–23.

OpenAPI. (2017, December 26). Retrieved 26 December 2017, from Open API Initiative. Retrieved November 20, 2019, from https://www.openapis.org/

Oreizy, P., Gorlick, M., Taylor, R. N., Heimbigner, D., Johnson, G., Medvidovic, N., ... Wolf, A. L. (1999, May/June). An Architecture-Based Approach to Self-Adaptive Software. *IEEE Intelligent Systems*, *14*(3), 54–62. doi:10.1109/5254.769885

Orso, A., & Rothermel, G. (2014). Software testing: a research travelogue (2000–2014). *Proceedings of the on Future of Software Engineering*, 117-132.

Owterweil, L. (1996). Strategic directions in software quality. *ACM Computing Surveys*, *28*(4).

Page, R. (2011, October). Property-based testing and verification: a catalog of classroom examples. In *International Symposium on Implementation and Application of Functional Languages* (pp. 134-147). Springer.

Paharia, R. (2013). *Loyalty 3.0: How to revolutionize customer and employee engagement with big data and gamification*. New York, NY: McGraw Hill Professional.

Pal, K. & Campbell, J.A. (1997). An application of rule-based and case-based reasoning within a single legal knowledge-based system. *ACM SIGMIS Database: the DATABASE for Advances in Information Systems, 28*(4), 48-63.

Pal, K. (1999). An approach to legal reasoning based on a hybrids decision-support system. *Expert Systems with Applications*, *1*(1), 1–12. doi:10.1016/S0957-4174(99)00015-9

Pal, K. (2017). Supply Chain Coordination Based on web Service. In H. K. Chan, N. Subramanian, & M. D. Abdulrahman (Eds.), *Supply Chain Management in Big Data Era* (pp. 137–170). Hershey, PA: IGI Publication. doi:10.4018/978-1-5225-0956-1.ch009

Pal, K. (2019). Markov Decision Theory-Based Crowdsourcing Software Process Model. In V. Gupta (Ed.), *Crowdsourcing and Probabilistic Decision-Making in Software Engineering: Emerging Research and Opportunities* (pp. 1–22). Hershey, PA: IGI Global Publishing.

Pal, K., & Palmer, O. (2000). A decision-support system for business acquisition. *Decision Support Systems*, *27*(4), 411–429. doi:10.1016/S0167-9236(99)00083-4

Panetto, H., & Whitman, L. (2016). Knowledge engineering for enterprise integration, interoperability and networking: Theory and applications. *Data & Knowledge Engineering*, *105*, 1–4. doi:10.1016/j.datak.2016.05.001

Pang, C. Y. (2001). A Design Pattern Type Extension with Facets and Decorators. *Journal of Object-Oriented Programming*, *13*(13), 14–18.

Pang, C. Y. (2015). Ten Years of Experience with Agile and Model Driven Software Development in a Legacy Platform. In A. Singh (Ed.), *Emerging Innovations in Agile Software Development*. Hershey, PA: IGI Global.

Pang, C. Y. (2016). An Agile Architecture for a Legacy Enterprise IT System. *International Journal of Organizational and Collective Intelligence*, *6*(4), 65–97. doi:10.4018/IJOCI.2016100104

Pantiuchina, J., Lanza, M., & Bavota, G. (2018). Improving code: The (mis) perception of quality metrics. In *Proceedings of the IEEE International Conference on Software Maintenance and Evolution* (pp. 80-91). Piscataway, NJ: IEEE Computer Society Press. 10.1109/ICSME.2018.00017

Park, J.-G., & Lee, J. (2014). Knowledge sharing in information systems development projects: Explicating the role of dependence and trust. *International Journal of Project Management*, *32*(1), 153–165. doi:10.1016/j.ijproman.2013.02.004

Parnas, D. L. (1972). On the Criteria To Be Used in Decomposing Systems into Modules. *Communications of the ACM*, *15*(12), 1053–1058. doi:10.1145/361598.361623

Pautasso, C. (2014). RESTful web services: principles, patterns, emerging technologies. In Web Services Foundations (pp. 31-51). New York, NY: Springer. doi:10.1007/978-1-4614-7518-7_2

Petersen, K., Feldt, R., Mujtaba, S., & Mattsson, M. (2008). *Systematic mapping studies in software engineering.* Paper presented at the Ease. 10.14236/ewic/EASE2008.8

Pettichord, B., Kaner, C., & Bach, J. (2008). *Lessons Learned in Software Testing: A Context-Driven Approach* (1st ed.). John Wiley & Sons.

Pfleeger, S. L., & Atlee, J. M. (2006). *Software Engineering: Theory and Practice.* London, UK: Pearson.

Piña, I. L., Cohen, P. D., Larson, D. B., Marion, L. N., Sills, M. R., Solberg, L. I., & Zerzan, J. (2015, April). A Framework for Describing Health Care Delivery Organizations and Systems. *American Journal of Public Health, 105*(4), 650–659. doi:10.2105/AJPH.2014.301926 PMID:24922130

Popplewell, K. (2014). Enterprise interoperability science base structure. In K. Mertins, F. Bénaben, R. Poler, & J. Bour-rières (Eds.), *Enterprise Interoperability VI: Interoperability for Agility, Resilience and Plasticity of Collaborations* (pp. 417–427). Cham, Switzerland: Springer International Publishing. doi:10.1007/978-3-319-04948-9_35

Porcello, E., & Banks, A. (2018). *Learning GraphQL - Declarative Data Fetching for Modern Web Apps* (1st ed.). Retrieved November 20, 2019, from http://shop.oreilly.com/product/0636920137269.do

Powell, M. (2007). The mixed economy of welfare and the social division of welfare. In M. Powell (Ed.), *Understanding the Mixed Economy of Welfare* (pp. 1–21). Bristol, UK: Policy Press. doi:10.2307/j.ctt1t89b4m.6

Prahalad, C. K., & Mashelkar, R. A. (2010). Innovation's Holy Grail. *Harvard Business Review, 88*(7/8), 132–141.

PropEr. (2018). *PropEr: a QuickCheck-inspired property-based testing tool for Erlang.* Retrieved from https://github.com/proper-testing/proper

Pulparambil, S., Baghdadi, Y., Al-Hamdani, A., & Al-Badawi, M. (2018). Service Design Metrics to Predict IT-Based Drivers of Service Oriented Architecture Adoption. In *Proceedings of the 9th International Conference on Computing, Communication and Networking Technologies* (pp. 1-7). Piscataway, NJ: IEEE Computer Society Press. 10.1109/ICCCNT.2018.8494072

Quast, L. (2012). *Why knowledge management is important to the success of your company.* Retrieved September from https://www.forbes.com/sites/lisaquast/2012/08/20/why-knowledge-management-is-important-to-the-success-of-your-company/#673aceac3681

Queiroz, M., Tallon, P., Sharma, R., & Coltman, T. (2018). The role of IT application orchestration capability in improving agility and performance. *The Journal of Strategic Information Systems, 27*(1), 4–21. doi:10.1016/j.jsis.2017.10.002

QuickCheck. (2019). *QuickCheck: Automatic testing of Haskell programs.* Retrieved from http://hackage.haskell.org/package/QuickCheck-2.13.2

QuviQ. (2019a). *QuviQ.* Retrieved from http://www.quviq.com/contact-2/about/

QuviQ. (2019b). *QuviQ testing tools.* Retrieved from http://www.quviq.com/products/

Rakitin, S. R. (2001). Manifesto Elicits Cynicism: Reader's Letter to the Editor by Steven R. Rakitin. IEEE Computer, (34), 4.

Ramesh, M., Wu, X., & He, A. J. (2013). Health governance and healthcare reforms in China. *Health Policy and Planning, 29*(6), 663–672. doi:10.1093/heapol/czs109 PMID:23293100

Ranasinghe, G., & Jayawardana, A. (2011). Impact of knowledge sharing on project success in the Sri Lankan software industry. *Sri Lankan Journal of Management, 16*(1).

Rantanen, J. (2007). *Acceptance Test-Driven Development with KeywordDriven Test Automation Framework in an Agile Software Project.* Helsinki University of Technology, Software Business and Engineering Institute.

Rashmi & Bajpai, N. (2012). A Keyword Driven Framework for Testing Web Applications. *International Journal of Advanced Computer Science and Applications, 3*(3), 8–14.

Rehkopf, M. (2019). User Stories. *Atlassian Agile Guide.* Retrieved May 22, 2019, from https://www.atlassian.com/agile/project-management/user-stories

Rehman, F., Maqbool, B., Riaz, M. Q., Qamar, U., & Abbas, M. (2018). *Scrum Software Maintenance Model: Efficient Software Maintenance in Agile Methodology.* Paper presented at the 2018 21st Saudi Computer Society National Computer Conference (NCC). 10.1109/NCG.2018.8593152

Reyes, W., Smith, R., & Fraunholz, B. (2007). *Agile approaches to software maintenance: an exploratory study of practitioner views.* Paper presented at the Managing worldwide operations and communications with information technology: 2007 Information Resources Management Association International Conference, Vancouver, British Columbia, Canada.

Rezaei, R., Chiew, T., & Lee, S. (2014). A review on E-business interoperability frameworks. *Journal of Systems and Software, 93*, 199–216. doi:10.1016/j.jss.2014.02.004

Richards, M. (2015). *Software Architecture Patterns.* Sebastopol, CA: O'Reilly.

Richardson, M. (2006). Guideline: Use-Case Realization. *IBM Corp.* Retrieved May 22, 2019, from http://www.michael-richardson.com/processes/rup_classic/core.base_rup/guidances/guidelines/use-case_realization_C690D81F.html

Riege, A. (2005). Three-dozen knowledge-sharing barriers managers must consider. *Journal of Knowledge Management, 9*(3), 18–35. doi:10.1108/13673270510602746

Robson, K., Plangger, K., Kietzmann, J. H., McCarthy, I., & Pitt, L. (2016). Game on: Engaging customers and employees through gamification. *Business Horizons, 59*(1), 29–36. doi:10.1016/j.bushor.2015.08.002

Ross, A., Rhodes, D., & Hastings, D. (2008). Defining changeability: Reconciling flexibility, adaptability, scalability, modifiability, and robustness for maintaining system lifecycle value. *Systems Engineering, 11*(3), 246–262. doi:10.1002ys.20098

Royce, W. (1970). Managing the Development of Large Software Systems. *Proceedings of IEEE WESON, (28),* 1-9.

Rubin, K. S. (2012). *Essential Scrum: A Practical Guide to the Most Popular Agile Process.* Reading, MA: Addison-Wesley.

Ruiz, F., Vizcaíno, A., Piattini, M., & García, F. (2004). An ontology for the management of software maintenance projects. *International Journal of Software Engineering and Knowledge Engineering, 14*(03), 323–349. doi:10.1142/S0218194004001646

Runciman, C., Naylor, M., & Lindblad, F. (2008). SmallCheck and Lazy SmallCheck. In *Proceedings of the first ACM SIGPLAN symposium on Haskell (Haskell '08).* ACM. 10.1145/1411286.1411292

Runeson, P., Andersson, C., & Höst, M. (2003). Test processes in software product evolution—a qualitative survey on the state of practice. *Journal of Software Maintenance and Evolution: Research and Practice, 15*(1), 41-59.

Runeson, P., Andersson, C., Thelin, T., Andrews, A., & Berling, T. (2006). What do we know about defect detection methods? *IEEE Software, 23*(3), 82–90. doi:10.1109/MS.2006.89

Rus, I., Lindvall, M., & Sinha, S. (2002). Knowledge management in software engineering. *IEEE Software, 19*(3), 26–38. doi:10.1109/MS.2002.1003450

Saad, M. (2019). How to Develop Test Scripts Using Top 5 Most Popular Test Automation Frameworks. *Software Testing Help*. Retrieved September 09, 2019, from https://www.softwaretestinghelp.com/automation-testing-tutorial-5

Saaty, T. L., & Vargas, L. G. (1991). *Prediction, Projection and Forecasting: Applications of the Analytic Hierarchy Process in Economics, Finance, Politics, Games and Sports*. Retrieved November 20, 2019, from https://www.springer.com/kr/book/9789401579544

Saaty, T. L. (1980). *The Analytic Hierarchy Process: Planning, Priority Setting, Resource Allocation*. New York, NY: McGraw-Hill.

Sadiq, S. (2019). 7 Ways to Make Test Automation Effective in Agile Development. *DZone*. Retrieved November 07, 2019, from https://dzone.com/articles/7-ways-to-make-test-automation-effective-in-agile

Sagenschneider, D. (2019). Local Microservices: Object Orientation Behavior Coupling Problem. *DZone*. Retrieved June 6, 2019, from https://dzone.com/articles/local-microservices-object-orientation-behaviour-c

Saha, S., Beach, M. C., & Cooper, L. A. (2008). Patient centeredness cultural competence and healthcare quality. *Journal of the National Medical Association, 100*(11), 1275–1285. doi:10.1016/S0027-9684(15)31505-4 PMID:19024223

Samdantsoodol, A., Cang, S., Yu, H., Eardley, A., & Buyantsogt, A. (2017). Predicting the relationships between virtual enterprises and agility in supply chains. *Expert Systems with Applications, 84*, 58–73. doi:10.1016/j.eswa.2017.04.037

Sawyer, X. (2014). A Test to Remember: Testing Your Web Application. *Perl Dancer Advent Calendar*. Retrieved May 26, 2019, from http://advent.perldancer.org/2014/12

ScalaCheck. (2019). *ScalaCheck User Guide*. Retrieved from https://github.com/typelevel/scalacheck/blob/master/doc/UserGuide.md#stateful-testing

Scaled Agile. (2019). Story. *Scaled Agile Framework*. Retrieved July 20, 2019 from https://www.scaledagileframework.com/story/

Schmidt, D. C. (2006). Model-Driven Engineering. *IEEE Computer, 39*(2), 9. Retrieved from https://citeseerx.ist.psu.edu/

Schoen, C., Osborn, R., Squires, D., Doty, M., Pierson, R., & Applebaum, S. (2011). Survey of patients with complex care needs in eleven countries finds that care is often poorly coordinated. *Health Affairs, 30*(12), 2437-2448.

Schwaber, K., & Beedle, M. (2001). *Agile software development with Scrum*. Upper Saddle River, NJ: Prentice Hall PTR.

Scrum Expert. (2016). User Stories Are Not Requirements. *Scrum Expert*. Retrieved July 20, 2019 from https://www.scrumexpert.com/knowledge/user-stories-are-not-requirements/

Scrum. (2019). Scrum (software development). *Wikipedia*. Retrieved July 20, 2019 from https://en.wikipedia.org/wiki/Scrum_(software_development)

SDLC. (2013). Software Development Life Cycle. *SDLC*. Retrieved December 11, 2014, from http://www.sdlc.ws/

Seba, I., Rowley, J., & Lambert, S. (2012). Factors affecting attitudes and intentions towards knowledge sharing in the Dubai Police Force. *International Journal of Information Management, 32*(4), 372–380. doi:10.1016/j.ijinfomgt.2011.12.003

Sebega, Y., & Mnkandla, E. (2017). Exploring Issues in Agile Requirements Engineering in the South African Software Industry. *EJISDC, 81*(5), 1–18.

Sessions, R. (2008). *Simple Architectures for Complex Enterprises*. Redmond, WA: Microsoft Press.

Shao, Z. L., Bai, X, Y., & Zhao, C.C. (2006). Research and implementation of a reuse-oriented test design model. *Journal of Mini-Micro Systems, 27,* 2150-2155.

Shaw, M. (2001, May). The Coming-of-Age of Software Architecture Research. *Proceedings of the 23rd International Conference on Software Engineering, ICSE 2001,* 656-664. 10.1109/ICSE.2001.919142

Shaw, M., & Garlan, D. (1996). *Software Architecture: Perspectives on an Emerging Discipline.* Prentice Hall.

Shepperd, M., & Schofield, C. (1997). Estimating software project effort using analogies. *IEEE Transactions on Software Engineering, 23*(11), 736–743. doi:10.1109/32.637387

Shiff, L., & Rowe, W. (2018). NoSQL vs SQL: Examining the Differences and Deciding Which to Choose. *Bmc.* Retrieved July 11, 2019, from https://www.bmc.com/blogs/sql-vs-nosql

Shoemaker, N. (2014). Can Universities Encourage Students Continued Motivation For Knowledge Sharing And How Can This Help Organizations? *Journal of College Teaching and Learning, 11*(3), 99–114. doi:10.19030/tlc.v11i3.8757

Shtatnov, A., & Ranganathan, R. S. (2018, December 10). *Our learnings from adopting GraphQL.* Retrieved 9 February 2019, from Netflix TechBlog. Retrieved November 20, 2019, from https://medium.com/netflix-techblog/our-learnings-from-adopting-graphql-f099de39ae5f

Şimşit, Z., Günay, S., & Vayvay, Ö. (2014). Theory of Constraints: A Literature Review. *Procedia: Social and Behavioral Sciences, 150,* 930–936. doi:10.1016/j.sbspro.2014.09.104

Singh, S., Burns, K. K., Rees, J., Picklyk, D., Spence, J., & Marlett, N. (2018). Patient and family engagement in Alberta Health Services: Improving care delivery and research outcomes. *Healthcare Management Forum, SAGE Journal, 31*(2), 57-61.

Singh, A., & Pandey, D. (2017). Implementation of Requirement Engineering in Extreme Programing and SCRUM. *International Journal of Advanced Research in Computer Science, 8*(5).

Smith, S., & Kandel, A. (2018). *Verification and validation of rule-based expert systems.* CRC Press.

Sneha, K., & Malle, G. (2014). Research on software testing techniques and software automation testing tools. *IEEE Xplore.* Retrieved May 26, 2019, from https://ieeexplore.ieee.org/document/8389562

Software Crisis. (2010). Software Crisis. *Wikipedia.* Retrieved July 26, 2010, from http://en.wikipedia.org/wiki/Software_crisis

Software Engineering. (2010). Software Engineering. *Wikipedia.* Retrieved July 26, 2010, from http://en.wikipedia.org/wiki/Software_engineering

Software Engineering. (2010). Software Engineering. *Wikipedia.* Retrieved July 26, 2019, from http://en.wikipedia.org/wiki/Software_engineering

Sommerville, I., & Sawyer, P. (1997). *Requirements Engineering: A Good Practice Guide.* West Sussex, UK: John Wiley & Son.

Soora, S. K. (2014). A Framework for Software Reuse and Research *Challenges. International Journal of Advanced Research in Computer Science and Software Engineering, 4*(8), 441–448.

Sousa, M. J. C., & Moreira, H. M. (1998). A survey on the software maintenance process. *Proceedings of the International Conference on Software Maintenance* (Cat. No. 98CB36272). 10.1109/ICSM.1998.738518

Souza, E. F., Falbo, R., & Vijaykumar, N. L. (2013). *Using ontology patterns for building a reference software testing ontology.* Paper presented at the Enterprise Distributed Object Computing Conference Workshops (EDOCW), 2013 17th IEEE International. 10.1109/EDOCW.2013.10

Stahlbauer, A., Kreis, M., & Fraser, G. (2019, August). Testing scratch programs automatically. In *Proceedings of the 2019 27th ACM Joint Meeting on European Software Engineering Conference and Symposium on the Foundations of Software Engineering* (pp. 165-175). ACM.

Stark, G. E., Oman, P., Skillicorn, A., & Ameele, A. (1999). An examination of the effects of requirements changes on software maintenance releases. *Journal of Software Maintenance: Research and Practice, 11*(5), 293–309. doi:10.1002/(SICI)1096-908X(199909/10)11:5<293::AID-SMR198>3.0.CO;2-R

Steele, R., Min, K., & Lo, A. (2012). Personal Health Record Architectures: Technology Infrastructure Implications and Dependencies. *Journal of the American Society for Information Science and Technology, 63*(6), 1079–1091. doi:10.1002/asi.22635

Stellman, A., & Greene, J. (2015). *Learning Agile: Understand Scrum, XP, Lean, and Kanban.* Sebastopol, CA: O'Reilly.

Stellman, A., & Greene, J. (2015). *Learning Agile: Understand SCRUM, XP, Lean, and Kanban.* Sebastopol, CA: O'Reilly.

Strauss, A., & Corbin, J. M. (1997). Grounded theory in practice. *Sage (Atlanta, Ga.).*

Strazdiņa, L., Arnicane, V., Arnicans, G., Bičevskis, J., Borzovs, J., & Kuļešovs, I. (2018). What Software Test Approaches, Methods, and Techniques are Actually Used in Software Industry? *Joint Proceedings of Baltic DB&IS 2018 Conference Forum and Doctoral Consortium.*

Stuart, M. (2018, October 16). *GraphQL: A success story for PayPal Checkout.* Retrieved 17 January 2019, from PayPal Engineering. Retrieved November 20, 2019, from https://medium.com/paypal-engineering/graphql-a-success-story-for-paypal-checkout-3482f724fb53

Stubailo, S. (2017, June 27). *GraphQL vs. REST.* Retrieved 3 December 2018, from Apollo GraphQL. Retrieved November 20, 2019, from https://blog.apollographql.com/graphql-vs-rest-5d425123e34b

Szulanski, G. (2002). Sticky knowledge: Barriers to knowing in the firm. *Sage (Atlanta, Ga.).*

Tao, Q., Wu, W., Zhao, C., & Shen, W. (2010, November). An automatic testing approach for compiler based on metamorphic testing technique. In 2010 Asia Pacific Software Engineering Conference (pp. 270-279). IEEE. doi:10.1109/APSEC.2010.39

Titi Amayah, A. (2013). Determinants of knowledge sharing in a public sector organization. *Journal of Knowledge Management, 17*(3), 454–471. doi:10.1108/JKM-11-2012-0369

Tooranloo, H. S., & Saghafi, S. (2018). The relationship between organisational agility and applying knowledge management. *International Journal of Agile Systems and Management, 11*(1), 41–66. doi:10.1504/IJASM.2018.091360

Torikian, G., Black, B., Swinnerton, B., Somerville, C., Celis, D., & Daigle, K. (2016, September 14). *The GitHub GraphQL API.* Retrieved 17 January 2019, from GitHub Engineering. Retrieved November 20, 2019, from https://githubengineering.com/the-github-graphql-api/

Tran, H., Zdun, U., Oberortner, E., Mulo, E., & Dustdar, S. (2012). Compliance in service-oriented architectures: A model-driven and view-based approach. *Information and Software Technology, 54*(6), 531–552. doi:10.1016/j.infsof.2012.01.001

Tsui, F., Karam, O., & Bernal, B. (2016). *Essentials of Software Engineering* (4th ed.). Burlington, MA: Jones & Bartlett Learning.

User Story. (2019). User Story. *Wikipedia*. Retrieved July 26, 2019, from https://en.wikipedia.org/wiki/User_story

Vasanthapriyan, S. (2018). *A Study of Software Testing Practices in Sri Lankan Software Companies*. Paper presented at the 2018 IEEE International Conference on Software Quality, Reliability and Security Companion (QRS-C). 10.1109/QRS-C.2018.00066

Vasanthapriyan, S., Tian, J., & Xiang, J. (2015). *A survey on knowledge management in software engineering*. Paper presented at the Software Quality, Reliability and Security-Companion (QRS-C), 2015 IEEE International Conference on, Vancouver, Canada. 10.1109/QRS-C.2015.48

Vasanthapriyan, S. (2019). *Knowledge Sharing Initiatives in Software Companies: A Mapping Study. In Human Factors in Global Software Engineering* (pp. 84–108). IGI Global. doi:10.4018/978-1-5225-9448-2.ch004

Vasanthapriyan, S., Tan, J., Zhao, D., Xiong, S., & Xiang, J. (2017). An Ontology-based Knowledge Sharing Portal for Software Testing. *IEEE International Conference on Software Quality, Reliability and Security*, 472-479. 10.1109/QRS-C.2017.82

Vasanthapriyan, S., Xiang, J., Tian, J., & Xiong, S. (2017). Knowledge synthesis in software industries: A survey in Sri Lanka. *Knowledge Management Research and Practice*, *15*(3), 413–430. doi:10.105741275-017-0057-7

Vázquez-Ingelmo, A., Cruz-Benito, J., & García-Peñalvo, F. J. (2017). Improving the OEEU's Data-driven Technological Ecosystem's Interoperability with GraphQL. *Proceedings of the 5th International Conference on Technological Ecosystems for Enhancing Multiculturality*, 89:1–89:8. 10.1145/3144826.3145437

Von Krogh, G. (1998). Care in knowledge creation. *California Management Review*, *40*(3), 133–153. doi:10.2307/41165947

Von Krogh, G., Back, A., Enkel, E., & Seufert, A. (2004). *Putting knowledge networks into action*. Springer-Verlag.

Wake, B. (2003). INVEST in Good Stories, and SMART Tasks. *XP123*. Retrieved May 25, 2019, from https://xp123.com/articles/invest-in-good-stories-and-smart-tasks/

Wake, B. (2018). Back to basics: Writing and splitting user stories. *Medium.com*. Retrieved May 25, 2019, from https://medium.com/agile-outside-the-box/back-to-basics-writing-and-splitting-user-stories-8903a931499c

Waldmann, J. (2017). How I Teach Functional Programming. *Workshop on Functional Logic Programming (WFLP 2017)*.

Walz, S. P., & Deterding, S. (2015). *The gameful world: Approaches, issues, applications*. Cambridge, MA: MIT Press. doi:10.7551/mitpress/9788.001.0001

Wang, H., Xing, J., Yang, Q., Song, W., & Zhang, X. (2016). Generating effective test cases based on satisfiability modulo theory solvers for service-oriented workflow applications. *Software Testing, Verification & Reliability*, *26*(2), 149–169. doi:10.1002tvr.1592

Wang, Y., Huang, Q., Davison, R. M., & Yang, F. (2018). Effect of transactive memory systems on team performance mediated by knowledge transfer. *International Journal of Information Management*, *41*, 65–79. doi:10.1016/j.ijinfomgt.2018.04.001

Watson, I. (2003). *Applying Knowledge Management: techniques for building corporate memories*. San Francisco, CA: Morgan Kaufmann Publishers.

Weerakoon, S., & Wijayanayake, J. (2016). *Propensity of Knowledge Sharing in Software Development Case in Sri Lanka*. Paper presented at the International Conference on Multidisciplinary Approaches.

Wendt, C., Frisina, L., & Rothgang, H. (2009, February). Healthcare System Types: A Conceptual Framework for Comparison. *Social Policy & Administration, Wiley*, *43*(1), 70–90. doi:10.1111/j.1467-9515.2008.00647.x

Werbach, K., & Hunter, D. (2012). *For the Win: How Game Thinking can Revolutionize your Business*. Philadelphia, PA: Wharton School Press.

Wickramasinghe, V., & Widyaratne, R. (2012). Effects of interpersonal trust, team leader support, rewards, and knowledge sharing mechanisms on knowledge sharing in project teams. *Vine*, *42*(2), 214–236. doi:10.1108/03055721211227255

Wiegers, K., & Beatty, J. (2013). *Software Requirements* (3rd ed.). Redmond, WA: Microsoft Press.

Wikipedia. (2019). *QuickCheck*. Retrieved from https://en.wikipedia.org/wiki/QuickCheck

Wittern, E., Cha, A., & Laredo, J. A. (2018). Generating GraphQL-Wrappers for REST(-like) APIs. In T. Mikkonen, R. Klamma, & J. Hernández (Eds.), *Web Engineering* (pp. 65–83). London, UK: Springer International Publishing. doi:10.1007/978-3-319-91662-0_5

Wlaschin, S. (2015). *An introduction to property based testing*. Paper presented at Functional Programming eXchange Conference, London, UK.

World Health Organization. (2008). *Framework and standards for country health information systems*. Geneva: Health Metrics Network.

Xiao-Li, L., Wei, G., Xin-Li, C., & Ke-Gang, H. (2006). Designing a test case library system of supporting sharing and reusing. *Journal of Computational Science*, *33*, 290–291.

Xu, R., Chen, B., & Chen, B., Wu, M., & Xiong Z. (2003). Investigation on the pattern for Construction of Reusable Test Cases in Object-oriented Software. *Journal of Wuhan University*, *49*(5), 592–596.

Yang, H., Ma, K., Deng, C., Liao, H., Yan, J., & Zhang, J. (2013). Towards conformance testing of choreography based on scenario. In *Proceedings of the International Symposium on Theoretical Aspects of Software Engineering* (pp. 59-62). Piscataway, NJ: IEEE Computer Society Press. 10.1109/TASE.2013.23

Yip, S. W., & Lam, T. (1994). A software maintenance survey. *Proceedings of 1st Asia-Pacific Software Engineering Conference*. 10.1109/APSEC.1994.465272

Yourdon, E., & Constantine, L. L. (1979). *Structure Design: Fundamentals of a Discipline of Computer Program and System Design*. Upper Saddle River, NJ: Yourdon Press.

Zammit, J. P., Gao, J., & Evans, R. (2015). *A framework to capture and share knowledge using storytelling and video sharing in global product development*. Paper presented at the IFIP International Conference on Product Lifecycle Management.

Zammit, J., Gao, J., & Evans, R. (2016). Capturing and sharing product development knowledge using storytelling and video sharing. *Procedia CIRP*, *56*, 440–445. doi:10.1016/j.procir.2016.10.081

Zanero, S. (2017). Cyber-physical systems. *IEEE Computer*, *50*(4), 14–16. doi:10.1109/MC.2017.105

Zichermann, G., & Cunningham, C. (2011). *Gamification by design: Implementing game mechanics in web and mobile apps*. ⌈O'Reilly Media, Inc.

Zimmermann, O., Tomlinson, M., & Peuser, S. (2012). *Perspectives on Web Services: Applying SOAP, WSDL and UDDI to Real-World Projects*. New York, NY: Springer Science & Business Media.

About the Contributors

Pedro Aguiar received his degree in Informatics Engineering from Instituto de Engenharia do Porto (ISEP) in 2017 and is currently finishing his studies for a master's degree in Software Engineering. He became proficient in a wide variety of tools and programming languages over time and by the beginning of 2019 he started developing a project based on gamification and Model-Driven Engineering (MDE), about how an MDE approach can mitigate some of the problems identified when developing gamification strategies.

Isabel Azevedo holds a Ph.D. in Informatics Engineering from the Faculty of Engineering of the University of Porto (FEUP). She is an Associate Professor in the Department of Informatics Engineering of ISEP, and a researcher at the Games, Interaction and Learning Technologies (GILT) research group at ISEP. Isabel Azevedo previously worked in the area of Technological Infrastructures at FEUP, and in the Documentation Service of Aveiro University. Her main research topics include model-driven engineering, decentralized applications, and learning technologies.

Kuhaneswaran Banujan has received his first degree B.Sc. (Hons) in Computing & Information Systems from Sabaragamuwa University of Sri Lanka in Sri Lanka, in 2019. He is currently working as a Lecturer at Sabaragamuwa University of Sri Lanka in Sri Lanka.

José C. Delgado is an Associate Professor at the Computer Science and Engineering Department of the Instituto Superior Técnico (University of Lisbon), in Lisbon, Portugal, where he earned the Ph.D. degree in 1988. He lectures courses in the areas of Computer Architecture, Information Technology and Service Engineering. He has performed several management roles in his faculty, namely Director of the Taguspark campus, near Lisbon, and Coordinator of the B.Sc. and M.Sc. in Computer Science and Engineering at that campus. He has been the coordinator of and researcher in several international research projects. As an author, his publications include one book, 25 book chapters and more than 50 papers in international refereed conferences and journals.

Pooja Kaplesh is working as an Assistant Professor in department of CSE in Chandigarh University, Punjab.

Mafalda Landeiro received her bachelor in Computer Engineering from the Porto School of Engineering in 2014. In 2014, she also starts her professional career, having been a focus on backend development, mainly in Java. In 2016, decided to take the master degree in Software Engineering, at the same school, which is currently being finished.

Kalpani Madushika is an undergraduate at Department of Computing and Information Systems, Faculty of Applied Sciences, Sabaragamuwa University of Sri Lanka and have the experience in the area of Agile software development.

Nuno Malheiro was born in Portugal in 1972. He received his M.Sc from Faculdade de Engenharia da Universidade do Porto in 1997 and his Ph.D. from Universidade de Trás-os-Montes e Alto Douro in 2005, both in Electrical and Computing Engineering. Since 1997, he has been with the Instituto Superior de Engenharia do Porto, where he is currently a Professor. His main areas of research interest are Temporal and Model Based Reasoning and Software Quality.

Kamalendu Pal is with the Department of Computer Science, School of Mathematics, Computer Science and Engineering, City, University London. Kamalendu received his BSc (Hons) degree in Physics from Calcutta University, India, Postgraduate Diploma in Computer Science from Pune, India; MSc degree in Software Systems Technology from Sheffield University, Postgraduate Diploma in Artificial Intelligence from Kingston University, MPhil degree in Computer Science from University College London, and MBA degree from University of Hull, United Kingdom. He has published dozens of research papers in international journals and conferences. His research interests include knowledge-based systems, decision support systems, computer integrated design, software engineering, and service oriented computing. He is a member of the British Computer Society, the Institution of Engineering and Technology, and the IEEE Computer Society.

Severin Pang graduated from the University of Bern in a combined field of economics, mathematics and statistics. He has also received the Swiss state diploma in application programming and has attended a number of courses in data science, machine learning and AI. He has 8 years of application development experience for large companies such as Swiss Re, Zurich Insurance and IBM in Switzerland. At IBM, he worked on the program to develop the AI functionalities of a hovering robot to assist ISS astronauts. He currently works as a Data Scientist for Cognitive Solutions and Innovation AG. Severin Pang has contributed to publications in the fields of data science, AI and software engineering.

Kanak Saxena, Ph.D. in computer Science from the Devi Ahilya University, Indore, India. She is professor in the computer Science & Information Technology Department at the Samrat Ashok Technological Institute affiliated to Rajiv Gandhi Technical University, Bhopal. Her Current research focuses on Database Systems, Parallel computing, Data Uncertainty and design and other interests include Network security and performance and Software Engineering. She is the member of editorial board of various international journals. She is the member of the international committee of the International Conference on Computer Science and Its Applications. She Published more than 80 research Papers in Various Conferences and Journals National/International).

Shanmuganathan Vasanthapriyan has received B.Sc. (Hons) in Computer Science degree from University of Peradeniya, Sri Lanka, in 2004. He was awarded with Ashoka Amunugama Memorial award for the best performances in University of Peradeniya. He obtained his Master of Science in Computer Science and Engineering at Eindhoven University of Technology in The Netherlands in 2010. In 2017, he obtained his Doctor of Engineering Degree in Computer Science in Wuhan University of Technology in PR China. He received a number of prestigious international awards including Nuffic Fellowship Awards (in 2007) and Chinese Government Scholarship (in 2014). He is currently working as a Senior Lecturer at Sabaragamuwa University of Sri Lanka in Sri Lanka. He is a Senior Member of IEEE. For More: http://www.sab.ac.lk/staff-directory/216.

Index

Ensure Quality Research is Introduced to the Academic Community

Become an IGI Global Reviewer for Authored Book Projects

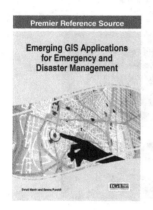

The overall success of an authored book project is dependent on quality and timely reviews.

In this competitive age of scholarly publishing, constructive and timely feedback significantly expedites the turnaround time of manuscripts from submission to acceptance, allowing the publication and discovery of forward-thinking research at a much more expeditious rate. Several IGI Global authored book projects are currently seeking highly-qualified experts in the field to fill vacancies on their respective editorial review boards:

Applications and Inquiries may be sent to:
development@igi-global.com

Applicants must have a doctorate (or an equivalent degree) as well as publishing and reviewing experience. Reviewers are asked to complete the open-ended evaluation questions with as much detail as possible in a timely, collegial, and constructive manner. All reviewers' tenures run for one-year terms on the editorial review boards and are expected to complete at least three reviews per term. Upon successful completion of this term, reviewers can be considered for an additional term.

If you have a colleague that may be interested in this opportunity,
we encourage you to share this information with them.

IGI Global Proudly Partners With eContent Pro International

Receive a 25% Discount on all Editorial Services

Editorial Services

IGI Global expects all final manuscripts submitted for publication to be in their final form. This means they must be reviewed, revised, and professionally copy edited prior to their final submission. Not only does this support with accelerating the publication process, but it also ensures that the highest quality scholarly work can be disseminated.

English Language Copy Editing

Let eContent Pro International's expert copy editors perform edits on your manuscript to resolve spelling, punctuaion, grammar, syntax, flow, formatting issues and more.

Scientific and Scholarly Editing

Allow colleagues in your research area to examine the content of your manuscript and provide you with valuable feedback and suggestions before submission.

Figure, Table, Chart & Equation Conversions

Do you have poor quality figures? Do you need visual elements in your manuscript created or converted? A design expert can help!

Translation

Need your documjent translated into English? eContent Pro International's expert translators are fluent in English and more than 40 different languages.

Email: customerservice@econtentpro.com   **www.igi-global.com/editorial-service-partners**

Publisher of Peer-Reviewed, Timely, and
Innovative Academic Research Since 1988

IGI Global's Transformative Open Access (OA) Model:
How to Turn Your University Library's Database Acquisitions Into a Source of OA Funding

In response to the OA movement and well in advance of Plan S, IGI Global, early last year, unveiled their OA Fee Waiver (Offset Model) Initiative.

Under this initiative, librarians who invest in IGI Global's InfoSci-Books (5,300+ reference books) and/or InfoSci-Journals (185+ scholarly journals) databases will be able to subsidize their patron's OA article processing charges (APC) when their work is submitted and accepted (after the peer review process) into an IGI Global journal.*

How Does it Work?

1. When a library subscribes or perpetually purchases IGI Global's InfoSci-Databases including InfoSci-Books (5,300+ e-books), InfoSci-Journals (185+ e-journals), and/or their discipline/subject-focused subsets, IGI Global will match the library's investment with a fund of equal value to go toward subsidizing the OA article processing charges (APCs) for their patrons.

   Researchers: Be sure to recommend the InfoSci-Books and InfoSci-Journals to take advantage of this initiative.

2. When a student, faculty, or staff member submits a paper and it is accepted (following the peer review) into one of IGI Global's 185+ scholarly journals, the author will have the option to have their paper published under a traditional publishing model or as OA.

3. When the author chooses to have their paper published under OA, IGI Global will notify them of the OA Fee Waiver (Offset Model) Initiative. If the author decides they would like to take advantage of this initiative, IGI Global will deduct the US$ 1,500 APC from the created fund.

4. This fund will be offered on an annual basis and will renew as the subscription is renewed for each year thereafter. IGI Global will manage the fund and award the APC waivers unless the librarian has a preference as to how the funds should be managed.

Hear From the Experts on This Initiative:

"I'm very happy to have been able to make one of my recent research contributions, 'Visualizing the Social Media Conversations of a National Information Technology Professional Association' featured in the *International Journal of Human Capital and Information Technology Professionals*, freely available along with having access to the valuable resources found within IGI Global's InfoSci-Journals database."

– Prof. Stuart Palmer,
Deakin University, Australia

For More Information, Visit:
www.igi-global.com/publish/contributor-resources/open-access or contact IGI Global's Database Team at eresources@igi-global.com.

Printed in the United States
By Bookmasters